9789401504232

INTERNATIONAL UNION OF LOCAL AUTHORITIES

THE STRUCTURE OF LOCAL GOVERNMENTS THROUGHOUT THE WORLD

by

SAMUEL HUMES

and

EILEEN M. MARTIN

MARTINUS NIJHOFF / THE HAGUE

THE STRUCTURE OF LOCAL GOVERNMENTS
THROUGHOUT THE WORLD

INTERNATIONAL UNION OF LOCAL
AUTHORITIES

THE STRUCTURE OF LOCAL GOVERNMENTS
THROUGHOUT THE WORLD

by

SAMUEL HUMES

and

EILEEN M. MARTIN

THE HAGUE / MARTINUS NIJHOFF / 1961

Discarded by
Dartmouth College Library

Copyright 1961 by Martinus Nijhoff, The Hague, Netherlands
All rights reserved, including the right to translate or to reproduce this book or parts thereof in any form.

352
H883s

Max. Goot.
Jan. 16, 1964

PRINTED IN THE NETHERLANDS

TABLE OF CONTENTS

List of Exhibits — XI
Patterns of Government Units and Structures of Municipal Government — XII
Preface by N. ARKEMA — XIII
Foreword by ARTHUR W. BROMAGE — XVII
Foreword by HENRY MADDICK — XIX
Foreword by C. H. F. POLAK — XXIII
Introduction to Part I by SAMUEL HUMES — XXVIII
Introduction to Part II by EILEEN MARTIN — XXXIII

PART ONE

1. LOCAL GOVERNMENT AND ITS STRUCTURE — 1
1. Sovereignty and local government — 1
2. Three types of local government — 3
3. The reasons for local government — 6
4. The process of local government — 8
5. The structure of local government — 9

2. THE UNITS OF LOCAL GOVERNMENT — 12
1. Number of tiers — 12
2. The municipalities and other basic units of local government — 14
3. The uniform and diversified patterns of basic units — 16
4. The population size of municipalities — 18
5. The sub-municipal units — 21
6. The local special-purpose authorities — 23
7. The intermediate units — 27

3. THE RELATIONS WITH THE CENTRAL GOVERNMENT — 31
1. Local representative government and the central government — 31
2. Local representative government and the central government ministries — 32

TABLE OF CONTENTS

   3. The creation, alteration, and termination of local units ... 34
   4. The authority of the municipalities and other local units ... 34
   5. The review of local decisions ... 39
   6. The financial status of the local units ... 44
   7. The appointment and dismissal of local officials ... 47
   8. Other means of control ... 48

4. THE PROCESS OF LOCAL ELECTIONS ... 51

   1. Elections and the local representative governing process ... 51
   2. Who can vote ... 52
   3. Who does vote ... 55
   4. Personalities, the press, and pressure groups ... 56
   5. Indirect elections ... 57
   6. Proportional representation ... 59
   7. Plurality choice ... 62
   8. Consent by acclamation ... 64
   9. The delimitation of constituencies ... 67
   10. Nominations ... 68
   11. The local political party organizations ... 70

5. THE COUNCIL ... 72

   1. The council and representative government ... 72
   2. No councils ... 73
   3. The advisory councils ... 74
   4. The councils with some authority to govern ... 75
   5. The nature of council deliberations in representative government ... 79
   6. The popular assembly and the referendum ... 82
   7. Selection of members ... 84
   8. The size of the council ... 86
   9. The council chairman and the secretary ... 89

6. THE COMMITTEES OF COUNCIL ... 93

   1. The committees and council ... 93
   2. Specialization of the committees ... 95

3. The preparatory committees 97
4. The administering committees 97
5. The composition of the committees 101
6. The committee chairmen and secretaries 104

7. THE BOARD 107

1. The board and the executive function 107
2. The selection of the board members 110
3. The board and its members: collectively and individually 111
4. The board and the council 113
5. The board and the staff 114
6. The board chairman and the board secretary 115

8. THE CHIEF EXECUTIVE 119

1. The chief executive and the executive function 119
2. The chief executive and the council 122
3. The chief executive and the staff 125
4. The chief executive as local agent of the central government 127
5. The chief executive as the ceremonial head 130
6. The quasi-chief executive 131
7. The village headman 134
8. The chief executive appointed by the central government or other higher units 135
9. The chief executive elected by council 139
10. The chief executive elected by popular vote 142
11. The chief executive appointed by council 144
12. The terms of office 147

9. THE STAFF 149

1. The staff and the local government process 149
2. The selection of the staff 151
3. The departments 154
4. The department heads 156
5. The chief administrative officer 158

10. TOWARD RESPONSIBLE LOCAL REPRESENTATIVE GOVERNMENT — 162

1. Problems and trends — 162
2. Problems and trends: the central government — 167
3. The two purposes of local representative government structure — 169
4. The representative organs — 171
5. The staff officers — 176
6. The functions of the chief executive, the ceremonial head, and the chief administrative officer — 179
7. The establishment of the executive — 182
8. Toward responsible local representative government — 186

PART TWO — 187

(0) THE GEOGRAPHICAL GROUPS — 189

0. The countries and the geographical groups — 189
1. The Anglo-Saxon group — 192
2. The North Europe group — 194
3. The Central and North-West Europe group — 196
4. The East Europe group — 197
5. The South Europe group — 199
6. The South and Central America group — 202
7. The West Asia and North Africa group — 203
8. The South Asia and East Africa group — 204
9. The East Asia group — 206

(1) THE ANGLO SAXON GROUP — 208

The United Kingdom — 208
Australia — 217
South Africa — 221
Canada — 227
The United States of America — 233

(2) THE NORTH EUROPE GROUP — 243

Sweden — 243
Finland — 247

TABLE OF CONTENTS IX

	Norway	251
	Denmark	256
	Iceland	260
(3)	CENTRAL AND NORTH-WEST EUROPE	263
	The German Federal Republic	263
	Austria	268
	Switzerland	272
	The Netherlands	276
	Belgium	281
	Luxembourg	286
(4)	THE EAST EUROPE GROUP	290
	The Union of Soviet Socialist Republics	290
	Poland	293
	Bulgaria	299
	Yugoslavia	302
(5)	THE SOUTH EUROPE GROUP	309
	France	309
	Italy	319
	Greece	324
	Spain	329
	Portugal	334
(6)	THE SOUTH AND CENTRAL AMERICA GROUP	342
	Brazil	342
	Ecuador	346
	Colombia	351
	El Salvador	356
(7)	THE WEST ASIA AND NORTH AFRICA GROUP	362
	Tunisia	362
	Iran	366
	Lebanon	368
	Turkey	370

TABLE OF CONTENTS

(8) THE SOUTH ASIA AND EAST AFRICA GROUP	379
India	379
Ceylon	386
Burma	390
Malaya	395
The Sudan	400
Ethiopia	405
(9) THE EAST ASIA GROUP	411
Thailand	411
The Philippines	419
Japan	424
Peru	428
Index	433

LIST OF EXHIBITS

Facing page

Exhibit 1. (Chapter 1)	– Three types of local governments	4
Exhibit 2. (Chapter 2)	– Table of local government units	14
Exhibit 3. (Chapter 2)	– Simplified geographical diagram of some intermediate units	18
Exhibit 4. (Chapter 2)	– Comparison of population medians of selected local governments	28
Exhibit 5. (Chapter 6)	– Specialization of committees	96
Exhibit 6. (Chapter 6)	– A contrast between administering and preparatory committees	97
Exhibit 7. (Chapter 7)	– A comparison of the organization of municipal boards	114
Exhibit 8. (Chapter 9)	– Examples of organization of municipal departments	158
Exhibit 9. (Chapter 9)	– A contrast in the relationship of chief administrative officer and the department heads	159

Following page

Exhibit 10.	– World map showing countries included in survey and geographical groups	449
Exhibit 11.	– Table of municipal government structures	449
Exhibit 12.	– Table of intermediate government structures	449

PATTERNS OF GOVERNMENT UNITS AND STRUCTURES
OF MUNICIPAL GOVERNMENT

Facing page

United Kingdom	208
United States of America	234
Norway	252
Switzerland	272
The Netherlands	276
Poland	294
Yugoslavia	304
France	310
Brazil	342
Japan	424

PREFACE

In 1955/56, the International Union of Local Authorities, at the request of the United Nations Educational, Social and Cultural Organization, undertook a broad enquiry into local government throughout the world. This enquiry covered many aspects of local government including organization and structure, functions and activities, local democracy and the rôle of the citizen. To ensure the success of the enquiry a detailed questionnaire was sent to key officials or organizations in 74 countries, asking their co-operation in drawing up a report on local government in their country on the basis of this questionnaire. The response was most gratifying, reports being received from 42 of these countries.[1]

In accordance with our agreement with Unesco, five countries representing different types of local government were selected, on the basis of this enquiry, for a further study. Experts from these countries, namely Brazil, Sweden, Thailand, Tunisia and Yugoslavia, were requested to write a monograph on local government in their own countries. The monographs on the first four of these countries will be published in English shortly.[2]

The material received in response to the enquiry was so voluminous and valuable that it prompted us to attempt to make a comparative study on local government in the 42 countries concerned. Appreciating the size of such a study, we felt that it should be restricted to certain aspects of local government and not cover the entire field of the enquiry. The information on local government functions and on local democracy being often scanty, it was decided to limit the study mainly to local government structure. This had the additional advantage that a large amount of background information and documentation was available on this subject over and above the material received in response to the enquiry.

This choice, however, forced us towards an institutional ap-

[1] After the conclusion of this study a report was received from Peru which was summarized in accordance with the other countries and added at the end of this publication. No information on Peru is, however, included in the rest of this publication.
[2] Unesco published the French version in one of their series of publications.

proach of the study, so that it will be, understandably, subject to criticism from those who claim that the functional approach is to be preferred. In consequence of this approach, it was not possible to give, at the same time, a full picture of the rôle and functions of local government as such, nor was it our intention to do so.

From the outset, we have been well aware that an international comparative study of this size would necessarily have many defects, some of which we have mentioned earlier; I will not go further into the difficulties to be encountered and the shortcomings inherent in such a study, as these will be properly explained and evaluated in subsequent pages in the forewords by three international experts on local government and by the authors themselves.

In spite of possible shortcomings, we felt justified in undertaking this study. Comparative local government is still in its infancy, and the importance of developing this subject should not be underestimated. Local government systems in many countries have undergone strong foreign influence either by imposition or by free choice. Among the striking examples of the acceptance of a foreign system of government was the tendency in many countries on the European continent after the French Revolution at the end of the 18th century to follow the French pattern, which is still apparent in today's local government structure of many countries. Similarly the system of people's committees originating in Russia has been adopted in East European countries. In another sense the former British and French colonies have undergone strong British and French influences. The history of local government can testify to many other cases of one country borrowing certain features from the other. This proves the value of an international study of this kind on comparative local government.

This ambitious study would never have been possible without the enthusiasm, energy, and perseverance of two young Americans: Mr. Samuel Humes, a Netherlands-America Foundation fellow, and Miss Eileen Martin, a Fulbright fellow, who joined the IULA staff in December 1956 and September 1957 respectively and who both worked continuously on this project until the autumn of 1959. Mr. Humes undertook the purely comparative part of this project. It was, therefore, he who had in the first place to solve the many problems involved in an international comparative study of this kind. He has carried out this difficult task with much zeal and inventiveness and his work has been crowned by its acceptance by the University of Leyden as a thesis for a doctorate of law. Miss Eileen Martin wrote the summaries on local government in 43 countries. Hers is the achievement of having sifted out the basic essentials from the great volume of material before her. The systematic presentation which she has made of local government in many countries will be of much help to students needing a comparative view of these structures.

We owe special thanks to two other persons. Firstly to Mr. A. F. Leemans, assistant Secretary General of the International Union of Local Authorities, who directed this enquiry on local government from beginning to end and was responsible for the final editing of this publication. He also gave constant advice and guidance to Mr. Humes and Miss Martin throughout the study. Secondly we are very grateful to Prof. C. H. F. Polak of the Law faculty of Leyden University, who, as Mr. Humes' academic mentor, gave much of his time to consultation on this study, in particular on the comparative part contained in part I.

To these four persons goes the principal credit for this book. Besides, there are innumerable other persons to whom we would render our thanks. Most of them have been acknowledged by the authors in their presentation. I therefore will not repeat their names, but only mention Mrs. Van de Poll who did the tedious but indispensable work of indexing. Moreover, I wish to thank the many people who provided the original national reports which were the essential basis of this study and without whose unselfish contributions this project could never have been undertaken.

Being well aware that this project is a hazardous one, we have requested a number of experts of international renown to give their opinion on an international study of this kind in general. and on the merits and defects of the present study in particular, Prof. Arthur W. Bromage, of the University of Michigan, U.S.A., Prof. Henry Maddick, of the University of Birmingham, U. K., and Prof. C. H. F. Polak, of Leyden University, Netherlands, have kindly consented to express their views in the short Forewords which follow.

The Hague. N. Arkema
September 1960. Secretary General
International Union
of Local Authorities

FOREWORD

Many case studies exist of local government in particular countries, but few volumes appear of a comparative character. Yet, everywhere political scientists and students struggle with similar questions. Are local governments relatively free to manage their own affairs through locally representative councils? How much central administrative control is exercised over local officials? In a given culture and tradition what is an appropriate design of the structure for representative local self-government? How effective are national parties as instrumentalities in local government elections? Are local units decentralized arms of central administration or instrumentalities of local government? There are almost as many answers as there are sovereign and quasi-sovereign states. Comparative studies can shed light on the similarities and differences in forms and in realities.

The specific systems in particular countries are related to culture, tradition, and capacity of populations for local self-government. Many systems of local government exist and can be classified only in a general way by geographical groups of countries or cultural transplantations. The task of producing a meaningful analysis of comparative local government is one of magnitude. Even the preparation of digests pertaining to local government in particular areas is complex.

This monograph published by the International Union of Local Authorities undertakes to give a systematic classification of local government in many countries. The result is a readable demonstration of central-local relationships and variations in local governmental design. The first major theme concerns the nature and technique of central control. Of necessity the analysis is restricted to the facts and to their classification into systems. Value judgments as to the validity of different kinds of central control can be made only after more intensive research by many scholars. But the emphasis in this work is upon the importance of local representative government which can be stifled by too much central control.

A second major concern is the design of local representative institutions at the local level. Electoral systems are reviewed, including the one-party method of consent by acclamation, a process in which the realities of political life are more significant than the formalities. Stress is put on the interrelations between representative policy-makers and administrators, and this leads to such matters as the design of councils, council committees, types of chief executives, executive boards for administrative co-ordination, chief executive and staff problems. One of the key issues is the selection of chief executives whether by central appointment, direct election, council election, or council appointment. This monograph seeks clarifications by indicating in various countries the true nature of the chief executive office in local government.

A third basic concern is the classification of local governmental systems into geographical groups, where local government has been influenced by similar cultures, traditions, and philosophies. These are rather loose classifications, and the Anglo-Saxon "group" does not fit any geographical configuration. Yet the geographical scheme is helpful, for in the East Europe group the Soviet model is dominant with its emphasis on the extrastructural aspects of one-party dominance over institutions. The influence of the French administrative system appears in the West Asia and North Africa group. Cultural interrelationships are important in understanding the evolution of local systems and in making comparisons. British influence on local governments which has been significant in many areas, emphasizes the council-committee approach in which committees are the work-shops of policy and administration.

Where the objective is to continue, or to move forward to, responsible and representative institutions of local representative government, this monograph will be viewed as a constructive contribution to the literature. It will be valuable to political scientists, councilmen, administrators and students. It will deserve a place in the libraries and classrooms where local government is taught and local administrators are trained. The way has been opened for further comparative studies which may in the future give us even greater understanding of the realities of local government which lie in and around the law and the structure of organization.

Arthur W. Bromage
Michigan State, University, U.S.A.

FOREWORD

At no other time in its history has the world been so much governed and known so much about the government of its separate countries. This is undoubtedly for the good for in every country the peoples are faced with problems which bear a remarkable similarity to each other and it can be of value to know the solutions that others are applying. These problems arise as a result of the predominant challenge of the times, namely the challenge of the pressure of population upon the world's resources combined with a revolution in the expectation of those peoples. More people wanting more in the common description of popular demand in all countries whether in Western Europe or North America or in Africa or Asia, whether the political system favoured by these countries be Communism or some other form of Government. How to satisfy these demands, how best to utilize the resources, and what methods of administration will yield the best results – this is the common ground on which the student of politics and the administrator alike must approach problems of government and administration.

In the first part of this book, Mr. Humes has chosen to examine certain aspects of the structure of local government. He has taken this term "local government" on the assumption that thereby he can make an abstraction from the governmental systems of some forty countries and draw comparisons between them. His study directs our attention to certain main aspects of this branch of government. These predominantly are the ways in which local government is constituted, the different forms in which public opinion is represented and its desires and wishes put into effect, not only through elected or nominated representatives, but through executive members of the representative body and the staff itself. It is significant here that he touches on relations with central governments because in so doing we should be reminded that this problem of central-local relations has long been the concern of students and has often warped the whole approach to the study of the proper rôle of local government in the State. It has been treated as though local and central governments were not within the same state at all, but were seen as rival powers with the same sphere of interest which caused jealousy and emotional outbursts and, one must admit, frequently very bad solutions to the problems of the well-being of the majority, which was often of only secondary importance to the contestants.

In studying the various aspects of local government that are dealt with here, the student has two difficulties to overcome. The first is the wide variety of forms and devices adopted for any one section of the structure. The second is that whilst the subject can be dissected in this way for study, a local authority is a complex living organism adapted to its own locality. Whilst we may talk of staff, or of executive, or of representatives, or of central-local relations, all the parts are interlocked and the whole develops relationships and attitudes that are, in a sense, unique. Whilst, when dissected, the structure may look the same, actual results are often markedly different.

Evaluation of the various forms that any part of the machinery of local government may take, must allow for the different demands which are being made upon the system as a whole. In the case of war, say, unity and security dominates any plea for local autonomy. With its history of dictatorship, a Latin American country may consider that the plea of local autonomy far outweighs that of being an effective agent for development. For this, local government must be able to give expression to the needs of its inhabitants in a way which will capture their enthusiasms and harness their energies to the national programme for development.

There is another problem for the student of local government systems as they are analysed here. He has to think, also, of the background in which local government is going to operate, and whilst one may argue persuasively in favour of, shall we say, a mixed system of the single transferable vote and of the plurality system of election, one has to consider the societies in which this system is to be applied. In how many countries in the world would this sophisticated system be readily accepted as a practical and satisfactory method of representation? In arguing the merits of different systems of voting or different arrangements of staff-council relationships, it must always be remembered that the social and ecological setting in which government has to operate differs greatly from one country to another, and that governmental machinery must be adjusted to meet the circumstances of a particular situation.

Particularly is this the case of relations between central and local government. It may be argued that in England or the United States of America the staffs and capabilities of the units of local government are such that central control is not necessary in order to ensure proper standards of administration and of technical efficiency. Yet, outside Western Europe and North America, tutelle is, in fact, a valuable influence in the total system of government. Especially is this so for rural sections of a country whose understanding of modern techniques and modern methods is extremely elementary, and whose ability to provide technical advice is extremely limited. The extent of this application of tutelle can be divined from the second part of the book.

This book is concerned, in the main, with the larger unit of local government. Quite rightly, the criticism is made that the majority of units of local government are too small to be in any way effective, but it would be unfortunate if the student thought that in making the larger unit, the problem was then solved. Clearly, there remains the issue of how to provide government which is, at one and the same time, effective and convenient for those who live in villages and hamlets. They are a very considerable portion of the population, accounting for some three-quarters of the total population of developing countries. Here is a question of such importance that it cannot be pushed on one side as unfortunately so many politicians and administrators are inclined to do. If they can establish good government in the capital and reasonable government in the centre of the district, they are satisfied with their work. The fortunes and misfortunes of those vast numbers of people living outside the urban areas are too often ignored.

The countries covered by this survey are divided into areas according to certain common cultural influences, thus providing a basis for comparison. An equally valid and probably more vital basis for comparative evaluation must lie in the division between the developed and the less developed countries. The essential difference for administration is not language, nor yet features of terrain or climate of a particular country or group of countries, but whether or not there are adequate financial resources and sufficient personnel, both those lay gents to participate in the deliberations of the council and those technical and professional gents who provide the backbone of the service through its staff. This, I would suggest, is the essential demarcation line, for these factors determine how local government will work in practice whatever it may look like in the paper analysis of its constitution.

In the second part of this study, Miss Martin has recorded some of the basic facts relating to the formal structure of local government in 42 countries. These will be very useful to the student who wishes to make a comparison between systems.

Whilst structure in every case must be seen as being within a cocoon of conventions, lists of functions must not be regarded as concrete reality. The countries which supplied this information have listed the totality of obligatory and permissive activities regardless of whether they are actually performed or not. The greater the degree of underdevelopment, the fewer will be the functions performed. Very often, owing to inadequate revenue, even the 'obligatory' duties are not carried out. Unfortunately, all problems of finance, other than matters relating to audit, have been omitted from this enquiry, as they were dealt with in an earlier publication by the IULA. Viability of a system and of an authority is fundamental to the working of any structure of local government.

Basically, and this is the justification for any study of local government which attempts to straddle five continents, the tasks of government are everywhere the same. They are how to meet the demands for a higher standard of living, both materially and spiritually, and furthermore, how to utilise new skills and new techniques which are known, if not always available. If by discriminatory selection developing countries will learn from the mistakes and the successes of others, the time taken to proceed along this road of development should be much reduced. This study points to the variety of solutions. These, and the questions raised explicitly and implicitly in the book, need to be studied in depth in the setting of different societies to aid the process of selection by the practitioner and the understanding of the student.

Henry Maddick
University of Birmingham, England.

FOREWORD

The publication of the present book is a bold venture. In any international comparative study there are difficulties, almost insurmountable difficulties, which leave their scars on the final product.

A study of "the structure of local government throughout the world" is beset by all those problems which characterise international, comparative enquiries. The endless variety of systems, the subtlety of the distinctions, the difficulty of examining these from a comparative point of view, all these and similar factors influence the result of such an enquiry. It has been recognized by eminent scholars that a comparative study of local government requires that the student spend a considerable time in each country concerned in order to become familiar with the actual functioning of local government and to get to know the heart of the matter. But even then, the student of local government will be faced with the difficulty that inside one and the same country considerable differences exist between local governments, especially between the large and the small, the urban and the rural municipalities, differences which are sometimes based on law, but very often deriving from actual practice. A comparative study of local government could be set up within the borders of one country. A British expert of local government stated with regard to his own country: "local government's infinite variety makes generalizations dangerous" (Jessup, Problems of local government in England and Wales, p. VIII). In the same spirit Harvard's John M. Gauss wrote in his foreword to John C. Bollens' "Special District Governments in the United States":

"All writers on questions of local and state government face the insoluble problem of treating comparatively variations of a particular practice or institution among forty-eight states or among thousands of local governments, while at the same time indicating that in any one state or local government the practice or institution must be examined as part of a particular local setting, with its own peculiar governmental, social, physical, cultural and historic characteristics. Too much emphasis on the first, and you are accused of counting sewer covers and lampposts. Too much on the second, and meaningful generalization is strangled by the local variables."

We must take for granted that a very high degree of generalization is inevitable in a study so ambitious as to compare the local government of no less than forty-three countries. However, the real importance of local government, its influence on the course of events, can only be judged against the background of the historical development of a country and its social, economic and cultural circumstances.

Nevertheless, I am glad that two young Americans have given their time and energy to this project. I saw them working at their strenuous task and had the privilege to be often consulted by them. Hence I realized that one must be inspired by fresh enthusiasm and possess a certain youthful recklessness to be able to tackle and persevere in a study like the present, which necessarily shows gaps and defects. The authors deserve our gratitude for having undertaken and completed this work. Now that local government in many countries is subject to heavy strains and considerable changes, even crises, comparative studies in this field are all the more useful.

Many voices have advocated the active participation of the local population in the government of local affairs and have thus pleaded for a strong local government with a wide scope of activities and freedom of decision and action. Describing democracy in the U.S. in the early years of the 19th century, the famous French author Alexis de Tocqueville writes:

"C'est pourtant dans la commune que réside la force des peuples libres. Les institutions communales sont à la liberté ce que les écoles primaires sont à la science; elles la mettent à la portée du peuple; elle lui en font goûter l'usage paisible et l'habituent à s'en servir. Sans institutions communales une nation peut se donner un gouvernement libre, mais elle n'a pas l'esprit de la liberté."

This conception of democracy has been accepted in many countries and has inspired their governmental structure. However, the trend towards the Welfare State, which has developed during the 20th century, and whose purpose it is to secure the highest possible standard of living for everybody, made a strong central government direction a necessity. Herman Finer rightly observed in his well-known "Theory and Practice of Modern Government" (p. 595) that

"Local government has become integrated with the work of the central authority, so that today there is hardly any real localization of an important subject of government."

This is even more true in the underdeveloped and less developed countries where only centralized and centrally co-ordinated programmes and efforts will be able to achieve a relatively rapid economic and social progress. The lack of capable men and adequate means in the local communities constitute a serious obstacle to the improvement of the population's living conditions.

Consequently, local governments tend to become merely administrative units of the complex structure of an administrative state. These tendencies have several implications. Firstly, they have shifted the emphasis from (good) government to (good) administration, and consequently, a different type of person is required for the management of the community. This aspect of good administration will gain in force, and will be of particular importance for inspiring the central government's confidence in local government in those countries where local government has to be thoroughly transformed.

Secondly, the centralizing trend, which deprives local government of much of its powers, will tend to diminish the interest of the citizens in local government, as it reduces the opportunity for them to make a really important contribution towards the welfare of their community. And it is this participation of the citizens which is the very lifeblood of local government. Besides, the interest of the citizen in local government is no longer a matter of course. With better communications and the development of region- or state-wide social services and public utilities, the local community has lost much of its importance for the average citizen, whose horizons are steadily widening.

One must never lose sight of the fact that good administration is not an end in itself, it is but a prerequisite for good government, just as good government is a prerequisite for a good society. And a good society means much more than that people are well-fed, well-clothed and well-housed. Age-old communities have been disrupted; it is one of the most urgent tasks of our time to create new ones. We must try to evolve structures of local government which will offer to the people who live in this brave new world of mass-circulation newspapers, electronics, atomic energy and jetplanes, the opportunity to take part in the management of what they rightly feel to be their own affairs and stimulate them to give their best efforts to the common weal.

Fortunately, the authors, too, have realized that one cannot describe the structure of local government without giving due regard to its relations with the central government. In this field, too, legal regulations are less important than the factual means of power. The decisive factor, perhaps, is whether, and to what extent, local governments still dispose of their own sources of income. The central governments of the great majority of countries have been compelled, by the expansion of their tasks, to a considerable increase and extension of taxes, and every opportunity of raising taxes is eagerly grasped, with the result that the municipalities are deprived of any possibility of collecting more than the smallest sums. Besides, public opinion nowadays tends to reject any inequality of taxes between citizens, even though they live in different municipalities. The regulations concerning local and central government may remain unchanged, but the independence of local government is done for if it no longer disposes of itw own sources of income. The initiation and development of new schemes and activities become dependent on the approval and financial aid of the central authorities, who are usually averse to precedents and above all seek to impose uniformity.

Politicians should bear in mind that there is not necessarily a fundamental incompatibility between the demands of good government and a sound and vital democracy. The ever increasing governmental tasks can only be accomplished by means of a far-reaching decentralization or at least deconcentration.

By leaving decisions of local interest to local authorities who are responsible to the representatives of the community, a strong safeguard is created against slow and ineffective government. A state is stronger in such measures as its units have more vitality and the more people feel their responsibility to the public cause. The system of government whereby all decisions, even those of purely local interest, have to be taken by the central authorities, is seldom competent to pass fair judgement on questions where an intimate knowledge of local conditions is required. Decisions will be postponed and, worse still, nobody will be really responsible for them. A minister rarely resigns because of a decision in a purely local affair and a parliament usually lacks the time and zeal to call a minister to account for his administrative decision in such a matter.

Local government will only be able to accomplish important tasks in the modern world if it is adapted to the effects of a rapid economic and social development. This holds good not only for countries with a long established independence, but also for the new ones.

Many of these latter are in search of a proper system of government and administration. In this search they must give due attention to local government. A recent study by the United Nations on Public Administration Aspects of Community Development Programmes stated that the rôle of local government in community development is of fundamental importance. To quote one of the conclusions of the report: "As a general rule, programmes to improve local government should be planned and executed simultaneously and in co-ordination with community development programmes."

This publication of the International Union of Local Authorities has assembled information which so far was not readily available. It will, therefore, fill an important need.

C. H. F. Polak

University of Leyden
Netherlands

INTRODUCTION TO PART I

1. The purpose

The purpose of this study is to gain an insight into and make an introductory comparison of the structure of local government in many countries throughout the world. More specifically the aim is to define and describe in a comparative fashion the various organs of local government and their relationships.

The need for, as well as the obstacles encountered in, such a survey are perhaps equally obvious. It is said that he who understands only his own language knows none. It may just as easily be contended that he who understands only his own governmental institutions knows none. Governmental comparisons are useful not only to find out how others are governed but also to more fully comprehend the role which one's own governmental institutions play.[1]

From a pragmatic point of view there is a still further value in making comparisons of local governments. Local government institutions are constantly undergoing changes. The changes are both formal and informal; they may be evolutionary and revolutionary. A comparative study of local government can help many countries to take advantage of the experiments and experiences of others. From the beginning of recorded history there are indications of man borrowing heavily from the institutions of his neighbour in organizing his own institutions. In local government there are several examples of countries which have set up their local government systems by wholesale copying the model of another. Although such slavish adaptations are no longer considered desirable, fortunately for the vitality of our local government systems there are frequent examples of one country adopting pertinent features of the government structures of other countries.

The rapid changes and many experiments in local government systems since the end of World War II have made it of special current importance that countries be able to share the successes

---

[1] For a fuller explanation of the need for comparative surveys see Gunnar Heckscher, *The Study of Comparative Government and Politics* (London 1958), pp. 13–16.

and to profit by the mistakes of others. Moreover, it is particularly important that the nations just embarking on programs of broad local government revision be able to utilize the ideas that have already been tried and found good in other countries.

One of the most important reasons why such a study has been undertaken is because there is a lack of material, and especially comparative material, which is available to the general reader. Moreover, in many countries there is relatively little literature concerning local government at all and much of this is limited to legal codes and government reports, a large proportion of which are highly technical, out-dated, and in the native language of the country concerned. Of the few books which attempt to be comparative, most are limited to a comparison of local governments in Europe. The growth of a world-wide consciousness of local government along with the marked increase in the concern for the development of local representative government in Asia and Africa has made it especially important to have a world-wide description and comparison of local government.

Another limitation of most of the comparative surveys is that they have tended to emphasize the individual descriptions of the systems of local government in the various countries. This emphasis has usually been at the expense of an over-all comparison which might develop terms of reference, classification, and common denominators, by which the institutions may be compared. The lack of even such fundamentals as a consistent terminology is demonstrated by the variation in the use of such basic terms as "municipality" and "council" which are interpreted in various ways in different countries.

Just as the rapidly changing structures of the local governments of many countries, the scarcity of documentation, and the lack of a consistent terminology in this field are reasons why a survey such as this was needed, they are also among the severe handicaps to be faced in undertaking such a project. As might be expected, in a broad survey such as this there are many inherent difficulties, numerous possible approaches, and many different points of view. Primarily, of course, local government institutions are an inter-related part of the governmental system and culture of a country. It is impossible, therefore, for any one observer to present the institutions of each of many countries in a context which is fully satisfying to all of the readers.

I am, therefore, aware that (in the words of K. C. Wheare):

> "In writing this book I am attempting to fly before I can walk. I can explain and, I hope, justify the attempt. The student ... has to make a choice. Either he can try to hack his way through the jungle on foot or he can try to get a bird's eye view of the terrain from the air. If he chooses the first alternative, the most he can hope for is to clear a portion of his territory; if he chooses the second, the most he can hope for is to produce a rough sketchmap of the whole area. Each course has its advantages and its defects. The explorer on foot will know a part, but he will not understand its relation to the whole; the explorer from the air will see the whole but he is certain to miss or to misread or to misunderstand some at least of the parts. I have chosen to attempt a reconnaissance from the air, in spite of its dangers, for it seems to me that when you are exploring a jungle an aerial map is the first essential. I hope that, others will persevere with the exploration on foot and that, while they correct and amplify my map, they may testify that it had some rough working value for them."[2]

This study, then, is an attempt to fill the need for a broad worldwide comparison of the structures of local government. The purpose of such a broad survey is not to analyse the complete field of local government, which would be impossible, at least at this stage, but rather to compare the various organs of local government by describing their relationships with one another and to introduce a consistent terminology in the field. It is hoped that this world-wide comparative survey may serve to provide a basis for and lend encouragement to more specialized and penetrating studies of local government.

2. *The scope*

Probably the fundamental restriction to this study of local government has been to limit it to a comparison of the structure of local government. Although there are various other possible approaches, especially the study of functions, the material available lent itself best to a study from the structural point of view. Furthermore, before one can start to understand the functions, the problems,

---

[2] These are the opening lines in the Preface of the book by K. C. Wheare, *Government by Committee* (Oxford 1955).

the role of local governments in various countries one must understand the structure of the local units. This is the basic framework without which the other aspects of local government are like quotations taken out of context. To know, for instance, that the local government units are responsible for the police function is relatively unimportant until one knows whether the local units have representative government or are local branches of the central government bureaucracy.

The choice also had to be made whether the comparison of the structure of local government was to be made primarily from a legal or a sociological point of view. Each of these possibilities has its advantages but also its disadvantages. Although it is usually convenient to begin with the law as a basis for classification, a strictly legal analysis tends to be misleading since it does not tell much about how the organization actually works. On the other hand a sociological comparison, such as those dealing with community power structure, can only be undertaken by means of a vast number of individual community case studies; there are too many variations to attempt a general comparative survey. Although probably neither lawyers nor sociologists will applaud the choice, a middle way was chosen. An effort has been made to describe how most of the structures of government within a given country tend to operate; that is what are the general inter-relationships among the various organs, within the formal structure of government, in making and carrying out the local government process.

Furthermore, the description also had to be limited to the broad general outlines of the systems in given countries. This left little and often no room for mentioning minor variations, many of which may seem major to those in the country in question. The large federal countries presented a particular problem in this regard because their structure varies to such a large degree from state to state. I also chose not to discuss the variation in the local government structures of very large cities from the general patterns.

The major emphasis in this survey has been on the units of local representative government. For it is in these units, and in the development of these units, that most of the interest in the field of local government is focused. Furthermore, it is these units whose organizational structures show the greatest variety and whose organizational problems are most complex. Nevertheless, the units of local non-representative government will be mentioned if only to provide an overall perspective of the patterns of local government. In fact, the emphasis of this survey is narrowed even further, for most of the attention will be on the municipalities, that is the basic units of local government. Although the scope of this survey is limited in several regards, in at least one respect, however, it has been made as wide as possible – for 42 sovereign and independent countries have been included which is a fairly broad cross-section of the countries throughout the world.[1]

3. Acknowledgements

A survey such as this would not have been at all possible without the encouragement and indispensable help of several organizations and many persons. Among them are the Netherlands-America Foundation which financed the first part of my stay in The Netherlands.

Most important I wish to acknowledge the help and encouragement of the International Union of Local Authorities who in conjunction with UNESCO took the initiative in selecting this topic for study and, through Prof. Charles Ascher, the IULA representative at the United Nations, arranged for me to work on this project. IULA has been more than generous in offering its facilities and advice in the project.

Each member of the IULA staff has also been helpful, particularly Mr. A. F. Leemans, Assistant Secretary-General of IULA,

[1] In order to secure material for this survey, IULA in co-operation with UNESCO sent questionnaires to organizations or persons in 74 different countries. Replies were received from 42 countries. In one of these countries, though, later political events have so changed the system of local representative government that it was considered inadvisable to include it in the survey. On the other hand, Australia was included in the survey despite the fact that a report was not received from that country; sufficient material was able to be found in other sources.

Thus, there are 42 countries in this survey, which is as broad a cross-section of the countries throughout the world as appeared possible. It is to be regretted, though, that there are not more African, Asian, and particularly South American countries. For comparative purpose, it is also to be regretted that there are no countries in which there is no formal local representative government.

whose constant advice was indispensable, Miss V. Kyjovská who helped reading the foreign language documents, Mrs. C. J. J. de Bruijn who typed most of the manuscripts often from illegible drafts, and Miss E. Martin, who wrote the second part of the IULA publication in which this study is the first part.

In gathering material for this study I have drawn heavily on numerous sources. I wish to acknowledge my general indebtedness to a wide range of people, including Professor James M. Burns of Williams College and the faculty of the Institute of Local and State Government of the University of Pennsylvania, at which institutions my interest in local government was inspired and encouraged. More specifically I am grateful for the information received from over forty organizations or persons in answer to the IULA questionnaire regarding local government in their countries. The relative lack of footnotes in the text is due primarily to an effort to use their reports as the basic source material. A great amount of books and magazines have been read for corroborating information. Furthermore, interviews have been extensively used as a means of gaining insight into the actual operations of the local government units. Finally, a number of persons made comments upon the original draft manuscript; among them were Professors Charles Ascher, Arthur Bromage, and Fred Riggs, as well as Messrs S. O. van Poelje, Orin F. Nolting, and Pierre Poutout.

Although I am indebted to many sources including IULA, the respondents, and the persons who have commented on the survey, and countless others whose books or articles I have read or with whom I have talked, the responsibility for the text and the opinions contained therein are mine.

The Hague, June 1959   Samuel Humes

INTRODUCTION TO PART II

Part II of this book contains summaries of the local government structures of 43 countries throughout the world. As was mentioned in the preface to this entire study, much of this information was contained in the replies of the various countries to the IULA-UNESCO questionnaire of 1955. In addition, or where information was not forthcoming from a country, any available literature on that country's local government was consulted, including unpublished theses, the country's Constitution and local government laws, government reports, articles in newspapers and journals, and books on local government in general as well as local government in that specific country. Whenever possible, too, further information was obtained from local government officials and experts, either personnally or by mail.

After having been written, each of the following summaries was then sent to a local government official, agency or organisation in its respective country for correction and approval. In most instances this contact person or organization was the original respondent to the questionnaire; in a few instances it was not. Moreover, when corrections submitted by a country were extensive, the revised summary was again sent to that country for final approval. In those few instances where official or expert approval of a summary was not forthcoming the IULA gave the responsible person or organisation adequate notice that unless corrections and comments were received within a stated length of time it would be assumed that the report was approved as submitted by the IULA. In these cases mention of a lack of official or expert approval has been made in a footnote to the summary.

It might be mentioned at this time that perhaps the greatest number of corrections submitted by the individual countries concerned the matter of terminology. This was bound to be so as an attempt was made in the summaries to use the standardized terminology established in the first part of this book. It was felt that only in this way could a great deal of confusion be avoided and an adequate basis for comparison be established. To many this attempt to avoid confusion has only led to further confusion. It is hoped, however, that this number is far outweighed by those who have found in a standardized terminology a clearer understanding of the likenesses and differences among countries in those aspects of local government which have been described in these summaries. Another confusion may be the grouping of countries in Part II by geographical locations rather than by alphabetical order. This too was done to aid the comparative section of this book. In most instances the geographical groupings show similar governmental patterns and structure; in other instances the relationship cannot be so easily seen. Again this was an arbitrary decision and, like most arbitrary matters, is subject to debate. It is to be hoped, however, that these groupings will not detract from the value of the information contained in the individual summaries of the 43 countries included in this study.

Following the completion of both parts of this book a report was received by the IULA concerning the local government structure of Peru. Although it was then impossible to consider this country in the comparative section of the book, the information received has been summarized and included in Part II. It was felt that this summary of local government in Peru should be included in this book primarily because there is such a dearth of information available on many countries in the southern part of the Western Hemisphere. Hopefully this will prove a stimulus for the further study and dissemination of information on countries in this as well as other parts of the world.

Acknowledgements

Were it not for the United States government, the Netherlands government and the International Union of Local Authorities my work on this study would not have been possible. To the American government goes my deep appreciation for having been granted a Fulbright Fellowship for nine months as an interne in local government research at the International Union of Local Authorities in The Hague; to the Dutch government goes my gratitude for accepting me in this capacity. To the IULA I extend my gratefulness for having been given the assignment of writing these summaries, for keeping me on this job one year longer than my original grant and for the honour of having this work published.

Specifically I should like to acknowledge the guidance and supervision of Mr. A. F. Leemans, who devoted much time and thought to the development of the general outline used in these summaries as well as much encouragement and support throughout a long task. I should also like to thank Miss V. Kyjovská and Mr.

C. J. Cossey who cheerfully gave of their time in the reading of foreign language documents, Mrs. C. J. J. de Bruijn who did much of the typing and Samuel Humes, the author of the first part of this book as well as the chapters in the second part. It was he who developed the standardized terminology for this study and conceived of dividing the 42 countries into nine geographical groups. Mr. Humes is also responsible for the charts in part II.

My further appreciation and gratitude go to Prof. Mr. C. H. F. Polak of the University of Leyden who also read and commented on the manuscript in addition to his many other tasks and responsibilities. And last, but certainly not least, many grateful thanks go to those people throughout the world who were responsible for reading their country's summary and making corrections and comments on it. May the extra effort and time this involved be counter-balanced by the knowledge that they have had a part in the further dissemination of information among the peoples of the world, if only in a small measure.

Batavia, New York, U.S.A. Eileen Martin
June 1960

PART ONE

I

LOCAL GOVERNMENT AND ITS STRUCTURE

1. Sovereignty and local government

IN our present-day, sovereignty-conscious world there are essentially four types of government. These are the supra-sovereign, the sovereign national, the quasi-sovereign (federated-)state, and the infra-sovereign local governments. Supra-sovereign governments, such as the European Coal and Steel Community, are still very few and relatively undeveloped; but they may be helping to make the term "sovereignty" obsolete. Today it is the sovereign national governments which exercise most authority and power, have the most fully developed bureaucracies, and upon which most public opinion is focused.

A quasi-sovereign[1] (federated-)state is a part of a federal form of government, either in constitutional theory or in practice or both. The essential principle of a federal form of government is that the sovereignty, that is, the supreme political authority and power, is in principle divided between the national government of the country as a whole and the federated-state governments of the major constituent geographical parts, so that each of them within its own sphere is supreme and independent of the other.[2] One of the spheres which is in principle reserved to the

---

[1] According to *The Shorter Oxford Dictionary*, "quasi" is defined as "(a) kind of; resembling or simulating, but not really the same."

[2] For a fuller description of "the federal principle" and the distinction between "a federal government" and "a federal constitution" see K. C. Wheare, *Federal Government* (London 1953), especially the first two chapters. Professor Wheare maintains that although many countries have a federal or quasi-federal constitution, only four countries, the United States, Switzerland, Australia and Canada, have a federal form of government in actual practice.

In determining, though, which countries in this survey have quasi-sovereign

federated-state government is local government. Thus the laws establishing and controlling local government are generally state laws, and the administrative controls over local government in countries with federal constitutions are usually exercised by state officials. From a local government viewpoint, then, both the state as well as the national governments are considered "central governments"; the states are quasi-sovereign and are not, therefore, considered to be local governments.

Local governments are infra-sovereign[1] geographic units contained within a sovereign nation or quasi-sovereign state. They include provinces and other intermediate units as well as municipalities and other basic units. Like all units of government, local government units have a defined area, a population, a continuing organization, and the authority to undertake and the power to carry out public activities. Many of them are legal persons, which means that they can sue and be sued and enter into contracts. Some may levy taxes and most have independent budgets. The main distinguishing characteristic of local governments is that they are infra-sovereign, that is, they do not have any aspects of sovereignty.[2]

---

constituent parts, I have deliberately included Brazil, West Germany, India, the Soviet Union, and Yugoslavia, which according to Wheare have a federal or quasi-federal constitution but do not operate as federal countries. I have also included Malaya and Austria whose constitutions were adopted after Wheare wrote his book. Partially I used this broader interpretation in order to avoid unnecessary controversy on a point which I do not consider crucial to this presentation. Moreover, whether or not a form of government in these countries is federal in practice, the major constituent parts appear and are considered by those in the countries concerned, to have some aspects of sovereignty, therefore they are in this survey defined as quasi-sovereign and are not considered to be local government. In fact I am doubtful if there are any fields in which the major constituent parts of any of these so-called federal countries, including the United States, are in fact sovereign, that is supreme and completely independent of the actions of the other.

[1] According to *The Shorter Oxford Dictionary*, "infra" is defined as "Denoting 'below' or 'beneath' (i.e. 'lower down than') in respect of status or conditions." It is also defined as "Denoting 'within' (as in medieval Latin), as *infra-territorial* etc."

[2] The local units may possess "inherent competence," however, which closely resembles the authority of some of the quasi-sovereign states. See page 38 in Chapter 3.

2. Three types of local government

Local governments are the infra-sovereign geographic subdivisions of a sovereign nation or quasi-sovereign state, providing public services in a particular area. In the broadest sense "local government" may be understood as all government which is local, that is, it might be interpreted as covering all the local organs of the central government, including the local posts of the national police and all other special-purpose field offices of one of the central government ministries. Generally, though, even a broad definition of local government, and the definition used in this survey, includes only those local units which are either "general-purpose," or "representative" or both.

"General-purpose" local governments are those which carry out most, and in some cases all, of the public activities within a particular area. The general-purpose local units may be contrasted with the "special-purpose" or "limited-purpose" local units which carry out only one or a few public activities within a particular area.

"Representative" local governments are those which have one or more legally constituted plural representative organs, that is organs all or most of whose members are elected (directly or indirectly) by the local citizens, which organs have some authority to govern. Local representative governments contrast with local non-representative governments which either do not have plural representative organs-or whose plural representative organs do not have any authority to govern.[1]

---

[1] I have used the terms "local representative government" and "local non-representative government" in preference to the terms "local self-government" and "local State government" which are employed by some writers. See, for instance, G. Montagu Harris, *Comparative Local Government* (London 1948), p. 9:

"(1) the government of all parts of a country by means of local agents appointed, and responsible only to, the central government. This is local government of a kind, but is part of a centralized system and may be called 'local State government,' or

(2) government by local bodies, freely elected, which, while subject to the supremacy of the national government, are endowed in some respects with power, discretion and responsibility, which they can exercise without control over their decisions by the higher authority. The extent of power, discretion and responsibility which the local bodies possess is a matter of degree, which varies considerably in the various countries. This is called in many countries, 'communal autonomy'; in others, 'local self-government.'"

I believe, though, that the terms "local representative government" and

In this survey most of the emphasis will be on local bodies which are both general-purpose and representative and are called units of local representative government.[1] Many European cities had some form of representative or limited representative government as early as the tenth, eleventh and twelfth centuries. For instance, the charters of many English cities date back to the Norman kings. Many French cities acquired prerogatives of limited representative government at least as early as the English cities, these prerogatives being guaranteed by charters which were sometimes gained by force of arms, sometimes by mere bargaining, and were in fact treaties or agreements with feudal lords. Similar developments occurred in other European countries such as Germany and Denmark. Local representative government of some form also has a long history in such countries as Sweden and Finland, not only in the urban municipalities but also in the rural areas. And in India a form of limited representative government existed in many villages long before it developed in the European cities.[2]

"local non-representative government" give a more precise indication of the differences between these twot ypes of local units, that is, the one has representative governing organs and the other has not. Furthermore the term "local State government" is confusing because the word "State" is in this study used to mean a quasi-sovereign constituent part of a federal country. The term "local self-government" I also find confusing. In the first place no local government is really self-governing for if it were it would not be infrasovereign. In the second place, the term "local self-government" may be interpreted to include units with no representative organs whose executives have opportunities to make a large share of the decisions concerning the local public activities.

My terminology may, of course, also be criticized. For instance, it may be argued that I have used the word "representative" too narrowly and that representative governments should include one or both of the following kinds of local units: (1) Those units with representative organs with no decisive authority and (2) those units with no plural representative organs but whose chief executive or headman may be considered "representative." I have chosen not to include the first group precisely because the "representative" organs do not govern. The second group I have not included because of the difficulty in finding adequate indices for judging when the head of a local government without a council can be considered to be "representative."

[1] The most descriptive title of these bodies would be general-purpose units of local representative government. For sake of simplicity, though, they will be called units of local representative government. Moreover, when the context makes it clear what is meant, they may even be referred to simply as "local governments" or "local units." In the same way the term units of local non-representative government will always indicate general-purpose non-representative local units. On the other hand, the special-purpose local representative units, or special-purpose authorities, will always be denoted as special-purpose units in order to distinguish them from the general-purpose local units.

[2] Harris, 10–11.

EXHIBIT 1 – THREE TYPES OF LOCAL GOVERNMENTS

Conditions	General-Purpose	Special-Purpose
Representative	*Units of Local Representative Government* Examples: French Municipality (*Commune*) French Province (*Département*) English Municipalities and Counties (Most of the emphasis of this survey will be on this type of local unit).	*Special-Purpose Units of Local Representative Government* (*Special Purpose Authorities*) Examples: French intermunicipal bodies (*Syndicat*) U. S. *School Board* (This type of local unit will be discussed in one section of chapter II, but only occasionally in other parts of this survey).
Non-Representative	*Units of Local Non Representative Government* Examples: French District (*Arrondissement*) Tunisian rural basic unit (This type of local unit will be discussed relatively little-mainly for purposes of contrast and comparison with the units of local representative government).	*Local Special-Purpose Organs of Central Government* (*Not Units of Local Government*) Possible Examples: Local Post Office Local Post of National Police (These special-purpose local organs of the central government bureaucracy will not be discussed in this survey).

These forms of limited representative government in Europe as well as other continents were in fact, though, mostly forms of oligarchy rather than forms of government based on a widespread suffrage. In some cases it was the guilds which ran the city. In other cases the oligarchy was composed of the members of a few leading families. Only a relatively few municipalities, including the Swiss, had forms of representative government in which a large percentage of the local inhabitants were actually represented.

It was not until the latter part of the nineteenth century that units of local representative governments based upon widespread suffrage took general root. Not until 1835 did English cities have councils which were elected by a significant portion of the local citizenry. It was not until 1884 that the French municipal councils had the authority to make decisions, although these councils had been elected bodies since 1831. In the latter part of the nineteenth century and the first half of the twentieth century though, forms of local representative government have spread to many other countries in Europe as well as to other continents.

In contrast to the general-purpose local representative governments are the second type of local units, called units of local non-representative government. They are general purpose but are not representative. Either there are no representative organs or these organs are only advisory.

About a hundred years ago in most countries the emphasis was on local non-representative government with the local governments serving as agencies of the central government. Systematized in France and other parts of continental Europe during the generation of the French Revolution and Napoleon, this pattern spread over most of Asia, Africa and South America. Regarding its development W. Hardy Wickwar has pointed out: "One reason for introducing this administrative pattern was, in fact, an effort to put an end to semi-autonomous provincial governors and substitute for them salaried agents of the central authorities. Another reason was that the creation of regular armies... removed the need for a feudal system under which land was held in return for the performance of military and administrative duties, and left a gap which needed to be filled."[1]

[1] Wickwar, W. Hardy, "Notes on Local Government Administration Areas

The third type of local units are the special-purpose units of local representative government, frequently called special-purpose authorities. They are limited –, instead of general –, purpose bodies and are governed by representative organs through which the citizens may exercise some control over the carrying out of the public activities. These representative organs may be either popular assemblies (as in Switzerland), or popularly elected organs (as in some of the U. S. school authorities), or more frequently, indirectly elected organs, whose members are selected by other governmental units. Special-purpose authorities are usually inter-municipal bodies organized to handle one or a few activities over an area which includes two or more units of local representative government.[1]

The two types of general-purpose units, that is the units of local representative and the units of non-representative government, may be said to make up the general pattern of tiers of contiguous non-overlapping local units. The special-purpose units are additions to this general pattern. Each of these three types of local units may be found co-existing with one or more of the other types in many countries. On the other hand in some countries such as the United Kingdom, there are no general-purpose units of local non-representative government. And there are several countries, of which none are included in the survey, which do not have any units of local representative government.

3. *The reasons for local government*

The reasons for having general-purpose geographical subdivisions or local units of a country or state are primarily historical and expeditious ones.[2] In the first place many of the local units of today, particularly the populous urban ones, had their origin as community governments earlier than the sovereign nations of

and Local Government Units in the Middle East," *Revue Internationale des Sciences Administratives*, Vol. XXIV, No. 2 (1958), p. 148.

[1] There are, though, some intra-municipal special-purpose authorities for many of the districts in the United States and a large number of the special authorities in Switzerland exist entirely within the boundaries of one municipality.

[2] The reasons for having special-purpose local authorities will be explained in the Chapter 2 in the section on special-purpose authorities.

which they are now a part. It was natural, therefore, that the local entities continued to exist as units of local government; in fact, political and administrative considerations usually made it imperative that they be retained.

Historical reasons are not the only factors, however, accounting for the widespread use of local government units. Probably the most important reason is the fact that the different public services must be integrated or arranged according to some criteria. Almost every country, with the possible exception of such historical anachronisms as San Marino, find it convenient to integrate their public activities by considerations of both function and area. Area integration of activities at the local levels is used in conjunction with the functional arrangement of ministries at the central government levels. Without geographically dispersed general-purpose local units a central government would be obliged to co-ordinate all public activities at a single central location, which would be impossible in all but the smallest countries. In any country larger than a city-state, therefore, the question is not whether to have general-purpose units of local government, but rather to what extent the general-purpose local units should be developed and assigned functions. These reasons for local government consider the local units from the central government point of view and apply with equal validity to local non-representative government and local representative government.

Having discussed the reasons for local government from the central government point of view, perhaps it is even more important now to consider them from the local point of view; these apply with greater validity to the units of local representative government. There are some public interests which are primarily local, that is they are interests which vary widely in intensity and are not common to all local areas. These are activities in which the opportunity for local discretion, not only in determining how to carry out the activity but also in many cases in deciding whether to undertake it, usually proves to be an advantage in effective administration. Furthermore the use of local units gives more opportunities for the local residents to have contact with, to take an interest in, and to have an understanding of, to exert influence upon, and even to participate in the public affairs of the communities. The local citizen has easier access to the local unit and can exert more influence on it than he can upon the central government. Furthermore local representative government forms a valuable training ground for the elected leaders at higher levels of representative government.

Local governments serve, then, at least one and often two main purposes. First of all, the local governments serve as geographic subdivisions of the sovereign or quasi-sovereign entities carrying out some portion of the public activities; and secondly, the units of local representative government give an opportunity for the local residents to determine and achieve desired objectives.

4. *The process of local government*

The process of local government may be succinctly described as the determination and implementation of decisions regarding local public policy.[1] The making and the carrying out of policy decisions are, of course, two almost indistinguishable phenomena in the process of local government, for the implementation of all but the most minor decisions requires making further decisions of an elucidating and clarifying nature; in fact wherever there is action involving decisions there is some degree of policy-making.

Policy-making, for the purposes of this survey, is the deciding of the actions to be taken. This includes five steps: (1) The determination of what is needed. (2) The determination of what most of the electorate will accept. (3) The determination of what can be done from an administrative, a financial, and sometimes a partisan political standpoint. (4) The determination that the action should be undertaken. (5) The determination of how and when the action should be undertaken.[2]

The making of local public policy is not, therefore, a task which is performed by only one type of organ. The local staff in units

---

[1] In this regard I have avoided making the familiar contrast of policy and administration because of the large amount of ambiguity now attached to both words. One might refer to Paul Appleby, *Policy and Administration* (University, Al. 1949) and Brian Chapman, *The Profession of Government* (London 1959), however, for an interesting treatment of this subject.

[2] Compare with Clarence E. Ridley, *The Role of the City Manager in Policy Formulation* (Chicago 1959), pp. 9–10.

of representative and non-representative forms of local government participates in the decision-making process. In units of local representative government the representative organs, that is those composed wholly or mainly of elected persons, make a large share of the decisions. Organs of units of higher governments also have a major part in the making of policy decisions in both the representative and non-representative processes of governments.

5. The structure of local government

The structure of local government is the framework within which local public policy is determined and implemented. In organizing any government one must take into account such contrasting, but not mutually exclusive, emphases as individual liberty and corporate authority, local political initiative and central government direction, citizen participation and professional management, and popular responsiveness and effective administration. Structures are the syntheses, albeit usually temporizing ones, of these apparently opposing values. The structure of an organization not only determines the relationship between the organs but also the balance between these apparently opposing values, and thus provides its inherent character and strength.

Pope once said "For forms of government let fools contest; Whate'er is best administered is best." Pope appeared, however, not to recognize that the way in which a government is organized has an important effect upon how the decisions are made, co-ordinated, and carried out. Structure is not an end in itself but it is an indispensable means to the end of government performance and results; "structure can increase or decrease the effectiveness of those who operate under it and can make the getting and retaining of able men more or less likely."[1]

In discussing organizational structure, one must draw a distinction between the formal static structure and the more informal kinetic structure. The static structure may be reduced to a set of laws and an organizational chart which diagrams the skeleton and organs. The informal structure, by contrast, is a

[1] Dennison, Henry, *Organizational Engineering* (1937), pp. 123–4.

complex living body which is best described in terms of what the body does rather than how it is made up inside. The description and analysis of organizational structures, like the description and study of animals, appears to offer a choice between classification according to skeleton and organs or identification according to performance. In fact, some type of combination of these two is desirable. Although it is readily apparent that a unit of government is more than the sum of its organs, the constitution of an organization defies quantitative comparative description. Therefore, although analysis of organizational structure must in practice begin with a description and classification of the skeleton and organs of the static structure, to be meaningful it must make some attempts to describe and correlate aspects of the kinetic structure.

Just as one may draw a distinction between formal static structure and the more informal kinetic structure, so one may also distinguish between the terms "authority" and "power". Authority is a more formal static term, referring to a legal ability to make decisions. Power, on the other hand, is a more informal kinetic term, referring to the actual ability to influence the decision-making process.

The most fruitful approach to an introductory study of the structure of a large number of local governments in many different countries appears to be through a comparison of the organs which comprise the local structures. One must analyse the role of each of the organs in the over-all structure by determining its authority and power and its inter-relationship with the other organs in the local government structure. This involves "responsibility," which may be defined as accountability to some body for carrying out some task.[1] Accountability to some organ is important because it is the most practical means of ensuring that public administrative acts will be in accord with the public needs as interpreted in the political process. The corollary of this is that responsibility means being accountable for some-

---

[1] In local government this term "responsibility" may have a wide variety of precise shades of meanings. For instance, a council member is responsible to the public, for it may choose not to re-elect him, and a civil servant is responsible to his superior, for the latter can order an action to be done. The word is used in very different senses. An attempt has been made in some places to indicate the different uses of the word but it has not always been possible to be precise.

thing for the doing of which there is the necessary authority and power. In this regard the difference between representative and non-representative local government is that the former is ultimately accountable to the electorate. For in units of local representative government the elected officials have some control (the control varying with the degree of representative government) of the decision-making process and these persons can be held accountable for their actions through the electoral process. If, after a decision is reached, the persons responsible for it are accountable for their actions in elections, then the electorate has an indirect control over the decision-making process. The public may not participate directly in the making of decisions, but by approving or disapproving the candidacy of members of the representative organs who have made some of the overall policy decisions the public is holding a weapon of control over these men.

Thus local representative government may be seen as a process involving different organs whose inter-relations are such that the electorate, through its authority to select the representative body, can, albeit indirectly, control both the policy-making as well as the policy implementation by the executive organs and the staff.

It is important, therefore, in any study of local government to examine the various organs of a local government and their relations to one another in order to obtain a perspective of the various types of local government structures.

2

THE UNITS OF LOCAL GOVERNMENT

1. *Number of tiers*

Considering the large variation in population and geographical size of the countries included in this survey it is remarkable that there is so little variety in the number of tiers of governmental units to be found in each. The largest number are to be found in some parts of India, Burma, and Ethiopia where there are as many as six tiers of government, counting the tiers of central as well as local government. All the countries in this survey, including Luxembourg and Iceland, have at least three tiers (again counting the national government as one tier). The only countries in which two tiers of local government are not generally found are Canada and Switzerland, whose major constituent parts are quasi-sovereign units of government.

Many factors influence the number of tiers and the number and size of the intermediate units. Some of the most obvious are the geographical size of the country, the population of the country, the number of basic units, and the degree of centralization. When all the policy decisions are centralized in the national capital there is an increased amount of administration needed at the intermediate levels to convert this central political direction into local administrative action.

In many countries there is a greater number of tiers in the rural areas than in the urban. This is particularly marked where the degree of development between the different areas varies greatly. To some extent this is also due to the tendency of the rural units to be smaller in population than their urban counterparts and to have fewer financial resources, political leaders and skilled administrators. The urban municipalities are often the equivalent of an intermediate unit in a rural area (district or province) in all respects except area.

There are often fewer tiers in the vicinity of the headquarters of the intermediate units. In a few countries such as Turkey and Iran, the local units in the vicinity of the seat of government of a province are directly supervised by the provincial offices, while the outlying area is divided into districts and supervised by the district officers. Likewise, if there are sub-districts, the district office will only directly supervise the local units in the immediate vicinity of its headquarters, leaving the supervision of the others to the sub-district offices. A similar situation exists in the French provinces (*départements*) whereby the chief assistant (*secrétaire-général*) to the provincial governor (*préfet*) is in theory the head of the district (*arrondissement*) in which the seat of the province is located. The administrative staff of both the district and province are identical.

In the United Kingdom and Germany as well as in a few other countries the large cities have a quasi-intermediate unit status, that is they themselves are not only municipalities but also provinces or another type of intermediate unit.[1] Furthermore, in France and Belgium all the municipalities over a certain population (in France 40,000; in Belgium 5,000) are supervised directly in the first instance by the provincial staffs while the municipalities under this size are supervised in the first instance by the district staffs. In most of the other countries with uniform systems the smaller municipalities, with consequently smaller and less specialized staffs, are supervised more closely.

Although in most European countries the total area, with a few minor exceptions, is included in the general municipal system, there are large portions of many countries which do not have any basic units of local government. Such unorganized areas are generally sparsely populated and local government activities may be administered directly by an intermediate unit of government or directly by the central government either as special territory or by various field offices of the individual ministries of the central government.

---

[1] These large cities are called quasi-intermediate units and will be mentioned later at the end of the chapter.

The pattern of geographical sub-divisions provides a framework within which the two different kinds of local government may be practised: local representative government and local non-representative government. In some countries, including the Anglo-Saxon, East European Communist, and some other European ones, all units of all tiers of local government have some form of representative government. In most other countries, though, not all the local units have councils – but generally most if not all of the basic units have representative organs.

2. *The municipalities and other basic units of local government*

The basic units of local government are those which make up the basic level in the pattern of general-purpose local government units; they are the municipalities as well as the basic units of non-representative government.[1] Usually the basic level is the lowest of the tiers of local government in a country; there are, however, exceptions. The municipalities of Portugal, Yugoslavia, the Philippines, and Brazil for instance, are on the next to the lowest tier. The lowest tiers in these countries are made up of units which are organs of the municipal governments and which have relatively few functions to fulfill. Often it is difficult to tell which of two layers of local units should be considered the level of municipal units. It is difficult to decide, for instance, whether to call the English *parish* or the *rural district* a rural municipality. The *rural districts* rather than the *parishes* have been considered the rural municipalities in this study not only because they are more nearly comparable to the urban municipalities (*urban districts* and *boroughs*) but also because the *rural districts* have so many more activities than the *parishes*.

In this survey the basic units of local representative government are called municipalities. In France the municipalities are called *communes*, and in the United Kingdom they are known as *boroughs, urban districts* and *rural districts*. In the United States the municipalities are generally called *cities, towns, boroughs,*

---

[1] Special mention should be made of those larger urban municipalities which are quasi-intermediate units in some countries. These units will be mentioned again at the end of the chapter.

villages and *townships*. Just as there is a wide variety in the degree of local representative government among municipalities, so do they vary in number and type of public activities, geographical size, number of inhabitants and degree of urbanization. Many municipalities cover only a few acres. Others, such as those in Brazil or the Sudan, mayer covhundreds and even thousands of square miles. The range in population is even more spectacular. Most are relatively small. In France several municipalities have no inhabitants; other municipalities have several million inhabitants. Municipalities which have a relatively large population and consist almost entirely of densely populated area, are the more stereotyped concept of municipalities. There are, however, an overwhelmingly greater number of municipal units in the rural area. These municipalities may include one or more hamlets or larger, more densely populated areas.

In the more rural areas general-purpose local government units were slower to develop. Local public activities were generally undertaken and co-ordinated at the initiative of either the local lord or the church. In fact most of the basic units of local representative government in the rural areas of Europe found their origin in the parish church councils. When the local government bodies were separated from the ecclesiastical units, the areas governed by each generally remained identical.[1]

The development during the last few centuries of the municipal systems in the non-European countries has been crucially influenced by the European example. On both of the American continents the forms of local government resembled those of their mother countries. Toward the end of the nineteenth century some of the countries in Asia as well as Europe adopted many aspects of the French system when setting up their own systems of local government. In other Asian and in African countries, too, the structures of the urban municipalities show a close resemblance to those of the European countries with which they have been associated. In the rural areas of many countries on these two continents the traditional village representative bodies were often undermined by the strengthening of the central governments that accompanied colonialism and the development of

[1] Jennings, W. Ivor, Laski, Harold, and Robson, W. A., *A Century of Municipal Progress* (London 1936), p. 32.

modern communication and transportation, which made stricter central control possible. Attempts to graft non-indigenous structures onto the village pattern of a different cultural environment have not been altogether successful.

The need for local government developed first, and has remained the greatest, in the large urban areas. Later came recognition of the fact that rural citizens have as much need for many local government services as do their urban neigbours. A great disparity between the public services provided in the rural and urban areas has, nevertheless, generally continued to exist. Only in recent years in a few countries has an extension of the size in the standard of living to the rural areas tended to reduce this disparity. In many countries, though, the disparity has not only continued but is also reflected in a diversified system of basic units.

3. *The uniform and diversified patterns of basic units*

In most countries there is a legal distinction made between different types of basic units with some having more authority than others. This may be called a diversified pattern of basic units. The basic units in urban areas have a more densely populated area and therefore a more obvious need for public services than do their rural counter-parts. Also the units in the urban areas usually have greater resources not only in terms of facilities and finances, but also in terms of able elected and staff officials. In those countries with diversified systems (such as the United Kingdom) most units in the urban areas are granted a broader competence than their rural neighbours. Often there are several categories of so-called urban municipalities, each category being authorized to perform a different number of activities. Among the urban municipalities are many with very small populations, some of which have achieved the urban municipal status because of historic, political and other (in some cases apparently irrelevant) factors. It should be emphasized therefore, that the distinction between urban and rural municipalities in this survey is one of legal, not of sociological, differences.

The rural basic units, which in many countries have a municipal status, generally have smaller populations, even though the areas are in many cases larger than those of the urban units. In the countries with diversified systems these are the units that have not qualified for the legal status of an urban municipality and the consequent broader authority which goes with such status. There are, however, many so-called rural municipalities which are densely populated and have an urban character. Among these are several North American municipalities (*townships*) which have close to 100,000 inhabitants and are part of a metropolitan area. Nevertheless, they have not requested nor have they been granted the legal status of an urban municipality.

In a few countries, such as Iran and Tunisia, where the difference in degree of development between the urban and rural areas is especially marked, the legal distinction between the urban and rural units is particularly significant. For in these countries the urban units have representative governing organs, whereas their rural counterparts do not.

In several countries, among them most of the South European and South and Central American countries, all the basic units have the same legal status. They are organized in the same manner and have the same rights and duties. This is commonly called a "uniform pattern" of municipalities. It was introduced in France during the Revolution and has become increasingly prevalent since 1800. During the nineteenth century, many European countries, including the Netherlands and Italy, adopted the uniform system; since World War II Sweden and Norway have approached this system by consolidating the rural units and increasing their legal competence.

In practice, of course, the principle of legal equality seldom means actual equality, unless the rural units are large enough to support activities equivalent to those of their urban counterparts. In those countries which have a uniform system of municipalities one or more of several conditions are generally to be found. Among the more obvious are the transfer of some of the functions of the basic units to a special-purpose local authority or to a higher unit of government.

A still further possibility is that the central government may step in and run a service for the less populated units, while the more populated units run such services as a matter of local government. In the Netherlands, for example, the municipalities above 25,000 population recruit and operate their own police force, while those under 10,000 have police assigned to them by the central government (for those in between 10,000 and 25,000, the type of police is determined individually for each municipality by the central government).

In many cases the smaller units can hardly afford to undertake the services which the law directs to be done; they rarely have the resources to take advantage of many of the powers which the law allows. A further result of this apparent inability of most rural units to meet the standards expected of them is that in practice the central government supervises and controls the activities of these units more strictly and in greater detail.

4. The population size of municipalities

The size of the units of non-representative government is not of great importance, for these units are merely field offices of higher organs whose activities are co-ordinated in the normal process of administration. The number of inhabitants of the municipalities, however, is a more important factor. Twentieth century municipalities are faced with a dilemma. To meet increasingly greater and more complex technical demands the local units should be large enough to maintain an adequate staff and facilities. The units should be also small enough to preserve the local community atmosphere and spirit in which each citizen feels he has an opportunity to be politically effective.

One of the most salient characteristics of our age is the booming growth of the urban areas. The metropolitan areas keep growing even when the central core appears to be past its prime of life. In the urban areas towns have expanded to cover rural areas and in their expansion have often grown into adjoining towns. Many urban municipalities have been forced, in most cases belatedly and insufficiently, to amalgamate in order that the joint problems of the area can be more effectively tackled. Nevertheless, most of the larger cities do not include within their borders large portions of the residential areas.

EXHIBIT 3 – SIMPLIFIED GEOGRAPHICAL DIAGRAM
OF SOME INTERMEDIATE UNITS[1]

a. THE NETHERLANDS

M	M	M	M	M
M	M	M	M	M
M	M	M	M	M
M	M	M	M	M

An example of the uniform municipal system

b. UNITED KINGDOM

An example of a diversified system with Quasi-Intermediate units (*County borough*) and Sub-Municipal units (Parishes).

c. UNITED STATES – SOME WESTERN STATES

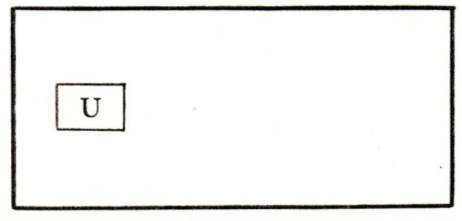

An example of secondary units which is not sub-divided in rural areas

[1] Symbols:
   U = urban municipality
   R = rural municipality
   M = uniform municipality
   QIM = Quasi-intermediate municipality

Boundaries
——————— secondary unit
——————— basic unit
·················· sub-municipal unit

d. GREECE

U	U	R	R	R
U	R	R	R	U
R	R	R	R	R
R	R	R	R	R

An example of a diversified municipal system

e. GERMANY

M	M	M	M	M
M	M	M	M	M
M	QIM	M	M	M
M	M	M	M	M

An example of uniform municipal system with Quasi-Intermediate unit

From the point of view of local government large cities have major disadvantages. The amount of activity on the part of the staff is greater and more complicated; consequently, the organisation tends to become more bureaucratic, the departments tend to become strongly separated services, and it is more difficult for the representative organs to retain a perspective of the overall program and keep control over the individual activities. The result is a diminished influence of the representative organs over the administration and a lack of opportunity for effective citizen participation. Only relatively few large urban areas, however, have experimented with federated metropolitan units of local government as a possible approach to diminishing these problems.

Although the problem of the oversized municipality is currently receiving much attention, the problem of most municipalities is their inadequate size. The vast proportion of municipalities have fewer than 2,000 residents. Such is the case, for example, with 85% or more of the Swiss, German, Austrian and French municipalities, a large percentage of which have fewer than 200 people. Generally these are rural municipalities whose boundaries have remained static over many decades.

The case against the very small municipality has probably been best expressed by Mill in his classic *Representative Government*: "Such small places have rarely a sufficient public to furnish a tolerable municipal council; if they contain any talent or knowledge applicable to public business, it is apt to be concentrated in some one man, who thereby becomes the dominator of the place. It is better that such places be merged in a larger circumscription."[1] With the passage of time the small size of many rural municipalities has become an even more acute disadvantage, for the developments of the technical age, in conjunction with higher standards of living and increasing demands for services requires larger units to more effectively carry out the activities that are expected of local governments. The result is that small local units have the alternatives of amalgamating or of losing their functions to higher units or special-purpose districts.

It is generally agreed that in principle larger municipal units

[1] Mill, J. S., *Representative Government* (London: Everyman's Library Edition 1957), p. 352.

are administratively desirable; but there are political obstacles. Most local politicians will use every political argument and weapon they know to prevent their positions from being legislated out of existence. Since local and national policy and politics are intertwined, it has proved politically difficult to change the boundaries of the local units.

But the arguments against amalgamation are not limited to selfish cries of personal self-preservation. It is argued, and often correctly, that the amalgamation creates an artificial basic unit by joining together several different communities. The municipal hall is no longer close and easily accessible to the people. Many times the larger community within the municipality is able to dominate the area with the result that the interests outside this community are sub-ordinated or even ignored. This is, for instance, one of the chief criticisms of the Brazilian municipal system. On the other hand the amalgamation program in Japan was aided by large grants to help build bridges and new community centres to foster a feeling for the larger community.

The dichotomy between desirable administrative size and desirable sociological size need not, however, continue to be a problem. The more frequent use of modern services, the telephone, the bus and the bicycle are undermining the claims of each individual centre of population to be the natural centre of a local community, especially in the more developed countries. People are more likely to work, to shop, and to have friends living at greater distances than would have been usual a century ago. A municipal headquarters need no longer be within easy walking distance to be close and accessible to the local inhabitants. Until the problem of inadequate size is tackled, many activities that might have been local government tasks will go by default to other units or will not be done. Without enough resources or enough capable political and administrative leaders to support the local government activities local representative governments become either do-nothing governments or façades for activities of the central government.

5. *The sub-municipal units*

There are two types of units of government which may be found wholly confined within the borders of a municipality. One is the intra-municipal special-purpose local authority which is organized to perform one or more particular functions as to operate the schools or to supply the water for a municipality. The second is the sub-municipal unit which is a geographical, although not necessarily an organizational, sub-division of a municipality.

Like other units of local government, sub-municipal units have a defined area, a population, and one or more officials, either voluntary or paid. They are, then, more than electoral geographical sub-divisions of a municipality (such as the *wards* in many Anglo-Saxon municipalities). Although the competence of a sub-municipal unit may cover most of the elementary services, the scope of its responsibilities is almost invariably more limited than that of a municipality.

In practice one must be somewhat arbitrary in drawing a distinction between a municipality and a sub-municipality.[1] The English sub-municipal units and the Danish rural municipalities resemble each other in many respects. The Danish local units, however, have a wide range of responsibilities and must still be considered the basic rural units of local government, that is rural municipalities. On the other hand, the English *parish* is a typical result of the British tendency not to discard historical institutions which appear to have out-lived their usefulness. The *parishes* have relatively few functions compared to the rural municipalities (*rural districts*) of which they are a geographical part.

For the most part sub-municipal units are a characteristic of large municipalities. In countries in which the main portion of the municipalities are large in both area and population, as in Yugoslavia, Brazil, Portugal, Ecuador, and the Philippines, the sub-municipal units form a part of the general pattern of units of local government. The municipalities are large enough to be administratively effective, while the sub-municipal units are small enough to retain immediate contact with the citizenry. Outside the urbanized area of the municipality, the sub-municipal units usually conform to the sociological communities, and the

[1] This was discussed in the second section of this chapter.

degree of representative government attributed to these varies. In the less developed countries each sub-municipal unit is generally governed by one man, the headman, with councils, where they exist, being confined to an advisory role.

The Philippine sub-municipal units (*barrios*), for instance, are the historic community units. They are headed by a headman who is appointed by the municipal councilman in charge of the unit and approved by the council. The headman may be aided by an advisory council which is also appointed. The sub-municipal units at the outskirts of the municipality are, in fact, virtually autonomous, if only because the municipal bureaucracy bothers little about them. Few functions, and often none at all, are carried out by the municipality in these areas; the headman is left to keep public order and to collect the taxes. On the other hand the sub-municipal units in the vicinity of the municipal headquarters have little, if any, individuality. Their officials have no duties other than to assist the municipal officials in the performance of their tasks.[1]

In Yugoslavia each centre of population within a municipality has a local committee composed of five to nine members, who are elected by the people of that community. Among the committee members may be two or more members of the municipal council (people's committee). In some respects this committee is similar to the administering committees discussed in a later chapter.

In Brazil the sub-municipal unit is headed by a vice-mayor who is usually appointed by the mayor although in one state he is popularly elected. The sub-municipal unit in this country is usually nothing more than a branch office of the municipal hall.

The sub-municipal units are not always deconcentrated offices of the municipal hall. In Turkey, as in England, the sub-municipal units are local units with representative organs. In the former country the sub-municipal unit (*mahalle*) is a geographical subdivision of an urban municipality, although it has no organizational ties with the municipality. Its work is reviewed by the district or provincial organs of the central government, and not by the municipality. Each sub-municipal unit has an organization similar to that of a rural municipality, with an elected

---

[1] Romani, John H., "The Philippine Barrio," *Far Eastern Quaterly*, XV, No. 2 (Februari 1956), pp. 229–239.

"council of elders" headed by a chairman, all of whom serve a two year term of office. The representative organs have few decisions to make, however, since all their functions, such as keeping the vital statistics and notifying conscripts for the army, allow very little discretion.

Sub-municipal units may also be found in the larger cities of many countries. This is particularly true of those cities which have quasi-intermediate unit status, such as Warsaw, and Beirut. Many other large cities have one or more special organs of a less formal character for dealing with matters affecting one area within the municipality, but it is difficult to determine whether they have a sub-municipal character.

6. *The local special-purpose authorities*

The importance of local special-purpose authorities in the over-all pattern of units of local government is twofold. They are a medium for undertaking many of the local activities which the general-purpose units are unable to handle adequately due to one or more limitations. The use of special-purpose authorities, however, sometimes creates a muddle of overlapping units superimposed on the over-all pattern of general-purpose units of local governments.

Special-purpose local authorities may be differentiated from a general-purpose unit of local government by the fact that to them is devolved only one or a few activities, such as education, health, or certain public utilities. This *ad hoc* authority, as it is sometimes called, has its own staff, its own budget, and a defined geographical jurisdiction which may cover the territory, or parts of the territory, of one, two, or more general-purpose units of local government.

The special-purpose authority is distinguished from the special purpose deconcentrated agencies of the central government bureaucratic hierarchy by the fact that it is outside this administrative hierarchy and has a representative governing organ, whose members may be selected in one or more of the following ways. First of all many inter-municipal special-purpose authorities are composed of representatives of the municipal organs of the constituent municipalities. Sometimes the representative organs may be composed of persons selected by the special groups, such as professional organizations, chiefly concerned with the activities. Other representative organs are directly elected, as is the case with many of the "school boards" in the United States. In a few intra-municipal special-purpose authorites, such as some of the Swiss local "relief communes," all the electors form the representative organ of the unit. In some cases a few (but not a majority, for then it would be classified as a deconcentrated agency of the central government) of the members of the representative organs may be central government appointees or officials serving ex-officio on the organ.

There are, of course, many special-purpose authorities with more than one of these four main types of members of the governing bodies. One not so well known example is the "sanitary authority" in Thailand, whose governing body consists of ex-officio members and four directly elected members. The former are the provincial governor, a deputy provincial governor, the local police head, finance and health officers, and all the village and village group headmen whose jurisdictions lie within the sanitary district; and the latter are generally elected by the inhabitants of the sanitary district. This authority has a limited number of activities which are devolved to it by the Ministry of Interior and it operates according to ministerial regulations.

There are a variety of inter-related historical, geographical, legal, financial, and constitutional reasons for the existence of special-purpose local authorities. The geographical considerations of determining the area most convenient for the inhabitants and most efficient for administration have often been among the basic reasons for setting up and continuing special-purpose local authorities. Different local public activities often need areas which are arranged in basically different ways; the most practical area for an elementary school, for instance, will not usually be the same as for a water or sewage utility district. Quite often it is necessary to organize special-purpose local authorities because the arrangement of the boundaries of the general-purpose local units is unsatisfactory for specific types of local public activities. Although an alternative is to arrange the boundaries of the local general-purpose unit in such a way that all of its local public activities may be carried on in a practical manner, this is seldom possible.

Considerations of size are probably the primary reasons for the presence of inter-municipal special-purpose authorities. These are found in a wide variety of countries, particularly those with many small units. Thus the small units must co-operate to supply such services as a hospital, for example, which each cannot provide separately. Perhaps the most complete recognition of the need for small basic units to work together to provide local public services is in Germany, where municipal unions have been formed which have their own council, board and administration, as well as a chief executive officer.

The intra-municipal special-purpose local authorities (as contrasted with the inter-municipal ones) are found mainly in such British-influenced countries as the United States, Canada, Australia, New Zealand and India. Although in the nineteenth century England, too, carried out many of her local public activities through special-purpose local authorities, in the twentieth century English local government has been almost completely integrated into a pattern of general-purpose local units. Switzerland is another country with a large number of special-purpose intra-municipal local authorities. In most of the cantons there are special-purpose religious (*paroissiales*) and relief (*bourgeoises*) authorities in each municipality.

The reasons for the establishment of intra-municipal special-purpose authorities are more complex than are those for the establishment of inter-municipal ones. The primary ones are constitutional and other political considerations. Professor Alderfer points out that the large number of school authorities in the United States, for example, is a product of the early nineteenth century, when it was considered important to separate education from the "politics" of municipal government.[1] For the same reason watch (police) committees of many Canadian municipalities are virtually independent. On the other hand, many of the public utility special-purpose local authorities which are intra-municipal in character were set up to escape debt or other financial and legal restrictions which are imposed upon the general-

---

[1] Alderfer, Harold F., *American Local Government and Administration* (New York 1956), p. 16.

purpose local units by the constitutions and other laws of the central governments. A consequence has been that in the last few decades there has been a rapidly increasing number of special-purpose authorities in the field of public works and utilities.

Special-purpose authorities may be organized and have their activities devolved to them by either central or local government units and sometimes by both. When two or more municipalities form an authority to carry out an activity jointly, they devolve an activity to this new authority. Special-purpose authorities may also be established by the central government to carry out activities for a certain given area.

Though the reasons for setting up special-purpose authorities are obvious, such a solution brings its own problems. For instance, Professor Robson points out that:

> "The most serious drawback of the *ad hoc* body is that there is no method of co-ordinating its work with related activities carried out by other bodies. It has one, and only one, object in view; and it is in a sense failing to discharge its duty if it attempts to take a comprehensive view of things... Housing, planning, transport, highways – how can one separate such a group as this? And housing in turn involves education, drainage, public health, gas and electricity and many other services. There are hundreds of other points of contact between the various public and social services where the single eye is needed to obtain the best result."[1]

The second main drawback of the special-purpose authority is precisely what many of its advocates consider as its virtue. It is isolated from politics and therefore from direct popular control. "Taking an agency out of politics" is a fallacious argument, for no agency can be taken out of politics as long as its operations are to be guided by public policy. The question is not whether the authority should operate in a vacuum but to whom the agency should be responsible. The interest of the public can probably best be served by having the responsibility for local activities focused in one central representative organ, which can integrate them with others being carried on in the same area, whenever this is possible.

Despite these drawbacks to the establishment of special-purpose local authorities they will continue to be found useful, if

---

[1] Robson, W. A., *The Government and the Misgovernment of London* (London, 2nd Edition), pp. 333–4.

only quasi-effective, solutions. In many cases the only alternative arrangement would be for the local units to amalgamate or to pass their functions on to the secondary units or to the central government; such arrangements have their own undesirable or inexpedient features.

7. *The intermediate units*

The intermediate units of local government are those units making up the intermediate levels of general purpose units of local government that is the levels between the basic level and the national or state governments. In principle the general-purpose intermediate units contain within their borders two or more basic units, although in fact, many have either no or only one such basic unit. The intermediate units may be units of local representative or local non-representative government.

Like many other aspects of local government, intermediate units are difficult to discuss, because there is no accepted vocabulary. In the English language they are generally referred to as provinces, districts, and counties.[1] In this survey, whenever there are two layers of intermediate units within a given country, the units on the higher level will be referred to as provinces and the lower as districts. When there are three or more tiers of intermediate units, the words sub-province and sub-district will also be used. The tier immediately above the basic tier may be called the secondary tier and the units at this level secondary units.

In many European countries the intermediate units trace their origin to the feudal ages and their present-day areas are almost identical to the principalities, duchies, and counties of former times. Only a few European countries (outside of East Europe) have as thoroughly re-organized their pattern of intermediate units as did France around 1800.

---

[1] The term *county*, which is generally synonymous with district, will be used for the Anglo-Saxon intermediate units. The word *county* is used partially because it is generally accepted, partially because a large number of counties are in fact basic units, and partially because the nature of the relationship of counties to the municipalities contained therein generally differs substantially from the relationship of the intermediate units in other countries to the basic units contained within them (i.e. the counties have little if any authority to review the decisions of the local units within its geographic borders.)

There is a wide variety in the population and size of the intermediate units. Some of the Indian provinces, for instance, are larger than many sovereign countries. On the other hand, many intermediate units are relatively small and include only a few centres of population.

The intermediate units generally have more deconcentrated and fewer decentralized activities than the basic units. At the intermediate levels, too, there is generally less emphasis on the representative aspect of the governmental process.

The activities of intermediate units fall broadly into four main categories. First of all, like the basic units they often directly carry out many local public services according to policies determined by the central government. Secondly, many intermediate units are responsible for co-ordinating the local activities of central government ministries in their area. Thirdly, except in the Anglo-Saxon countries, intermediate units are generally responsible for supervising the activities of the local units within their jurisdiction. And finally, in addition to the above deconcentrated activities, those intermediate units which have organs of local representative government undertake some decentralized activities.

A majority of intermediate units are units of local non-representative government which are responsible only for deconcentrated activities and have no representative governing organs. Examples include the French districts (*arrondissements*), and the provinces of Iran, Thailand, and Finland. Other examples are the Portuguese and Greek provinces, which have only advisory councils.

A second frequently found kind of intermediate unit operates in some respects like a unit of local non-representative government, although it does have a representative governing organ. The decentralized authority of these units is so limited, that the councils tend to be more appendages than vital parts in the governing process. The French province *(département)* is the most well-known and copied example of this type of intermediate unit. First, it directly carries out some duties as an agency of the central government. Secondly, the provincial governor (*préfet*) is the legal superior of all the other central government offices in the province and is charged with the co-ordination of their duties. Thirdly, the

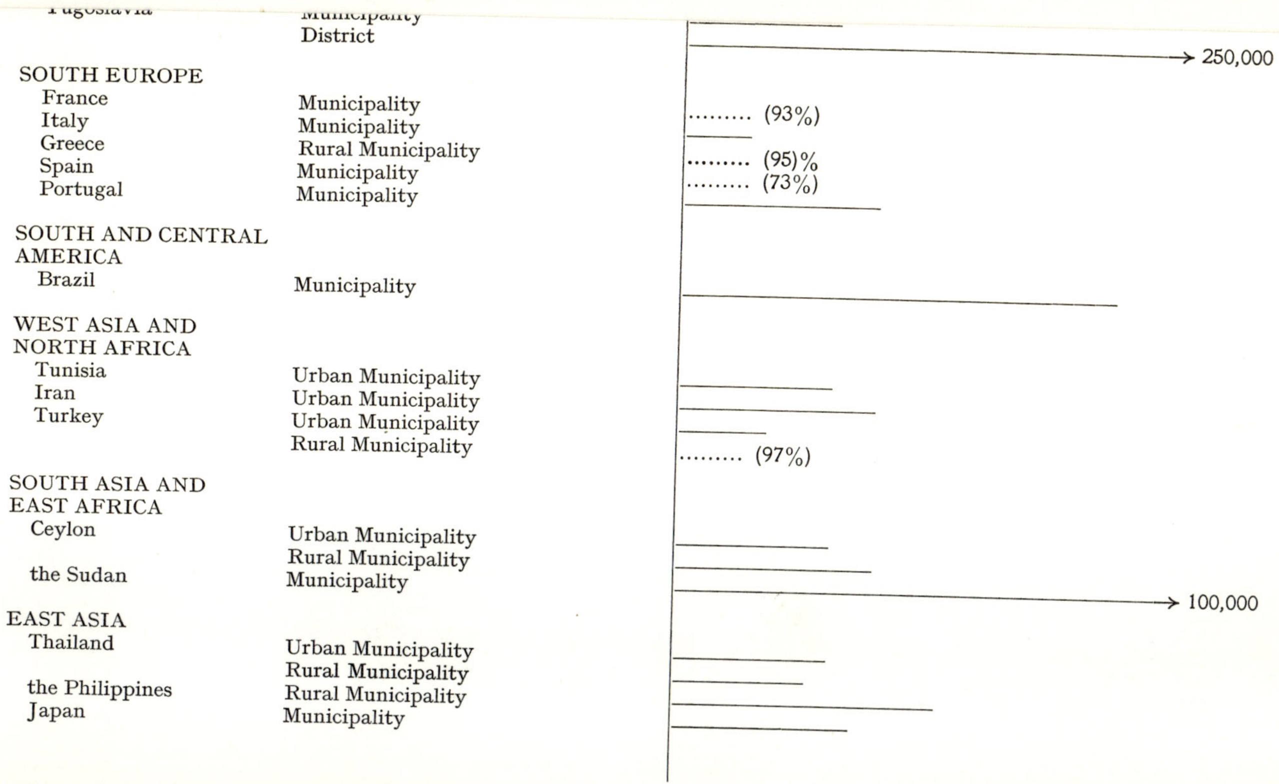

District
250,000
SOUTH EUROPE
France
Italy
Greece
Spain
Portugal
Municipality
Municipality
Rural Municipality
Municipality
Municipality
(93%)
(95)%
(73%)
SOUTH AND CENTRAL AMERICA
Brazil
Municipality
WEST ASIA AND NORTH AFRICA
Tunisia
Iran
Turkey
Urban Municipality
Urban Municipality
Urban Municipality
Rural Municipality
(97%)
SOUTH ASIA AND EAST AFRICA
Ceylon
the Sudan
Urban Municipality
Rural Municipality
Municipality
100,000
EAST ASIA
Thailand
the Philippines
Japan
Urban Municipality
Rural Municipality
Rural Municipality
Municipality

Median means "situated in the middle," therefore, half of any group of local governments will have a population greater than the median, half will have a population less than the median.

The large majority of local units have medians somewhere between 0 and 2,000. In these local units the exact median can not be determined from the figures available; however, the approximate percentage of local units with populations lower than 2,000 is included between parentheses following the appropriate line .... (75%). Many of these municipalities may have only a few residents; for instance more than 500 of the approximately 38.000 French municipalities have less than 50 inhabitants.

provincial government closely supervises the activities of each of the basic units. Finally, the provincial administration, under the immediate direction of the governor, carries out some functions which are the decentralized responsibilities of the provincial council.

A third type of arrangement for carrying out local government activities at the intermediate levels is that found in the Swedish and Italian provinces. In both countries each province has two government organisations (with separate chief executives) which serve the same area and population. One organisation is purely a unit of local non-representative government; the other is a unit of local representative government. This same arrangement is also found in many of the districts in India.

There are also many intermediate units which have well developed representative governing organs and a relatively large number of decentralized activities. In this category may be listed the Dutch and Norwegian provinces.

The intermediate units of local representative government in several countries may be described as "quasi-municipal." Thus, in Denmark, Germany, the United Kingdom, and the United States, the relatively smaller size of most of the intermediate units of representative governments, along with the frequent inability of the basic units to fulfil their roles adequately, has meant that these intermediate units are assuming more and more the role of municipal units.

In many western and southern states of the United States the county is the rural basic unit. Although here urban areas may be incorporated as municipalities and theoretically remain within the county, for most purposes they are generally ignored by the county administration. In some other U.S. states the rural basic units (*townships*) exist in theory, but they are extinct or dying out in practice. In many relatively less developed countries, such as Malaya, the districts directly govern most of the rural area, although there are many small rural municipalities, or villages, also included within and responsible to the district.

Many large urban municipalities may be referred to as quasi-intermediate units, for they have simultaneously the legal status of both a municipality and an intermediate unit. Tokyo, Warsaw, Stockholm, Moscow, and Beirut, for example, have the status of a province. Some cities, like Hamburg, even have the status of a quasi-sovereign state. In the United Kingdom, Germany and Poland a large number of the medium sized as well as large cities have a quasi-intermediate status. This is often referred to as one-tier local government. Many of these large cities then have sub-municipal units.

3

THE RELATIONS WITH THE CENTRAL GOVERNMENT

1. Local representative government and the central government

No unit of local government is, by definition, completely self-governing. If it were, it would no longer be a unit of local government but rather a sovereign city-state such as ancient Athens or modern San Marino. Although historically a central government may have developed later than most of the local units now contained therein, legally speaking all units of local government are dependent upon and derive their authority from the central government. In theory the authority of the central government over the local non-representative government units is absolute; however, in practice some of these units may be so remote that the central government has difficulty in exercising its power.

The central government also has the authority to exercise some control over units of local representative government. This is regarded as both necessary and desirable to guarantee that these local units conform to certain minimum standards. The maintenance of a proper standard of local government is a matter of more than purely local concern, since the effects of poor government rarely are confined to the locality in which they occur. On the other hand, central government control tends to weaken the sense of responsibility of the local people for the proper handling of local affairs. Nor is the judgement of central government officials necessarily always superior to that of local organs. Central government supervision becomes objectionable when it tends to deny local representative government the opportunity to take the initiative, act upon it, and to realize its objectives. Thus the needs of central government supervision must be balanced with those of local representative government.

The control exercised by the central government over the local units is not, strictly speaking, a part of the structure of local representative government. Nevertheless, even where the degree of control is relatively small, the relationship between the local units and the central government has a critical influence on the local government structure and, more important, on how the local units operate. Whereas the representative council may be described as the foundation of local representative government, it is the relationship with the central government which provides the groundwork upon which these foundations are laid.

It is difficult to describe how the relationship between a central government and the local units influences the municipal structures and their degree of local representative government. Like an iceberg, only the small proportion that appears on the surface is easily analysed. A far larger proportion is beneath the surface, where its significance and consequences are more difficult to determine. The central government may exercise control over the local units by many inter-related means, including the right to review some or all of the local decisions and to check, and even to interfere in, matters concerning personnel or finances. Ultimately, moreover, the central government has the prerogative to create, change, and even terminate the existence of the local units as well as to determine their competence.

2. *Local representative government and the central government ministries*

Most of the central government ministries participate in the regulation, supervision, and tutelage of the units of local government by directly or indirectly supervising the activities of the local units in their respective field of concern. A ministry of health, for example, usually works closely with the local units to see that they carry out their public health activities in a manner that conforms to the central government statutes and regulations, and ministries of housing and of education have similar responsibilities in their respective fields.

From the point of view of local government a few central government ministries have especially important roles. These are the ministries charged with finance, police, and the co-ordination of local government activities. The ministry of finance may be important, at least in part, because of its part in determining the availability of money for subsidies to supplement the locally raised revenues of the usually hard pressed local government units.

A crucial role in local government is also played by the ministry that has control of the police. Usually it is the "ministry of the interior" and sometimes the "ministry of justice." Maintaining the security and enforcing the peace is probably the most basic activity of local government. In several countries, especially in West Asia and North Africa, the police function is virtually the only local public activity in the rural areas.[1]

One central government ministry is generally directly charged with the over-all co-ordination of the local activities. In many countries, particularly the centralized ones such as France, the deconcentrated geographically dispersed field agencies of this ministry, which is the ministry of the interior, are the executive and staff organs of the intermediate units and they are often charged with co-ordinating all the local activities of the other central government ministries. On the other hand, in a few countries such as the United Kingdom this co-ordinating ministry, the Ministry of Housing and Local Government, has a much less dominant role. It serves more as a clearing house for the collection and disposal of reports, statistics, and information in addition to its other activities. It does not have the direct relationship with the local units as does the ministry of the interior in France.

The ministry charged with the co-ordination of local government activities is also almost invariably charged with one of the other local government-related activities, usually that of the police (as is the case with the ministry of the interior in France). In many countries the ministry of the interior is considered one of the most important cabinet posts, and from the point of view of local government in a highly centralized country this ministry is without a peer. The minister of the interior and his chief assistants

[1] Wickwar, W. Hardy, "Patterns and Problems of Local Administration in the Middle East." *The Middle East Journal* (Summer 1958), p. 253.

are often in crucial positions to help or hinder the development of responsible local representative government.

3. *The creation, alteration, and termination of local units*

The control over the very existence of the local units in theory is the most fundamental prerogative of the central government in the field of local government. The creation, alteration of boundaries, amalgamation, improvement of legal status, and termination of the existence of local units are essential aspects, albeit often politically inexpedient ones, of the authority of a sovereign country or quasi-sovereign state. Each of these actions can only be taken in accordance with a central government statute or in some cases a regulation.

In some countries each change affecting the creation, alteration, or termination of a local unit requires an act of legislature. In many countries, though, the statutes merely set forth the conditions which must be met to accomplish one of these objectives. Other central government organs, either executive or judicial, are charged with the determination of whether specific municipalities have met these conditions as well as with the implementation of the change. For instance, a few countries such as Turkey have statutes governing the minimum population of rural municipalities and most countries set forth definite conditions under which a rural municipality may achieve urban status.

There are several countries with planned programmes of amalgamation although most are not as comprehensive as those which have recently taken place in Sweden and Japan. Specific changes in the boundaries, status, or existence of the local representative governing units in other countries are usually left by law to the initiative of the local population. Political conditions usually make such changes by local initiative impractical.

4. *The authority of the municipalities and other local units*

The authority of the local governmental units is their legal *raison d'être*; it is their basic legal ability, or competence, to enact by-laws and make other decisions involved in carrying out their functions. The number of activities, the degree to which the local units act in their own right or as agents of the central government, the juridical source of the authority to carry out these activities, and the degree to which the courts protect the right of the local units to exercise these functions are the major factors in determining the extent of the competence of a unit of local government. The autority of a unit of local non-representative government is generally limited to making relatively unimportant decisions regarding carrying out policies determined by the central government. On the other hand, units of representative government may have the authority to make a wide range of decisions, including passing by-laws.

There is a marked contrast between the large number of functions exercised by most of the northern European municipalities and the minimum exercised by many of the rural units in the less developed areas of the world. In the latter areas the functions often consist only of collecting the taxes, registering the births and deaths, and maintaining the public security, which includes the police and minor judicial functions. In many of the northern and central west European countries, on the other hand, the number of local functions is comparatively large. This is due primarily to the following reasons:

1. national constitutional clauses allow the municipalities the right to undertake any local government "domestic" activities without specific authorization by national statutes;

2. the large number of functions that are deconcentrated to the municipalities, often directly to their executive organs as agents of the central government, and

3. the relatively satisfactory state of their finances.

There is a variety of different interpretations of the terms "decentralization" and "deconcentration." (Moreover some use other terms, such as "autonomous" and "delegated" to make a similar – although not the same distinction). In order to give a clear idea about the relationship between the central government and the local ones and to define the manner in which the functions of government are exercised locally, it is necessary in the course of this survey to be able to draw a distinction, albeit a relative one, between (1) those functions in the carrying out of which the representative organs of a local unit may exercise a significant degree of discretion and (2) those other functions in the implementation of which the local units have no opportunity to exercise discretion. For the purposes of this survey, therefore, decentralized functions are to be interpreted as including not only permissive functions (that is those functions which the local units may do – but are not obliged to do – and may carry out in a manner to be determined by themselves), but also those obligatory functions in the carrying out of which the representative organs may exercise a significant degree of discretion. Deconcentrated functions, on the other hand, are to be interpreted to include those obligatory functions which the local units must carry out in a manner which is precisely specified in the law or directive by which the function is deconcentrated – and the implementation of deconcentrated functions is closely controlled by the staff of higher units.

According to this interpretation units of local non-representative government may be said to have only decondentrated functions, and units of local representative government almost invariably have deconcentrated as well as decentralized functions. The degree to which units of local representative government exercise decentralized or deconcentrated functions varies widely not only from country to country but also from activity to activity.

In some cases directives issued by the executive or staff organs of the central government or of the other higher units are used to spell out exactly how a deconcentrated task is to be carried out. These directives may be either general or specific in nature. General directives are equally applicable to all local units and are used in almost all countries. Specific directives are applicable only to certain specific local units cited by the directive; this type of directive is in most cases used in countries with relatively less local representative government. The effect of the use of directives on local government depends to a great extent on how and by whom the directives are issued and enforced. In France, and many other countries, the directives are enforced by the executive organs of the central government and in effect the provincial governor may "order" to local mayors to undertake certain actions. The penalty for not complying may be the dismissal of the local officials. In several countries, if the local officials refuse to act, the directives cannot be enforced without court action; the juridical penalties include fines against the local officials.

In the last few decades, and particularly since World War II, there has been in almost every country a marked increase in the number of deconcentrated activities undertaken by the local units, often at the expense of the number of decentralized activities, with the result that the local units appear to have less opportunity to exercise discretion on whether and how to carry out many activities. Whereas formerly the local units often had decentralized authority which was unused, now they must undertake these activities in a specific manner. Danish local government, as described by Arneson, is only one of many examples of this trend:

"It is clear from this brief description that the parish (s. c. rural municipality) not only takes care of matters of a purely local nature but that it also partakes in a large degree of the nature of an administrative agency for the central government. This development is so marked that it has led some Danish commentators to say that the present status of local units in Denmark should not be discussed as *local government* but rather as *local administration*.[1]

This phenomenon is even more obvious in some of the Asian countries. In Japan, for instance, the distinction between the rural municipality as an autonomous entity and as a national agency breaks down, and central government exercises general guidance without regard to this dual character of the village:

"There exists thus a hyperthophy of nationally assigned functions which is accompanied by an atrophy of proper local functions. The situation may be illustrated by the fact that village mayors are usually unable to indicate the range of independent functions of the village. When they venture an estimate of the percentage of their own time and effort devoted to funct ons which are assigned by the national government, the figure given is generally about 80 per cent."[2]

The degree to which municipalities exercise activities in their own right is in part dependent not only on the total amount of legal competence but also on the source of their authority. The

[1] Arneson, Ben A., *The Democratic Monarchies of Scandinavia*, (New York, 1949), pp. 184–5.
[2] Steiner, Kurt, "The Japanese Village and Its Government," *FEQ*, Vol. XV, No. 2 (February 1956), p. 191.

local units derive their autority from three types of central government documents: constitutions, statutes, and administrative regulations. Activities derived by virtue of administrative regulations inevitably are deconcentrated functions for which the local councils have little, if any, discretionary authority. Such activities are usually deconcentrated directly to the chief executive, or in some cases the board, although they may also be deconcentrated to the council. Activities devolved by statute may be either deconcentrated or decentralized. Functions derived by virtue of clauses of the central government constitutions are considered decentralized functions for which the units of local representative government have more discretionary authority. Many of the European countries as well as Brazil, for example, have constitutions that guarantee to the municipalities local government "domestic" functions. What these functions are is, however, determined by the central government statutes, or the lack of such statutes. Fire protection, for instance, may be considered a local government "domestic" function until such a time as the central government passes a law which assumes for itself the authority to regulate fire protection, at which time it may deconcentrate certain fire protection tasks to the municipalities.

A unit of local government may, then, have either a specific authority or a general authority to undertake decentralized activities. In countries in which there is constitution-derived competence, the local units have been devolved a general authority, usually called "inherent competence", to do anything which is not specifically forbidden or is not granted exclusively to another unit of government. On the other hand in Anglo-Saxon law the competence of the local units must be specifically granted by statutes. In England, for example, if a unit of local government wants to do something there must be a specific central government statute directly authorizing the local unit to do it. It is pointed out by Jackson that "The recasting of English local government in the nineteenth century led to a very different doctrine which is that local authorities (s.c. units of local government) have only those powers that have been given to them."[1] Anglo-Saxon local units have no such thing as inherent com-

---

[1] Jackson, R. M., *The Machinery of Local Government* (London 1958), p. 38.

petence, for if there is no competence to undertake something, it is beyond their competence, or *ultra vires.*

The extent to which activities are actually decentralized or deconcentrated, depends in fact on the various organs of the central government The central government legislature has the authority to enact the statutes that determine the statute-derived competence or define the constitution-derived competence; and the latitude of the executive organs in their supervision of the local units determines to a great extent the degree of discretion allowed at the local level. In the few countries in which courts have the authority to pass judgement on the central government's legislative statutes and render them null and void, if they trespass on the autority of the municipalities, there is at least some degree of protection against the encroachment of central government authority. In the other countries, however, the legislative and executive organs of the central governments are not hindered from such encroachment.

5. *The review of local decisions*

The authority to review is the prerogative of the higher units of government to check and annul, or refuse to render valid, decisions made by the local units. Such review has two possible aspects. One is to prevent the local units from making decisions in an unproper or illegal manner or taking actions in matters that are outside of their competence. This may be called legal review and is a characteristic common to the process of review in every country. The second aspect is to prevent the local units from making decisions or taking actions which are, in the opinion of the central government organs, contrary to the general interest, even though they may be legally acceptable. This may be called merit review and is not as widely used as its counterpart.

In the Latin countries, and most of those that are Latin-influenced, all local resolutions are usually closely reviewed for both lack of legality and lack of merit. Regarding the practice in French local government Chapman observes that "*All* decisions of the *conseil municipal,* no matter what their content or authority, have to be deposited at the Prefecture or Sub-Prefecture for a certain time before they can be put into effect."[1] Decisions concerning finance, contracts, property, and the appointment of local officials must be approved by the provincial governor before they become operative; and the approval is discretionary. Not only must the communal budget receive approval prior to becoming valid, but also the provincial governor (*préfet*) or sub-provincial governor (*sous-préfet*) may make item additions or deletions. Furthermore, the decisions of the mayor as well as of the municipal council are subject to a strict higher control. Any decisions which the mayor takes in this capacity of a state official directly subordinated to the provincial governor, may be changed or annulled at the discretion of the governor.

In Italy since the last war the power of review has been divided between the two intermediate units covering the same area but with separate executives and administrative organs. One of these is a unit of local non-representative government (prefectorate) headed by the provincial governor, and the other is a unit of local representative government with a board. The provincial governor, who is head of the prefectorate and as such is an agent of the central government, exercises the prerogative of legal review. The board of the intermediate unit of local representative government exercises the prerogative of merit review.

In Germany decisions of the local units regarding deconcentrated activities are reviewed by the district chief executive for reasons of merit as well as legality. In addition, all important financial decisions are usually subject to review for the same reasons. Most decisions in the decentralized field are, however, only reviewed to see that they do not conflict with the central government law. The local units may appeal adverse decisions to the state or the federal courts.

In Sweden the situation is somewhat similar to that of Germany. The Swedish provincial governor as the representative of the crown may exercise the prerogative of review. Actually he seldom reviews the local decisions unless there is an appeal made by an interested citizen. The protest period is at present three weeks and an appeal from an adverse decision of the provincial governor may go to the supreme administrative council (*Regie-*

---

[1] Chapman, Brian, *Introduction to French Local Government* (London 1953), p. 129.

rungsratt). Appeal of a municipal decision in the field of the so-called "free" functions can be made by any citizen but only on the basis of its legality. An appeal of a decision in the so-called "regulated" sphere may be made only by a citizen affected by the decision; in this case the merit of the decision may also be challenged and a new decision may be forced upon the local unit.

In the Anglo-Saxon countries the pattern of review differs from that in other countries. There are no provincial governors or other executive organs of intermediate units which have authority as agents of the central government to review the resolutions and ordinances, including the budget, of the council. Furthermore there are no municipal chief executives serving in a dual capacity as officers of the local unit and as agents of the central government; therefore, the central government cannot directly supervise or control their activities. Thus some of the better known forms of central control are absent.

Instead, however, there are many more subtle means of control, some of which are mentioned in other sections. One of the most noticeable is that with the increase in central government financial aid to local units there has come a corresponding increase in central control. Central government ministries have statutory authority of many kinds affecting the activities of the local units. Thus, the units of local government must submit their school development plans to the Ministry of Education, for example, and this ministry makes regulations concerning the standards to be observed by the local units in building new schools and hiring teachers. Moreover, many individual acts of the local units require the assent of a minister. In the Anglo-Saxon countries, as in many others, the judicial system plays a role in the process of review, for decisions of the local units may be challenged in the court for being *ultra vires*.

In India, and most South Asian countries the control over the various activities of the local bodies such as education, health, and public works, is exercised by the appropriate departments of the state government through their field officers. The control in general and in residuary matters is vested in the department of local government, of which there is one in each state. In most states this department has no field agency of its own and acts through the provincial and district heads, which are state officials.

In India the state governments have the power to annul district and municipal council resolutions which are likely to affect adversely the general welfare. Local by-laws concerning taxation, staff qualifications and salaries, and the budgets of indebted municipalities must be approved by the state officials before they become valid. The districts in turn exercise supervisory powers over the rural municipal councils. In the other Asian and most South American countries, decisions are generally reviewed for both legality and merit.

In the East European countries the process of review is in form a task of a legislative organ. Decisions of the municipal councils may be reviewed and annulled by the district councils, in turn the decisions of the district councils may be annulled by the provincial councils and so forth up the hierarchy. In addition the respective committees at each level may have their decisions overruled, not only by the council at their level but also by the counterpart committee at the next higher level. Constitutionally the units of local government are guaranteed certain areas of decentralized authority, although these areas are not precisely defined. Furthermore, the courts do not play a role in defending the constitutional prerogative of the local units.

Review, then, may be a function of the executive, legislative, or judicial organs of the central government. With the exception of the Anglo-American countries, however, the task is generally, at least in the first instance, a function of the executive organs of the intermediate units of government. Adverse decisions may be appealed to the executive organ of a higher unit of government (and in some cases ultimately to the minister of interior) or to the courts. A few countries, such as France and Sweden, have a council of state to which certain types of adverse decisions may ultimately be appealed.

The review of the measures passed by the municipal councils may occur before or after the measures have actually become valid. In almost all countries, except the Anglo-American ones, some of the more important local resolutions, including these pertaining to finance, must receive the approval of higher units before they become valid. In France, other Latin countries, and most of the Latin-influenced countries, all the local decisions must be submitted to the provincial governor for a certain period of time before they become valid, some must then receive explicit approval, while with others the approval is implicit if there is no objection raised. Generally speaking, pre-review is a stricter control than post-review. Before a law becomes valid a reviewing officer is in a much better position to insist on some changes. By way of contract, once a law becomes valid, a reviewing officer can insist on a minor change only by rejecting the whole law. This he generally hesitates to do.

The authority to review local decisions is an effective and powerful means of control. The maze of national legislation affecting the competence of the local units is in many countries so pervasive that only a skilled legal expert is capable of finding his way through it in such a manner that proposed resolutions are not invalid. This is at least a partial explanation for the large number of local chief administrative officers who have legal training. However, relatively few decisions are actually rejected at the formal review stage. The local officials generally check the proposed measures with the officials of the higher units before the council officially enacts the by-laws. This informal preliminary clearance is thus used to avoid rejection at the formal review stage. Formal review, like most other effective means of control, is most effective as a threat and an impetus to using the more informal means of review.

Almost invariably the process of review is stricter and more thorough with the rural units than with the more populous urban municipalities. The urban units generally have larger and more specialized and experienced staffs and often more capable chief executives and councilmen. There is, therefore, a greater possibility that the decisions will be well thought out and legally correct. Furthermore the decisions made by the larger units are so extensive and so complicated that it would be extremely difficult for the higher units to review all the decisions of those larger units in a thorough and an informed manner.[1]

---

[1] In the previous chapter it was pointed out that the councils of the more populous local units also had difficulties controlling the activities of staff for much the same reasons.

6. *The financial status of the local units*[1]

The authority, or the competence, to undertake functions is generally useless unless the local units also have the financial power or means to undertake the task. For without money the local units can not pay for the men, the machinery, or the materials with which to carry out the local activities. The two most important criteria for determining the financial status of a local unit are its total income and the extent to which this income is dependent upon central government grants and contributions.

The amount of the total income of a local unit is important in determining the number and quality of the tasks it can undertake. In many countries there is a lack of adequate funds and a precarious state of local government finances. Some municipalities such as many of the Scandinavian units have, however, a relatively high percentage of the total governmental income of their countries.

On the other hand, the impoverished state of the finances of most of the municipalities in the less developed countries is a severe handicap to responsible local government. In the less developed Asian countries there is an acute inadequacy of revenue, for the national governments absorb the greatest portion of easily tapped revenues for the national programmes. The small rural units are not prepared financially to undertake new public responsibilities. The local units are often forced to depend upon the services of the intermediate units and central government organs if any local functions are to be performed.

In many countries this destitute state of local government finance is sometimes partially self imposed. Thus in many rural municipal units political apathy manifests itself in an unwillingness to undertake any activities which cost money, unless the money is given them by the central government. Under such circumstances it is almost impossible for a unit of representative government to gain sufficient electoral support to undertake any but the most essential services to which support has always been given.

---

[1] For the material in this section the author has relied heavily on the material in IULA's publication, *Local Government Finance and its Importance for Local Autonomy*, prepared for the Rome Congress 1955.

The percentage of central government grants and subsidies in the income of the local governments is a second important criterion in determining local government financial status. Prof. Meyer points out that "Of course the backbone of Local Government is financial autonomy. As soon as Local Governments have to live on income derived primarily from the central government... the future of Local Government does not seem bright."[1] Brian Chapman adds that "Adequate financial resources, which are independent of the State (s.c. central government), are a *sine qua non* of proper local government. Without them local authorities become mere agents of the central Government, and elected representation loses most of its point."[2] The question of central government aid is not, however, that simple, it is more of a paradox. In many cases it is central government aid which is keeping the local units alive both directly with money and in directly with the ideas and encouragement pushed along with the money. Nevertheless, it is usually only successful in preserving the forms, not the spirit, of local representative government.

In several countries such as Austria, Italy and Yugoslavia, less than 10% of the local funds are central government grants. In contrast more than 60% of the municipal income in the United Kingdom, Japan, Belgium, and the Netherlands is in the form of grants from the national government. In the U.S.S.R., Poland and Bulgaria the local government budgets are a part of the central government budget.

The importance of central government grants forming a large part of the municipal income depends largely on the extent to which the grants are allocated according to a prescribed formula or according to the discretion, and perhaps the whim, of the central government organs. For instance, in Japan, the large national subsidies are granted almost completely at the discretion of the provincial governor.[3] Under such conditions hardly any degree of financial or administrative autonomy can flourish. On the other hand, grants in the Netherlands and the United King-

---

[1] Meyer, Ernst Wilhelm, "Local Self-Government in Germany," *Civic Affairs — Monthly Journal of Local Government and Public Administration in India*, Vol. 4, No. 5 (December 1956), p. 115.
[2] Chapman, *Introduction to French Local Government*, p. 167.
[3] Steiner, *FEQ*, Vol. XV, No. 2 (February 1956), p. 193.

dom are generally allocated according to a legal formula so that representative government is not as greatly impaired.

The use of subsidies or grants conditioned upon the acceptance of certain stipulations by the local units is another effective use of the financial power. Such subsidies are widely used to promote highway and educational programmes, and the local units find it difficult to refuse money even when its acceptance brings with it many implicit as well as explicit controls. Many municipalities depend to such a large extent on grants-in-aid from the central governments that in reality local officials have little power over municipal activities. In many lethargic municipalities, particularly the small rural ones, grants-in-aid appear to be the only means of arousing activity; therefore subsidized, and usually strictly controlled, programs are by far the major portion of their local government activities.

In most countries one of the cardinal problems of local government is to improve the critical financial condition caused by the lack of revenue. As the central governments have increased their expenditures they have taken the most lucrative sources of revenue for themselves and often seem to have left too little for the local units. Because of their small size there are many taxes which the municipalities inherently have more difficulty in assessing and collecting than the larger units (for example, cities often hesitate to levy sales taxes since this often causes people to make their purchases in neighbouring towns). A further obstacle to improving the condition of local finances is the unequal distribution of wealth over the various municipalities. As the money needed to support the municipal services continues to increase, the inadequacy of the tax base in the less wealthy local units has become more serious. These are some of the fundamental reasons why the local units tend to look more and more to the central government for additional sources of money.

The importance of a municipality being able to raise enough local revenue to support itself is demonstrated by the number of countries that classify their municipalities depending on their ability to pay their own expenses. The Philippines, for example, has two categories of rural municipalities, the one with less revenue having a greater degree of control exercised over it.

7. *The appointment and dismissal of local officials*

The authority of the central government to appoint and dismiss local officials is one of the most effective and obvious means of supervising the activities of the local government units. By this means the higher unit may exercise its control from within the municipal organizational structure.

Many central governments such as Italy, have the right to appoint some of the top administrative officials. In other countries, for example the United Kingdom, the appointment of such officials as the medical officer of health, and the chief police officer, must be approved by the appropriate central government ministry. Chief executive officers, chief administrative officers, and sometimes even council members and members of council committees may be appointed by organs of the higher units. Examples of this appointment power will be set forth in the following chapters.

The authority of the higher units to remove officials is often even more extensive than its power to appoint, for in many European as well as Asiatic and South American countries the higher units can decommission elected as well as appointed officials. In most of these countries the right to dismiss elected officials from office is limited to situations where there is gross incompetence, proved persistent disobedience of orders, corruption, or a failure to perform their functions due to a political stalemate. In practice, however, the power is relatively little used and is confined mainly to the Latin and Asiatic countries. Of the approximately 38,000 French municipalities, about 300 councils are decommissioned annually, in many cases for the latter reason.[1] In Ceylon, between the years 1952 and 1955,

[1] Chapman, *Introduction to French Local Government*, 127. He points out that "The *conseil municipal* as a body can be dismissed if it is unable to function, if it deliberately abuses its power or if it refuses to perform duties legally incumbent upon it. Local politics sometimes lead to such acrimony and such cleavage into hostile groups that no clear majority is possible, and the Mayor is unable to obtain support to continue to administer efficiently or to get the communal budget voted. Nearly every week there are examples of ministerial decrees dissolving *conseils municipaux* which are unable to function, and nothing remains but the hope that the local electorate will decide to choose other representatives. It is much rarer to find dissolutions for abuse of power and neglect of duties, but this is considered a necessary reserve power."

A footnote goes on to point out "On an average some 300 *conseils municipaux* are dissolved every year. The principal cause is that the numbers fall below a

14 chairmen were removed, and two local councils dissolved by the central government.[1] The central governments usually do not find it politically expedient to dismiss elected officials more than is felt to be absolutely necessary. In most cases, the dismissed elected officials are replaced by new elections. In a relatively few more serious cases central government appointees are assigned to manage the local affairs for an interim period.

The effect of the central government's power of dismissal cannot be measured, though, only in terms of how many officials actually lose their offices. The constant knowledge of the possibility of losing one's office, even when the threat is not directly posed, is usually enough to encourage most local officials to act in such a way that there is little reason for dismissal.

8. Other means of control

Inspections, reports, and technical and other advice are more indirect forms of control than those already mentioned. So far we have examined the means of control one by one, but to understand fully the nature of the central-local relationships, one must have a perspective of the whole inter-connected maze of relationships. The use of the more indirect forms of control becomes important when seen in connection with the use of such controls as financial assistance, review, and the right to appoint and to remove officials. Indirect means of control are effective means of supplementing the more direct means of control.

Inspections and reports are means by which the central government may check to see if the municipalities are keeping up to prescribed minimum standards. More important perhaps is that the municipalities often try to keep up to these standards in anticipation of preparing the reports or being visited by an inspector.

Technical advice is perhaps one of the most important means of aiding and thereby controlling the activities of the local government units. Most municipalities, particularly the small ones, can-

---

quorum due to the death of councillors, but it may result from an irreconcilable disagreement on policy inside the council."
[1] *Report of the Commissioner of Local Government* (Colombo 1955), p. 214.

not afford large staffs with many specialists. As a result they are frequently forced to depend heavily upon the large and often highly specialized staffs of the organs of higher units. In France, for example, the rural mayor often leans heavily upon the sub-provincial governor for advice. Neither the mayor nor the municipal secretary, both of whom are usually part-time, have either the knowledge or the experience to deal with many matters and the sub-provincial governor is thus the most likely person to whom to turn for advice on such matters as drawing a budget.

Such technical advice often assumes even larger proportions. In many countries, particularly in the less developed ones, the central government organs will work with the local government units in carrying out programs such as mosquito control. The "co-operation" may consist of the municipal council deciding to have the job done at the urging of a higher unit and the higher unit sending in men and equipment to do the job. In countries with a relatively short tradition of local representative government, the relations of the local officials with the higher units is further complicated by the fact that the officials of the central government are reluctant to part with their duties in the local government field. Their reluctance is primarily due to their confidence that they know their job and are better qualified to perform the activities.

Nor is the central government advice limited to technical advice. Many central governments and other higher units are generous in issuing advice by means of bulletins, discussions, and other media. The municipalities frequently find it more convenient to heed the general advice and to enact the central government proposed resolutions than to risk an unfavourable relationship with the higher units. Frequently the central governments even supply model local ordinances; the municipalities often find it easier to accept these than to draft their own original ordinances that may have to be re-drafted before they are acceptable to the reviewing authorities.

Units of local government, by the very nature of their subordinate legal, if not historical status can never be more than junior partners in their relationships with the central government. There is a vast maze of means by which the central governments often through the medium of the intermediate units can control the decisions and actions of the local units. To a certain extent these means are necessary and desirable to achieve minimum standards and a co-ordination of services among the local units. Furthermore many local units would be incapable of undertaking any appreciable tasks without some form of help from the central government, and such help brings with it some form of control. A large number of local units in many countries will never be able to achieve even the role of junior partners until they have a larger degree of competence and more opportunity and facilities for exercising it. Local representative government can live up to its potential only if it is given the opportunity to make, and learn by, what the central government may consider to be mistakes. Local government can never be responsible to local citizens if the central government controls everything.

4

THE PROCESS OF LOCAL ELECTIONS

1. Elections and the local representative governing process

THE fundamental prerequisite for representative government is that the public has an opportunity to elect representatives (the only alternative is that they represent themselves as in a popular assembly) who play a responsible role in the governing process. W. J. M. Mackenzie in his book *Free Elections* maintains "that free elections though not a supreme end are yet a device of the highest value, because no one has invented a better political contrivance for securing in large societies two conditions necessary for the maintenance of government in any society. First, elections can create a sentiment of popular consent and participation in public affairs even when government is so complex as to be beyond the direct understanding of the ordinary citizen. Secondly, elections can provide for orderly succession in government, by the peaceful transfer of authority to new rulers when the time comes for the old rulers to go, because of mortality or because of failure."[1]

In a system of local non-representative government, the local residents are at best limited to a relatively unorganized and indirect role in their local government affairs. The public must play an active and direct role if representative government is to be dynamic and not a static mechanical and lifeless process. Citizen interest and influence may manifest itself in many ways, but the most fundamental one is in purposefully voting for its representatives.

[1] Mackenzie, W. S. M., *Free Elections* (London, 1958), pp. 13–14.

In most units of local representative government only the members of the council are directly elected by popular vote. Only in a small number of countries are the mayors also directly elected. In a few other countries, the village headmen are informally selected and approved in the local community but their assumption of office must be approved by the higher units of government. In only a very few countries, including the United States, are judicial or administrative officers, other than the mayor, directly elected by popular vote. This chapter will concentrate mainly on elections for councils; the method by which other officials are selected will be dealt with more thoroughly in later chapters.

Any system of elections includes a number of aspects, all of which are inter-related and of almost equal importance. These deal with the qualifications and disqualifications of voters, the method of voting, the type of (including the secrecy of) balloting, the nomination of candidates, the division of the electorate into constituencies, the prevention of corruption and intimidation during the campaign, the judicial and administrative provisions for seeing that the law is observed, the interest of the voters in public affairs and the role of the political party or parties. Each of these aspects is meaningless in isolation from the others and the lack of any of these aspects can render the whole system futile. Moreover, some of the technical aspects of the electoral process become especially important and more complicated in the more popular local unit. Thus, although some of the more salient aspects of the electoral system will be discussed in this chapter, a fuller discussion of local government electoral systems (including the more informal political aspects of them) will have to wait for more adequate source material and a survey specifically devoted to this topic.

2. *Who can vote*

A general suffrage is the basis of representative government and its extension has been one of the most significant phenomena associated with the development of modern local representative government. In the early nineteenth century, many of the countries included in this survey did not have elections for local government positions. In others the privilege of voting was often restricted to a relatively small percentage of the population. For more than a century now, however, there has been a steady progress in turning the privileges of a few into the rights for all, or more accurately for almost all for even in the most widespread system of suffrage there are some who are not qualified to vote.

Almost invariably the right to vote for representatives to local bodies is restricted to persons who are citizens of the country of which the locality is a part. An exception, however, is the case of the British Commonwealth under whose citizenship law the citizen of any country in the Commonwealth can vote in the United Kingdom, if he is otherwise qualified.

Local residence is another electoral qualification in general use. In some U. S. states one must be resident in a municipality for twelve months before one is entitled to vote in the local elections. On the other hand, in England it is sufficient merely to be living in the locality on the registration day preceding the election. The local units of many countries have a new registration of voters for each election, in others the list of those entitled to vote is carried over from one election to the next with provisions for amending and deleting names of individual voters. In a few countries persons are allowed to vote in local elections of municipalities in which they own property as well as the ones in which they are resident. (They may not, however, vote twice for any one candidate; that is, they could not vote in both their home municipality and the additional local unit of the same province in a provincial election). It is usual to grant the vote to persons who have reached a "responsible age." This varies in different countries from eighteen to twenty-five with the most usual age being twenty-one.

Until the twentieth century women were generally not entitled to vote, but within the past few decades they have gained the right to participate in elections in almost every country. Switzerland is one of the increasingly rare exceptions to this generalization, although one finds a similar limitation in Spain and Portugal where only the heads of families vote.

Literacy requirements are still current in a number of countries; this is an important question in those countries with a high proportion of illiterates. This is an especially acute question in countries in which there are two or more distinct racial groups, one of which has a high percentage of illiterate persons. It may be argued that one should be able to read and understand the issues before one can become well-enough informed to cast an intelligent vote. On the other hand, if there are to be literacy qualifications, questions are raised concerning what the standards should be and who shall administer the necessary tests. Too often literacy tests have been manipulated to prevent literate members of minority groups from exercising their right to vote.

Tax-paying also used to be a widespread requirement for local voting, but this limitation is also decreasing. Now Ethiopia is one of a few countries in which only tax-payers are eligible to vote in the urban municipal elections. (The Ethiopian rural units do not have representative government and therefore do not have local elections). Moreover, in many municipalities of southern United States one is not eligible to vote unless one has paid a *per caput* "poll tax." It is, however, generally felt that the financial prerequisites for voting have less validity in today's world where it is becoming generally recognized that government is not an exclusive domain of the privileged but is an institution in theory serving the best interests of all.

There are two further qualifications for voting which are most naturally expressed in a negative fashion. It is usual to disenfranchise persons certified to be lunatics or mental defectives. It is almost equally usual to disenfranchise convicted persons serving sentences in prison. Furthermore, having served a long prison sentence often disqualifies one from voting.

The gradual extension of the suffrage was accompanied by an apprehension on the part of some who feared that the enlargement of the right to vote would force the local government to become responsive to a large number of relatively uninformed voters. Universal suffrage, it was thought, would lead to a tyranny of the masses; since government could not be run by a mass that did not understand all the intricacies of the issues, some reasoned that it would no longer be as purposeful, as co-ordinated, or as effective as it had been. But time has shown that the forebodings of the pessimists were overstated. The running of the government is still concentrated in the hands of a few although now they must seek the periodic approval of the many. The significant change is that the persons holding power must be capable of obtaining the electoral support of the voters.

3. Who does vote

Not everyone who has the right to vote takes advantage of his opportunity. A large proportion of the population of many countries do not vote, not so much because of governmental restrictions but because of lack of personal interest. Most of the European countries have high turn-outs at elections, but in many other countries only a small proportion of those qualified to be voters bother to cast a ballot, especially in the local elections. Such apathy and lack of interest on the part of the local voters, if spread to a considerable extent, could mean an abdication of local government by the majority to local government by a small minority. In short, this is perhaps one of the most telling manifestations of the plight of local government.

In several countries, mostly European, voting is compulsory, that is qualified voters must cast a ballot. A variation of compulsory voting is found in the Netherlands; according to Dutch law a qualified voter must present himself at his polling station but he need not cast a ballot. It should be pointed out, though, that there are several countries, such as Brazil, in which the voting is in theory compulsory, but in which no legal action is taken against those who do not vote. The result is that a large proportion of qualified voters, often as many as one half, do not vote.

The advocates of compulsory voting hope that it not only increases the number of voters but that the voter is also thereby encouraged to become acquainted with the local political situation since he knows he must make some electoral decisions. Others feel that compulsory voting only increases the number of uninformed voters and does not, therefore, contribute to the development of responsible local government; it is more important, they feel, to increase the intelligent voting than to merely increase the number of voters. One consequence of the compulsory voting scheme is that there seems to be less need for political advertising. The use of compulsory voting does mean that a valuable thermometer for the registering of the presence or lack of public interest is lost. Furthermore, it may be argued that a qualified voter may have the moral right to show his lack of interest in government issues or his disdain for all the candidates by not voting.

4. *Personalities, the press, and pressure groups*

Personalities, the press, pressure groups, and political parties (the latter of which will be dealt with at greater length in a later section of this chapter) are among the most important catalytic agents for arousing and organizing public interest and participation in local government. In the larger units they play an essential role in the representative governing process. In the many small local units, however, these factors are not necessarily as important. Such units are small enough for the individual citizen to be closer to his local government and thus it is easier for him to make personal judgements on the local government issues and candidates.

The lack of economic development in many countries, has precluded the development of a middle class, especially in the rural areas. This along with the lack of any significant development of these four P's already mentioned means that there is less opportunity for informal thinking about public issues. There is, therefore, relatively a small group from which to derive local government leadership, and perhaps even more significant the group from which to draw the actual support is also too small to be adequate.

Personalities are important in developing and focusing political interest, especially in the younger countries, including the United States. Except for the most dramatic, and usually oversimplified, issues, it is far easier to arouse and crystallize public support for personalities than for programs. This is one of the factors accounting for the *boss* (or the *caudillo* as he is called in many Latin American countries), who runs many units of local representative governments in what often appears to be an undemocratic manner.[1]

[1] MacDonald Austin F., *Latin American Politics and Government* (New York 1954), p. 2.

The press and other media of mass communication play an important part in bringing government closer to the people. Outside of the smaller municipalities mass communication media seem to be indispensable means of presenting political parties and candidates to the public, explaining public issues, and crystallizing public sentiment. While the press as a means of conveying information to the public is fairly obvious, it is also a means of conveying public opinion to the political leaders.

Organized pressure groups are not as important in local elections as they are at national and state levels. Formally, at least, they have less need to bring their organized pressure to bear. For at the local level the citizens can exert an influence more easily than they can at higher levels.

The public, if it is to exercise its role intelligently, must be well informed and well led. The extent to which the public is well informed depends not only on the public itself, but also on governmental and non-governmental institutions. The council, the committees of council, and the mayor individually and collectively, have a responsibility not only for keeping the public informed, but also for providing the political leadership necessary for arousing the public interest and participation that is vital to the local representative governing process.

5. *Indirect elections*

In discussing methods of elections one must first make a distinction between direct and indirect elections. In the former one votes directly for a candidate, who if successful wins a public office; the plurality and proportional representation methods of voting are both direct ones. In indirect voting on the other hand, the person who is elected to public office does not gain it by virtue of having won a sufficient number of the votes of the public but by having won a sufficient number of the votes of an electoral organ whose members were themselves elected by the public, or perhaps by even another such electoral organ. In a sense, of course, almost all elections, especially those with large electorates, are indirect elections because they depend to some extent on pre-selection of candidates by party organizations and other limited extra-governmental groups.

Indirect elections may be organized in several different ways, depending partly upon local factors and partly upon the objectives desired in using the system. The electoral organs, as one example of indirect elections, may be composed of persons elected especially for the purpose of selecting the person for the public representative position; or these electoral organs may be composed of persons selected primarily for another purpose, such as a local council. In either case the procedure for voting for these electoral organs themselves can take any of the forms described in the following sections.

When used to elect intermediate unit councils, indirect voting has the theoretical advantage of encouraging co-operation and similarity of political outlook on the part of both the municipal and secondary units. Nevertheless, it retains the disadvantages already mentioned. The recently organized intermediate unit councils in Burma are elected in this manner. A variation of this scheme of indirect elections is found in Scotland; the persons who are elected to the county councils are by virtue of their election members also of the rural municipal council from which they are elected.

In England some of the members of the municipal councils are chosen by the directly elected councilmen instead of directly by the people. These indirectly elected councilmen, called aldermen, have the same rights and duties as other councilmen. The theoretical advantage of the method is that some valuable people may be persuaded to serve on the council who would not stand for election. In practice, however, those who have the longest tenure on the council as elected members are chosen for these indirectly elected seats. The result is that many of the indirectly elected council members are super-annuated men who no longer feel any need to be sensitive to the current political thinking.

In some less-developed areas, such as parts of rural Sudan, specially chosen electoral organs are used to permit a wide suffrage of voters while restricting the actual ability to vote for the council members to those considered better qualified to make a choice. Indirect elections in such a situation are in some cases considered to be a necessary and helpful step in preparing the way for direct elections in countries where the range of mass communication and the degree of literacy is at present small.

6. *Proportional representation*[1]

Electoral, and hence representative, government rests on the general acceptance of the convention that it is necessary and permissible in certain circumstances to take the formally expressed opinion of a part for the opinion of the whole. The choice of a method of election is a major factor in determining how this part shall be composed. Each method of election (plurality choice, proportional representation, and consent by acclamation, as well as indirect) affects the composition of the local councils in a different manner and thus affects what will be the expressed opinion of the whole. In addition there is a large number of combinations of one or more of these methods, of which many can not be described in these pages.

A method of proportional representation may be defined as a "system of voting which includes some device for allocating seats proportionately to the votes cast for each candidate (or affiliated groups of candidates) in the constituency concerned."[2] Multi-member constituencies are essential to proportional representation since one seat cannot be divided proportionally. There are two main types of proportional representation, the "list system" and the "single transferable vote" (or Hare) system which is virtually never used in practice except in a few cities in some Anglo-Saxon countries. Each has many variants and it is possible to combine them with one another, or even mix them ingeniously with the plurality choice method.

The list system of proportional representation may be described as one in which the voter makes a choice between two or more lists of candidates, each of which is sponsored by a party or by some other organization. With the list system there are multi-member constituencies in which each party submits on its list

---

[1] For further information regarding elections, see G. Van den Bergh, *Eenheid en Verscheidenheid* (Alphen aan den Rijn 1946); pp. 10–15 deal with elections to organs with more than one person.
[2] MacKenzie, 61.
[3] *Ibid.*, 75.

as many candidates as there are seats, and the voter casts only one vote, a vote for the list he prefers. By this plan the seats on a local council are assigned according to the proportion of the total vote which each party obtains. As a rule the voter's choice of candidates is confined to the party list which he decides to support, but practice varies with respect to the extent of his discretion in making selections within the list. Usually the candidates heading a party's list, the exact number depending on its proportion of the total votes, are declared elected. Where the voter is allowed to make selections among the candidates of his party, candidates from the bottom have a theoretical opportunity to be elected although in fact they seldom are. The list system gives the party managers a crucial role in determining which individual members will be elected by votes cast for the party, thus the party discipline is strengthened.

The list system is extensively used, particularly on the European continent, for local as well as national elections. In a few countries, though, the smaller municipalities do not necessarily use proportional representation to elect their local council. In Iceland, for example, the rural municipalities have proportional representation only when three-fourths of the population live in a built up area, or when one-tenth of the electorate or twenty-five voters, whichever is smaller, request it.

The proportional representation method of election by the list system is the natural and almost inevitable method of voting in all but the smallest constituencies of countries whose citizens are internally split by deep traditional divisions, such as those of language and religion, which often are not easily susceptible to political compromise. These countries have evolved party systems in which each party acts for a particular clientele, often closely associated with other kinds of organizations as well. Thus, in the Netherlands for example, there are deep confessional and philosophical differences and in France and Italy economic and philosophical differences assume an intensity of feeling which exceeds that in most other countries.

In a few countries the internal splits are so deep and so pronounced that the citizens form distinct "communities" (here used not in the geographical but in the sociological sense). The Lebanon, which stands at what may be called the religious crossroads of the world, is an excellent example of this phenomenon. Intensity of religious feeling plus a multiplicity of religious traditions has divided the country into many fervent religious groups, with the result that the urban municipal councils are elected by direct vote with each religious community entitled to a certain number of seats in proportion to the respective number of municipal voters as ascertained in the last census. In fact, this is not a method of proportional representation since the seats have been allocated according to the census and prior to the election, not according to election results. Such a manner of conducting elections is considered necessary because of the basic cleavages in the Lebanese people which affect not only the composition but also the operational effectiveness of the councils. The religious cleavage was one of the reasons for the postponement of the local government elections in the Lebanon which are supposed to take place every four years. In 1953 were held the only post-war elections.

The principal advantage claimed for proportional representation is that the composition is more likely to be a heterogeneous group which reflects fairly accurately the amount of support given to each party by the voters and thus represents a broad cross-section of the local unit. A party with a majority of the votes will have a majority of the council seats but significantly sized politically organized minority groups are also assured a representative voice. Provisions are made, though, in most local units to discourage very small new parties by making them post a sum of money which is forfeited if they fail to get a certain minimum number of votes.

Another advantage of proportional representation by the list system is the continuity of the councils. It is a landslide when two or three seats change from one party to another. Furthermore, since the same party leaders are likely to continue to head a party's "list," many of the leading councilmen are likely to return to office after successive elections.

The main argument against proportional representation by the list system is that it encourages the formation of numerous parties and a multi-party system. Therefore, it reduces the possibility of any one party obtaining a workable majority and securing the support for the executive organ. As long as any group is able to secure representation in proportion to its numerical voting strength, people are less likely to subordinate their special interests to considerations of general welfare. The reduced possibility of achieving a workable majority increases the necessity of arranging coalition governments composed of parties whose positions are in some respects irreconcilable. In many cases the coalitions are able to work together so that coalition or minority governments hold office for long periods, often undisturbed by the very slight changes in representation which take place at elections. On the other hand, when the parties are not capable of working together endless bickering and temporizing at the expense of far-sighted and effective plans may occur. In practice, though, the presence of a one, two, or many parties and the extent to which the parties are capable of working together appears to depend at least partially on the basic economic, religious, political, and sociological factors operative in a community and on the intensity of feeling aroused by them, as well as on the method of election.

7. *Plurality choice*

The plurality choice method of election combines two distinctive features:

1. the expression of a single choice by the voter for each office to be filled, and

2. the use of the plurality rule for determining the winning candidate.

Where three or more candidates are competing for one office the candidate with the largest number of votes wins, regardless of whether or not it is by a majority of all the votes. The plurality choice method of election is usually used with single-member constituencies. It may also, though, be used with multi-member constituencies in which the usual practice is to allow each voter one vote per position to be filled. Both the single-member and multi-member plurality choice methods are in some cases modified to provide for some type of minority representation. The plurality choice method of election has been the traditional English practice from the thirteenth century onward. It is now by far the commonest form of voting in the English-speaking countries. In other countries it is rarely used.

With the plurality choice method of election it is mathematically possible for one party to gain all the council seats with only a plurality of the vote; frequently a 55% vote can win 75% of the council seats. It is also possible for one party to gain a majority of the seats when it has less votes than a competing party. Each of these possibilities depends on the distribution of the voting strength of the parties and the delimitation of constituencies.

In as much as the composition of a council elected by the plurality choice by district method depends to so great an extent on the territorial distribution of the adherents of the competing parties, there is often a temptation to adjust district boundaries (in the United States called "gerrymandering") in order to distribute one party's adherents to the greatest advantage. The plurality plan tends to over-represent the majority or plurality group at the expense of the minority groups. It can also over-represent a minority whose members are strategically distributed.

The most important advantage of the plurality choice method of election is that it seems to increase the possibility of workable majorities. When only the candidates who receive the largest number of votes win the elections, there is a tendency for politicians and voters to group themselves into a few large parties capable of gaining a plurality of the votes rather than to diffuse themselves over many smaller parties or factions. The result is that there is a greater possibility that one party can gain a majority of the seats of a council. Instead of coalitions, compromises, frustration, and division of responsibility between parties, there can be workable majorities capable of supporting the stable leadership necessary for effective governments.

Another corollary of the plurality choice method of election is that there can be a rapid change in the political complexion of a council. Where a 55% vote for one party can win 75% of the seats, a 10% shift can often bring a 50% shift in seats. This increases the degree and speed with which the complexion of the council can respond to changes in public opinion. In areas where the balance of political forces is approximately equal, as is the case in many local units in the Anglo-Saxon countries, the council can be plagued by a lack of continuity and therefore of experience.

Simple plurality voting almost invariably favours the biggest organized groups at the expense of the smaller ones. There are various ways of counteracting this tendency without having resource to proportional representation, but only a few of the more usual ones shall be mentioned here. A method of limited voting may be used in connection with multi-member constituencies. For instance, in a three-member constituency each party may be allowed only two candidates, thus providing a minority party a greater opportunity of capturing one seat. This system is used for electing the representative organ in a few of the local units in the United States (e. g. Pennsylvania counties).

Another device for assuring minority representation is to set up a system of "communal" representation alongside the system of general territorial constituencies. A system of communal representation links together voters throughout the local unit on the basis of characteristics other than that of residence in a particular geographical area. In many of the urban municipalities of India, for instance, seats on the council are reserved for certain minority groups, such as Moslems or "untouchables." Representatives are then elected to these seats by the voters on these communal rolls. The use of such "communal" elections has disadvantages in that they tend to fragmentize the over-all community. Like proportional representation though, it is a means of assuring minority representation.

8. *Consent by acclamation*

Consent by acclamation is one of the simplest methods of election. With this method of election the voters merely endorse the candidates that have been selected by the political leaders. Generally, the political leaders select exactly as many candidates as there are positions to be filled. Elections of this type often appear not to leave the voters any valid choice. When contests do occur, it is result of the system breaking down or changing.

In a sense consent by acclamation is a type of simple plurality method of election since one who received all, or almost all, the votes has also a plurality. Furthermore, when a contest does occur the candidate who has a plurality wins the election. Nevertheless, consent by acclamation operates in such a basically different manner that it is probably best to discuss it separately. This case does serve to illustrate the similarities and overlapping of the various methods of elections and the difficulty of placing specific methods into airtight compartments. In the social sciences one is forever plagued by this problem.

Consent by acclamation is the natural method of voting in two basically different political environments. First is the essentially one-party political environment in the East European countries in which the elections conform to most of the procedural aspects of elections in other European countries. Second is the traditionally non-party atmosphere present in the rural, less developed areas of many of the African and Asian countries in which the elections are open and relatively informal, at least as judged from a European point of view.

In the Communist countries there is only one party. It is part of the Communist ideology that more parties are superfluous since the one party is capable of crystallizing the policies, selecting the leaders, and otherwise guiding the destinies of the units of government. Current Marxist doctrine bases the Communist party's right to govern on historical necessity, since it is the vanguard of the proletariat, the governing class in the stage of transition to Communism. This single party cannot, therefore, admit a rival without self-contradiction, and a governmental unit which admits more parties than one cannot, therefore, be truly Marxist.[1]

In units of local government in Communist countries candidates for local councils are selected by discussions in the factory, farm, cultural, and other non-political public bodies. Party members play an active part in these discussions. In Yugoslavian local elections, for instance, the local council as well as all the other organs of government in Yugoslavia, rely on the support of the Socialist Union of the Working People of Yugoslavia which is the general political organization in which the leading role is played by the Yugoslav League of Communists. The Union has its municipal and district organizations. These organizations appear in the role of initiators in calling the meetings of voters at which candidates to membership in local councils are proposed.

[1] *Ibid.*, 173.

Thus, the candidates proposed by the meetings of voters are considered as the candidates of the Union. There is no other local political party beside the Union, which is the sole political organization in Yugoslavia.

In the end only one candidate is usually proposed for each seat in the local council. (In Yugoslavia, though, some local units now have twice as many candidates as there are seats available). Under these conditions the results of the elections are never in doubt; the electorate merely has the opportunity to make a public act of approval. Voting statistics may be pushed to unheard of levels, for instance, 99% of the electorate voting with 99% of the votes cast in favour of the proposed slate.

Most village elections in the rural parts of Asia and Africa are also foregone conclusions, but the reasons for the consent by acclamation type of election are historically and basically different from the causes for this type of election in the Communist countries. The custom in most of the African and Asian villages is for the village leaders, or "elders", to meet together in advance of a general village meeting to discuss and select a candidate for any vacant post. Theoretically, of course, the villagers are free to propose alternate candidates, but they seldom do. The village leaders usually have chosen the candidates wisely and the village assemblies endorse their selection. Secret ballots are not generally used.

Many village elections in India, for instance, may be described as consent by acclamation.

> The political process at the village level is very simple. The elders of the village and the younger leaders determine the membership of the panchayat council. Elections register the formal approval by the village of choices already decided upon by the leaders ... Where there is rivalry between two families or two communities for leadership, the village tends to range itself on one or the other side regardless of the merits of the case... In recent years political parties have invaded the countryside. Party alignments in the villages tend to follow the older divisions of the community along factional, family, or personal lines. This is perhaps to be expected since the parties as such have no substantial programs for the villages. Local civic work has not benefited by this intrusion of national and state party politics into village affairs.[1]

To point out more strikingly the manner in which competitive

---

[1] Srinivasan, N., "Village Government in India," *FEQ*, XV, No. 2 (February 1956), p. 211.

elections are successfully avoided, in elections for the Japanese village assembly, the informal leadership parcels out the available seats among the various sub-municipal communities, one candidate is nominated for each seat, and the sub-municipal community votes for him as a group. Even on a nation-wide basis, the number of candidates only slightly exceeds the number of vacant positions. In 1951 there were on the average only 1.3 candidates for each municipal council seat. This includes the urban municipal councils for which there is usually less effort to avoid competitive elections. In mayoralty elections the informal leadership also attempts to avoid competitive elections, but here it is not quite as successful as in council elections. Various sub-municipal communities or groups of sub-municipal communities may put forward their own candidate for the single position that is at stake. In municipalities where only one candidate is nominated, no election needs to take place. This is usually the case in about one-third of Japan's municipalities. Campaigns are usually not based on issues. Almost all candidates run as independents. Campaigning is neither necessary nor considered desirable. The avoidance of competitive elections and of campaigns ties in with the high value put on the appearance of harmony and on individual self-effacement. Balloting is largely a formality. Nomination thus becomes particularly important. Given the conservative colouring of the informal leadership group and the fact that nomination is based mainly on family or personal status, it is not surprising that most village councils in Japan have a conservative majority.[1]

9. *The delimitation of constituencies*

Perhaps it has not in earlier sections been stressed sufficiently that in all local council elections the matter of constituencies, or districts, is involved. The local unit may form one single at-large constituency or it may be divided into several constituencies. In the vast majority of municipalities, including most of the ones with small councils and almost all of those local units which use proportional representation, the municipality forms one single

[1] Steiner, *FEQ*, XV, No. 2 (February 1956), 195.

constituency. In those local units, though, which have not only larger councils but also the plurality method of voting, there are generally several constituencies each of which elects one or more members of council. (It is possible to have multi-member constituencies in a municipality which elects its representatives by proportional vote; it occurs, however, in only a few of the larger cities).

The advantage of having only one at-large constituency is that the elected members are more likely to think of themselves as representatives of the whole local unit rather than of special geographical districts. On the other hand there is a tendency for the more populated portions of the municipality to capture more than their fair share of the seats in this type of election. This is the case, for instance, in many of the Brazilian municipalities.[1]

In local units with several constituencies, however, there is the advantage that each district has its own representative whom the inhabitants may consider as their personal representative. On the other hand, the council member elected in this manner tends to be sectionally minded and contending for the interests of his own constituents as against those of the larger community as a whole. Representation by district also reduces the availability of good candidates for council membership; one residential area of a municipality may have several excellent candidates while another may have none. Another disadvantage of the district system is that some votes of the electorate seem to be wasted and those voting for the losing candidate in any one district often feel unrepresented. As has been said before, another difficulty encountered in using several constituencies is that district lines may be manipulated to the advantage of the party in power.

10. *Nominations*

The process of elections almost invariably consists of two stages. One is the relatively informal stage in which one or more slates of candidates are pre-selected by a limited number of persons. The second is the relatively more formal stage at which one

[1] Lordello de Mello, Diego, *Local Government in Brazil*, Monograph in preparation.

candidate is elected or endorsed for each position. The situation, particularly in large cities, is often that in practice each party chooses its candidates, the electorate chooses between the parties, paying perhaps some attention to the personal merits of individual candidates, but moved primarily by the reputation and arguments of the parties. In cases where one party is supported by a large majority, or when the local leader has the general support of the community, the first stage is the decisive one; nomination as a candidate is tantamount to election.

So far this chapter has concentrated chiefly on the second aspect of the electoral process. But the first aspect is equally important and so closely inter-related with the first that one must often discuss the two together. It was not without reason that a prominent American political "boss" once commented that he did not care which party won the elections as long as he controlled all the nominations.

Generally, the political parties have an essential role in the electoral process through the process of selecting the candidates who stand for election. The vote in most local elections is restricted to those candidates whose names have been placed on the ballot by the party organizations. This role in the nominating process strengthens the party organization. In countries with the list form of proportional representation the nominating process is a task of the party organization. In the one-party East European countries many groups suggest a candidate, but the party controls the situation in such a way that only candidates acceptable to it are placed on the ballot.

In many countries, caucuses or conventions determine party candidates. In the United States in which primary elections are used to determine the party's nominees for the general election, the local party organizations are generally weak unless they take a leading role in supporting candidates in the primary elections which are used to nominate the parties' candidates.[1] In the relatively small local units in countries with a lack of strong party discipline the party organizations do not play as important a role in the nominating process. In these units, though, an informal local leadership generally plays an important role.

[1] About 60% of the cities in the United States with populations over 5,000 have non-partisan local elections and therefore do not have partisan primaries. Even where the local elections are "non-partisan," though, the political parties are not necessarily inactive.

11. *The local political party organizations*

The party organizations play an important role in the electoral and political processes of many of the local government units, especially the ones with large electorates. They act as catalytic agents in developing slates of candidates and arousing public interest and support for these slates. Usually the local party organizations are branches of the national political parties. Not only do the local political leaders generally find it advantageous to have organizational ties with the national organizations in order to get financial and other types of support, but the national parties usually also find it helpful to have local organizations to arouse local support for their national slates.

Although there is a general tendency for the local government units to share the same type of one, two, or multiple party system that exists at the national level, the geographical disparity of the strength of the national parties frequently reduces the number of parties in any one unit. The strengh of the local party organizations varies greatly, depending on a large number of factors including

1. the population of the municipality and the complexity of political and sociological interests in the community,
2. the method of election and the nominating process, and
3. the role of the local political leadership.

In the larger municipalities, particularly those that have a mixed and an overlapping maze of interest groups, the role of the parties tend to be more important since they can sift the popular sentiments and coalesce them into workable programmes that can arouse public support. The parties are political tools that can be used to bring the people and the organs of representative government into closer political contact with one another.

The parties may have a heavy responsibility in the processes of local representative government. Prof. Wheare has said "The right use of party in local government is therefore at the very root of its effective working."[1] In our modern complex society parties are important aids in transforming the multitude of uncoordinated public wills into an evident public will. They perform the increasingly important role of brokers between the public and

[1] Wheare, *Government by Committee*, 201.

the policy leadership by offering the electorate alternate slates of candidates and focusing attention upon issues. Whether parties aid in making the local governments responsible to the electorate depends for the most part on the ableness of the political leadership in making the parties both responsive and effective.

5

THE COUNCIL

1. The council and representative government

THE council is, in principle, the main representative organ of a unit of local government. There may be other representative organs, such as the board, with considerable authority and power, but it is primarily the council through which the public is represented in the affairs of government.

A council is an essential part of every unit of local representative government (exept in a few local units in which there is, however, a popular assembly which is formally constituted by law and which has some authority to govern). In some countries all units of local government have councils (or popular assemblies) while in others the pattern varies. In the Anglo-Saxon, East European Communist, and many of the other European countries, for example, the general pattern of all local units at both basic and intermediate levels is one of representative government. In France, on the other hand, all the municipalities (*communes*) and provinces (*départements*) have councils but the districts (*arrondissements*) do not. In still other countries, such as Iran and Ethiopia, only the urban basic units have councils with decisive authority. In most countries there is a tendency to develop councils or popular assemblies at the lowest level of governmental units. That is, representative government is most prevalent at the level "closest" to the people.[1]

The role of the council as a representative body is a complex one. It varies not only with the evolution but also with the

---

[1] The sub-municipal units, many of which do not have councils, are the exception to the principle.

mechanics of the processes of local government in each country. Nevertheless the degree to which a local unit has a representative government depends largely on two factors. One is the extent to which the membership of a council represents and is answerable to the public and the other is the extent to which the council has the authority and power to define the local policy objectives and to have these objectives implemented.

2. *No councils*

Units of local non-representative government may either have no councils or councils without decisive authority. In either case the local government organs are simply deconcentrated local organs of the central government whose chief executives hold their position at the discretion of the central government. With the increased acceptance of the principle of local representative government, the number of local units with no council is decreasing. Although there are a sizeable number of countries not included in this survey which have no local councils, all of the countries in this survey have councils at least in the urban municipalities. There are, however, several countries included in this survey such as Tunisia and Ethiopia in which there are no local councils in the rural units. These are in areas which tend, in general, to be underdeveloped and to have relatively few local government services performed. Few other units provide more than the elementary functions such as collecting taxes, maintaining the public security, and registering the vital statistics.

The lack of resources is a major reason for the lack of local representative government in these areas. Without money, the few services there are must be centrally supported and often consequently centrally controlled. In Tunisia, Ethiopia, and Iran the largeness of the area and sparsity of the population of the rural units also contribute to the difficulty of setting up councils. The duties of these units are to such an extent limited to mandatory deconcentrated activities that councils would have few if any decisions to make.

3. *The advisory councils*

Power without representation denotes an absence of representative government; the same is true of representation without decisive authority. In terms of authority one may divide councils and popular assemblies into two categories: those with governing or decisive authority and those without. Councils without decisive authority have only consultative or advisory tasks, and in some cases also some elective duties.[1] They are limited to the not altogether unimportant role of a forum focusing the opinions, hopes, and disappointments of the local inhabitants. Only a relatively few countries have advisory councils in the local government units; all are highly centralized countries. In this survey there are no counils at the basic units which are formally constited by law but do not have any authority to govern. Such councils are, however, found in a few sub-municipal and intermediate units.

The chief executive of this type of local government unit is responsible to the higher units, not to the local council, for the implementation of the local programs. The chief executive appointed by a higher unit often need not seek the advice of council, nor need he wait for its approval of his programs. In many cases, though, the advice of the council may be followed and it may exert considerable influence on the decision-making process. Its power depends on the personal prestige of the council members, the relations between the chief executive and the council, and the importance of the organ as a channel for communication and as a means of initiating proposals, which may be listened to and perhaps even approved of by the chief executive and the higher units of government.

The councils without authority may have, then, a varying extent of power. Some such councils, like those in the Philippine sub-municipal units (*barrios*) are completely powerless although they have a few nominal duties. Romani points out that the headman and members of the sub-municipal councils apparently

---

[1] To be precise, of course, a council without decisive authority can not elect anyone for that in itself is a decisive action. I hope the reader will understand that I have used this inaccurate expression as an alternative to allowing the terminology, the sentences, and the text to become more complicated than they already are.

were conceived as being similar to the chief and elders of the pre-colonial Philippine village. The sub-municipal officials of today, though, are simply "unpaid administrative assistants of the municipal government having no real role in policy determination nor any significant function in policy execution."[1]

On the other hand, some of the local advisory councils in the Sudan, which are unofficially established by the head of the district, are far from powerless. Although they do not have decisive authority and therefore cannot pass local ordinances, their recommendations are almost invariably accepted. In the Sudan, as in several other relatively less developed countries, advisory councils are being used as a means of preparing the unit for responsible representative government.

4. *The councils with some authority to govern*

A unit of local representative government has one of more representative organs with some authority to govern. Almost invariably one of these organs is a council.[2] Such a council not only has the opportunity to talk and give advice about local issues, but it also has the responsibility for making decisions authorizing or directing the local staff to perform tasks. Such a council not only discusses policy, but also makes decisions. It may pass the budget, enact ordinances and by-laws, and make or approve some appointments. The council approves and in many cases amends proposals submitted to it, and generally may take the initiative in making proposals.

A council with decisive authority may take decisions regarding matters of overall policy objectives, or relatively more minor matters concerning the routine co-ordination of the staff, or both. How the local councils use their decision-making competence is an indication of the role of the council in the local government system, both in regard to the central government and in regard to the local executive organs.

In discussing the competence of a council one must be careful to distinguish between the authority of a unit of local govern-

---

[1] Romani, *FEQ*, Vol. XV, (Februariy 1956), 233.
[2] The only exceptions to be found in this survey are: about 2,400 of the almost 11.000 English and Welch sub-municipalities (*parishes*) which do not have a council but do have a popular assembly with authority to govern. See Charles Arnold-Baker, *Parish Administration* (London 1958), p. 9.

ment and the authority of the council of the unit. In several conutries the council is responsible in the final analysis for all the activities of the unit of local government. In most countries, though, the competence of the council is not synonymous with that of the unit of local government. The chief executives of these local units are answerable to the council for some functions, for others directly to the central government hierarchy. This is the case in many countries of Europe, Africa and Asia.

In most of the municipalities in the Anglo-Saxon and Scandinavian countries the authority of the councils is broad and in principle covers all decisions. These units of local government have a relatively large degree of representative government, and their councils are ultimately responsible for the actions of the staffs. The concentration of such a large load of decision-making in the councils of the local units means that a large amount of the decisions are actually made in the committees.

In the East European countries a local council, in theory, is responsible for all the government activities, which includes almost all social and economic activity within the territorial confines of the local unit. In practice, the power of the council is severely restricted by its inferior role in its relation to other local government institutions, including the board, and the party. Despite the numerous activities for which the Russian councils are responsible, the sessions are few, and only a few subjects are discussed.

In other countries, too, the councils may be relatively powerless, although in theory they may have decisive authority. For instance, Burma has recently created rural local councils in many areas of that country. Regarding this development the Public Administration Service reports:

"Many village councils have been at a complete loss to decide what functions to undertake, particularly in the absence of guidance or financial support other than payment of the salary of the village clerk and the village constable by the district council. Many local activities sponsored by the central government ministries have been so organized as to bypass the elected representatives of the village residents. Committees for this and that activity, such as schools, land nationalization, tenancy distribution, defence, mass education, and others, continue to be appointed by the ministries concerned (or in some cases elected) without reference to the elected village councils. Since many of the activities and decisions of these committees constitute a considerable portion of the village business of a governmental nature, there is all too often very little left for the village council to do, except to perform the judicial function laid down for it in the Democratic Local Government Act. Often, there has been a marked reluctance even to undertake this activity, owing to lack of initiative, for fear of error, or other reasons."[1]

The decision-making power of the local councils in most of the Latin, Asian, and African countries is mainly confined to routine staff matters – at least when judged from the point of view of countries with a long tradition of local government. In these countries a relatively larger percentage of policy decisions regarding local government matters are made at the central government and other higher levels rather than the local level. There is a tendency in these countries for the role of the council to be weak in comparison with that of the chief executive, an important reason for which is that much of the activity of the councils consists in implementation of national policies.

There are other councils whose decision-making power is mainly exercised in setting overall objectives. Among the possible examples are most of the councils in Switzerland and Germany, and the strong mayor-council and council-manager cities in the United States. These are municipalities which have a relatively high number of decentralized activities and in which the responsibility for the implementation of the local services is focused in a strong chief executive or board. A large number of the decisions concerning the work of the staff in other municipalities are made without the specific authorization of the council. The emphasis of these councils on overall objectives may be attributed to several different factors. The separation of powers theory, for example, is one factor influencing the role of the council in the U. S. strong mayor-council cities.

In the U. S. council-manager cities the councils, whose competence is synonymous with the competence of the unit of local government, exercise their autority over the more routine matters both by setting the overall objectives which determine the framework of the consequent staff decisions and by having the ability to remove the manager at any time. The American city manager is responsible to the council for every action of the staff;

[1] Public Administration Service, *The Local Government Democratization Program of the Government of the Union of Burma* (Chicago, Ill.) p. 10.

he is not directly responsible to either the electorate or the central government.

The German municipal councils generally do not exercise as much control as the councils in the U.S. council-manager municipalities over the staff activities, partially because the chief executive is directly responsible to the central government for some of his activities, and partially because he has a traditionally stronger position in the structure of German local government. His very term of office, which is often 12 years or "for life," is an indication of this; usually he cannot be dismissed except for gross misconduct.

Another factor influencing the type and number of decisions made by a local council is the number of members which it has. Large representative organs by their very nature can discuss and arrive at only a small percentage of the decisions which must be made in running a local unit. On the other hand, a small body generally can arrive at decisions more easily. Furthermore, it tends to meet more often and for longer periods of time. The smaller body is therefore more likely to concern itself with more routine matters as well as overall objectives. This tendency is made even more obvious because the smaller councils are generally in the less populous municipalities which have fewer decisions to be made, and therefore it is easier for the council to concern itself with the more routine details. Examples of small councils which concern themselves with details of staff work are particularly evident in some of the North American municipalities, including most of the rural ones. Many of these small councils may in fact be considered as plural executive organs.

Committees and directly-elected administrative officers such as the clerk or solicitor can also detract from the governing power of a council. Most of the counties and rural municipalities in the United States have a large number of independently elected administrative officers such as sheriff or constable, clerk, treasurer, and solicitor, who are not responsible to the council for their actions. The extent of the power of a council, therefore, must be measured not only in terms of its direct decision-making power but also in terms of its power to select and dismiss and to define the decision-making latitude of the officials who are taking the leading role in initiating and implementing the local governmental decisions.

5. *The nature of council deliberations in representative government*

A strong tendency is present in many council meetings for most of the decisions, although not necessarily the more important ones, to be made by common consent. For every decision taken amid heated public controversy there are many more routinely adopted with only a few perfunctory comments. The large majority of decisions are taken without a dissenting vote. Even when sharp discussion takes place the end result in many cases is that the councilmen are able to agree on a decision that is acceptable to all. The atmosphere then may not always be one of mutual cordiality but it is in most cases not one of deliberate obstruction. Many factors contribute to this apparent unity in the council meetings. Probably among the main causes of this atmosphere are a natural desire for harmony, an eagerness to get a job done, the presence of leaders who have the respect of the others, and an acceptance of the attitude that most of the problems of local government can best be solved in an atmosphere of mutual co-operation rather than antagonistic argument.

Another contributing factor is that most decisions on local government matters appear to be obvious. At least by the time they reach the voting stage the choice of which way a councilman should vote generally appears clear. In many local units the councils appear to do little more than ratify the suggestion of the local chief executive or the board, some of which are merely implementations of national policies. Furthermore, many councils tend to avoid decisions on issues on which there is a strong division of opinion until the subject is forgotten or a compromise is found which is generally acceptable. In many U.S. small rural units the desire for unanimity is closely interrelated to a low-cost-and-do-nothing philosophy of local government and lack of citizen interest; councils tend to vote for spending money only on continuing old activities, and they are reluctant to approve any new ones.[1] This is an important reason why subsidies are such an important factor in local representative government.

In some countries the tendency toward unity is made even stronger by the national and local customs. In Japan, for example,

[1] See Arthur J. Vidich and Joseph Bensman, *Small Town in Mass Society* (Princeton, N. J. 1958), pp. 211–217, for further comments on this.

voting is scrupulously avoided because the resulting division of the community into a majority and minority would show a lack of group solidarity. Steiner points out:

> "The meeting aims at achieving the appearance of consensus by a method which is often referred to as recommendation without objection (*sansuiiginashi*). It involves long and somewhat indirect discussions out of which ultimately an acceptable compromise solution emerges. This solution is then formally announced as the consensus of the meeting in the absence of objection. Because the appearance of conformity is highly valued, objections are seldom raised. These methods are usually reflected in the village assembly so that its decisions, too, are nearly always adopted by recommendation without objection. The village prides itself on a record of unanimity as a show of the harmony existing within it. Since almost all by-laws are proposed by the mayor, the process greatly favours his predominance."[1]

The effect of the local party organizations upon the deliberations of the local councils is generally not as great as upon the local elections. The local council members of any one party do not usually group together as closely as their counter-parts at the national level. The local problems are generally not ones that readily inspire party loyalty, the local issues do not as easily orient themselves around party principles as the national issues do. Moreover the local issues are often ones that the local council member and his constituency are more capable of understanding, and the council member is often, therefore, less readily inclined to follow the party leadership. Furthermore, a local council member has a small constituency and is therefore more likely to be able to build up a personal following which is not dependent on the party organization. In addition the local voters are more likely to know their local councilmen on a personal basis and are therefore more likely to vote for a personal rather than a party choice, if the arrangement of the ballot affords them this discretion. Correspondingly, the lesser population and smaller geographical size of the local political units often means that the working relations between the elected representatives are influenced to a greater degree by personal friendships.

Party loyalties appear to be playing an increasingly important role, though, in the activities of many of the local councils in several

---

[1] Steiner, *FEQ*, XV, No. 2 (February 1956), 190.

countries, particularly in the larger cities. To a certain extent this is due to the increasingly obvious inter-connection between local and national interests and the increasing extent to which local attention is focused on national issues. Another reason may be the decline in the social homogeneity of the local community. Furthermore, a central party organization may use its control of large campaign funds, patronage, and sometimes even its influence upon the local nominating processes, to tie the local party organization and the local coulcilmen belonging to the party more closely to the central organization.

The local party organizations, including both the local branches of the national parties and the independent local parties, have a two-edged effect upon the deliberations of the local councils. A high degree of party consciousness upon the part of the voters lessens the possibilities of a non-party council member being elected, and, if elected, lessens the possibility of the non-party council members having an effective role. There is a danger, though, that what are in fact essentially technical questions may be transformed into party issues. Increased party loyalties on the part of the council members may also make it more difficult for professional administrators to retain their impartial neutrality when the issues dividing the council become matters of strong party feeling.

On the other land, the rivalry of parties tends to make the local issues more understandable – perhaps with the danger of over-simplification. Harold Laski has said in this regard that if there is a tendency to over-emphasize the political motive where it is, in fact, out of place, the greater clarity of objective achieved probably more than compensates for its presence.[1] Competition is also often the most effective catalyst for striving to promote new and improved services as well as raising and retaining the interest and participation of those who should be concerned. In large councils which rely heavily on use of committees, the parties can be effective instruments for helping to develop an integrated and coherent programme and for co-ordinating the representative process.

With an effective local party organization the local elections can become a test of the record the majority has been able to

[1] Jennings, Laski, and Robson, *A Century of Municipal Progress*, 87.

make: there is something to be measured by the attitude public opinion will take. Just as a local council whose members are of one or of no political complexion may tend to lose its driving power from the absence of competition, so one in which party allegiances are strong tends not only to discover concrete objectives, but also to relate those objectives to a general orientation of outlook which gives meaning and vitality to the work of a council. One might add that a local government which is devoid of any policy issues suitable for political dispute is local government which is carrying out only deconcentrated functions.

In the last analysis the role and value of party politics in local government depends upon many factors, some tangible and some intangible. Included among these are the presence or absence of other cohesive forces, the quality and spirit of the members, and the degree to which politics is approached with a constructive or destructive attitude.

6. *The popular assembly and the referendum*

There are two opposing elements affecting the optimum size of a representative body. One element favours the election of relatively few members in order to permit them to have a more effective part in the representative process. The argument for having a small body is a recognition of the fact that the presence of a large number of people tends to give less opportunity for many members to discuss the problems thoroughly. If there is insufficient time to allow each member to express his views on the matters considered for discussion, the representative function of those members who cannot speak is severely limited.

The other element favours securing as wide a representation as possible in order to make certain that the wishes of the different groups and interest of the community are heard and the problems of the local unit understood. Theoretically the ideal situation is that in which all the residents of the local unit meet together in a "popular assembly" to conduct the governmental affairs that concern them. An alternative is that all the questions are submitted to them in a "referendum," that is the referring of certain questions to the electorate for a direct decision by a general vote.

Each voter may then in theory participate in and directly influence the actions of his local government. When units of government were smaller and the issues less complex, the popular assembly and referendum had fewer disadvantages. Today it is becoming increasingly questionable whether one can expect a whole population to be adequately enough informed to give proper consideration to the questions of government policies and programs. A large group has many inherent difficulties in systematically discussing and making decisions, unless the decisions have been prearranged.

The need for a relatively small representative organ is such that almost all municipalities with a popular assembly have a smaller, representative organ (which in this survey is called the council) which handles many of the less important policy and programming decisions. For instance, both the municipalities in Switzerland and north-eastern United States with popular assemblies have such organs. They prepare and approve the agenda and proposals for the popular assembly; more important they make many of the decisions. In the Polish, Turkish, and Icelandic rural units so many of the decision-making responsibilities have been transferred to this smaller organ that the popular assembly is merely a supplementary organ.

In practice, only smaller units of government are governed by popular assemblies and their number is declining. The only higher units with popular assemblies as representative organs are the three smallest Swiss states (*cantons*). Switzerland is the best-known example of a country with most of its smaller units still governed by assemblies composed of all the electorate. In approximately 90% of the municipalities the local legislative power is exercised by an assembly (*assemblée communale, conseil général or Gemeindeversammlung*) of all the local electors. This popular assembly approves all local statutes and resolutions, including the budget; it also elects the board, which is the collegial executive authority of the municipality.

The popular assembly is also used widely in the rural municipalities of some north-eastern U. S. states, and in a few of the German municipalities with less than 200 inhabitants. As mentioned earlier, in many of the English and Welch sub-municipalities (*parishes*) popular assemblies (with some authority to govern) are also used. In Sweden, too, until the 1953 consolidation of rural units, many of the municipalities had representative organs composed of all the electors. In the Turkish rural municipalities the popular assembly is, in theory at least, charged with all the powers of the urban municipal councils. In a few other local units, such as a few of the Asian and African rural basic units, popular assemblies are convened but their duties are generally limited to elective and advisory functions.

Aside from the local units which have popular assemblies there are only a few municipalities which have legal provisions for directly deciding policy matters by popular vote. These are the municipalities in which referendum is used. United States and Canada are the only countries in which a significant number of municipalities use referendum to decide a variety of types of local issues. In the United Kingdom and Norway referendum may also be used to decide a few types of questions.

7. *Selection of members*

The manner in which the council is selected is, for all practical purposes, the crucial factor in determining its representative nature. In terms of the selection of membership, one may divide the main representative organs of local governments into three main groups: (1) those in which all the members are elected either directly or indirectly, (2) those in which some are elected and some are appointed by organs of higher units of government, and (3) those in which all the voters participate as members, that is the popular assembly in which each voter may represent himself. (An organ with a majority of appointed members is for the purposes of this study not considered to be representative. A discussion of the so-called "administrative councils" with a majority of department heads and other appointed officials will, therefore, be omitted).

With the exception of the municipalities with electorates small enough to make popular assemblies practical, there is no satisfactory substitute for election by the people as a means of selecting all, or at least some, of the members of an organ which is to be representative as well as responsive and responsible to the public." For representation, elect" is an axiom of representative government. In most of the countries included in this survey all the local councilmen are elected and the tendency in the remaining countries is in this direction.

There are two approaches by which a central government may assure itself that the local councils will not make too many decisions which it considers wrong. One approach is to minimize and check the authority of the councils. The other is to maximize the number of council members who may be expected to guide the municipalities in what the central government considers to be good programs and policies. At least from the central government's point of view the most expedient means of guaranteeing a certain number of such members is to have them appointed by organs of the central government or other higher units.

Councils in which some of the members are appointed by higher units are found among the urban municipalities of India, Malaya, and the Philippines as well as the municipalities of the Sudan. These are all countries whose local government has been influenced, particularly in the urban areas, by the Anglo-Saxon tradition.

The proportion of council members appointed by higher units varies. Where the pattern is flexible within the country the tendency has been to reduce the proportion of appointed councilmen. For example in India the proportion of appointed members has been steadily reduced; in many cases the appointed members have been replaced by members selected by the council. The appointed members may be either government officials or private citizens; they may have definite or indefinite terms of office.

The government officials who are appointed to seats on the local councils may serve either on local or central government staffs. They may receive their appointments either as corollaries of their government posts or in addition to and distinct from these posts. In some of the urban municipalities of a few Indian states, for example, the public works director and the local chief of the central government police force have seats on the council by virtue of their official positions, while other central and local government officials may receive appointments as councilmen which are not linked with their government posts. Having acquired experience and training in government administration, these government officials are able to play an influential role in shaping the policies and programs of the representative bodies. Frequently they have been appointed to the council because the central government considers it advantageous to have their work co-ordinated with that of the council. Because of the large proportion of able, trained men in the central government service in these countries it is a somewhat natural tendency to use them in either elective or appointive capacities on the councils.

The private citizens who are appointed to council seats are frequently leading people in the community who have been recommended by the local political leaders. They are often the hardest workers on the councils. In some cases their appointment has been a means of securing minority representation, which is a difficult problem in countries in which the minority groups often make up distinct subcommunities. Although there are some considerations of expediency in having appointed members of council, it is generally recognized that the elimination of appointed council members is the desirable goal for all units of local representative government.[1]

8. *The size of the council*

The number of members of the local councils varies in general with the population of the unit of local government. The size of the council, however, is also closely inter-related with its role in the local government structure. The largeness or the smallness of the body affects the representative character, the effectiveness, and the nature of the deliberations of the council.

The size of councils varies immensely. Many large European cities and provinces have councils with more than a hundred members. Probably the largest city council in the world is that of Moscow, which has approximately 1,400 councilmen. On the other hand, many local councils have only a handful of members. In the United States, for instance, many of the rural municipal and county councils have only three members and a large number of the city councils have only five or fewer councilmen.

In the Communist countries the councils are relatively large. The emphasis in composition is upon having broad representation

[1] Sharma, M. P., *Local Self-Government in India* (Bombay 1951), p. 58.

and popular participation; in general the councils are too large to be effective as the actual governing organs of the local units. In these units, therefore, a large amount of the work-load (which in most countries is undertaken by council) is passed on, or delegated, to other bodies.

In order to be effective large councils must rely heavily on the executive organs or on the committees of council or on both. This can be a workable arrangement. It can also become in effect an abdication of power to bodies which are at best only indirectly answerable to the electorate.

The principal argument advanced for large councils is that it increases the ratio of councilmen to the population. It is felt that a large council makes it possible to have more citizens who participate in local government work, therefore making local government more representative and closer to the people. In the days when politics depended to a greater extent on direct personal communication, it was more important perhaps to have a high ratio of councilmen to citizens. With the development of mass techniques of communication, today's need for a low ratio is probably not as great. Size is a relatively minor factor in the determination of the representative character of a council; more important are the methods of selection and the degree to which the members of council can responsibly and effectively represent the will of the electorate.

In a few countries such as the United States and Canada, the tendency is toward small councils, particularly in the rural units and in the urban municipalities with either the "commission" or "council-manager" forms of government. The small size generally allows each of its members a greater opportunity for participation in the decision-making process. It is argued that its smaller membership and greater opportunity to play an effective role in the governing process increases the prestige of a position of a councilman and the possibility of obtaining good candidates for all the seats. The principal argument advanced for small councils is that small size increases the opportunity for efficient and effective consideration and decision of the local issues. The increase of efficiency in the handling of the public business may, though, decrease a council's role as a public forum of local political opinion. A council with a very small membership often allows little opportunity for minority opinions. Such small councils may be at a disadvantage in feeling the thinking, desires, and needs of the people. In many U. S. cities the council uses a large number of committees, many of which are composed mainly of non-councilmen, to overcome this obstacle. In fact, in respect to the nature of their activities the small councils in the United States correspond in some respects to the boards in European cities.

A principal argument for having at least moderately sized councils is that there may be enough members to represent the heterogeneous aspects of the people of the local unit, that is to recognize and understand the various interests and needs of the community or communities. This is especially true in the local units with large areas, large populations, or other factors which tend to increase the number and complexity of interest groups and special needs. In a council with more than a few members the different members may specialize in certain types of problems on which the council is expected to be informed.

In general, councilmen are not paid, although they may receive honorariums or nominal amounts to cover, or partially cover, their expenses incurred in serving on the council and in some cases to cover, or partially cover, their lost time from work. Many local units do, though, pay councilmen who have additional duties such as serving on the board, especially if this entails a major portion of the person's time.

The terms of office for which the councilmen are elected do not vary as greatly as the size of the councils. In France the terms are for six years. Many of the Swiss and smaller North American municipalities have one and two year terms; these are the countries where the traditional concept of "direct democracy" has taken the deepest root. In many of the Anglo-Saxon and East European municipalities the terms are three years. In other European, as well as the West Asian, the East Asian, and the more populous U. S. municipalities, the usual term is four years.

Terms of office for a council member should be short enough to provide for electoral control, but long enough to provide time for effective action and continuity. Except perhaps in basic units whose functions are small and the issues simple, one year is hardly adequate to learn the job and to become effective as a councilman. One may also question whether six years is not too long to assure a councilman's responsiveness to the public will.

The use of overlapping, or staggered, terms of office is another approach to the problem of providing continuity to the councils. By this arrangement only a fraction of the total number of council members are elected at any one election; the balance of members being selected at one or more later elections. Since the terms of office are equal, the terms of the various councilmen do not cease at the same election. This device has proved particularly useful in countries such as the United States which use the plurality choice method of election where there is often a sweeping change in the composition of the council.

Almost invariably the councils are single-chambered bodies.[1] A large number of Yugoslav municipalities, though, have bicameral structures. One chamber is the political chamber, composed of representatives elected by popular vote. The other chamber (called the *Producers' Council*) is composed of representatives of producing organizations. In those municipalities with two chambers, both bodies pass upon the municipal statutes, elect the municipal officers, and select the committees. The *Producers' Council* has a special jurisdiction in the co-ordination of the work of the economic activities within a municipality. The political chamber has special jurisdiction over such services as education, culture, and health.

9. *The council chairman and the secretary*

No council can operate without a chairman. His function, to put it at its irreducible minimum, is to promote and maintain an orderly discussion. His position will be affected by such factors as the method of his appointment, what his other roles are, and whether he or another person is the policy leader of the council. It is from his primary function of being responsible for order and from his unique position of being the focus of all remarks in the course of a council meeting from which spring his opportunities as chairman for guiding the discussions.

In terms of his voting, the prerogatives of the chairman are

[1] A board should not, and in this survey is not, be considered as one of two chambers in a bicameral council.

relatively less important. In those cases in which he is elected chairman by and from among the council he generally retains his right to vote. In many councils the custom is for him to vote after everyone else; in some cases he has the right to vote only if there is a tie. When the council chairman is not elected from among the council members he generally is not entitled to a regular vote; usually, though, he is entitled to cast a ballot if this is necessary to break a tie vote.

The chairman has some opportunity to influence the council decisions from the fact that he is entitled to have at least some control of the agenda of council session. Usually it is drawn up in co-operation with the secretary or clerk but in any case the chairman is in a crucial position to influence what items will be discussed and the order in which they will be discussed.

One of the reasons for the important role of the chairman in preparing the agenda is that he is the one who must act as the moderator or traffic policeman of the discussions once the meeting has been convened. He may exert influence over a discussion by his recognizing and encouraging speakers as well as by discouraging others by the manner in which he accepts, defers, and declines motions and amendments, by adding his own comments concerning the subject under discussion, and even by the timing with which he calls the meetings. Wheare adds: "A chairman has an opportunity to lead his committee also because of the desire, natural in a presiding officer, to bring a discussion to a close and get the question settled. This desire is often strong in members of a committee also, and chairmen are urged to get a decision and 'give a lead'... from his function as the conductor of the discussion a chairman may suggest solutions and in this way affect the course of policy."[1]

The influential role of a chairman, Wheare goes on to say, is increased by other factors. A chairman often tends to get himself identified with his council not only in his own eyes but also in the eyes of his fellow members and of the public. On many occasions he acts for the body as their representative at public gatherings or private consultations. Furthermore in times of emergency he may act on their behalf, seeking their confirmation for his actions later, while in normal times it is not uncommon

[1] Wheare, *Government by Committee*, pp. 39–40.

for them to authorize him to act for them upon routine or even upon exceptional matters.

The extent to which a council chairman exercises his opportunities for leadership depends somewhat on his other roles. In most municipalities the post of a council chairman and chief executive is filled by the same person, the mayor. In a lesser number of municipalities the position of council chairman is not combined with that of the chief executive. The latter type of council chairman usually does not as fully use his chairmanship opportunities for leadership. His position is one of high prestige and honour but generally he views his role as that of the impartial moderator rather than the forceful leader. Council election is the general method for choosing council chairmen who are not also chief executives.

The English council chairman, for example, presides over the council in a relatively impartial manner and is the ceremonial head of the municipality. He is not expected to play an active political or administrative role during his term of office. The council chairman is elected annually by the council, generally, but not necessarily, from its own membership. In urban municipalities the position is seldom held by any one person for more than one year so that eventually almost all the senior members of council have served as mayor.

In Sweden the municipal council chairmanship is also not identical with that of the chief executive. The council chairman is the ceremonial head of the municipality. Here, too, he is elected annually by the council, although frequently the same person is returned to office for many years in succession. The chairman is expected to exercise an impartial role. For this reason he is usually not a member of the municipal board. In fact the leader of the minority party is frequently elected to this post while the leader of the majority party is almost invariably elected board chairman.

When the posts of council chairman and chief executive are combined in the same person, he generally plays a more forceful role as council leader. If he is a chief executive, he is frequently the leader of the majority party or coalition. He has an intimate contact with the staff and is thereby acquainted with the staff routine and problems. The administrative officials supply him with proposals and answers to questions and criticisms. He has the opportunity to be the best-informed man regarding what the municipality has done, is doing, and will do. His opportunity to take the initiative and "lead" council is therefore greatly strengthened. The way in which the combination council chairman – chief executive is selected, is an important factor affecting his relationships with council. This will be discussed further in a later chapter.

While the opportunities which the chairman has for guiding council discussions are fairly obvious, not so conspicuous is the important role of the secretary. A secretary of the council has the task of recording the minutes, keeping the records, and usually the actual preparing of the agenda. This official must work closely with the council chairman and usually is in a strategic position to give the latter advice on the initiation and guidance of council deliberations. Usually the council secretary is a salaried full-time career official in the local administration, often he is the municipal chief administrative officer. His knowledge of administration and his experience in local government make his advice valuable and therefore less likely to be ignored.

Committee chairmen, particularly those of the crucial committees, are also in favourable positions for exercising leadership in guiding council as well as committee discussions. A study of the role of the committee of council is necessary to understand the importance of the committee chairman.

6

THE COMMITTEES OF COUNCIL

1. The committees and the council

"A committee is" says Wheare, "a body to which some task has been referred or committed by some other person or body. It may be asked or required or permitted to carry out this task. But that is not all. The notion of a committee carries with it the idea of a body being in some manner or degree responsible or subordinate or answerable in the last resort to the body or person who set up or committed a power or duty to it. There is inherent in the notion of a committee some idea of dependent status, in form at least; it lacks original jurisdiction. It acts on behalf of or with responsibility to another body."[1]

Among the reasons for the existence of committees are the privacy and the more informal procedure generally found in smaller bodies. The smaller size of the committees makes these bodies more effective organs for thoroughly discussing and understanding an issue. The use of committees also permits members to specialize in the matters which most interest them. Some small councils such as many U. S. ones, use committees to increase popular participation and thus allow for a more heterogeneous representation of the public interests. Furthermore, since most councils are by law open to the public (although aside from members of the press this opportunity is in most municipalities seldom used), use of committees generally permits matters to be discussed less publicly in an atmosphere where there can be a greater give-and-take of discussion with less fear of the members

[1] *Ibid.*, 5–6.

finding themselves publicly committed to particular positions.

The most important reason for the existence of committees, though, appears to be the need for a means for a council to relieve itself of some of its work load. The use of committees as part of the process of local representative government is, therefore, most pronounced in those countries in which the local councils have a large volume of decisions to make. A heavy work load for the council may be the result not only of a large number of activities being devolved to the council but also of the manner in which the council exercises its authority either in determining overall policy objectives or in deciding more routine matters concerning work of the staff, or both. Consequently the committees of council play a particularly important role in such countries as the United Kingdom, Yugoslavia and Sweden in which the councils, through the committees, directly manage the work of the staff.

A further factor affecting the development of committees is the size of the councils. The sheer size of the large council is an impediment to constructive discussions. Councils with a large membership, particularly those with many decisions to make, must pass some of their work load on either to administrative officials, a chief executive, or to committees of council.

Therefore, since the larger urban municipalities generally have large councils and a large number of decisions to make, there is a tendency for them to develop a committee system. Some of them have, in fact, a plethora of committees. A few of the larger English municipalities have as many as 25 to 30 standing committees in addition to the special committees. Furthermore some of these committees, such as the education committee in some populous U. K. municipalities, may have as many as 30 sub-committees. Even the sub-committees may be sub-divided. In contrast, there are some large U. S. urban municipalities with small councils which do not have any council committees.

In discussing committees of council a distinction has to be made between standing committees and special committees.[1] Special committees, or *ad hoc* committees, are appointed for a specific task and their existence is expected to terminate upon completion

---

[1] The board, which is the executive committee of the council, will be discussed in the next chapter.

of that task. A standing committee is a continuing body although its membership may change. It is considered to be permanent at least until there is a general re-organization of the system of committees of a council. It is the standing committees which play the more important roles in the continuing process of local government and to which this chapter will be devoted.

Councils generally have a wide latitude in setting up committees. The central government through statutes may, however, require the local council to have a committee for some particular purpose. Examples of the so-called statutory committees in English local government are the committees for education, health, and public assistance. Among other duties these commitees are charged with carrying out some relatively deconcentrated activities.

2. *Specialization of the committees*

Councils with more than one committee must have some criteria for allocating the work among them. Most committees specialize on matters dealing with one particular geographical area, activity, or management aspect of the local government activities.

Relatively few councils have committees organized to deal with matters affecting one geographical area within the local unit. Examples, though, are the Yugoslav municipal councils, which have a "local committee" for each sub-municipal unit.

The large majority of the committees of council are set up to deal with matters affecting a particular purpose or activity such as libraries, education, or public health. Often the arrangement of these committees corresponds to a certain degree with the organization of the departments of the local unit.[1] This arrangement allows the education committee for instance, to work closely with the education department. Committees set up along these lines are often called "vertical" committees.

Other committees deal with matters affecting a particular aspect, such as finance and personnel, of the management of the local government activities. These may be called the "horizontal" committees. They deal with matters that affect each of the local

[1] See the section on the departments in chapter 9.

government activities. This type of committee is in a favourable position to co-ordinate all the activities of the unit of local government in their respective fields. Often a "horizontal" committee has a leading co-ordinating role in the activities of a council. The finance committee is especially well-suited to develop a paramount position among the committees. This is particularly obvious in many of the Danish, Norwegian, and Swedish municipalities. In a large number of them the finance committee is legally established as a board; in others it is legally only one among equals among the committees of the council.

There is no standard practice in the organizing of committees. It is not at all unusual for one council to have all three types of committees. Generally, though, most of the committees are "vertical." Among the councils which have committees, though, all but the smallest have at least one horizontal committee.

There is a wide variation in the status and power of the committees of councils. Some, such as those in French local government, are supplementary adjuncts of the council. In contrast, the English council committees play such an important role that local government in the United Kingdom may be described accurately as government by and through committees. Many English local committees act in an apparently independent fashion, with council approval of their action appearing to be almost a foregone conclusion. In fact, the English local council meetings tend to be dull reading and routine approval of the minutes of the committee meetings.

In some respects the manner of operation of the more independent committees may resemble that of the special purpose units with which they are not to be confused. Unlike the special-purpose authorities, though, the decisions of the committees of council must receive the approval of the council. No matter how routine or automatic the approval may appear, the opportunity for control does exist. Furthermore a council, through its leaders, may exercise its control over the committees in an informal manner, and much of the control of committee decisions may be exercised through informal contacts between committee and council leaders. The administrative officers as well as the chief executive officer may also play an important role in this respect.

EXHIBIT 5. – SPECIALIZATION OF COMMITTEES

Management Aspects \ Activity	Fire	Police	Health	Education	Recreation	Health
Personnel						
Finance						
Planning						
Supplies						
Law						
Records						
Maintenance						

The use of two types of committees means that any one matter is within the jurisdiction of at least two committees. A matter concerning school health finances could be, for instance, within the jurisdiction of at least three committees. Furthermore, the use of geographically oriented committees would add a third dimension to this chart.

EXHIBIT 6 – A CONTRAST BETWEEN ADMINISTERING
AND PREPARATORY COMMITTEES

a. An example of the relationship of preparatory committees to the council and the departments in a U.S. council-(strong) mayor city

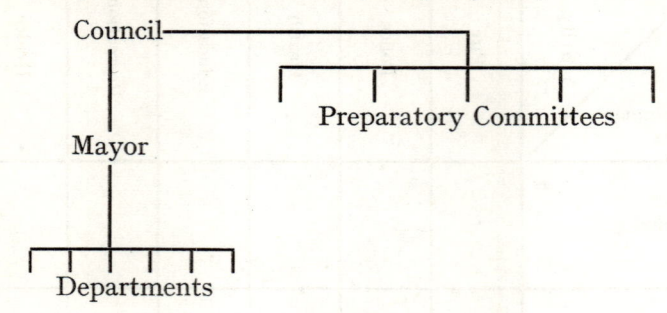

```
     Council─────────────────────┐
        │                ┌───┬───┼───┬───┐
        │                        Preparatory Committees
      Mayor
        │
   ┌──┬─┼─┬──┐
      Departments
```

b. An example of the relationship of administering committees to the council and the departments in an English municipality.

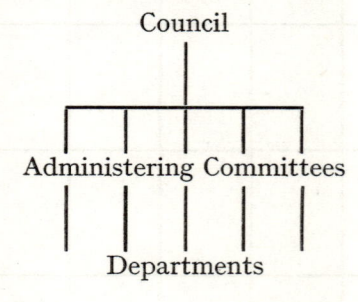

```
                Council
                   │
           ┌───┬───┼───┬───┐
              Administering Committees
           │   │   │   │   │
                Departments
```

3. The preparatory committees

In discussing the operations of the committees of council an important distinction must be made between "preparatory" and "administering" committees. Preparatory committees may play an important role in preparing policy decisions. They do not make them, however, for that is the task of the council. Many committees of council fall clearly into one or the other category, but there are some which would be difficult to categorize.

Outside of the Anglo-Saxon, Scandinavian and East European Communist countries, committees of council are generally preparatory bodies. In many countries, such as France and Germany, the use of preparatory committees is more often a feature of the larger councils of the more populous local units.[1]

The role of the preparatory committees in the decision-making process of local government is, generally speaking, relatively more confined than that of the administering committees. A few preparatory committees may have little more to do than to examine the texts of proposed ordinances and resolutions to correct poor drafting. Other preparatory committees may have a broader mandate to amend or reject a proposal. Some may study and analyse the problems in their field, make inquiries concerning the means of meeting the problems, and after discussion arrive at tentative decisions for recommending to the board or council. Some local government preparatory committees, such as in some U.S. cities, even have their own staffs. The preparatory committees cannot, however, supervise the implementation of decisions approved by the council. The implementation of these decisions is left to the executive organs.

4. The administering committees

Students of public administration have often discussed the question whether it is better to entrust the direction of the process of implementation to single individuals or to groups of

[1] Despite the important role the preparatory committees may have in the process of local government, their less formal character makes it difficult to write a general description of their manner of operation. In fact there is very little information available on the subject in any country.

individuals, that is, whether the unitary executive is preferable to the plural executive. In local government we may find examples of each, plus combinations of both. The administering committees as well as the boards mentioned in the next chapter, are examples of implementation directed by a group.

The use of administering committees, some of which are statutory, is widespread among the local units of the East European Communist, Scandinavian, and Anglo-Saxon as well as some of the Anglo-Saxon-influenced countries. In the East European Communist countries administering committees were adopted as a means of extending popular participation in the mechanics of government. In most of the British and Scandinavian local units the use of the administering committees developed in the years when a large amount of the local government work was performed directly by the volunteer labour of the committee members. In a few countries, such as India and the Sudan, administering committees were developed mainly in imitation of the British model.

The administering committees play an important role in the process of local government. They have an extensive amount of power both in formulating policy and in determining how it should be implemented. "It is in the committees of a Council" Laski has said of the English local committees "that policy is really made; it is in the committees, also, that the supervision of its execution is really effected."[1]

Like the preparatory committees the administering committees may study local problems and propose decisions for the council. But their power is usually much greater. The administering committees tend to take the lead in initiating proposals more often than do the preparatory committees. Whereas most of the work of the preparatory committees generally comes to them after it has been referred by the council or board, the main bulk of the work of the administering committees comes to them before going to council. This difference may partially be accounted for by the fact that the flow of ideas from the staff tends to go via the committees (and via the board if there is one) to the council when there are administering committees, and, to a les-

[1] Laski, Jennings, and Robson, *A Century of Municipal Progress*, 82.

ser degree, via the board or the council to the committees when there are preparatory committees. In any event, before going to the council for discussion, proposals are generally referred to the administering committees for their comments.

In addition, the administering committees frequently make decisions and act upon them without waiting for the approval of council. Most of the more important decisions are generally approved by the council before they are acted upon; but less important decisions, which are within the framework of a course of action already approved of by the council, often do not have specific approval of council before they are acted upon. Also in emergency situations, an administering committee often acts without the explicit approval of the council. In these cases the council may review the decisions after the actions have taken place. If there is a board, this body generally plays an important role in controlling most of the decisions of the administering committees. The most salient difference between the administering committees and the preparatory committees is that the former not only participate in the preparatory stages of the decision-making process, but that they also actively participate in the process of implementation.

In some of the smaller municipalities the committee members may actually perform all, or almost all, of the work performed by the staff in larger units. In other units of local government the committee members may directly supervise and work with the employees. In larger units each of the committees generally works with the relevant department head or in some cases with the chief administrative officer or one of his assistants.

The decisions and the activities of an administering committee are always subject to review by the local council. In some cases they are also subject to review by organs of higher units of government. In the United Kingdom, the interested ministry reviews the decisions of the committees regarding deconcentrated activities carried out by the committees. In Sweden the organs of the central government also show a particular interest in reviewing the work of the committee dealing with the so-called "regulated" activities. In the East European Communist countries all the decisions and actions of each of the municipal committees may be reviewed not only by the municipal council but also by the counter-part committees at the next highest level. In these countries each committee is thus simultaneously accountable both to the local council, actually the board, and to the parallel committee on the next highest tier.

The degree of independence of an administering committee may vary widely. A council may insist upon closely reviewing and frequently amending or nullifying the decisions of some committees. Other committees may appear to operate with complete freedom, with apparently automatic approval of any decisions submitted for approval.

The use of a committee system in which a large amount of power is delegated to the committees can result in council meetings becoming mere formalities, and hence the councils becoming mere façades. The role of the council may be reduced to merely ratifying the previously made decisions. Sometimes the ratifications are made on a log-rolling (or "I'll scratch your back, you scratch mine") basis. The council then fails to perform its role as the main representative body. "The tendency toward oligarchy, which the use of smaller and smaller bodies ... exhibits," says Wheare in describing the inclination for the real decisions to be made in committees and sub-committees instead of the council, makes the larger organ "at the best a screen and at the worst a sham."[1] Administering committees may become in effect relatively independent special-purpose bodies.

"Committees must bear some sort of subordinate relations to the body which creates them."[2] By their very nature administering committees require a great deal of co-ordination if their work is to become part of a harmonious whole, which is necessary if there is to be a minimum of misdirected effort and wasted public funds. Although the British local government units do not have committees with a clearly defined co-ordinating task, many of the larger councils have committees which have developed leading roles; often they are finance committees.

Political parties, particularly in the East European countries, also have an important unifying role. In many municipalities the mayor, chief administrative officer, or board may play an

---

[1] Wheare, *Government by Committee*, 195.
[2] *Ibid.*, 175.

important part in co-ordinating the activities of the committees. For instance, in the Sudan, India, Australia, South Africa and Ceylon, the position of the mayor is much stronger than that of his counterpart in the United Kingdom. These possibilities, however, will be examined further in later chapters.

5. *The composition of the committees*

In a discussion of the composition of committees of council, one must include a description of the size of the committees, how the committee members are selected, and what proportion of the committee members are council members.

The size of the committees can vary from a "committee of the whole" to a "committee of one" but mostly they have between three and twenty members. As has been pointed out, an argument for the use of committees is that it enables fewer people than the whole council to be associated with a particular process. It allows the work load of the council to be passed on to smaller organs which may assess more thoroughly the factors in making a decision. When the committees themselves are too large to deal with the volume of work presented to them they themselves tend to subdivide into smaller bodies. A committee may be used, though, not only to enable fewer people to be associated with a particular process but also to enable more people to be associated with a particular process. The points are not contradictory. The smaller membership of a committee of council does not preclude the possibility of using committees as an opportunity to expand public participation in the representative governmental process.

Almost invariably the members of council committees are chosen by the council, or more accurately the nominations of committee members are approved by the councils. Councils whose committees consist mainly of council members generally have a small group prepare a list of which members shall serve on which committees. This small group is in some cases formally constituted as a special committee, and generally consists of the leading men on the council with the council chairman sometimes playing a leading part in its deliberation. Usually a council member who has been selected to serve on a given committee continues in this position as long as he is re-elected to the council.

Among the committees which include a large number of non-councilmen, the tentative selection of the committee members from outside the council is in many local units a duty of the committee itself, although the council in most cases makes the formal selection. In the U. S. S. R. the chairman of a council committee generally has an important role in determining the membership of his committee.

Some councils, particularly those with administering committees, may be required to include among the members of some of the statutory committees persons with a special knowledge who are not members of the council. In the United Kingdom, for instance, an education committee may be required by law to have a teacher on it, or the public health committee may be required to have a medical doctor on it. Swedish law requires that certain public officials serve on those committees in which the central government has particular interests; furthermore, the provincial governor may appoint members to some of the committees dealing with deconcentrated functions.

In the units of local government with preparatory committees, the membership of these bodies is generally confined to councilmen; for instance, the French and Dutch standing committees of the local councils are composed solely of councilmen. In contrast, many of the administering committees such as those in the Scandinavian and East European Communist countries include non-council members, and frequently only one or two of the members of any one committee in these countries are council members. In fact, many committees in U.S. cities have no council members on them. In the United Kingdom up to one-third of the membership of most committees of council (which are administering ones) may be non-members. In practice, however, in this country as well as most other Commonwealth countries non-council members are not appointed to council committees with a great deal of frequency. Only council members, though, may be appointed to council committees in Australia.

There are several arguments for using non-council members on the council committees. One is to increase the popular participation in the work of the local government. Another valid argument for including non-councilmen on the council committees is that there are many persons whose specialized education or background would make them an asset to the membership of certain committees. For instance, a public health committee might profit enormously by including in its membership not only professional medical people but also representatives of organizations such as labour unions and educational institutions whose co-operation could aid in the implementation of the public health program. In fact, though, the appointments to the committees are not usually thought out in such an idealistic manner. More often than not the appointments are based on political considerations, family relationships, or other personal ties.

These non-councilmen committee members are nevertheless among the hardest workers on the committees. They are persons who are usually not willing to be nominated for the council, nor would they necessarily be good council members. But they are often willing to give much time to work in the particular activity which interests them and their counsel can be quite valuable. Furthermore the use of these non-council members for this more specialized work can free the regular council member so that he may better concentrate on the more general representative duties.

The selection of non-council members for committee membership raises the question, though, whether it is consistent with the concept of local representative government to have persons who have not been chosen by public election participate in the policy formulating process. The answer, it would seem, depends on whether they only recommend decisions or, in fact, make them. The council should act as a trustee of the general public; therefore, part of its role as a representative body is listening to the criticisms and advice of the members of the community among whom may be experts on particular subjects. The use of non-council members on committees is only a formalization of this process if the council retains its role as the main representative organ by making, not merely ratifying, the policy decisions. As long as the committees are, in fact, responsive and responsible to the popularly elected council, the concept of representative local government is secure.

6. *The committee chairmen and secretaries*

A committee, like a council, says Wheare, must be wisely led and wisely fed if it is to be effective. The extent to which a committee is wisely led and wisely fed depends largely on the role of its chairman and secretary. Both have positions of considerable importance.

The chairman of a committee is generally a senior or leading member of the committee who is selected by the committee itself or by the council. Once selected, a chairman often continues to be re-elected to this post; in some councils committee chairmen tend to retain their positions as long as they are in the council.

In the United Kingdom, for instance, the chairmen of the local committees are usually elected by the committees themselves. In the larger local units the committee chairmen may be nominated by the major political group. The chairmen of most of the Swedish council committees are also elected by the committees. However, the chairmen of the finance, poor relief, and child welfare committees are selected by the council as a whole, generally on the recommendations of the board or the leaders of the majority faction of the council.

In some countries the usual practice is for the board to select, or tentatively select the chairmen; this is the case in Norwegian municipalities. In the U.S.S.R. on the other hand, the board members themselves serve as chairmen of the committees and together determine which board member will chair which committee.

To a large degree the effectiveness of the committee is dependent upon the chairman's personality and ability, for the chairman of a committee, like the chairman of a council, can do much to determine the scope of the discussions and guide the conclusions of the group over which he presides. In fact a committee chairman may in some cases exercise more power in his relations with his committee than a council chairman can with regard to the council as a whole. The smaller membership of a committee, combined with the more private meetings, may give more opportunity for a dominating role on the part of the chairman.

The role of the chairman of the preparatory committees as well as that of the chairman of the administering committees is a significant one. But the role of the latter is especially important if only because of the relatively broader scope of decision-formulating powers of the administering committees. The chairman of an administering committee is normally an amateur. His relations with the administrative official charged with implementing the committee's decisions are similar, as will be seen, to those between a mayor and a chief administrative officer. In theory, the committee chairman takes the leadership in determining policy objectives, the department head in matters regarding how these policies are to be implemented. In practice, though, this is seldom a helpful distinction, both because policy formulation and implementation blend so much into one another and because the focus of power depends so completely on the personalities and the ability of the two men. Whereas many committees are dominated by the department head, there are also many committee chairmen who interfere excessively with the activities of the staff.

Legally, the committee is supreme in certain respects. It formulates the policy, approves the schemes prepared by the staff and supervises their implementation. A committee secretary, in some cases the chief administrative officer or his assistants and in many cases a department head, renders advice, furnishes statistical information, and explains and answers criticisms concerning the working of the department. He has to undertake the execution of any work after obtaining the financial and administrative sanction of the committee. In theory at least, therefore, he is the servant of the committee. In fact, however, he may be more a master than a servant. The reasons for this possibility are obvious. An honest, able and energetic chief administrative officer or department head can almost always win a committee to his point of view. In the ultimate analysis a committee, unless it is an extraordinarily strong or strong-headed one, usually approves the schemes prepared by the administrative staff. Staff officers do not await orders as to what ought to be done. Instead it is they who generally initiate the policies and tentatively formulate the programs for the execution of the policies. This tendency is particularly apparent in the Asian countries in which the administrative officials are often better informed and "superior in many respects to the average member of the committee."[1]

[1] Rao, V. V., "A Hundred Years of Local Government in Andhra and Madras," *Quarterly Journal of Local Self-Government Institute* (July 1958), p. 116.

The committees of council are among the least studied bodies in the local representative government process. Generally they are understood only in relationship to the other organs whose positions in the organizational structures are more clearly defined. The effective power of the committees of council is especially dependent upon their relationship to the board, the chief executive, other administrative officials, and the political parties.

7

THE BOARD

1. *The board and the executive function*

AN executive organ of a unit of local government is one which has the central over-all task of directing, initiating, and co-ordinating all or most of the activities of a local unit. At one time political theory under the influence of Locke and Montesquieu considered an executive organ to be one which carried out the decisions made by another organ, but now it is generally recognized that the making and carrying out of decisions cannot be delineated so sharply. In modern representative governments an executive organ is expected to take the general initiative not only in directing and supervising the implementation of policies but also in formulating proposals, recommending them to and guiding them through the representative assemblies, and in fact making a significant share of the policy decisions. Thus the executive organ is the focus of power in both the representative and staff aspects of the local representative government process.[1]

There are three essential duties of an executive organ: initiative, integration, and interpretation. All three facets are inter-related and run through each other. An executive organ is, above all others, expected to take the initiative in developing and implementing those measures which are in the best interest of the public and those which are necessary for the efficient administration of the local services. This does not mean that it must have all the new ideas itself: far from it. But it must encourage an environ-

---

[1] See John Locke, *Two Treatises on Government* (Morley, ed.), Bk. II, Chap. 14, §§ 159–166 and Edward S. Corwin, *The President – Office and Powers* (New York 1948), pp. 1–7.

ment of opinion in which new ideas can germinate, be recognized, and be brought to fruition.

A second essential duty of an executive organ is integration; it is expected to integrate and co-ordinate all the various local activities into one effective whole. It is favourably located to co-ordinate the work of the staff and representative organs. Strong executive leadership is also necessary if local government policy is not to be splintered among competing centres of power. Its efforts in the co-ordination of the different organs help to determine the balance and the character of the organization.

Another essential duty of an executive organ is interpretation. In fact the making and implementing of policy is one continuous process of interpretation. It should be obvious that policy objectives must be interpreted to those who help with the implementation if the tasks are to be carried out meaningfully. Also the ideas of the employees should be communicated and interpreted to those charged with determining the policy objectives, if the local unit is to be well run. Perhaps even more important for representative government, though, is that the public be convinced that the policies are necessary and beneficial as well as properly carried out; the corollary to this is that the ideas of the electorate must be communicated and interpreted to both the policy-makers and implementers. Interpretation is a two-way street; it is the key to arousing the enthusiasm of not only the voters and elected persons but also the employees. Without the support of both of these groups, representative government cannot succeed. In any vigorous local representative government, political leadership, informed electorate, and enthusiastic employees are essential elements. Each is an invaluable complement and catalyst to the other.[1]

An executive organ may consist of one or more than one person, that is, it may be a single chief executive or a plural executive organ (usually a board, but also in some cases a small council). Furthermore, a considerable number of municipalities have two executive organs, that is, they have a plural executive as well as a single one. By their very nature, however, there cannot be two or more separate focuses of executive power. In those

---

[1] See L. F. Urwick, *Leadership in the 20th Century* (London 1957), pp. 44–45 and Paul Rigors, *Leadership and Domination* (Boston 1935).

local units in which there is a plural executive in addition to the chief executive, the focus of power within the plural executive is in the position of the chief executive (who is almost invariably the board chairman).

The board of a local government is a plural executive organ composed wholly or mainly of elected persons and which is responsible to the main representative organ for the preparation and the implementation of the decisions of the larger organ.[1] The board is expected to prepare and guide the deliberations of the larger body and supervise the activities of the staff. Unlike most other local committees the scope of the authority and power of the board extends across the whole spectrum of local public activities. More than any other committee it has a pivotal role in formulating and elaborating the decisions of the council, and in many cases it makes decisions on its own authority.

The board is a part of the structures of many local units, especially in European countries. In those cases in which there are relatively large councils, the small size of the board makes this body especially effective for discussing, and arriving at, decisions; thus the roles of the board and the council complement one another, for the larger size of the council makes it more effective for representing the various aspects of the community but less effective for formulating policy and supervising the day-to-day management of the local unit.

The board is a relatively small organ; generally it has fewer than eight members. Larger boards are found, though, in many of the municipalities with the larger councils. Many of the larger boards have small unofficial and informal executive committees of their own. In the Soviet Union, in which both the councils and the boards (presidiums) tend to be exceptionally large (the board of the city of Moscow has sixty members), there are formal official executive committees (bureaus) of the boards of the urban municipalities.

---

[1] So-called "administrative boards," composed solely of members of the staff as well as the chief executive, do not come within the scope of this study. Although the municipal boards in Luxembourg are officially appointed by the central government, they are considered as boards, because in fact they are nominated by the local council majority.

2. *The selection of the board members*

A board may include non-elected as well as elected persons. For instance, in the Turkish urban municipalities up to one-half of the board members may be department heads who are staff officers. In the Finnish urban and some of the rural municipalities, too, the board chairman is the council-appointed manager, that is the chief staff officer. (In the larger municipalities the assistant chief staff officers may also be members of the board). Other examples of a non-elected person who is not only a member of a board but also its chairman is the council-appointed chief executive in some German urban municipalities and the centrally-appointed chief executive in all the Dutch municipalities. All of the members of the local boards in most countries, though, are elected persons.

Generally the elected persons on a board are elected by and from the council or lacking a council by the popular assembly. There are a few Canadian cities and some of the more populous Swiss municipalities, though, which have councils in which the members of the boards are directly elected by the voting public.

The manner in which the members of the boards are elected by and from the council varies both by law and by custom. In French municipalities the assistant mayors (*adjoints*), who along with the mayor may be said to comprise a board, are elected following the election of the mayor; his influence on the selection of the assistant mayors is considerable. In Finland the municipal law provides that at the elections of members of a board (not including the manager or his assistants) a system of proportional representation should be adhered to, provided that this system is requested by one-fourth of the councilmen who are taking part in the election. In the Netherlands, in which most of the local councils have three or more parties represented, the board members (not including the chief executive) are elected by the council by majority vote but the custom generally is to allocate the places on the board among the parties approximately in proportion to their seats on the council. In Swedish municipalities, on the other hand, the usual practice is for the majority faction to nominate all the members of the board; in this way the board is a relatively homogeneous organ prepared to undertake the collective responsibility to the council for formulating the over-all program of policy of the local unit.

In most countries the term of office for the elected board members coincides with the term for the councilmen. (One exception is the Swedish board; a new local board in Sweden takes office one year after a new council is inaugurated and the term of the board expires one year after the old council has left office). In several countries, though, the board generally stays in office only as long as it has the support of the council. A vote of non-confidence can, for instance, bring the resignation of the French mayor and this brings with it the termination of the terms of all the assistant mayors. In practice, though, a board usually serves out its full term of office. First of all, the council usually retains confidence in those whom it originally elected to the board, especially since among the members of this organ are generally several of the leading members of the council. Furthermore, since the board is in close contact with the council and it generally understands the feelings of the members, it is usually able to avoid presenting measures which antagonize a majority of council members.

3. The board and its members – *collectively and individually*

Some tasks of a board are exercised collectively by all the members acting together. On the other hand, there are some tasks which are carried out by individual members of the board. In many local units, such as the urban municipalities in Denmark and Greece, only the board chairman as mayor has specific individual executive duties in addition to his more general collective duties as a member of the board. In some other local units the board is composed partially of those who only have the duties of a more general collective nature and partially of those who also have specific individual executive duties. For instance, the Polish and Austrian urban municipal board is composed of the mayor and assistant mayors plus several other board members; the mayor and each of the assistant mayors have specific individual executive duties which the other board members do not have. In still other boards, such as those in the more populous Belgian cities, every board member has specific individual executive duties in addition to his collective tasks as a member of the board.

The nature of the specific individual executive duties of the members of the board varies. For example in Finland, each of the elected members of the local boards is charged with looking after the affairs of a particular area of the municipality. In most local boards, though, in which members other than the mayor have specific individual executive duties, each of these persons is charged with looking after the affairs pertaining to one or more departments.

The extent to which the board acts as a whole or one or more of the members act individually is affected by many factors. One of the most important factors is that in those local units in which the board has developed from a finance, or other type of specialized, committee, the members, other than the chairman, seldom have specific duties. Another important factor is that in the more populous municipalities in some countries there is a greater tendency to spread the executive work load among the members.

In a few countries the municipal codes are a large factor in determining how much power is focused in the board chairman. Another factor is how many of the board members are paid full-time salaries, for usually the power tends to concentrate with the full-time officials; when only the board chairman is a full-time official the power tends to focus to a very large extent in him. Other factors are the customs of the countries and the localities as well as the capabilities and personalities of each of the board members, especially the chairman.

In many countries the tendency is for the board to work together as a group in fulfilling many of its tasks. The Norwegian and Swedish municipal boards, for instance, have relatively frequent meetings at which the work and problems of the staff are reviewed and proposals for future courses of action are discussed. A large percentage of their work is therefore collective action, even though much of the preparatory work for the meetings may have been concentrated in one or a few individuals. On the other hand, there are some boards (including some of the Thai cities) which meet relatively little and in which the large percentage of the work is not co-ordinated by board meetings.

4. The board and the council

The tasks of the board may be discussed from two different points of view. One is from the side of the council, to which the board is responsible, the other is from the side of the staff, for whose activities the board is responsible. In reality, of course, these two aspects of the work of the board cannot be separated, for they are merely viewing the same set of tasks from two different points of view.

In the representative aspect of the process of local government the board is the steering committee of the council and is expected, along with the chief executive, to provide the overall initiative in the policy-making process. It also goes over the council agenda and makes recommendations on the items to be discussed and the final form of the proposals submitted to council.

The opportunity for the board to exercise power occurs not only when it formulates the proposals for the council but also when it amplifies the decisions during the supervision of their implementation. A board generally has a broad latitude to exercise discretion as long as the decisions are in accord with the policy determined by the council. A board usually also has a fairly broad power to make decisions on matters which come up between council sessions and cannot be held over until a succeeding meeting. Law and practice varies concerning the extent to which these board decisions are subject to later review by the full council.

In addition to the decisions which the board may take for the council, the board in a few countries such as the Netherlands has the authority to make some decisions in its own right; these are decisions involving activities devolved by the central government directly to the board. Although legally the board is not accountable to the council for the manner in which these activities are managed, in fact there is not so distinct a separation.

In discussing the role of the board as regards the council one must, of course, also consider the other committees, which exist in many but not all the local units which have boards. In local units with specialized committees, the relationship of the board with the council is only one, although the major one, of the many relations among the various committees, the board, and the council. The board is able to exercise control over the specialized committees, in part, by its control of the council agenda and its power to influence the decisions of the council. It is the board rather than the council which most affects the course of the decisions of the committees. This is more evident in regard to the preparatory committees; it is perhaps less obvious and more complex in regard to the administering committees. In either case, though, the members of the board are almost invariably among the most influential persons on both the council and its committees. Quite often the board members are the chairmen of the committees and are thus in particularly strong positions to influence the course of their decisions.

5. *The board and the staff*

Collectively the board is responsible for the over-all co-ordinated implementation of the decisions of the council. Through the board chairman and the board secretary they collectively supervise the implementation and co-ordination of the local activities.

The individual board members, as mentioned in the previous section, may also have specific duties regarding the supervision of the implementation of certain aspects of the local government policy. The degree to which they are involved, though, in the management of the individual departments varies widely. In some local units, for instance in many of the Swiss and Thai cities, the individual board members have duties involving the direct management of one or more of the municipal departments with which they are charged.[1] (In this respect the Swiss and Thai boards are very similar to those councils in the United States cities with the "commission" form of government). More frequently, as in the Dutch municipalities, the board members are not themselves the department heads but they work closely with the department heads in many of the more important policy matters.

---

[1] See the section on the department heads in Chapter 9 for further information concerning board members as department heads.

EXHIBIT 7 – A COMPARISON OF THE ORGANIZATION OF MUNICIPAL BOARDS

a. Organization of a Thai Municipal Board

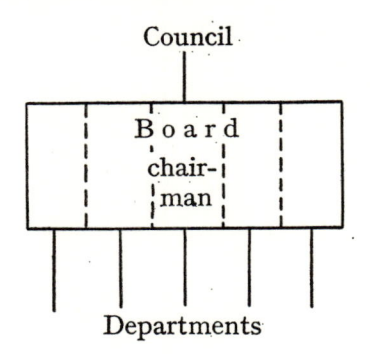

b. Organization of a Swedish Municipal Board

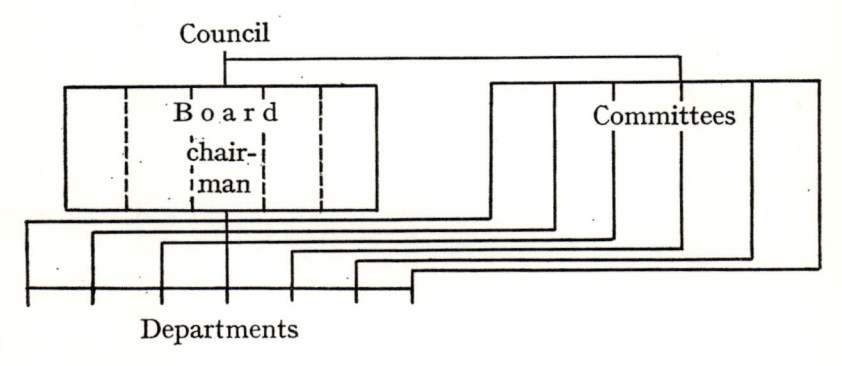

c. Organisation of a French Municipal "Board"

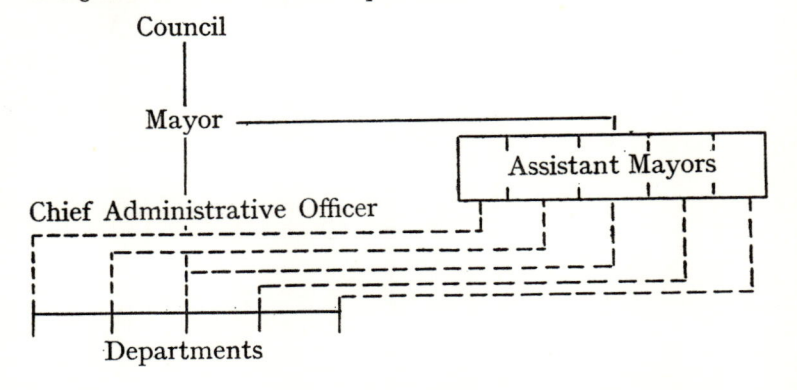

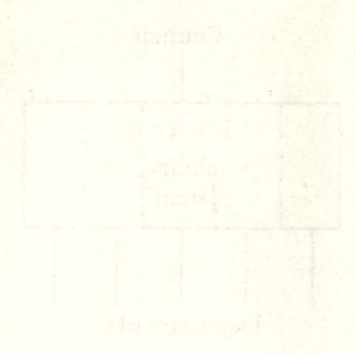

6. *The board chairman and the board secretary*

The importance of the board is demonstrated by the fact that its chairmanship is almost invariably the most important single position in the local government structure from which to influence the formulation, exposition, and implementation of municipal policy. That is, the tasks of the board chairman and chief executive are almost invariably combined in the same position. (In this line of thought one might contrast the position of many of the board chairmen in countries which have one of the Germanic tongues with that of most of the mayors in countries which have a Latin tongue, by saying that the former is a chief executive because he is a chairman of a board, while the latter is a board chairman because he is a chief executive). The Polish rural municipalities are, in fact, the only examples in this survey in which the chairman of the board cannot be considered the chief executive. In those local units the chairman of the popular assembly is the focal person in the process of government. He is the general liaison between the party, the public, the staff, the council, and the board (in whose sessions he is the foremost person, although he is a voteless non-member).

The board chairman may or may not be the council chairman. In most local units, such as those in the Netherlands, Norway and Italy, the board chairmen are also the council chairmen. On the other hand, the board chairman in some other municipalities is not also the council chairman. The board chairman may be selected in a variety of ways. Some are appointed by the central government or other higher units as in the Netherlands and Spain. Some Canadian and Swiss board chairmen, on the other hand, are directly elected by popular vote. Some of the Swiss boards elect their own chairman. Still other board chairmen are elected by the council, as in Austria and Sweden; in some cases the tentative selection has been made by the board but the approval rests with the council. In many cases it is a foregone conclusion that the leader of the majority faction will be the board chairman. In the Finnish urban municipalities and some of the rural municipalities the professional council-appointed chief executive officer, who is appointed by the council for an indefinite term, is the chairman of the board.

In order to understand the relationship of the board chairman to the board one must consider the extent to which the use of executive power, both as board chairman and in other capacities, is focused in him. It is inevitable that the collective power of the board is focused to some extent in the board chairman. His prerogatives as presiding officer of the board meetings give him a natural opportunity to present ideas, guide the discussions, and influence the decisions. His capacity to focus the collective power of the board in himself is generally strengthened by the fact that he is usually accepted by most, if not all, of the board members, as well as by the council as the leader and representative of the board.

The focusing of the collective executive power of the board in the office of its chairman is made all the more inevitable in those cases in which the board chairman also has some specific individual executive authority in his own right. Whereas some board chairmen have no authority aside from that which accrues to them as a member and moderator of the board, others may have specific individual executive authority. For instance the Swedish, Russian and some of the Swiss board chairmen have no specific individual executive authority; their individual power as chief executive depends solely on their power as board chairman. On the other hand, the office of the board chairman in many European, Latin American and Middle Eastern countries has specially devolved powers, many of which are in the important field of public security. Since the exercise of executive power in any one municipal field is inextricably linked with the exercise of such power in any other municipal field, the individual executive authority of the board chairman as chief executive tends to enhance his power as presiding officer of the board.

For this as well as other reasons, therefore, there is a significant variation in the extent to which the executive power is focused in the chairman. Many textbooks have contrasted the single chief executive and the plural executive forms of government A board is often considered to be a classic example of the plural executive. In fact, it generally represents some kind of compromise between the two forms for in practice no chairman is only one among equals.

To describe the chairman of some municipal boards, though, as a *primus inter pares* is not too much of an understatement. Some of the less forceful of those board chairmen who do not have a specific individual executive authority, could be so classified. Some of the Swiss and Thai mayors would fall in this category. Most board chairmen, though, have more power focused in their positions. In the Swedish cities, for instance, the focusing of power in the board chairman is substantial even though these chief executives do not have any individual executive authority. The local board chairman is almost invariably the acknowledged political leader of the majority party. Upon this informal political role of leadership depends an important degree of the focusing of power. The Russian board chairman also does not have any specific individual executive authority, but his close working relations with the head of the local party organization (in some cases he is the head) strengthen his position as chief executive.

In terms of executive authority at least, the Dutch and Austrian mayor also usually has a relatively strong position in his relations with the board. In addition to his power as the presiding officer of the board he has the authority to act as an agent of the central government and to thus carry out deconcentrated activities. These two roles tend to make his position an influential one for coordinating and guiding the decision-making processes of the board. In the smaller municipalities in which the other board members are not fulltime paid officials the primacy of the chief executive is even more obvious.

The French mayor may be considered as a "single chief executive." The organ composed of the French mayor and his assistants (called *maire et adjoints*) can hardly be called a plural executive organ although in some respects it resembles one. This "quasi-board" does not, however, have any collective authority. All the executive authority is vested in the mayor and he need not consult the assistant mayors at all. They act purely as his deputies carrying out duties as directed. Nevertheless, the delegated power of an assistant mayor may be substantial. An assistant may have a valuable role to play particularly if he represents a faction upon whom the mayor depends for support in the council. Furthermore, a mayor may often consult with one or more of his assistant mayors, particularly those in whom he has confidence.

The Spanish municipal board can also hardly be described as a plural executive organ. Collectively the Spanish board, unlike the French one, does have some authority. And all the members of the Spanish boards, except the chief executive, are chosen from among the members of council; however, they are personally selected by the chief executive and the selections need not be approved by the council.

At least in local government then, the frequent black-and-white contrast of the plural executive versus the single chief executive is overdone. Although the executive power is divided among the board members, there is a tendency for the chairman to take a leading role in guiding the decision-making done by the board as a whole and co-ordinating the policy formulation and implementation done by the individual board members.

Just as the importance of the board is demonstrated by the fact that the board chairman is almost invariably the chief executive, so the importance of the board is also pointed out by the fact that the board secretary is almost invariably the chief administrative officer. In most cases he is also the council secretary. As the secretary he is generally charged with the actual preparation of the agenda. As an official with a long intimate experience with local government his counsel is valuable and not easily ignored. As the person with perhaps the best grasp of the current local administrative, and perhaps even political problems, his advice is constantly sought. As the administrator with the closest working relationship with the chief executive he is able to influence the decision-making process in a manner that defies analysis. In a number of local units this chief administrative officer may play a leading role during the meetings in bringing up matters for consideration and in crystallizing the decisions to be reached. He generally meets with the chairman of the board to discuss the agenda prior to the board meetings. The secretary does not, however, have a vote (unless he happens to be a regular elected or appointed member of the board).

8

THE CHIEF EXECUTIVE

1. *The chief executive and the executive function*

THE post of the chief executive is essentially and pre-eminently the focal institution in a local government structure. He is the principal person co-ordinating the representative and staff aspects of the process of local government. The chief executive may be the chairman of the plural executive organ, or he may be a single chief executive with specific individual executive authority in his own right, or he may be both. He may be the mayor (*maire, Bürgermeister,* or *Alcalde*) or he may be another official such as a manager.

The chief executive is the focal point of the process of local government; this does not negate the fact, though, that he must work closely with others. He must work closely with the council in the co-ordination of the making of policy objectives, he must also work closely with the staff in co-ordinating the policy implementation. Furthermore, in many local units he works along with a board in co-ordinating both of these aspects of the local government process. The chief executive should be the captain or the pivot-man of the team, but he should never be the dominator if local representative government is to function successfully. For a concentration of local government power in one man seldom encourages him to engage in a public discussion of policy and thus deprives the council of the opportunity to represent the electorate and creates an unfavourable environment for popular participation and interest which is an essential aspect of representative government. Furthermore, one man seldom is able to fulfill each of the diverse tasks which must be performed in providing governmental leadership to a local unit.

The chief executive may share the executive power not only with other members of a plural executive (in those cases in which there is one), but also in many cases with a chief administrative officer. Furthermore in some local units a council chairman, who is not the chief executive, may share some of the policy formulation and exposition aspects of the task of the chief executive. In most countries the laws and customs are such that a general determination can be made concerning which position in the local government structure is that of the chief executive. In some cases, though, it is extremely difficult to judge which of two officials, (i.e. the council chairman/mayor or the chief administrative officer/manager) is actually the chief executive. Both share in the exercise of the executive power to a very large extent; the actual balance of power depends on the capabilities and personalities of the individual incumbents, the time the elected official can afford to spend on his public position, the local customs, and the local political environment.[1]

There has always been a natural tendency for men and their organizations to focus their attention upon key individuals to take the initiative in formulating and carrying out programs of action. Throughout history various theories from "divine right" to "charasmatic leadership" have been used to explain the roles of various chief executives. For the average man the chief executive is the government; he tends to judge his government, local as well as national, by the chief executive.

The chief executives of many units of local government original-

---

[1] Since one cannot in a survey such as this make a study of individual cases, for the purposes of this survey and its charts a general determination has had to be made concerning what position is that of the chief executive for each form of local government structure.

It is recognized, though, that there may be variations within some forms of government. For instance, in U. S. cities with the council-manager form of government some mayors may exercise more power than the managers. And in Ceylonese urban municipalities many chief administrative officers (*commissioners*) exercise more power than do the council chairmen. Several factors have influenced my choice concerning which position is generally that of the chief executive. Generally, I have leaned in favour of the elected political official, often called the "No. 1 man," who is expected to take the public and council leadership in defence of policy, particularly if the chief administrative officer tends to report to this single elected official more than to the council as a whole. Thus, in the Norwegian municipalities I have considered the council chairman-ly held a monopoly or near monopoly of local government power, for which they were responsible, to a greater or lesser degree, to the central governments. In the eighteenth century the positions of the *alcalde* in Spain and the sheriff in England, for instance, were in some respects comparable to the chief executives of the units of local non-representative government of today. With the development of local representative government, however, the local government power has been shared with other organs. Not only has much of the decision-making authority been transferred to the representative organs, but also the judicial functions have generally been transferred to other organs, generally outside of the local government structures.

Thus it happens that, whereas the duties of the courts and, to a lesser degree, of the councils today denote comparatively definite functions of government as well as fairly constant methods for their discharge, the duties of the local executive show a greater degree of variation and flexibility in method. It is consequently the executive organs which are most spontaneously responsive to emergency conditions; conditions, that is, which have not attained enough stability or recurrency to allow their being dealt with by rote. The tendency within recent years for the councils of many local governments to have a relatively less important role, as compared to the executive, in the presence of social changes and challenges presents, therefore, no cause for astonishment.

Indeed, it appears that the retention of meaningful organs of representative governments depends today largely upon the capacity of these representative organs to afford a matrix for strong responsible executive leadership which can provide the over-all initiative and co-ordination for both the representative and staff aspects of the process of local representative government. What opportunities do the local government structures offer in this respect? The answer brings under survey the roles of the chief executives in the various countries in this study.[1]

---

board chairman as the chief executive; on the other hand, in the United States council-manager cities I have considered the chief administrative officer (*manager*) as the chief executive.

[1] Many sentences in the last two paragraphs have been adapted from Corwin, *The President-Office and Powers*. 1.

2. *The chief executive and the council*

Just as the representative and staff aspects of the local representative governing process are so closely interwoven that it is impossible to segregate the two, so are the representative and staff aspects of the role of the chief executive impossible to distinguish clearly. Each of the two aspects is dependent upon the other. The leading role of the chief executive in the representative process enhances his ability to get things done as the top official directing the staff. On the other hand, his role as the over-all director of the staff puts him in a stronger position not only to formulate and initiate the ideas which are presented to the council, but also to influence the decisions which it makes.

In analyzing the influence of the chief executive upon the decisions of the council, an effort must be made to distinguish between the chief executive as the focal person charged with the overall co-ordination of the implementation of policy and the chief executive as either council chairman or board chairman, or both. As mentioned in previous chapters, the tasks of council chairman and board chairman are in many local units associated with the post of the chief executive, but there are many local councils in which the council chairman is not the chief executive. And there are many local units without boards which therefore have no board chairman. Since the influence of the board chairman and the council chairman upon the representative process has been discussed more fully in earlier chapters, in this section it is more pertinent to look at the influence upon the decisions of the council which the chief executive has as the focal person charged with the overall co-ordination of the implementation of policy decisions. It must be recognized, of course, that one can never clearly ascertain from which of his different roles the power of an official may spring.

The influence which a chief executive as the focal person charged with the overall co-ordination and implementation of policy decisions may have upon the representative process becomes clearer when one studies the manner in which the decisions of a council are developed, considered, made, and carried out. The determination of decisions is in reality a process which may be examined in four phases. The first stage is the preparation and formulation of the ideas. The second is the exposition of the proposals. The third consists in the council making its decisions by approving, modifying, or rejecting the proposals.[1] The fourth is the implementation of decisions which in itself involves decision-making and will be discussed in the next section. The important role which the chief executive plays in the first two phases as well as in the fourth profoundly affects his influence in the third phase of the process at which the actual voting of the proposals takes place.

To understand the role of the chief executive in formulation and exposition one must consider the sources of most of the proposals which are presented to a council. The possible sources of ideas which eventually become decisions of the representative organs are numerous. Although the raising of an issue in a council or board is limited generally to a relatively few persons, who are either members of the body concerned or top administrative officials who are granted this prerogative, numerous groups and individuals may by various means, including their appearance at the meetings of these bodies, be influential in seeing that a particular question is considered and discussed. Frequently, when the advocate of a proposal wishes to ensure its favourable consideration by a council or board, the support of the chief executive is solicited in advance of their meetings.

Furthermore, most of the ideas which eventually lead to decisions of a council, originate either with the local staff or in the higher units of government, and the most frequent channel of communication through which these ideas are eventually proposed to the council is the chief executive. By law the chief executive may be the only source for the proposal of some types of decisions; for instance in the Brazilian municipalities only the mayor may introduce proposals concerning changing salary rules or creating new positions. In many local units of some countries it is customary for the chief executive to have a virtual monopoly for proposing measures to the council. Thus the position of the chief executive is not only the best, but almost invariably the main, source for the initiating of proposals to these organs.

Not only does the chief executive take the leading part in formulating ideas, just as important is his expository role as the

[1] Ridley, 13.

mobilizer of support for the proposals. As the focus of the development of the proposals he is expected not only by the council, but also by his party and by the public, to play a leading role in ensuring their favourable consideration. The effective chief executive either directly or indirectly must not only build up enough support in council so that his proposals are adopted but he must also build up enough support with the electorate that he and those council members who support his proposals are re-elected to office. As the focal person charged with the co-ordination of the implementation of policy he has the resources to find out and thereby explain the various technical aspects which would be involved in carrying out the decision as well as how this specific decision would fit into the over-all local government policy.

In the local units of some countries the habits and the customs of the people, the frequent need to implement national laws, combined with the near monopoly of the chief executive to introduce proposals, virtually guarantee him a predominant role in the representative process. For instance in the Japanese municipalities the desire for harmony, the respect for the position of the mayor, and the impropriety of speaking clearly and forcefully against a proposal greatly favours the predominance of the mayor.[1] On the other hand there are a large number of local units in many countries in which the lack of council opposition to the proposals of the chief executive is due in large part to his care in proposing only those measures for which he has support of the whole council.

In some local units there is still another prerogative of the chief executive which affects the ability of council to make a decision. In more than half of the council-mayor cities of the United States and in the municipalities of some other countries, such as Brazil and Columbia, the mayor may veto a decision of the council. Councils generally may override such a veto, a two-thirds vote usually being necessary. On the other hand, in a few countries such as Spain there are no legal provisions for overriding the veto of the mayor. In some other European, Asian, and African units of local government the local chief executive may delay the enforcement of a council decision but the suspension loses its

[1] Steiner, *FEQ*, Vol. XV, No. 2 (February 1956), 190.

effect unless the decision of the council is annulled by a higher unit of government. In some of these countries the local chief executive is even obliged to delay enforcement of a decision if he thinks it is contrary to law or the general interest.

Despite the increasing extent to which the central government has taken an interest in and encroached upon local affairs, the formulation, initiation, and exposition tasks of a chief executive are becoming increasingly important and more complex. Policy formulation is more demanding as the scope of local services broadens and their complexity increases, even though a larger share of the major decisions are now made by the central government organs. Policy exposition also is more challenging as the local issues tend to be more complex, a larger portion of the local residents has more opportunities to be informed on public issues, the communities are more populous and their social composition more complex, and the political techniques more subtle. The chief executive as the focal point of the representative process has many opportunities to provide leadership to, and crystallize the thinking of, the councils, boards, and popular assemblies and thus aid them in playing a more important role in the process of local representative government.

3. The chief executive and the staff

A decision of a representative organ remains practically meaningless until it is transformed into action. This indicates why the role of the chief executive as the head of the local staff is as important as his part in the formulation and exposition of decisions of the council, board, or popular assembly.

Invariably the use of executive power involves some exercise of discretion. The amount of discretion exerted depends partially on the national and local customs, partially on the laws pertaining to the local unit, and partially on the rapport existing between the local chief executive and the other governmental organs, including the organs of higher units as well as the local representative organs and the staff.

The local chief executive as the apex of an administrative hierarchical pyramid is charged with carrying out the over-all policies made for the local unit by the organs of the higher units of government or by the local representative organs. He, often with the board, therefore, has the right and the duty to make such decisions as may be necessary to supplement and carry out the policies of the higher units, or of the local representative organs, or both. An essential aspect of this job is the duty to lead in preparing and controlling the execution of the budget. Perhaps most important, he has the duty to supervise the employees of the local units, to co-ordinate their activities and to maintain their efficiency. In most local units the chief executive has specific charge of the police.

Although the chief executive is the head of the local staff, in some cases the more immediate direction and co-ordination of the local employees may be the duty of a chief administrative officer who is the principal staff collaborator of the chief executive. For instance, in the more populous French municipalities the secretary-general is the official head of the municipal employees and administratively the department heads are responsible to him. This type of chief administrative officer will be more thoroughly examined in the next chapter.

There is recognition in most countries of the need for a chief executive with the prestige, power, and authority to integrate the activities of the staff. The increasing reliance upon the chief executive in the local representative government process is largely due to the extent and the complexity of local governmental activities and of their staffs. Local governmental problems are becoming more complicated, more varied, more technical, and more inter-related. They tend to require the type of expert knowledge which is more likely to be found in the staff than in the representative organs of the local unit. Furthermore, the more immediate experience of the executive organs in the local implementation of the programs and policies and their more complete knowledge regarding the plans and views of the central government officials, often virtually compels the council to follow their recommendations.

The tendency for power to focus in the hands of the local chief executive need not be, and often is not, at the expense of the power of the main representative organs. As long as the chief executive remains responsible to these bodies for the implementation of their decisions, they still can remain ultimately responsible to the public for the activities of the local unit.

4. The chief executive as local agent of the central government

In analyzing the position of the chief executive as head of the local staff it is useful to bear in mind that in some cases he is supervising the implementation of decisions of local representative organs and in other cases he is supervising activities directly devolved by the central government to him as the head of the local unit. In addition to the relationship between the council and the local chief executive, the relationship between the local chief executive and the central government is a major factor in determining his role. To whom is the local chief executive responsible, to the central government or to the local council? If he is responsible to both, to which one is he primarily responsible? This is a crucial question in determining the extent of actual local representative government.

In units of local non-representative government the chief executives are responsible solely to the higher units and ultimately to the central government. In many units of local representative government, too, the chief executives, and in some cases also the board, manage some activities which are directly devolved to them by the central government.

At the beginning of the 19th century most of the chief executives in the majority of countries still functioned exclusively, at least in theory, as agents of the central government. In the European countries most of them at that time were appointees of the central government. As the basic units developed elected councils, most of the local chief executives have taken on a dual role. They now serve as the chief executive officer of the local representative government charged with implementing the council's decisions and also as a local agent of the central government directly charged with certain functions such as maintaining public security. Even after the development of the local election of mayors, the local chief executive has continued this dual role in most countries. The French mayor is probably the best known example of a locally elected mayor with duties as an agent of the central government.[1]

The powers of the chief executive as an agent of the central government are mainly in special fields. The chief executive is responsible to the executive organs of the higher units of government and ultimately to the central government for the safety and public security within the local units. To perform this duty the chief executive may have the authority to issue "police" regulations. In France the mayor (within the local government structure) has a monopoly of the police powers, he alone is entitled to issue regulations to enforce or maintain public order, public hygiene and public morality.

Furthermore, the French mayor has to ensure the performance of certain administrative tasks devolved by the central government, such as the preparation and compilation of reports, statutes, and civil registers recording births, deaths, marriages and availability for military service. In these fields the local chief executive is subject to the hierarchical administrative control of the executive organs of the higher units of government. Ultimately he is responsible to the central government. The municipal council is not legally permitted to interfere with his activities in this field.

Generally the authority granted to the local chief executive as a local agent of the central government concerns the activities which are fundamental to any local area. For without police protection and the records of vital statistics (such as births, deaths, and marriages) most other governmental activities cannot be carried out. Not only are these fundamental activities among the first introduced in a unit of local government, they

---

[1] For a fuller account of the powers of the French mayor as an agent of the central government see M. Leon Morgand, *La Loi Municipale* (Paris 1923). See especially Art. 92 "Attributions exercées par le maire comme agent du pouvoir central" (p. 705–708) in Titre III "Des Maires et des Adjoints".

In contrast to the French *maire*, the English mayor is probably the best known example of a head of a local unit who is not a local agent of the central government. In England the local councils were set up apart from the then existing local government officials such as the local lieutenants, the sheriffs, and the justices of the peace (although the mayor has continued to be an ex-officio justice of the peace). In contrast in France and many other European countries the local councils were established with the then existing chief executive as the head of the council. It is difficult to determine the degree of historical interrelationship between the fact that the English mayor has never been a local agent of the central government and that he has never possessed the powers of a chief executive.

are also the functions which the central governments are most anxious to have performed adequately.

There are certain advantages to having the local chief executive as executive officer of the council as well as the local central government agent. The combination eliminates a certain amount of inherent duplication and lack of co-ordination that exists when both the municipal and the central government have local administrative organs, as happens in some countries, such as the United States. This combination of local and central government tasks has, though, certain obvious disadvantages. The fact that he is an agent of the local government responsible to the council for some duties and on the other hand responsible to a higher unit for certain other duties leaves open a distinct possibility of a clash of interest between the two roles. At some point almost any two masters are bound to have differing points of view; this is particularly true when one is a centralization-minded national government and the other is an autonomy-minded local unit. This conflict is particularly likely to occur when the double-roled chief executive has the power to delay the validity of council resolutions which appear to be contrary to the general interest. Such a position calls for great skill and tact if the effects of conflicts of interest are to be diminished.

In fact, a chief executive with a double accountability often tends to be more loyal to one or the other body. In the Netherlands, there is no direct central government supervision over the chief executive and the general practice is for the chief executive to work closely with board and council in all matters with which he is concerned. In some other countries, though, a chief executive may consider his accountability to the local council of secondary importance. In practice, the loyalty of the local chief executive depends on various interrelated factors such as the tradition of local representative government, the manner in which he is selected, and the extent of the powers and authority of the representative organs.

5. The chief executive as the ceremonial head

Another task generally associated with the post of the chief executive is that of the ceremonial head or "first citizen" of the local unit. He welcomes visiting dignitaries, presides over civic gatherings, and cuts the tape at the opening of new public works. Usually he is the one who must formally sign the local resolutions and ordinances. The ceremonial head is the personified symbol of the whole local unit. The position is generally one of dignity and prestige, especially in the more populous local units. In most local units the chief executive is the ceremonial head.

The combination of the roles of ceremonial head and chief executive has some advantages. The prestige attached to the position as ceremonial head is helpful to the mayor as policy leader in developing support for his programs. Frequently his role as the ceremonial head of the community is an inducement for developing policies that are acceptable to the community as a whole instead of just to the faction of which he is the political leader.

There are some units of local representative government, however, in which the chief executive does not fulfill the tasks as ceremonial head; in these units the duties of council chairman and ceremonial head are combined in one position. In the Swedish municipalities, for instance, the roles of ceremonial head and chief executive are separated; the council chairman is the ceremonial head and the board chairman is the chief executive.[1] In these local units the council chairman almost invariably considers himself primarily as a moderator rather than as a leader of the council.

There are certain advantages in having the tasks of the council chairman and ceremonial head separated from those of the chief executive, especially in the more populous local units with a long tradition of representative government. First of all, this

[1] Generally the role of the ceremonial head is combined with the role of the council chairman, whether or not the council chairmanship is identified with the chief executive. There are, though, some exceptions. In the Greek urban municipalities the role of the ceremonial head is undertaken by the chief executive instead of by the council chairman. Probably the best known exception is the French provincial governor (préfet), who is the chief executive as well as ceremonial head although he is not the chairman of the provincial council. Such a distribution of the duties associated with the executive function is not uncommon in some intermediate units of local government in which the councils have a relatively short tradition and have relatively little authority.

relieves the chief executive of many official duties which are not an essential aspect of the policy-formulating role. Secondly, the establishment of a separately constituted post of ceremonial head-council chairman post creates a position high in the organization structure whose incumbent may play an important stabilizing role in the conduct of local government affairs. The advantages of separating these different roles is accentuated and more recognized at the national level. Many countries, for instance, have a constitutional monarch or honorific president as well as a prime minister.

One may contrast the chief executive, whose primary task is to lead the majority and to gain support for the program of his faction, with the ceremonial head-council chairman, whose primary task is to represent all factions and to allow all factions to have an opportunity to express themselves. Both of these roles are important to governments, the one because of the need for initiative and forcefulness, the other because of the need for stability and moderation. The two roles are inherently different and they call for different personal qualities. A person who has both roles simultaneously is in a dichotomous, and therefore somewhat ambiguous position. For it is difficult to be both an unbiased statesman who rises above factional strife as well as an energetic politician capable of rallying support for new policies often against spirited opposition. To ensure both roles being performed well there appears to be much merit in having the ceremonial head-council chairmanship separately constituted from the chief executive.

6. *The quasi-chief executive*

Not all local units have a chief executive. In those local governments without a chief executive, however, there is an official who is regarded as the head of the local unit. His position has some of the characteristics generally associated with the job of the chief executive including the tasks of council chairman and ceremonial head as well as a limited role in co-ordinating the activities of the local unit. He is the closest approach to a chief executive, his position resembles or simulates that of a chief executive, but he is not really the same as a chief executive. Therefore, he may be called a quasi-chief executive. Most of the examples of quasi-chief executives are found in the United Kingdom and countries which have been influenced directly or indirectly by the English model.

The most well known example of a quasi-chief executive is the English local council chairman (called mayor in the boroughs) "who presides over the council and occupies a position of great dignity and civic prestige. But he possesses no executive authority and does not control the administration."[1] He is not at the apex of an administrative hierarchical pyramid although he does have an important relatively impartial role in the council. He may have, however, more influence than the apparently impotent executive nature of his office indicates. The degree of influence depends, though, upon the prestige and dignity of the office and the incumbent's personal status and ability. The English chairman is in a leading and respected position to act as a catalyst in the molding of policies and therefore he has a potentially important role as an advisory and stabilizing element in the local government structure. Even these possibilities of exercising power are reduced, however, by the fact that he is elected for only a one year term and by custom in most of the urban municipalities he is not eligible for re-election.[2]

Municipal governments in the Sudan, Ceylon, India and other countries which were formerly British possessions have been highly influenced by the English model. Nevertheless the mayors in these countries are not quite as weak. The position of the Indian council chairman is a rather ambiguous one which is probably best described by M. P. Sharma:

> "Though in common parlance the chairman or president is called the executive head, in reality the highest executive power is not concentrated in his hands. In fact our councils at present do not really have an integrated executive at all. There is on the contrary a division and dispersal of executive authority between the council itself, the chairman, the various committees, and the executive officer (s.c. chief administrative officer) or secretary. This is illustrated by the power to make appointments, or sanction contracts. The appointment of some of the highest officials is

---

[1] Robson, William A. (ed.), *Great Cities of the World* (London 1954), p. 39.
[2] In the urban and rural district as well as the county councils the council chairman is often re-elected, but this is not the case in the boroughs.

vested in the council itself (e.g. the executive officer, secretary, engineer, etc.), of the middle ones in the chairman, and of the lowest in the executive officer, secretary, or department heads. Contracts above a certain sum require the sanction of the council, and below that they require the sanction of one of the committees which are for all practical purposes autonomous in their own sphere.

In one sense, however, the chairman is the nearest approach to the council's head executive. He is charged with the duty of general supervision over the council's administration, and every item of executive power, which is not vested in any other authority, belongs to him."[1]

There are several factors which may contribute to the tendency of council chairmen in these countries to have more influence than their English counterpart. First of all, some of these mayors are popularly elected and therefore tend to have a stronger position. Secondly, the usually longer terms of office and the practice of re-electing the mayors allows them more time to consolidate their position. Furthermore, in most of these other countries the councils tend to be smaller than in England, which means there are fewer committees and sub-committees for the mayor to keep in contact with; thus it is easier for him to play a co-ordinating role.

In the United States, too, there are many cities with a quasi-chief executive, often called "weak mayor." The lack of a real chief executive is inter-related with the presence not only of administering committees but also of a large number of publicly elected administrative officers such as the clerk, the municipal attorney, the treasurer, and the auditor, who may work quite independently from the quasi-chief executive.

The Philippine mayors, too, are only chief executives in theory. In urban municipalities the heads of the staff departments are appointed either by the President or by the corresponding heads of the national departments. In the rural municipalities the department heads are appointed by the heads of the corresponding provincial departments, who are themselves national appointees. The mayors may appoint the subordinate employees in the departments but only upon the recommendation of the department head. The only department in which he actually appoints employees and directs the operations is the police department. The role of the mayor as regards the staff is limited to that of a co-ordinator; and this power is largely

[1] Sharma, 59. (The word council has been inserted in place of board in this quotation to indicate the main representative organ.)

dependent upon the strength of his political status, particularly the extent to which the President or governor will back him. Usually, the office of the mayor is primarily concerned with partisan political rather than policy matters.

7. *The village headman*

Another type of local unit "head" which should be dealt with separately is the headman in the rural basic units in some Asian and African countries (e.g. the Lebanon and Ethiopia). One may use the same term for the head of the sub-municipal unit in the Philippines. The local headman in many of these countries represents a continuity of tradition and the sedentary agricultural life. Over the past centuries this position has been one of the most stable characteristics of government in many less-developed countries. In many cases the headman is a carry-over from tribal society. His relationship to the higher units is similar to that of the native chief in the so-called "native administration" or "indirect rule" in many countries which are not yet independent.[1] In many cares the headman has a traditional "council of elders," which assists him in carrying out his duties. These "elders" are selected in much the same manner as he is.

The formal head of the local unit appears to be invariably the natural social and political leader of the village community, who is informally selected by the village elders and in some cases with the ratification of the village at large. In many cases hereditary factors influence the selection. Generally there is a contest for the position only when there are two or more hamlets within one village, both of which put forward their own candidate. The locally-selected headman does not formally, at least, acquire the authority of his post until his selection has been approved by higher authorities such as the district or provincial head. Once elected and installed, however, the village headman is usually in office for life although he may be removed by the executive organ of a higher unit. His pay is usually derived from various

---

[1] See Ansu Kumar Datta, *Tanganyika – A Government in a Plural Society* (The Hague 1955), pp. 57–59 and 68–78.

fees received for specific services, but the high prestige connected with the job is often the most important reward.

The headman's duties and powers are extensive. He combines several governmental functions with the traditional duties of a village head. Margery Perham describes the role of the Ethiopian headman of a village or group of villages by saying:

> "He was responsible to the governor's district chief for the proper performance by his own community of their duties and especially for their payment to the proper authorities of tithe and tax and of dues in kind and labour. He was the judge to whom, if wayside arbitration failed, the litigants would first apply. He would be present at local weddings; would preside at meetings of the local council, and would be especially concerned with all transfers or allocations of land and disputes about it... He manages the affairs of the village like his own, and his patriarchal authority is sacred."[1]

The local headman is, then, the most important personage in his own community although from the point of view of the central government he is merely a minor functionary. Once elected, his power is mainly dependent upon his superiors in the central government administrative hierarchy. Although he is not a civil servant, he is in the fullest sense of the word a functionary of the central government. He is directly responsible to his superior, usually the district head, for the performance of his numerous duties. His selection by the local population makes him no less a central government functionary, for it is a convenient device for securing a person with the necessary leadership qualities for carrying out the local headmanship duties. Like the Belgian mayor (who is formally appointed by royal decree but actually locally selected) the village headman is difficult to categorize in terms of manner of selection.

8. *The chief executive appointed by the central government or other higher units*

The role of the local chief executive is greatly influenced by the manner in which he is selected, whether it be by the central government, the council, or the voting public. This selection, in turn, is one of the important determinants of the extent of

[1] Perham, Margery, *The Government of Ethiopia* (London 1947), p. 275.

responsible local representative government. As recently as a century ago the vast proportion of the local chief executives were appointed by the executive organs of the higher units of government. With the spread of local representative government, however, this means of selection is used by fewer local units. In many local units the chief executive is now elected by, and generally from, the council. In several countries, including the United States, a large number of the local units elect their chief executive (mayor) by direct popular vote. A relatively recent trend in the United States as well as a few other countries, has been for the local council to appoint the chief executive officer (manager). Usually he is not selected from among the councilmen and has had previous experience and training in government administration.[1]

Although there is a trend away from the appointment of the local chief executive by the higher units, this is still the practice in some units of local representative government as well as the units of local non-representative government, especially in the intermediate units. There are many countries (among which are Norway, France and Turkey), in which all the basic units have locally elected mayors, but the chief executives of all the intermediate units, whether they have representative organs or not, are appointed by the central government.

Among the basic units the practice is more varied. In the Netherlands, Ethiopia, and Iran, all the basic units have chief executives who receive their appointments from the central government. In Brazil, in which the mayor is generally locally elected, the chief executives of the more important cities are appointed by the central government. On the other hand, in Iran the head officials of the basic units are appointed by higher units.

Many of the centrally appointed local chief executives are central government civil servants. In each of the Scandinavian countries, for instance, the provincial governors are officials of the national government. Such executives also may be members of an elite corps of central government officials. One example of such a corps is the French *corps préfectoral*. The chief executives

[1] The difference between council-elected and council-appointed chief executives is explained in section 10 of this chapter.

of the French districts *(arrondissements*, which have no representative organs) and of the provinces (*départements*, which have elected councils) are members of the same administrative pyramidal corps whose superior is the minister of the interior. Such a *corps* finds its counterparts in many other countries, especially in North Africa and West Asia.

In some of the Asian and African countries which were formerly part of the British Empire, India and the Sudan for example, there are often other types of centrally-appointed chief executives. Formerly the almost universal practice was for the district chief executive to be the ex-officio chairman of the urban municipal councils. (Another district official, a deputy, would, however, often actually preside.) This arrangement put the chief executive in a strong position to influence local decisions, particularly since the district administrative staff frequently also performed the administrative duties of the local units. The advocates of this arrangement point out that this co-ordinated the activities of the local and districts units and eliminated duplication of functions. More and more councils, however, now elect their own chairman, although a central government official may continue as chief administrative officer.[1] Today the centrally appointed municipal chief administrators in the Sudan and India are generally central government civil servants assigned (seconded) to the urban municipalities. Although keeping their central government civil service prerogatives and tenure, they serve fulltime as the local chief executives. In India these officials are not also the council chairmen. On the other hand, Malaya, the centrally appointed local chief executive is also the chairman of the local council.

In many countries, though, the local chief executives appointed by higher units, are not civil service officials of the central government. They are, though, persons with considerable administrative or political experience, or both. In Spain, the mayors of all the municipalities with less then 10,000 inhabitants are appointed by the provincial governors while the mayors of the larger municipalities are appointed directly by the minister of the interior; almost invariably the post of mayor and the post of the local leader of the party are held by the same person,

[1] This is further explained in the next chapter.

although it is possible for the mayor to be a henchman of the political "boss" (*caudillo*).

In the Netherlands a mixture of administrative and political considerations appear to come into play in the appointment of the mayor. The appointments are made by royal decree, which in effect means by the cabinet or the minister of the interior with the provincial governor usually playing the initiatory role; in the smaller municipalities the choice of the provincial governor is usually decisive. An effort is made to find persons who are administratively competent and whose political loyalties will enable them to work easily with the local councils. Generally the chief executive is appointed to a municipality of which he is not a resident, frequently he has served previously in a smaller municipality. Unlike their Spanish counterparts, most Dutch mayors do not engage in an active partisan politics while serving as mayor.

The power of an appointed local chief executive in his relations with a council is usually large. He has a fairly secure tenure, at least in most cases more secure than his elected counterparts, and as an acknowledged expert on government and political affairs, he has an authoritative and pre-eminent position among the elected members of the council. He is almost invariably chairman of the council; as such he is in a strategic position to influence its attitude and the decisions. As the chief executive he is usually in close contact with the central (and intermediate unit) government officials; thus he is in a favourable position to know what will be approved by the higher authorities.

The opportunity which the appointment of the local chief executive gives to the central government to exert some control over the local unit is fairly obvious, especially since appointment by higher units almost invariably carries with it the right to remove (even though the prerogative may be seldom used). What is not so obvious is the extent to which the appointed local chief executive is often the most effective advocate of the interests of the local unit. Because he has the confidence of the central government his suggestions are often more likely to be listened to than are those of a local politician. The role of an appointed local chief executive is often that of a channel of communication between the central and local government.

An important advantage of the appointed local chief executive is the stability he contributes to the unit of local government. His appointment is a way of guaranteeing that an expert in local government is directing the local activities. His relatively secure tenure contributes continuity to the programs and policies of the local unit and as a person who is not dependent on the local political tides of fortune he can afford to stay above the party and fractional strife as well as other local cliques and petty jealousies. As chairman of the local council he can play an important role in securing the cooperation of various groups and bringing about the necessary compromises. This consideration is especially important in countries which have traditionally deep social and religious cleavages that affect the political environment.

The objection to the selection of local chief executives by organs of higher units is a basic one. If units of local government are to be representative it appears logical that the chief executive, who is the most important formulator and expositor of public policy, should have the support of the council and be encouraged to be sensitive to the needs and will of the electorate. There appears to be no better method of choosing such an official than by local selection. Furthermore, there appears to be no better method of encouraging his sensitivity to the interests of the public than to make his continuance in office subject to some sort of local control, exercised either at periodic intervals of election or continually through the right of the council to force the termination of the term of office of the chief executive at any time, as with the French mayor or U. S. city manager.

9. *The chief executive elected by council*

Among the countries included in this survey, election by council is the most frequently used method of selecting a mayor. Many countries over the course of the last hundred years have turned from appointed mayors to council-elected mayors, as is now the case in the vast majority of European municipalities. In Asiatic countries there has recently also been a trend in this same direction. The election of a chief executive by a local council is generally a deliberate political and often a partisan political choice. The choice of the French mayor, for instance, can be a matter of involved internal political manoeuvering. Where one party has an absolute majority in a council, the nomination will depend on the balance of forces inside this party. If there is one recognized leader this may be simple, otherwise it can be a complicated matter. In the European countries the method of proportional representation used in the municipal elections often precludes one party capturing a majority of the seats. In these units the internal political manoeuvering may be quite complicated. Usually an effort is made to form a coalition of parties that together will have a majority; in this case a nominee for chief executive must be found who is acceptable to all the groups. Sometimes the prestige of one man is so great that the other parties back him even though his party is relatively insignificant. Almost invariably the person selected is a member of the council in which case he retains his seat on the council.

The organs of central government may have an opportunity to review the election of local officials. In France, for instance, the district head (*sous-préfet*) must be notified within one day of the election of the mayor and his assistants; as they do not come into power for five days after the election, this is a preventive measure allowing time for objections to be raised. In a few rare cases the elections are declared null and new ones called.

In Belgium the mayor assumes office only upon the receipt of the royal appointment. The majority or majority coalition of the local council submits a list of recommendations and almost invariably the first person on the list is appointed. In theory the Belgian mayor is a centrally-appointed local chief executive, but in practice he is a council-elected one.

A disadvantage of the council-elected chief executive is that he is often not adequately qualified for the implementation aspects of the chief executive job. An elected person may be excellent as a council chairman, and as a political leader, but they are usually not so successful as a head of the local staff. Part of the difficulties of an elected person successfully discharging the administrative aspects of his job, of course, are a result of his politically insecure tenure. Besides he usually devotes only a few hours a week to the job. Selection by council of the local chief executive has one important advantage, though, for he has, at least initially, the support of the majority of the council.

The tendency of the council and the executive to work together is increased when the council may force the resignation of the executive as well as elect one. In several countries (e.g. France and Ceylon), in which the local chief executives are council-elected, a vote of no-confidence may force the resignation of a chief executive. In some cases, though, a mayor will not resign after such a vote of no-confidence. Such a situation may cause a deadlock in the process of government in these local units. In France in such cases the provincial governor (*préfet*) may, and in some cases does, dissolve the local council and call for new elections. The new council may than elect a new mayor.

Selection and possible dismissal by council is at least in some respects, then, the most logical means of establishing a local chief executive. It is the best method to assure that the executive and council tend to work together instead of at cross-purposes. With this means of establishing the chief executive the council has control over the executive and hence the staff, although it does not itself direct the activities of the staff.

Nevertheless, from a pragmatic point of view, there are important disadvatages to the council-elected mayoralty. The very manner of his selection tends to emphasize the factionalism of the council, and often this factionalism tends to reduce the probability of the type of working relationships that produce effective programs. In France and Italy many municipal councils are so factionalized that they are frustrated to a point of inaction.

The role of factionalism in determining the selection of the mayor also means that he is identified with one political group of coalition. His outlook tends to be dominated and bound by political considerations, particularly when his tenure is subject to retaining the confidence of a majority of the council. As a party man bound by party or coalition considerations he may make an excellent policy leader, but it may be difficult for either the council or the public to think of him as a representative of the municipality as a whole.

10. *The chief executive elected by popular vote*

In a limited number of countries the local chief executives are elected by a direct popular election of the voting public. In the United States this is the case for almost all the mayors in the cities with the mayor-council form of government.[1] Many cities in Canada and New Zealand also have popularly elected mayors as do those in Japan and the Philippines.

The adoption of the practice of popular election of the local chief executive can, to a large degree, be attributed to the influence of the ideas of "separation of powers" as expressed by Montesquieu. The United States national government is probably the best known example of a political organization molded in accordance with these ideas and its state and many local government structures have been heavily influenced by the national model. In addition, the national as well as local government structure of several other countries, such as Brazil and the Philippines, have been modelled after the example of the United States.

In the popular election of a local chief executive each of the candidates is listed on the ballot and the candidate with the largest number of votes wins. Unless the election is a non-partisan (as in many U. S. cities) each party sponsors a candidate. The candidate of the party may have been selected at a primary election or at a gathering of party leaders. Generally the independent candidates have a poor chance of success at the polls; nevertheless, there are frequent examples of persons without organized party backing who have won the election. In some local units a popularly-elected local chief executive may be removed from office by a popular vote, after a petition by a specified percentage of the local voters (this is called *recall*).

There are many pros and cons to the direct election of the mayor. The campaign and election of the local chief executive is a helpful means of raising the interest of voters in municipal issues. In addition, unlike the appointed or council-elected chief

---

[1] According to the International City Managers' Association *The Municipal Yearbook* 1959, p. 81, 95% of the cities over 5,000 inhabitants with a mayor-council form of government have popularly elected mayors. Of all the cities over 5,000 inhabitants in the United States 74% have popularly elected mayors, some of which are the mayors of cities with the "commission" or "council-manager" forms of government.

executive, the popularly-elected chief executive is directly responsible to the public. Furthermore with both the council and the chief executive separately elected, these organs often check and balance one another.

On the other hand, since both the executive and the council have independent mandates from the electorate, there is an almost inevitable rivalry between them, particularly if a majority of the council is not politically in accord with the mayor. Alderfer points out that:

"the mayor and council share both legislative and administrative powers and when they do not agree politically or on specific issues, the warfare adversely affects the operation of the government and the citizens suffer – sometimes for an extended period. Many strong mayors have taken their fight with the council, which sometimes represented the party machine, to the people. This meant headlines but seldom improved administration while the battle raged. Strong leadership or diplomacy of a high grade is always necessary to smooth the operation of a government machine that is founded on the principle of checks and balances."[1]

The second weakness of the popularly-elected mayors which is pointed out by Alderfer is one which the council-elected mayors also share. He says that the elected mayors

"are often less than top-grade administrators or just do not have the time to develop good administrative practices and procedures. The modern metropolis is a big business and needs as much expert administration as big business in industry. The average mayor cannot be everything: a party leader, a civic personage, an executive, an administrator, without some part of his responsibilities being neglected and this has usually been administration."[2]

The stress for an elected person of combining the tasks of administrative head with that of political head has often proved to be too much of a burden. Such a chief executive tends to succumb to the weight of his administrative duties or tends to neglect them. The development of a locally-elected chief executive has tended to increase the local political responsiveness of the chief executive but it has also tended to decrease the potential for administrative expertness which is increasingly important in modern local government, with its wide range and increasingly technical complexity of services and a large number of employees,

[1] Alderfer, 293.
[2] *Ibid.*, 293.

many of whom are highly skilled specialists. This increasing need for experienced administrative leadership, coupled with the inability, in terms of time and training and experience, of many elected chief executives to provide it, has been a strong factor in the development of positions of executive leadership which are filled by local appointment instead of by election.

11. *The chief executive appointed by council*

The most recently developed means of selecting a local chief executive is by appointment of the council, probably the best known example of a council appointed chief executive is the manager in many U. S. municipalities. The difference between council-appointment and council-election is easier to recognize in practice than to define in precise terms. Perhaps one of the easiest ways of distinguishing the two is to contrast their comparative emphases. Elected posts are ones which are expected to be filled by amateurs or politicians, appointed posts are expected to be filled by professional administrators. In election the choice is generally limited to persons who are residents of that particular local unit, in appointment the choice is generally restricted to persons who have had public administration training and experience, and frequently the appointee is chosen from outside the local unit. Partisan political considerations play an important role in the election of a council-elected chief executive, and he is expected to continue his political affiliations after election. Almost invariably he is chosen from among the members of the council and remains a member of the council. On the other hand, the council-appointed chief executive is an employed member of the staff who is not a member of the council and who is not expected to engage in factional or partisan politics.

The appointment method of selecting a chief executive allows for the development of a local chief executive profession, for which a man can train and of which he can make a career. After specific training, he may start out as an assistant to the chief executive, than become a chief executive of a small municipality, and later become the chief executive of a more populous local unit. Another administrative advantage of the appointed chief executive is that he is a full-time official, whereas his elected counterpart can usually only devote part of his working hours to the job.

The position of the professional council-appointed chief executive officer varies not only in the number of roles he fulfils but also in the manner in which he undertakes them. The number of roles (e.g. council chairman, board chairman, ceremonial head, and agent of central government) he fulfills is dependent upon the statutes of the country, state and of the local unit of which he is chief executive. The manner in which he exercises the power potentialities of these roles depends more, though, on his personal capabilities and the attitude of the council with which he must work. The presence, and the degree of, authority of a separate council chairman also affects the relationship of the professional appointed chief executive with the council, and influences the degree of power which he may exercise.

In the Finnish urban and many of the rural municipalities the chief executive (or manager) is an appointed professional employee. He serves as chairman of the municipal board and is head of the staff. The chairman of the council is the ceremonial head of the municipality, whereas the position of the chief executive-board chairman is the one of strong policy leadership. He has an indefinite appointment. If the council wishes to dismiss him for a reason other than physical inability to do the job, the decision must be based on a 3/4 majority and must be submitted to the provincial administration for approval.

In Germany, some of the chief executive officers are also professional officials. The terms of office may be six years, but more often they are twelve or for an indefinite period of time. In the first two cases the chief executive officers are usually selected for additional terms.

In the many municipalities in the United States with the council-manager form of government, the manager is an appointed professional official who serves at the pleasure of the council. He can speak freely on the council and is in a focal position for exercising policy leadership, although he is not the chairman. The council chairman, who also serves as ceremonial head, usually does not exercise much leadership in the council. In fact in most municipalities the large majority of proposals to the council are presented by the manager, and it is usually the manager who leads the discussion at the informal off-the-record sessions at which most of the actual deliberation takes place. Like an elected chief executive the U. S. city manager is the chief source, innovator, formulator, and recommender of policy proposals. He has the resources and the techniques that enable him to withstand even strong attempts by some councilmen to take the policy leadership away from him.[1] In fact, the U. S. city manager often finds himself in the position of being expected not only to explain and defend proposals in council but also in public. The policy leadership of the manager is contingent, of course, on the confidence of the council in the manager and their acceptance of his lead. For without such confidence not only would the proposals not be accepted but the manager might be jobless. In this respect the position of the municipal professional chief in Germany is much stronger, both because of his longer term of office and because of tradition.

In those cities with a council chairman and separate chief administrative officer, as in the U.S. council-manager cities, the relative power of each may vary. In the United States the office of the council chairman in the council-manager cities generally does not have enough authority, power, or prestige to give the incumbent a significant advantage over other potential leaders. He is often not chosen on the basis of leadership ability or willingness to play a leadership role, and he is, in these cases, no more likely to serve as a policy leader than any other councilman. There are, though, many exceptions. Many council chairman in council-manager cities, usually in the more populous ones, play a leading role in policy leadership so that one might question which official is the chief executive or whether in fact in these cases the role of chief executive is shared between two posts, the council chairman and the manager. There are a few other countries, too, in which the role of the chief executive appears, in fact, to be shared by the council chairman and the chief administrative officer (e.g. many of the more populous Norwegian municipalities and many German municipalities).[2]

---

[1] See Harold A. Stone, Don K. Price, and Kathryn H. Stone, *City Manager Government in the United States* (Public Administration Service 1940), p. 243.
[2] See footnote page 120.

12. Tenure of office

The mayors, headmen, and other chief executives of local units may have tenures of office for a fixed term of years or indefinite appointments. Almost invariably those (including the village headman) who are appointed either by the higher units or the local councils, have, not necessarily in law but in practice, indefinite tenures of office. One should draw an important distinction, though, between different types of indefinite appointments. One type of indefinite appointment is that which is for "life and good behaviour"; such an appointee cannot be removed from office unless by death, proven criminal misconduct as specified by law, or by reaching a mandatory retirement age (if one exists). Another type of indefinite appointment is one in which the appointee can be removed, either at any time or at periodic intervals, without proving criminal misconduct.

In most countries (e.g. Germany and India) an appointed local chief executive does not leave his post until he is transferred (usually a promotion), resigns (usually to take a better job), retires, or dies. There are a few countries (e.g. the United States), though, in which a local council appointed chief executive may be, and in some cases is, dismissed at any time.

The elected mayors have terms of office that vary from one year in the U.K. municipalities to twelve years in some German municipalities. Four year terms have the widest general acceptance. In some countries the council-elected local chief executives, although elected for specific terms, resign before the end of that term if they lose the support of the council; in this way the mayor is forced to be continuously accountable to the council. Most of the popularly elected mayors in India can also be removed in this manner.

One faces the same dilemma in determining the optimum term for elected local chief executives as one does for councilmen. What term is short enough to encourage the mayors to be mindful of the coming elections and keep them from being unresponsive to and insulated from the electorate, but long enough that they have time to provide continuity and to make long range plans as well as to fight election campaigns?

Few people will argue that one year is an adequate term for a local chief executive; most would feel that he has barely had time to understand his job in that period of time. In fact, those mayors whose terms are limited to one year are generally those who are quasi-chief executives.

On the other hand, one cannot help but wonder if a twelve year term, and certainly a "life" term, is not too long. Long fixed terms reduce the possibility of removing incompetent or undesirable chief executives. It is perhaps sufficient to point out that where the local chief executives have terms of that length, there is also a long tradition of strong dominant executives, or conversely, relatively weak representative organs.

The problem of establishing a responsible and effective executive is a cardinal problem of representative government. If the executive is not responsible, his acts will not need the consent of the local electorate. If, on the other hand, the chief executive is held so continuously and immediately under control by the council that he cannot take decisive executive action, the unit of government is rendered ineffective because of a lack of opportunity for effective leadership. The solution of the problem of establishing a responsible and effective local chief executive is fundamental to local representative government.

9

THE STAFF

1. *The staff and the local government process*

THE staff of a unit of local government may be defined as the non-elected employees engaged in assisting the representative organs (and the chief executive) in the preparation and the implementation of the local policies.[1] It is that group of persons says J. S. Mill, "which constitutes the permanent strength of the public service, those who do not change with changes in politics, but remain to aid ... (s.c. the political official) ... by their experience and traditions, inform him by their knowledge of business, and conduct official details under his general control; those, in short, who form the class of professional public servants."[2] Staff members may be employed in the provision of a wide variety of activities; they may be clerical workers, manual workers, police and firemen, and professional workers such as teachers, doctors and engineers.

In a unit of local government without representative organs the staff members, along with the chief executive, are the only persons officially participating in the local government process. In units of local representative government, however, there are elected persons as well as non-elected staff members. In previous chapters much has been said concerning the importance of the members of the representative organs and the local staff working together. In fact, the success of local representative government

---

[1] Actually some council-appointed chief executives. such as the U.S. and Finnish city managers, are also considered to be members of the staff.
[2] Mill, 341.

may very largely be attributed to the effective combination of the different qualities which are contributed by elected representatives and non-elected employees.

The role of the staff of the local units has become increasingly important in the last few decades. One obvious reason is the increasing size and complexity of the local government bureaucracy. There is a marked increase, particularly since World War II, in the range, number, and quality of the services which are expected by and performed for the residents in many local units. The older services, such as street maintenance and fire protection, are being approached in some areas with a new consciousness of the challenge of advanced technology. In a large number of local units newer services such as many of those in the social field are being introduced for the first time. This development is readily apparent not only in the rapidly growing urban areas, but also in many of the rural areas which are quickly acquiring a larger consciousness of a need for more local government services. This has accompanied the general rise in the standard of living and the development of better means of transportation and communication. This growth in the scope and complexity of local services has been accompanied not only by an increase in the number of employees and the development of more complex administrative apparatuses but also by an ever-growing reliance upon the local staff members as well as organs of the central government to preparse and implement policy.

The process of local representative government is one continuous inter-action involving at the one end the public in their capacity as potential voters and at the other end the members of the staff. One might, for instance, compare the structure of local representative government to the span of an arc: the public acting through the electoral system being one of the foundation stones, the staff being the other foundation stone, and the chief executive, the council, and in some cases the board being key stones making up the arc.

Unfortunately information available on the organization of local staffs, just as information on local election processes, is meager in all but a few countries. (Further more, such information, except for that which affects the top staff employees, is not directly pertinent to the central theme of this study.) Nevertheless, the role of the staff, just as that of the electoral process, is so important that any organic survey on the structure of local government which did not describe it would be incomplete. This chapter, which will necessarilly be short, is limited to generalities and will not be able to get into many of the fundamental organizational problems of administrative structures.

2. *The selection of the staff*

The increasing reliance upon the staff in the process of local representative government makes the methods of recruitment and selection and the conditions of advancement and discipline of the local employees an important matter: consequently even a superficial survey of the most salient variations in methods is fruitful. The variations are especially noticeable in regard to who makes the selections and what protection the employees have against political and other prejudicial actions affecting their tenure of office.

The first factor to be taken into consideration is whether the appointment is made by a local or a central government organ. In most units of local non-representative government, the staff members are considered to be central government employees. In addition, in some units of local representative government, including many of the more populous municipalities in India, the top staff officers are central government civil servants who are assigned to the local unit.

In Italy, and other countries, many of the top municipal staff officers make their entire careers in municipal service and are recruited and appointed directly by organs of the central government, which also determine their promotions. Such a system not only enables the central government to centralize and standardize the recruitment, training, examination, and promotion of candidates for local chief administrative officer as well as other local governmental positions, but it also facilitates promotions and transfers in positions between local government units. In some countries local units are allowed a limited discretion in choosing an officer from a centrally compiled list and, perhaps more important in some cases, they may request a replacement for an officer who has not been satisfactory.

In a few other countries, such as Ceylon, a central local public service commission has recently been established which is linked with the central government. These bodies may merely certify the competence of an individual or they may actually recruit, make the appointments, the transfers, the promotions, and take the disciplinary actions. Appointment of the local staff officers by organs of the higher units or by other centrally located organs give the opportunity for securing, at least from the central government point of view, a certain minimum level of administrative competence in each municipality. The central government also is assured that local political considerations will not have an adverse effect in determining the calibre of the official chosen.

Although there are still a large number of local government officers appointed by higher units, an increasingly large proportion of local staff members are locally appointed. Among these one may contrast those whose positions are protected by statute, either central or local, and those who are not legally shielded from political and other interference. In the vast majority of local units most or all of the local employees are protected by such statutes; furthermore they are protected against violations of these statutes by having recourse either to personnel commissions, special administrative courts, or the regular courts.

Many local units, including those in the United Kingdom, have the prerogative to appoint, dismiss and impose discipline on their own employees but there is an elaborate system of restraints imposed by the central government laws which specify the necessary qualifications for certain positions, the conditions of working, and the circumstances and the procedures under which an employee can be dismissed. These stipulations are particularly exacting for the top-ranking and professional posts. For some positions the organ of the central government must give specific approval for the appointment and dismissal of an official.

On the other hand some local units have the virtually unfettered prerogative to "hire and fire" the employees. In some U. S. municipalities, for instance, the appointment and dismissal of the employees is under the full control of the council, the chief executive, or of both. Although this method allows the local representative organs the fullest possible control over its staff organs, by the same token it places the employees at the mercy of the representative organs. Appointments and dismissals may be strongly influenced by political motivations and consequently capable administrators have not been encouraged to risk their careers in such a politically insecure vocation.

In order to avoid this "spoils system" many North American cities have taken the control of local personnel appointments and discipline "out of politics" by setting up a form of local civil service commission. The tasks of such a commission may vary. It may merely certify the competence of a prospective employee or it may actually recruit applicants, make the appointments, determine promotions, and pass judgement on all disciplinary actions.

Regarding the advantages of local selections over central government appointment, Jackson has pointed out:

"Where there is some provision that requires the consent of the central government to the appointment, salary or dismissal of a local government officer, that provision is not intended to affect the position of the officer in respect of his work. It is meant to give him some security against his own council, but he remains bound to obey all their proper directions and he does not in any sense become a servant of the central government. There is, however, always a tendency for an officer whose ultimate fate may depend upon the central government, to look to the central government for guidance in the conduct of his work. All experience indicates that it is better to have a man whose concern and loyalty is entirely to the authority that he serves than an officer who may have some temptation to do things that he knows will keep him in good favour with the central government. Hence, local authorities should always regard any powers of the central government in this respect as being undesirable and to be justified only in exceptional circumstances."[1]

Perhaps this comment tends to overstate the case; nevertheless it is increasingly accepted that local selection of employees is more compatible with the local representative government than appointment by a central government organ.

The staff positions in many local government units, particularly in the less populous rural units in under-developed countries, often do not offer salaries, prestige, or prospect of advancement adequate to attract competent personnel; central government appointment can be helpful to mitigate some of these disadvantages of local government services in rural areas. In the more populous local units of many countries, though, the staffs are large enough and the top staff posts are important enough that capable young potential administrators are willing to train for

[1] Jackson, 104.

and make a career of local government administration. Thus the large city naturally has a comparatively larger reservoir of trained and experienced manpower to draw from in selecting the top officers, even if it limits itself to selecting from the ranks of its own staff.

In several countries, though, the chief administrative officers as well as other top staff officers, either by law or by custom, may now be non-local as well as local persons. This development has done much to enable local government service in both the less populous and more populous local units to be an increasingly promising vocational field. Therefore, more capable potential administrators are being drawn into the field and their services are available to a larger number of local units. Such mobility between local units is the general practice in many countries, including Italy and France as well as the U.K. and Sweden. These trends, along with others such as the development of special training institutes and professional associations for local government officers, have done much to develop a growing profession of local administrative officers.

3. *The departments*

In those local units with more than a few employees the almost inevitable tendency is for the staff to be divided into departments. Departments then are the major parts of the local staff structure. A variety of factors may influence the way in which these departments are organized. A few will be discussed in this section.

The primary consideration in the organization of most departments is that they handle all matters affecting a particular purpose or activity, or two or more closely related purposes or activities.[1] For instance, a city might have a police department to deal with all matters affecting public security and a fire department to handle all fire fighting, or it might have one public safety department dealing with all police and fire matters. Other departments may be organized to handle such activities as public works, water supply, education and health, and most of their

[1] See Exhibit 5 for chart and a similar discussion and diagram on the manner in which committees are organized.

employees may work outside the city hall. Such departments may be called the "line" or "vertical" departments. In a few of the local units, generally those with a large area, line departments or offices may also be organized to deal with matters affecting one particular geographical area.

Other departments, on the other hand, are organized to deal with matters affecting one or more particular aspects of the management of the local government activities. There may be, for instance, a finance department, a legal department, a records department, a personnel department, or a building and supply department. These may be called "auxiliary," "non-line" or "horizontal" departments because they deal with matters that affect all the local activities and thus every one of the departments.[1]

Whereas the line departments exist primarily to serve the public and a large proportion of their employees work outside of the local headquarters, the non-line departments exist primarily to assist the other departments in carrying out their activities. Because the duties of the non-line departments affect matters pertaining to all the departments, some of them, especially finance, may be in strategic positions to co-ordinate and sometimes to control the activities of local units.

The number and size of departments in a local unit vary greatly. Moreover, some of the departments may operate in a more independent fashion, that is, some may be relatively centralized and others decentralized. One of the most conspicuous factors affecting the extent to which the activities of the departments are loosely organized or closely co-ordinated is the type of body to which they are responsible. Thus, departments whose heads report to a chief executive or chief administrative officer tend to have their work more closely co-ordinated than do those which are directly accountable to a council, a committee or a member or a board whose chairman does not exercise a strong co-ordinating influence.

[1] See, for instance, Arthur W. Bromage, *Municipal Government and Administration* (New York 1957), pp. 313–324 and the International City Managers' Association, *The Technique of Municipal Administration* (Chicago 1947), pp. 48–62. The "auxiliary" or "non-line" department is in some cases also called a "staff" department; this terminology has not been used in this survey because the word "staff" has been used in a broader sense.

In French and Italian municipalities, for example, which have a strong chief executive and a chief administrative officer, the activities of each of the departments are closely co-ordinated with the others. On the other hand, in the U.K. local units each of the departments generally operates in a more independent manner, working more closely with the individual committee than with a central co-ordinating organ. In other local units, such as in Switzerland, the department heads work more closely with one of the board members. There are also many local units in which some of the department heads are directly supervised by the chief executive or chief administrative officer while others are accountable only to the council and thus operate more independently. For instance, in a large number of municipalities in the United States some of the department heads report to the mayor while others are responsible only to the council or even directly to the public. The relationship of the departments to the executive organs is inter-related to some extent with the manner in which the department heads are selected and to whom they are responsible.

4. *The department heads*

Among the most important positions in the staff are the heads of both the line and non-line departments. Not only does a department head direct the work of the employees in his department, but he also has an important part in the preparation and in the actual making of the decisions which determine the policies affecting his department.

In the process of local non-representative government, this tier of local government department heads forms just one of the levels in an administrative pyramidal hierarchy reaching up to the higher units. In the process of local representative government, however, this tier of officers has an even more important role for they work in close conjunction with the representative organs not only in carrying out the decisions of the councils, the boards, and the committees, but also in preparing the papers which lay the groundwork for the decisions of these bodies. To a limited extent these relationships have already been pointed out in previous chapters.

A department head, for purposes of this survey, must be strictly defined as the person who has direct charge of the staff of a department. One may think the term "department head" is self-defining. In fact, though, one must draw a distinction in many local units between the staff officer who directs the actual work of a department and the elected official, often a board member, who works closely with the department head in matters affecting policy objectives.

Almost invariably at least one of the top staff officers attends the meeting of the council and of the board; this is the one who acts as secretary to the organ and who is in most local units the chief administrative officer (he will be further discussed in the next section). In a relatively few local units (e.g. some U. S. municipalities) other top staff officers are invited to attend meetings of their organs; generally, though, they do not speak unless requested. In only a few municipalities are staff officers members of a council or board. Some chief staff officers, for example those in the Finnish urban municipalities, are chairman of the board. Some other staff officers in the larger Finnish cities and the Turkish urban municipalities are also board members. One also finds staff officers among the appointed members of the council in some of the larger cities in a few countries (e.g. India).

Most of the department heads are members of the staff who have secured their appointment either from the council, the board, the chief executive, or from a public (or civil) service commission such as was mentioned earlier. There are, though, a number of local units in which administration of each of the departments is directed by an elected official. These elected officials may be either board members, council members, or officers who do not have seats on either the council or board.

Direct popular election of department heads, who do not have seats on the councils or boards, is almost unknown outside of the United States; even in that country this practice is on the decline. Of the U. S. municipalities with more than 5,000 inhabitants about a third have elected treasurers, a fourth have elected clerks, a seventh elected assessors, an eighth elected auditors, and a twelfth elected attorneys; about a half of the municipalites with more than 5,000 residents elect one or more of their department heads.[1] This method of selecting administrative officers is largely a result of an antipathy to centralized control and a confidence in so-called "popular democracy" which existed in the early years of this republic; today this manner of selection is generally considered unsatisfactory.

In a few municipalities the elected councilmen themselves are department heads. In the U. S. cities with the "commission" form of government, for instance, each of the council members has the direct charge of a department of the city administration, with the councilmen determining among themselves who shall be in charge of each department. Moreover, in some of the smaller municipalities, including a few in the United States and Sweden, the municipal clerk is elected from among and by the council. The chief administrative officer in Russian local units is almost invariably elected from the council. In another country, El Salvador, one voting place on the council is reserved for the solicitor (*sindaco*), who is directly elected to this specific post; in many of the smaller municipalities in this country other councilmen are assigned the direction of a department. There are other municipalities in which the departments are directly administered by the board members; the Thai and Swiss municipalities have been cited as examples of this in the previous chapter on the boards.

There are also a few local units in which the department heads are appointed by an organ or an official of a higher unit. Examples of this are the Philippine municipalities whose department heads are appointed by and responsible to the head of the counterpart department at the next higher level. In fact in the provincial capitals the head of the municipal public works department and the provincial public works department may be the same man.

5. *The chief administrative officer*

A chief administrative officer may be described as the principal collaborator of the chief executive, or of the quasi-chief executive, charged with the over-all direction or co-ordination of the staff

[1] *ICMA, The Municipal Yearbook* 1959, 86.

EXHIBIT 8 EXAMPLES OF ORGANIZATION OF
MUNICIPAL DEPARTMENTS

a. Departments closely co-ordinated (e.g. French Municipalities)

```
                    Council
                      |
                    Mayor
                      |
          Chief Administrative Officer
          |  |  |  |  |  |  |  |
                 Departments
```

b. Departments not closely co-ordinated (e.g. English Municipalities)

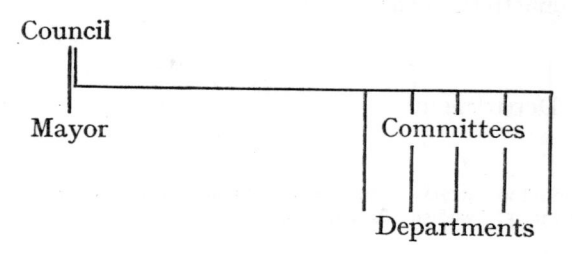

```
  Council
    ||_____
    |                  |  |  |
  Mayor            Committees
                     |  |  |
                  Departments
```

c. Mixture of Departments – some closely co-ordinated, others not (e.g. some U. S. council-mayor and council-committee cities)

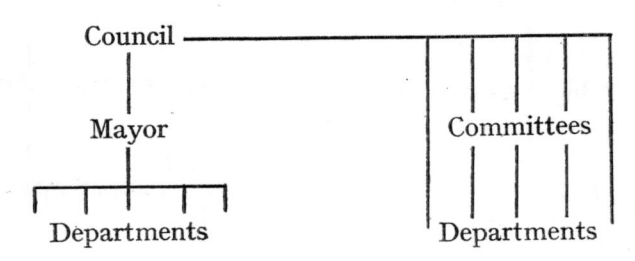

```
      Council _____
        |                |  |  |
      Mayor          Committees
      |  |  |           |  |  |
    Departments       Departments
```

EXHIBIT 9 – A CONTRAST IN RELATIONSHIP
BETWEEN CHIEF ADMINISTRATIVE OFFICER AND
DEPARTMENT HEADS

a. A chief administrative officer who is the hierarchical superior of the department heads (e. g. French Municipality)

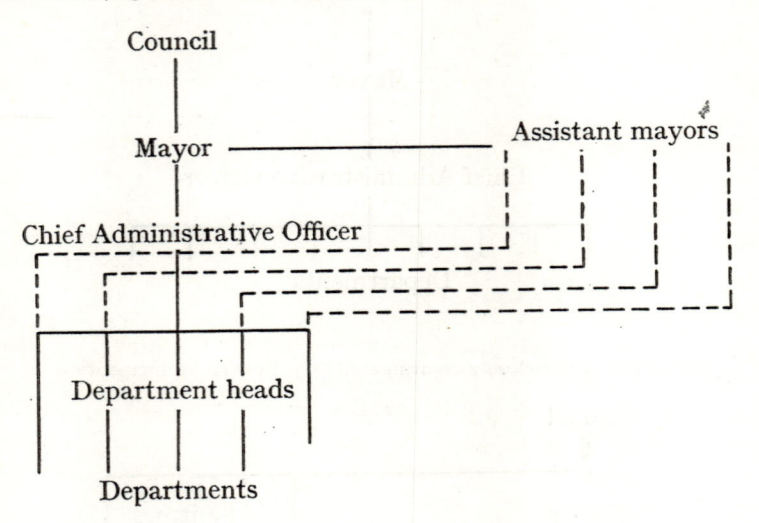

Council

Mayor —————————— Assistant mayors

Chief Administrative Officer

Department heads

Departments

b. A chief administrative officer who is *primus inter pares* among the department heads (e. g. Swedish Municipality)

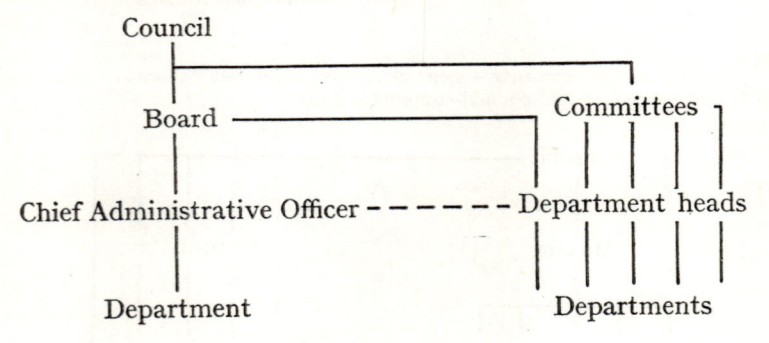

Council

Board —————————— Committees

Chief Administrative Officer — — — — — Department heads

Department   Departments

of a local unit. He may play an important role not only in co-ordinating the implementation, but also in co-ordinating the formulation and initiation of policy decisions. In those local units which do have such a chief administrative officer, this official is usually the secretary of the council or the board or both.

With the growth in the services and in the number of local employees, as well as in the increasing complexity of the local organisation, the position of the officer charged with the overall co-ordination has become more important. His role is especially important in countries with elected local chief executives, who often have many inherent difficulties in succesfully handling their duties regarding the staff. Their training and experience have in most countries generally been in other fields and have been limited to one community. In addition they are usually not prepared to devote themselves full-time to the task because of such factors as the inadequate pay and the need to continue in a more secure occupation. The locally elected chief executive is expected to be first of all a leader in the representative aspect of the local government process. It is primarily on these qualities that his re-election depends.

The growing importance of the chief administrative officer is a result of the need for the type of top administrative leadership which can usually be best supplied by full-time officials who have trained for and have had experience in the field. The development of council-appointed chief executives and the growing importance of the central administrative officer are inter-related trends with the same underlying causes.

One should distinguish two types of chief administrative officers. The first type is the hierarchical superior of all, or most, of the department heads. The second is in theory simply one of the department heads charged with one of the non-line departments, but whose duties are of such a nature that in effect he undertakes a general co-ordinating role and is therefore considered as *primus inter pares*.

Probably the best example of a chief administrative officer who is the hierarchical superior of the department heads is the secretary-general in the French and Italian municipalities. He is specifically the top staff officer directing the activities of the municipal administration. The heads of the various departments report directly to the secretary-general, and thus indirectly to the mayor, regarding the administrative activities of their departments and services. This type of chief administrative officer is found in many local units which have a strong elected chief executive. French local government, for instance, has no system of administering committees such as in England, even though the assistant mayors may be assigned by the mayor to supervise departments. In this regard Chapman points out that:

"In France committees of Council have no powers to act; only the Mayor and by delegation the Assistant Mayors can do so. Consequently all the measures requiring execution must pass through the hands of the communal executive. This naturally increases the power of the Secretary General."[1]

The second type of chief administrative officer is not the hierarchical superior of the department heads but is himself simply one of the department heads. In fact, though, he is far more important. He is also the secretary of the board or of the council or of both. Through his office pass the papers which are prepared for the consideration of the representative organ, or organs, of which he is secretary. The other municipal department heads generally make it a point to consult with this officer concerning their proposed programs not only because he can give expert legal or financial advice on the proposal, but also because his advice will carry a great deal of weight when the proposal is ultimately brought before the board or council. Moreover, his over-all co-ordinating position as regards staff activities is strengthened because the department which he heads is charged with one or more of such aspects of management as finance, records, and legal advice, through the control of which he is in a central position to co-ordinate the activities of the staff. Generally, though, the position of this type of central administrative officer is not as strong as that of the other chief administrative officers. Consequently the departments tend to operate more independently; often as mentioned in earlier chapters, they have more loyalty to individual committees or board members than to the council, to the board, or to the chief executive.

In most of the Swedish local units, which have a department head as the chief administrative officer, the person holding this

[1] Chapman, *Introduction to French Local Government*, 95–96.

position is the head of the financial department and generally has had his training and experience in finance administration. This is a natural corollary of the fact that the board or leading administering committee in most Scandinavian municipalities is concerned primarily with finances and the finance director is its secretary.

In the local units of the United Kingdom the chief administrative officer is the head of the department which handles the legal documents. His position as chief administrative officer is based on the fact that the council depends upon him for legal advice as well as for the preparation of the papers for consideration in the representative process. The municipal chief administrative officer in many European countries is also usually trained in law. In most of the mayor-council cities and rural municipalities of the North American countries, the chief administrative officer is the clerk who, although not trained in law, has some similarities to his English counter-part.

10

TOWARD RESPONSIBLE LOCAL REPRESENTATIVE GOVERNMENT

1. Problems and trends

THIS survey has been an attempt not only to make an organ-by-organ comparison of the structures of local government in many countries but also to assess some of the trends currently affecting these structures. It would be foolhardy, though, to attempt to generalize about local government structure throughout the world on the basis of this very broad and thus necessarily superficial survey. Nor would it be sensible to essay to postulate and defend a so-called ideal form of local government or to merely relist many of the conclusions already woven into the text. From the foregoing serial scrutiny of the constituent parts of local representative government it is now possible, though, to comment upon some of its more salient common and inter-related problems, to evaluate the general tendencies affecting these problems, and even to make some possibly constructive suggestions regarding the inter-relationships of the organs in the structure of local representative government. Of course, the extent to which such suggestions are, or may be, practical is, or would be, influenced by the local government environment in which one or more of them are, or would be, introduced.

Two inter-related sets of phenomena appear to underly, and to make more critically obvious, the problems now facing local government. They are particularly obvious in the more developed countries. One set of phenomena are the rapid mechanical developments, especially in transport and communication. The other set of phenomena, which has accompanied the mechanical evolution, is the growth of social services. The advances in techniques and methods in the social as well as engineering fields have opened whole new vistas of possible local government services. The possibility of new services and the improvement of older ones have meant a change in the whole scope of the quantity and quality of government services expected at the local level.

One of the most fundamental problems facing local representative government is that there are too many local units. Most of the municipalities, particularly those in the rural areas, are too small – not only in terms of population but also in terms of resources – to be able to undertake in an adequate manner any significant number of functions. The vast majority of municipalities have less than 2,000 residents and thus cannot afford the trained manpower or the equipment to undertake the increasingly complex and numerous public services which are expected of midtwentieth century local government; they are not capable of taking advantage of the efficiency and economy of doing services on a large scale. Fortunately, the development of rapid transportation and instant communication is making larger and more populous municipalities a more recognizable possibility. Two generations ago a municipal building in the next hamlet was a decided inconvenience, but today telephones and motor transportation, both public and private, are making it more easily accessible to a larger number of people, even in many of the less developed countries.

Whether municipalities are more or less populous is not the primary factor, of course, affecting the extent of local representative government. One can have the forms of representative government in either. But local representative government becomes meaningless if the local units are too small to perform a significant number of important functions. It tends to lose the interest of the voters and the confidence of the central government. The amalgamation of the "too small" municipalities, as has been done in several countries including Sweden and Japan, will not by itself bring stronger, more responsible local representative government, but such a measure will be a major step in creating the conditions in which responsible local representative government can flourish.

One of the possible approaches to the dilemma caused by the

presence of small communities and the need for larger local units may be the use of larger municipalities which are divided into sub-municipal units. In this manner the municipalities can be large enough to be administratively practical while the sub-municipal units can be small enough to conform to the local communities. The difficulty involved in this approach is to organize the sub-municipal units in such a way that there is sufficient opportunity for effective citizen participation and that there is a sufficient number of significant decisions to be made at the sub-municipal level by the representative organs to attract the public interest.

The use of sub-municipal units may also be a fruitful avenue for tackling the problem of the large cities. There is a need to have one single municipal government to co-ordinate the activities of a large city. At the same time such metropolitan areas are too large – in terms of area and population – for providing opportunity for broad-based citizen participation.

Closely connected with the problem of inadequately sized municipalities is the frequent existence of special purpose local units. A primary reason for the growth in the number of special purpose units is that the municipalities are too small – in area, population, and resources – to undertake a sufficient number of local government functions. To a certain extent the inter-municipal, but not the intra-municipal, special purpose local units are necessary, and justified by the fact that it is impossible to set up local jurisdictions which are suitable in terms of area and population for every local activity. The problem could, however, be considerably lessened by increasing the size of the municipalities and thereby reducing the number of "too small municipalities." In other cases the duties which the municipalities can not undertake might be undertaken by intermediate units instead of by special purpose units. In those cases in which an inter-municipal special purpose authority must be used in order to undertake a function for which the municipalities have the authority but not sufficient support in terms of area, people, or resources - the members of the governing bodies of these authorities should be appointed by, responsible to, and removable by the councils of the participating local units, including perhaps the intermediate units involved. In this manner the local councils can more completely fulfill their role as the representative organs of the local unit responsible to the electorate for the local public activities.

Another problem facing local representative government is the lack of adequate local financial resources. This may be attributed largely to three factors. One is that economically many local areas do not appear capable to support the array of local public services; as was pointed out earlier, this is often because they are too small in terms of area and population. Second is that the local units generally have a relatively limited authority for levying taxes, partially because most of the more lucrative fields have been appropriated by the central governments. Third, many local units only partially utilize the taxing authority which they possess because of the difficulty of raising sufficient public support for the tax levies. In an effort to circumvent this problem of inadequate local finances, the local governments have, to a greater or lesser extent, been forced to rely on the aid of the central government. With such aid, though, generally comes some degree of central government direction and supervision and increased central interference means decreased local discretion.

The degree of such central government direction varies widely; one of the crucial factors is whether the aid is distributed according to a fixed formula or not. In any case, no matter how the central government aid is distributed, the very fact that a significant portion of the money is not directly derived from local sources tends to undermine the local sense of financial responsibility; so the number of services which the local public wants tends not to be determined by what they are willing to pay for. Like some drugs, the central government aid has often kept the patient alive but also tends to render him an apparently permanent invalid dependent on the central government not only for money but also for policies.

Still another closely inter-related problem facing local representative government is the lack of a high calibre of elected and staff persons and in particular of persons who can provide the necessary leadership to the local units. Over a hundred years ago, J. S. Mill pointed out that "The greatest imperfection of popular local institutions, and the chief cause of the failure which has often attended them, is the low calibre of the men by whom they are almost always carried on."[1] The situation has not appeared

[1] Mill, 351.

to have improved sufficiently. The elected persons, too, often are not capable of determining the best public interests or of arousing the citizen support which is so necessary for healthy local representative government. Moreover, the staff members are frequently not capable of giving good policy advice to the elected persons nor of carrying out the policies in an effective and efficient manner.

The root of the problem of inadequate manpower seems to be that it is difficult to induce capable persons to take a share in local government if there are no important functions to perform. Only when the local government units have themselves the opportunities to guide, at least to some extent, their own destinies, will they be able to spark the interest of the electorate and attract the able leadership which together are the heart and brains of the local representative governing process. The tendency for the central government to play a greater role directly or indirectly, in determining the local policy objectives, has in many local units appeared to lower even further the incentives to seek an elected post in local government. On the other hand, the increasing amount of local government administration has tended to increase the incentives for staff careers in local government in many countries.

The lack of public concern for local government, and the consequent lack of public support for local government programs, is another crucial problem besetting local representative government. There must be an interested public, and in most cases this means active local party organizations as well, if there is to be an electorate which is willing to take the time and the energy to become informed on local public matters and use discretion in choosing its representatives. Without such a broad basis of popular support local representative government becomes a fiction. With the changing nature of our society, however, it appears to be increasingly difficult to attract the support of the public to local government. The focus of the public political attention is shifting to an increasingly greater extent from the local to national and even to international activities. The insufficient number of important functions and capable leaders at the local level seems to accelerate this trend.

2. Problems and trends: the central government

Closely inter-related with these problems is the increasingly more difficult challenge involved in the extension of the scope of central government interests and activities. To a large degree this extension of central government concern is the product of the two sets of modern phenomena, the rapid developments in transportation, communication, and industry as well as the growth of social services, abetted in many countries by the influence of war and economic depression. Many matters which formerly were considered local now appear to have assumed greater complexity and inter-relationships with national or even international interest. They are, therefore, subject to a greater degree of central government intervention. For the effects of poor health, mediocre schools, and bad roads seldom stop at the boundaries of local units and are now more than ever matters of concern to both local and central governments. Furthermore, better means of communication and transportation have not only increased the central government concern in some local matters, they have also made it easier for a central government to check and control the activities of the local units, and in some cases to manage some activities directly from the capital. Consequently in a large number of countries the general public is tending to look to the national government for more and better services as well as for determination of local policy objectives. To a degree the growth of the influence of the central governments has been made easy by the fact that the enlarging nature of our communities and their problems has made it difficult to determine how much the public functions at the local level should be controlled by the central government. In many cases, though, the central governments have found it necessary to extend, or continue, their control of public services at the local level precisely because of the apparent inability of the local units to undertake them in an adequate manner.

An increasing amount of interaction between the local and central levels of government appears, though, to be more necessary, more possible, and even more desirable in the world of today. In fact, autonomy and home-rule, the shibboleths of the past, appear to be giving way to co-operation and inter-dependence.

As transportation and communication become quicker and easier, and therefore distances appear to become smaller, there is a greater need for the central governments to have more concern for setting minimum common standards for local services. For today not only the indolent and incapable local units but also the active and capable ones need to have their activities financially assisted as well as guided and co-ordinated with the activities of other local units. But the general result of this increased central government participation is that in most countries local governments are in a somewhat paradoxical position. While a large number of local units have more duties and larger staffs than ever before, they appear to have a smaller share in determining their over-all policy objectives. The amount of activity at the local level has increased greatly, but the important decisions seem to be gravitating to the national, and in some cases to the supra-national and foreign capitals.

While in many countries, particularly the Asian and African ones, vast strides are being made in improving the forms of local representative government, and in almost every country an increasing number of tasks are being performed by the local governments, it appears that more and more of the over-all policy objectives are being made centrally, leaving the local representative organs with the duty to merely elucidate them. This presents a major challenge, for when the local representative organs do not have the power to determine, not merely ratify, their over-all policy objectives, then local reresentative governments tend to become merely a façade for the exercise of central government direction. While the more optimistic may speak of the need for a new era of central-local government partnership, the more pessimistic speak of the erosion of local representative government.

As long ago as 1931, Professor Robson wrote:

"Our municipal system is being subjected to a serious and perhaps dangerous strain by reason of the fact that burdens are being placed on the structure greater than those which it was designed to bear. An adjustment between structure and function is therefore urgently called for."[1]

[1] Robson, William A., *The Development of Local Government* (London 1931), Preface.

This comment is even more conspicuously valid today and it applies to local representative government in almost every country. In a later book Robson goes on to say that:

"An adjustment of this kind could be made in one of two ways. Either the structure could be improved so as to make it capable of carrying the functions more effectively, or, alternatively, the load could be reduced to correspond with the strength of the structure. Everyone who cares for local government and values its essential contribution... would desire to see the former course adopted. Unfortunately, however, the tide has been flowing strongly in the opposite direction."[1]

3. *The two purposes of local representative government structure*

Having outlined some of the more salient problems facing local representative government, one may now proceed, perhaps, to draw upon the analyses in the previous chapters in order to make some possibly constructive suggestions as regards improving the capacity of the structure of local government for meeting the problems of today. For the problems now facing local representative government make it particularly important that a local unit has a structure capable of achieving the maximum utilization and harmonization of the different qualities contributed by the elected representatives and non-elected employees, thereby making possible a synthesis of the virtues of popular control and effective administration.

In order further to clarify our concept of local representative government structure let us examine what is expected of the local units. The dichotomy between technical efficiency and popular responsiveness is reflected in the requirements for government structures. Responsible government, therefore, involves two aspects. One is the representation of the interests of the community in the determination of the local policy objectives and in the ultimate control of the implementation of these objectives. The other is the implementation of the policy objectives. Both tasks are, of course, closely inter-related and overlapping.

Local representative government needs, also, two main types of persons and, as the scope of the local activities becomes broad-

---

[1] Robson, William A., *The Development of Local Government* (London 1954), p. 15.

er and their complexity greater, the necessity for two distinct types of persons is becoming increasingly apparent. One is the representative person who is elected to represent the interests of the community; the other is the staff person who is appointed to implement the public policy. Both types of public officials tend to emphasize different kinds of personal characteristics, abilities, backgrounds and training. Consequently they tend to be selected and should be selected in basically different ways. Of course in local representative government each type of leadership must have a keen sense of appreciation for the contribution of the other. The ultimate central focus of both types of government persons is in the chief executive, but all the representative and staff persons are essential partners in the task of providing the initiative, integration, and interpretation to the process of successful local representative government.

Many commentators on local government have lamented the fact that the increased scope and more technical nature of local activities have tended to diminish the influence of the council as compared to the chief executive and the staff. Moreover, with the increased volume of work, the local councils have become so involved with the seemingly more easily understood administrative problems that some have tended to neglect determining what the longer range policy goals should be. The unfortunate results are that administratively inexperienced public representatives attempt to make technical decisions, which it appears could better be decided by trained staff members. The corollary is that the more important long range policy decisions are either made by the staff or, even worse, they are never consciously made.

As the basic representative organ, responsible to the public, the local council has two main duties as regards the executive organs and the staff. One is to determine over-all local policy objectives, that is those which set the framework for the other decisions which must be made by the executive organs and the staff. The other is controlling the implementation and the elucidation of those policy objectives. As will be suggested, the latter duty can probably be best performed when the council has the authority and the power to see to it that the persons who are selected to carry out the policies are not only administratively competent men, but also men with whom the council can work with confidence in their loyalty.

4. The representative organs

The collective responsibilities of the representative organs in the process of local government may be considered as four-fold. They are: (1) to ascertain not only the general public interest but also what various segments of the public think their interests are, (2) to set over-all policy objectives in accordance with the general public interest, (3) to control the implementation of the policy objectives through control of the administrative organs, and (4) to arouse the support of the public for the policy objectives and their appreciation of the way they are implemented. The representative organs, usually assisted by the party organization(s), especially in the electoral process, therefore, are the key to the popular participation and interest which are essential ingredients in the process of local representative government.

Although not a part of the actual local government structure, the parties have an important role as a catalyst in the representative aspect of the process of local government, especially in the more populous local units. Perhaps the most obvious contribution which can be made by political parties is to assist the representative organs in arousing the enthusiasm and focusing the support of the electorate. The parties are brokers in transforming the multitude of public interests into co-ordinated programs of public action, and in some cases they are indispensable means in aiding the public to select their representatives from among clearcut and, it is hoped, worthy alternatives. Perhaps a less obvious task of the parties is their part in co-ordinating the thinking and voting of party members who are in the representative organs. Where members of a council are linked together by party ties, they are no longer isolated individuals advocating a course of action or criticizing alone; such co-operation may even transcend local boundaries. They belong to an organization which aids in co-ordinating their actions. Whether in opposition or not, the party man is in a more effective and more responsible position than an isolated independent. And with all their faults the parties bring the opportunity for fixing responsibility in one faction or another of the councils.[1]

There appears to be little doubt that the best means of choos-

[1] Wheare, *Government by Committee*, 200–201.

ing the members of a council, the main local representative organ, is by direct popular vote. For there is no one person or organ better qualified to select the representatives of the general public than the public themselves, that is the public is the logical judge of which persons have won their confidence and the best, though not an infallible, judge of which persons can most successfully interpret their wishes. Furthermore, the periodic necessity of being re-elected by the electorate appears to be the most practical method of encouraging public representatives to be attentive to the wishes of the public.

In most countries all the members of the local councils are directly elected and the trend points to even more local councils having all their members popularly elected in the future. There appears to be much to be said in support of both the plurality vote and proportional representation methods of election, and yet there are several disadvantages to using either method totally. That is, the plurality vote method of election when combined with the single member constituency (as it usually is) has the merit of providing representation for the various geographical areas but tends to produce a sectionally minded council and one in which minorities are at a distinct disadvantage. By way of comparison, the proportional representation method makes provision for seats for the significantly sized politically organized minorities but frequently it provides an inadequate basis for stable governments. In addition some geographical areas away from the political centre of the local unit may be inadequately represented.

Might there not be many merits, and yet relatively few disadvantages, in combining these two methods: that is to elect up to one-half of the council members from single-member constituencies by plurality votes and the rest at-large by proportional representation? This appears to be the best method of securing a council which can perform the dichotomous task of representing the apparently increasingly more socially complex local units and also of providing a relatively stable support for an effective executive. The exact number of those elected from constituencies might best be left to the local unit so that it might vary according to the number of geographical sub-communities within a municipality. For instance, a municipality with a large area and several scattered centres of population would probably feel a greater need to use single-member constituencies in order that the smaller centres of population have a voice in the council. The fact that a significant segment of the council members are elected by plurality vote would probably be a discouragement to splintering the vote among an excessive number of parties. (This tendency for splintering would be further reduced by requiring each party to deposit a certain amount of money which is forfeited if the party fails to obtain a stipulated minimum percentage of the votes cast). Use of the plurality vote for some of the council seats will also make it more probable that the party with the plurality of the popular votes will win a sufficient number of council seats to support an effective executive.

On the other hand, the use of proportional representation for some of the council seats will assure some representation for the significantly sized politically organized minorities. By this means, also, a large percentage of the councilmen will be elected at-large, thus reducing the possibility of having sectionally minded councils. Furthermore the use of proportional representation for a sizeable proportion of the seats of the council improves the possibility of achieving a continuity of council membership. For the leaders of each political group, as the top men on their party lists, will usually be returned to the council at each succeeding election.

There is no noticeable trend toward the use of primary elections. A more widespread use of primary elections would, probably, though, be a useful adjunct to the election process. At present in most countries the voting public is forced to take a choice between the candidates presented by each of the parties, sometimes this reduces itself to choosing the lesser of two or more evils. A primary election can be used as a check on the selections made by each of the parties; it gives an opportunity for those who are discontent with the party selections to express themselves and perhaps alter the party slate without going over to the opposition. This opportunity can be especially important in a large number of local units, found not only in one-party countries but also in two- and many-party countries, in which there is in effect only one party in some of the local areas. In those local units which have a list form of proportional representation but do not have primary elections, a few of the merits of primary elections can be incorporated into the election system by allowing the voter to vote for individual candidates on the list. In this way the candidates who have been placed too low on the lists also have a possibility of being elected as council members; thus, to a limited extent the public can exercise some control over the selections of the party leaders without voting for another party.

From what has already been said about the role of the council in representing the interests of the public it follows that the number of members in a council should depend on the area and the number and complexity of political interests of the local unit as well as on the number of inhabitants; that is the council should be large enough that it can represent the various local public interests. At the same time, though, councils should not be so large that the individual positions lack the opportunity to make a creative contribution to the deliberations and thus do not attract the most capable men.

Interrelated with the size of the council is the question of the use of boards and committees. The general tendency is that local boards are used in countries with large local councils. Preparatory and administering committees tend to be used in conjunction with the councils of the more populous municipalities which have the larger workloads. These committees of council have an important role to play in aiding the larger councils in the more populous cities to perform their representative leadership role. They relieve the load of the council by doing much of the preparatory work. They make it possible for much of the work to be undertaken by smaller groups thus facilitating a thorough discussion. They also make it possible for a council member to become rather familiar with one or a few aspects of local government instead of spreading himself thin over the many. The danger in the use of committees is that individual members tend to think of their specialized interests ahead of the general community interests. This danger is especially acute in the use of administering committees.

A council in all but the small municipalities, if it is to be large enough to be representative of the public interests, generally needs a smaller organ to aid it in preparing the deliberations. There is undoubtedly value in having a board, or executive committee, which is small enough to be an effective organ supplying leadership to the council. Such a small organ can provide initiative to the council deliberations, integrate or co-ordinate the work of the council and its committees in making the over-all policy programs, and facilitate interpretation. Furthermore, within the framework of the policy objectives approved by the council, the board can actually make some of the local decisions, thus saving the time of the council and the councilmen for examining and discussing the more important over-all decisions. Most important, such a board can have a leading role in assisting the chief executive in supervising the activities of the staff.

The exact nature of the role of the board may vary from being primarily an executive committee of the council, in which only the chairman as the chief executive has specific individual duties of staff direction, to being a plural executive organ, in which all or most of the members have specific individual executive duties. There is a general tendency for the former to be the case in the less populous municipalities, and for the latter to be the case in some of the heavily populated local units, in which being a board member is a paid job taking up all or a major portion of a normal work week. This tendency appears to recommend itself, for in the larger local units there is a need for several full-time elected persons to be associated with the chief executive in providing representative leadership. Each board member may contribute to the effectiveness of the small representative organ by specializing in one or more aspects of local government, in connection with which he may supervise one or more departments or be a chairman of a committee of council or both. The fact that as a group, under the chairmanship of the chief executive, they are jointly accountable to the council generally encourages the members of such a board to put the general local interests above their specialized interests.

In general there are two ways in which the local boards are selected. In many local units the composition of the board is a miniature of that of the council; that is, by law or by custom the party groups are represented on the board in proportion to the percentage of seats they hold in the council. In other local units the board is composed only of representatives of the majority party or coalition. The former method permits a broader cross-section of the interests of the local units to be represented in the board; it is probably the most expedient method of forming a board in countries such as the Lebanon, in which there are deep cleavages between the religious communities, which affect the political life of the country and the local unit. Forming the board from among the majority of the council, however, has the advantage of securing a homogeneous group which is in comparative agreement concerning the ultimate goals of the local government policy. Such a board is generally better suited to the dual task of taking the general initiative in presenting an integrated program of action to the large, more broadly representative council and of directing the implementation of the decisions of the council. Furthermore, this method of forming a board enables the responsibility to be focused in one small group of persons who will defend one overall program of policies. Thus the functions of the broadly-based, more heterogeneous council and the more narrowly-constituted, more homogeneous board balance and complement each other.

5. *The staff officers*

It is necessary for strong local representative government to have a trained and experienced staff which can efficiently prepare and carry out the decisions of the representative organs. Moreover, the broader the scope, the greater the complexity, and the more technical the nature of the local functions, the larger are the local staffs, the more important is their part in preparing and implementing the decisions of the representative organs. The need to attract, select, and retain competent employees is an obvious one. In many countries it is generally accepted that most or all of the local staff members should be selected and promoted by means of examinations, which may be controlled by either a local or a central organ. In addition, it is also generally accepted that the positions of members of the local staffs should be made secure by statute in such a way that their tenure is protected from political interference; such statutes generally specify under exactly what conditions (e.g. criminal misconduct in office) an employee can be demoted, suspended, or dismissed from office, and they provide a means by which an employee can make an appeal to some tribunal concerning any actions which he feels are contrary to these statutes. Another factor which is tending to raise the quality of local staff members, and at the same time make a local government administrative career a more attractive one, is the extent to which local officials, especially those who hold the higher positions, may move, or be transferred, from one local unit to another in the advancement of their professional career.

It has already been pointed out that the larger the staffs, the more important are the roles of the top staff officers. For the larger the number of functions and the more technical and more complex they are, the more crucial are their roles in co-ordinating the preparation and the implementation of the decisions of the representative organs. The chief administrative officers, and in the more populous local units the department heads as well, not only must have administrative competence (the basic and primary qualification of a good staff officer), but also they should have the political confidence of the top elected officials. That is, the top elected officials should be able to be confident not only that the top staff officers are administratively capable, but also that their orientation in regard to policy principles permits them to prepare and implement the decisions of the representative organs with enthusiasm. Every competent department head has some sort of policy orientation, that is, there are some things he wants kept the way they are and there are other things he wants changed; and nothing is so frustrating to the implementation of a public policy, and to the officials who have decided upon it, as to have its implementation directed by those whose orientation is in fundamental contrast.

If one accepts the contention that the top staff officers should not carry out their duties reluctantly then it follows that not only the administrative competence but also the policy orientation of the candidates should be considered when appointing top staff officers. Furthermore, in those cases in which the policy orientation of an already appointed top staff officer differs so fundamentally from that of the decisions of the representative organs that he can carry out his duties only reluctantly, then there must be a means for permitting this staff officer to be removed from this particular position. A staff officer should, however, be granted an adequate separation allowance and have the right either to appeal his release to a higher unit or to explain is position publicly or both. (A further corollary of the right of the local unit to dismiss a top staff officer is that this officer should have as many opportunities as possible to continue his profession by finding a new job in which he can approach his task with more enthusiasm. The difficulties of finding a new position are noticeably less in those countries in which local government officers may move, or be transferred, with relative ease from one local unit to another).

From the foregoing it should be obvious that local representative government is dependent upon both its representatives and its staff officers. Moreover, each type of official is mutually dependent, each must not only appreciate and but also constructively cooperate with the other. To work ideally, though, there needs to be a fuller understanding, on both the elected and staff levels, about how to get the largest returns from the desirable interlocking of responsible representative direction and responsive staff implementation. The representative direction must have the vision to formulate and the capacity to gain support for worthy policies, but it must also create conditions for resourceful and effective administration, unhampered by unrestrained and irresponsible political considerations. The most basic concept to this team approach is, however, that a responsible representative government cannot unfold its full strength, except within a governmental structure that subordinates expert staff competence to lay representative direction. In a responsible local representative governing process the responsibility for running local public affairs should flow in an orderly manner from the public to the council to the executive to the staff.[1]

To a large degree the extent to which and the manner in which the elected persons and the staff work with, appreciate, and constructively exploit one another is dependent on the official who is the keystone or focal point of the local government process. For it is the chief executive plus his immediate collaborators who have the most important share in determining the balance of strength and the character of the organization.

---

[1] See Fritz Marstein Marx, *The Administration State* (Chicago 1957), pp. 186–187.

6. The functions of the chief executive, the ceremonial head, and the chief administrative officer

As has been pointed out earlier, the central and potentially most favourable position in the structure of local government for the exercise of policy leadership is that of the chief executive. He is essentially the most important co-ordinating element in the process of local government. For the chief executive, in some cases along with a board, is the focal point of both the representative and staff aspects of the local government process. As head of the government of the local unit he is expected to be the leader or the primary source of initiative, integration, and interpretation to the process of local government.

In most local units the chief executive is not able to fulfil each of the diverse tasks which must be performed in providing governmental leadership to a local unit. The difficulty is not so much that the chief executive of a local unit has too many duties. There will always be too many tasks involved in this position for any one man's working day; a large amount of the tasks must be delegated or shared with other persons. The problem is, however, more basic, for the duties which are generally linked with the job of the chief executive are too diverse to be performed well by one man. Like Pooh-bah, a character in the Gilbert and Sullivan operetta *The Mikado* who held every local government post except that of Lord High Executioner, many of the present-day local chief executives find some of their roles to be in conflict with one another. In many local units the chief executive is an agent of the central government, the ceremonial head, the council chairman, and the administrative head of the staff, as well as board chairman and leader of both the council and the public in matters affecting public policy. As pointed out in previous chapters, some of these jobs emphasize distinctly different attributes and require different backgrounds and character traits.

It would appear that three distinct characters are needed; in addition to the chief executive a local unit should have a relatively impartial ceremonial head or "first citizen" and a trained and experienced administrator. All three are most unlikely to be found together. Yet, in all three major areas there are important duties that must be discharged well if the local unit is to prosper.

There is only one conclusion: the chief executive in all but the smallest units can not be expected to undertake fully and successfully all the tasks which are generally associated with his position.[1]

The chief executive is the head of the government of the local unit, and as such is expected to take the initiative in advocating new and in some cases controversial programs. In those local units with boards he is generally expected to take an energetic lead in guiding its deliberations. This type of character then differs essentially from that of an impartial ceremonial head of the local unit. Like the constitutional monarch, who "reigns but does not rule," the ceremonial head of a local unit is expected to preside but not to govern. For this task the ideal person is one who considers himself to be above party strife and has the respect of most or all of the various factions. Such a person makes not only a good "first citizen" but also an excellent moderator of a council, one of whose main purposes is to give opportunities for the expression of minority as well as majority points of view. The ceremonial head, who is the symbol of the whole community, can use his official prestige and dignity combined with his personal stature to add a degree of stability to the local representative governing process.

The contrast between the backgrounds and abilities which are desirable in the chief executive and the chief administrative officer are even more obvious, and even more important, than that between the ceremonial head and the chief executive. The distinction between the roles of the chief executive and the chief administrative officer is a logical follow-through of the dichotomy between the two types of persons needed in local representative government: the representative and the staff. The political head should be a leader who has proved his adeptness at gaining the support of the council and the public by his ability to win public office; he is expected to feel the pulse of the political life of the community. In contrast, the top staff officer is a career man, trained and experienced in the methods of policy implementation and administrative techniques. As the chief administrative officer he is the principal administrative collaborator of the chief executive, charged with co-ordinating the activities of the staff, and may take a leading part in formulating policy; but it is

[1] Drucker, Peter, *The Practice of Management* (New York 1954), p. 168.

the political or elected head who should take the lead in the exposition of policy to the council and to the public. The successful functioning of such a team depends, of course, on a harmonious relationship between the two. Each must recognize that they are interdependent, and each must appreciate the complementary role of the other. In representative government, though, it is the elected element which must ultimately be supreme. It is the political head (rather than the chief administrative officer) who should be the No. 1 man or chief executive. That is, he should be the ultimate central focus of power, which is expected to co-ordinate both the representative and staff elements of the structure of local government. It is the chief administrative officer who should be the No. 2 man in the administrative hierarchy. Such an organizational set-up finds a close parallel not only in the partnership of the mayor and secretary (general) in French and Italian municipalities but also in the partnership of the cabinet minister and permanent department head in the central government departments of some countries (e.g. the United Kingdom).

In discussing the relationship of the chief administrative officer to the departments one must make an evaluation of the advantages of having one who is a hierarchical superior as compared to one who is a *primus inter pares*. It is difficult to discuss this question, of course, apart from such interrelated factors as the role of the board members and of the specialized committees. The general tendency, however, appears to be toward the use of one who is a hierarchical superior. From the point of view of effective, co-ordinated management this appears to be a desirable tendency. For an administrative leader is in a much better position to integrate and co-ordinate administrative activities when he is the hierarchical superior then when he has the status of a *primus inter pares*.

There is no substitute for effective leadership. In today's world it is more than ever important that the policy leadership as well as the administrative leadership be focused in vigorous, responsible leaders. Policy leadership has the increasingly important role of (1) developing dynamic visions of policies for the communities of tomorrow and (2) organizing support for these policies among the councils and the larger and more complex electorates of today. Likewise the chief administrative officer is the focal point of the work of the staff, which has the increasingly important role of utilizing the constantly advancing techniques of administration and technical progress for providing better services to the local citizens. Both the policy and administrative leadership roles complement each other, both roles are essential to the smooth responsible operation of the local representative governing process, they are, in effect, a team with the chief executive as captain.

7. *The establishment of the executive*

It is not without reason that Harold Stannard has called the problem of establishing a responsible executive "the cardinal problem of politics."[1] The difficulty is to establish an executive in such a way that it has sufficient strength to be the most important focus of power but is not so powerful that it eliminates other sources of power, or can act in a way that is contrary to the policy objectives as determined by the council.

As has been pointed out in previous chapters, this balance is hard to find. There are many local units, such as some of the Anglo-Saxon ones, in which the executive has insufficient power. On the other hand, there are many more local units in which the local executive has so much power that it is more aptly decribed as the dominator rather than the focus of leadership. The problem of finding the proper balance is made more difficult by the fact that the requirements for and the customs affecting leadership vary so much in different countries.

The fundamental elements in the establishment of the executive are the means by which it is selected and by which its term of office may be ended. Basically there are four methods by which the executive is selected: appointment by the central government or other higher units, direct popular election, election by (and generally from) the council, and council appointment. Each has its distinct advantages and disadvantages, the importance of which depends to a large extent on what the primary role of the

[1] Stannard, Harold, *The Two Constitutions* (London 1949), p. 167.

executive is expected to be. It is apparent that appointment by higher units is an acceptable means for a local executive who is considered to be mainly an agent of the central government, but it tends to promote a conflict of loyalties, on the part of the executive, between the local and central governments. Direct popular election is, likewise, a suitable means of determining the chief representative of the public, but it has its severe disadvantages, for the direct mandate of both the council and the executive is a standing invitation to a power struggle between the two. Council election is an ideal method of choosing an executive who is primarily a leader of the council, although in some cases this method appears to emphasize the factionalism of the council. On the other hand, council appointment is becoming increasingly accepted as a method of choosing an executive who is considered primarily as a chief administrative officer, but there are obvious disadvantages to his serving as the leading person in the exposition of public policy to the council and public.

Aside from the normal non-political contingencies, such as death, an executive may have varying degrees of security of tenure, depending upon the degree to which the executive is to be independent of control by the selecting organ. Some appointed executives have, by law or by custom, indefinite terms of office, which cease only upon reaching a mandatory retirement age, accepting a new position, or being found guilty of criminal misconduct in office. Other executives are elected for fixed terms of office and generally cannot be removed until the expiration of that specified term. Still other executives, both appointed and elected ones, may be removed from office at any time, if there is a lack of confidence upon the part of the selecting organ.

It appears that the interests of local representative government are served best by having an executive who is considered to be mainly a leader of the council and of the public. On the whole election by and from the council appears to be the most desirable alternative, for by this method the incumbents have demonstrated not only their ability to win a popular election but also to gain the support of the majority of the council. Inasmuch as the effectiveness of a council-elected executive depends, to a large extent, upon his ability to retain the support of a majority of council, it appears reasonable that a council should have the authority to elect a new executive to replace one who no longer enjoys the council's confidence.

There is still another method of electing an executive which might be tried. It is essentially a combination of a variation of direct popular election and of council election. By this suggested method the top man on the list of the party which gets the largest number of popular votes would be declared elected chief executive as well as a councilman. An essential element in this suggested method, though, is that the continuance of the chief executive in office would be dependent upon its ability to gain and retain the support of a majority of council. Since the chief executive won office as the head of the party list which had the largest number of votes, it is probable that he will have, at least initially, the support of the largest faction of councilmen. This does not prevent the possibility, though, that a coalition of factions, or dissidents from his faction plus another faction, may control a majority of the votes. In this case the council would be able to replace the chief executive.

In those local units which have a board, the chief executive would be selected in the same manner. In the event of one party winning a majority of the seats of the council the top persons on the electoral list of that party would be declared elected as board members. In the event, however, that no one party wins a majority of the seats, the selection of the board members, other than the chief executive, would have to await the forming of a majority coalition; in this case the already elected chief executive would be in a strategic position to take the leading role in forming the coalition. Whether the board is formed from among the members of one party or of two or more parties, though, the board members would be collectively responsible to the council. Furthermore, the council would have the authority to replace the board with a new one.

Use of this method of election permits the public to exert a more direct influence on who will form the executive (this is especially true if the determination of the top positions on the list was decided at a primary election). Furthermore, use of this method serves to focus the interest of the electorate and arouse their enthusiasm, for the public generally becomes more enthusiastic about voting for the candidates for executive, and especially the chief executive, positions than for positions on the council.

Another advantage to this method of electing an executive is, that it provides a means for the council to have some control over the implementation of its decisions through its control over the executive. It is obvious, from what has been said, that the executive occupies a focal position of power in the process of local representative government. And it is more and more inevitable that the executive should have such power if local activities are to be effectively managed. The provision that the executive should be (jointly) accountable to the council and that with the loss of the confidence of the council and the election of a new executive, its term of office would end, furnishes a means to exercise this control. Furthermore this provision reduces the possibility of that deadlock in politics which would ensue on a quarrel breaking out between an executive and a council, neither of whom, during an interval which might amount to years, would have any legal means of ridding itself of the other.[1]

The executive should not, however, be made unduly dependent upon the whims and votes of a council. The council should be encouraged to act responsibly in its use of the authority to cast an executive out of office. Otherwise the policy direction of the local unit may suffer from instability and lack of continuity. The possibility of the executive being unduly dependent on a vote of the council is considerably reduced, however, if its term of office is not ended until a successor has been selected – thus an executive cannot be removed by a purely negative "vote of no confidence" for the council must come forward with an alternative executive. Furthermore, though, the executive should have the authority (probably in most countries with the approval of one of the higher units) to dissolve the council in preparation for new municipal elections. Instead, therefore, of being merely turned out of office by a hostile vote, the executive is forced to the alternative of resignation or dissolution. In this manner the clash of wills can be referred to a decision of the electorate. In practice, clashes of interest between the French mayors and council are decided in this manner, although it is actually on the authority of the provincial governor that the new

[1] See Mill, 338.

elections are called. This combination of council and popular election, the possibility of replacing the executive, and the prerogative of the executive to dismiss the council and call new elections may be the most satisfactory method of establishing an accountable and effective executive in the process of responsible local representative government.

8. Toward responsible local representative government

From what has been written in the preceding pages, it is clear that, if local representative government is to work well, it is necessary to maintain a good supply of two types of persons – the representatives and the staff officers. "There will not be a supply of good laymen unless there is a demand for them," says Wheare, "unless, that is, local councils offer opportunities for them to exercise their talents, to show initiative and leadership, and to obtain some positions of power and influence."[1] By the same token there will not be a supply of good administrators unless there are opportunities for them to develop careers, that is the local units must offer chances to exercise administrative skill, to show initiative, to obtain promotions to high positions, and to work relatively secure from political interference.

The future of local representative government and its ability to meet the problems of today is dependent among other things on its structure and leadership. Responsible leadership is more likely to develop in those local units which have structures carefully prepared to evoke it.

[1] Wheare, *Government by Committee*, 201.

PART TWO

(0)

THE GEOGRAPHICAL GROUPS

0. The countries and the geographical groups

THERE is generally an obvious resemblance between the structures of local government in neighbouring countries. Naturally countries which are geographically close to one another have a greater tendency to be influenced by the same historical and environmental factors. Their cultures, including their languages, their religions, and their governmental traditions and philosophies, as well as the organizational implications of these traditions and philosophies, are historically closely related. The evolution of individual characteristics and the resulting synthesis of forms and systems of local government may be the product of the simultaneous inter-related development in countries with similar cultural backgrounds. Or it may be the result of the influence of one country upon the development of another country or group of countries either through colonization, subjugation, or more indirect means. This phenomenon of cultural inter-relationship is an important one not only for reviewing the manner in which local governments were developed and for understanding how they operate, but also for grouping the local government systems for any comparative study.

In any attempt to compare the institutions of as many as forty different countries it becomes necessary to group the countries. Such groupings are necessary not only for descriptive purposes but also for making the tables. The difficulty in determining such groups is that no one method is wholly satisfactory. In theory the ideal method would be to pick certain critical factors in the structures of local government and then to group the systems of the various countries by these factors. Among the more obvious reasons why it is not practical to do this, however, are the variation in the structures of local governments within the individual countries and the extent to which the more easily discernible superficial structural factors are not always an accurate reflection of the actual operation of the local government institutions.

The most practical method of arranging the countries appeared to be by geographical groups using such cultural factors as language and religion to aid in determining the boundaries between groups. This method recommends itself not only because of the greater ease in thus determining the groups, but more important because of the degree to which local government structures, and the way they operate, are aspects of the cultures of these countries. A geographical grouping of the countries in this survey appears to be a workable, although a somewhat arbitrary and imperfect, classification for convenient description. Accordingly the countries have been divided into the following major groups: Anglo-Saxon, North Europe, Central and North-West Europe, East Europe, South Europe, South and Central America, West Asia and North Africa, South Asia and East Africa, and East Asia.[1]

It will be interesting and useful in this chapter to survey local government in the various areas of the world, not only to describe the characteristics common to most or all of local government in the geographical groups, but also to report by which country or countries the countries of the geographical groups have been influenced. An effort will be made to summarize some of the more conspicuous common features of local government from a structural point of view in each of the nine geographical groups.

[1] As few as possible exceptions were made to this regional principle. The so-called Anglo-Saxon countries have been grouped together, though, since in every respect except geography they appear to make a useful group for the study of local government. Efforts were made to avoid miscellaneous or one-country groups; therefore, some countries such as Japan, Greece, and Ethiopia have been grouped with other countries with which they have relatively little in common. There are, of course, some countries such as Luxembourg whose systems of local government have been affected by two or more cultural patterns and are therefore difficult to place into a group. Other countries such as those that have been formed by colonization tend to resemble their parent country as well as the other countries that have been colonized by this mother country.

In making such a comparison of the structure of local government in different geographical areas of the world one is struck by the extensive influence of one or more of five countries namely France, England, Spain, the United States, and in the past few years the Soviet Union. In some cases the local governments of whole geographical groups of countries show the profound influence of one, and sometimes two, of these five countries. For instance local governments in the South Europe and the West Asia – North Africa group have been influenced by France. And most of the South and Central American local governments show the result not only of the Spanish influence, but also of the influence of their North American neighbour, the United States.

In a few countries there was an almost complete adoption of the forms and system of local government of one of these five countries. In Italy, for instance, local government was in the latter part of the 19th century an almost complete imitation of that of France. In other countries some features of the forms of local government of one of these five countries were adapted gradually over a long period of time.

In some cases this adoption or adaptation was due to the novelty and apparent usefulness of the characteristics. In many cases, of course, the features were logical developments which were not particularly novel, but nevertheless the role of each of these five countries in the world political situation at some particular period in history put them in a pivotal position to have an influence upon the local government as well as other aspects of the cultures in other countries. Interrelated with the position of these few countries as world powers was the fact that each of the four languages of these five countries is understood widely by people of many countries either as a mother or secondary tongue. The world-wide use of the French and English languages, in particular, has made them convenient conveyances for the spread of the features of government, including local government, as found in France, the United Kingdom, and also the United States. A more important factor, though, accounting for the spread of some of the characteristics of the Spanish, English, and French local government was the role of each of these countries as a colonial power.

1. The Anglo-Saxon group

The Anglo-Saxon group includes the United Kingdom, Australia, the Union of South Africa, Canada and the United States. Protestantism (and Anglicanism) is the major religious ideology and English is the (or a) major tongue in each of these countries. Each of the countries has been a part of the British empire and has been populated to a significant degree by British immigrants. Moreover, in each of these countries the council-committee form of local government as developed in England is widely used.

Local government as it has evolved in the United Kingdom has several distinctive features, among which are the extent to which the work is carried on by committees and the lack of a real executive organ. Perhaps the somewhat isolated position of the British Isles off the European continent partially accounts for many of the historic differences of local government between England and its European neighbours. Because of its position as a colonial power, however, many of the characteristics of British local government have been adopted for use in the local governments of several non-European countries, including those in the South Asian and East African group as well as those in the Anglo-Saxon group.

The popularly-elected council is the formal center of British local government. Its importance is made apparent by the fact that the county, borough, and district local governments are generally referred to as the "county councils", "borough councils," or "district councils." In the local units the authority for all municipal activity is vested in the councils, although the effective power is in the committees of council. British local government can, in fact, be described as government by, of, and through committees. The British local committees are probably the best known examples of administering committees which not only prepare decisions for the council but also act to implement the programs which have been agreed upon. Usually the council is content merely to review and approve the actions of its committees. Over half of the English sub-municipalities (*parishes*) have popular assemblies.

Probably the most conspicuous and peculiar feature of British local government is its lack of executive organs. The U.K.

and almost all of the other Anglo-Saxon local units do not have a board which can harmonize the many activities of the various committees. More important, there is no real chief executive in the U.K. local government units. The department heads work directly with the individual committees and are not responsible to the mayor. The clerk and, to a lesser extent, the treasurer, are virtually the only officials charged with the over-all co-ordination of local activities. In the other Anglo-Saxon countries the mayor generally has a stronger role.

In Australia and South Africa the form of local government is almost identical to that in the United Kingdom. The council-elected mayors, however, are generally not so administratively impotent as their U.K. counterparts. Some of the more important factors interrelated with the stronger role of the mayor is the fact that in most cases he has a longer term of office, that he is usually re-elected to office and that the councils are smaller.

In the two English-speaking North American countries there is a wide variation in the municipal organizational structure. The council-committee (often called the "weak mayor") form which closely resembles the English model is the earliest type of municipal government structure and is still the most prevalent form in both the United States and Canada. It is used by almost all the counties, the rural municipalities, and a large number of the urban municipalities. Two other types of local government have also developed in Canada. One is the council-board form. The other is the council-manager type which spread from the United States.

In the United States one may distinguish four main forms of local government. In addition to the council-committee form there is also the council-mayor (usually called "strong mayor"), the council-manager, and the "commission" form. Further interesting features of the U. S. system of local government are the large number of special-purpose districts and the number of officials, such as clerks or treasurers, who are elected by direct popular vote.

In reaction to the lack of co-ordination inherent to the council-committee system many of the urban municipalities in the United States have developed the so-called strong mayor-council form of local government, which was modelled after the U. S. national government and incorporated the "separation of powers" concept. The so-called strong mayor, who is almost invariably popularly elected, is a chief executive with the authority and power to direct the municipal activities. It is the strong mayor-council form of U. S. local government, with the popularly elected mayor, which has been copied in many South American countries. Furthermore this strong mayor-council form of municipal government structure in the Philippines, Japan, and some parts of Germany, was to a certain extent developed in imitation of the United States version.

A few of the U. S. urban municipalities (less than 10%) still use the "commission" form of local government. In this form each of the elected members (three to seven) of a small council also serves as a department head.

The most recently developed and most rapidly spreading form of municipal government in the United States is the council-manager form. The professional manager is appointed by the council, usually from outside the municipality. One of the council members serves as council chairman and as ceremonial head, the degree of power which he exercises varies widely. Generally he exerts very little leadership and the manager is the chief executive, in some cities though the mayor has considerable power.

2. *The North Europe group*

The North Europe, or Scandinavian group, consists of Norway, Sweden, Finland, Denmark and Iceland. All of them are Protestant countries and in each of them a Germanic tongue is officially accepted, although the leading language in Finland is non-Germanic. These five countries have had long inter-connected political histories. In fact, a major part of the life-span of each country has been spent as a part of political union with another. The Scandinavian countries present an excellent example of a simultaneous inter-related development of local government institutions in neighbouring countries with similar cultures. The local governments in each country have evolved in a similar fashion: each has benefited greatly from each other's experiments. The current trend toward larger municipalities and a uniform system is an evident manifestation of this tendency toward mutual interchange of ideas.

As in the United Kingdom, the North European local governments depend to a great extent on administering committees. A conspicuous difference, however, is that in the North European countries there is also a chief executive and a board. In each of the North European countries the board, which is chaired by the chief executive, plays a prominent role in the process of government in all or most of the municipalities. It initiates most council actions, co-ordinates the work of the committees, and guides and supervises the work of the staff.

The resemblance in structure is particularly obvious among the Norwegian, Swedish and Finnish local government units. In each of these three countries the municipalities have been consolidated and are therefore adequately sized. Although in these countries there is still a legal distinction made between urban and rural municipalities, the differences are relatively minor. The forms of municipal government in each of these three countries are also quite similar. Each municipality has a council, administering committees, a board, and a board chairman who is the chief executive. Furthermore there is a chief administrative officer in most of these local units who plays an important role in advising on policy matters as well as in co-ordinating the activities of the staff.

In Denmark and Iceland there is a clear distinction between urban and rural municipalities, the latter generally have a small number of inhabitants. In many respects the local governments are similar to those of their Scandinavian neighbours. Administering committees are composed largely of non-council members as in the other Scandinavian countries; however, boards are not used in the rural units and only in some of the urban municipalities. The council chairman, who is also the chairman of the board in those units which has one, is assisted in his executive functions by a chief administrative officer, usually the finance director acts in this capacity.

3. The Central and North-West Europe group

The Central and North-West Europe group includes Germany, Austria, and Switzerland as well as the Netherlands, Belgium and Luxembourg. A Germanic tongue is the official language or one of the official languages of each country. For purposes of description, this group may best be divided into three parts. The linguistic, cultural, and often the political ties between Germany and Austria have been exceptionally close. The local governments in the Netherlands, Belgium, and Luxembourg have many features in common. Swiss local government has many distinctive characteristics.

As in the Anglo-Saxon and North European groups, institutions of local representative government in the Central and North-West Europe countries have long, although sometimes interrupted, histories. In each of these countries the chief executive and the board has an important position in the structure of municipal government, and many of these executive organs have authority directly devolved to them by the central government. Unlike the North Europe and Anglo-Saxon units of local government, however, the Central and North-West Europe local units use their specialized committees for preparatory but not for administering tasks.

Until the 1930's both Germany and Austria had a council-board form of local government. Under Hitler, though, the form of government in both countries was one of a single administrator. After the war Austrian municipal government resumed the previous form of government in which the elected council selects a board and its chairman. In addition to being the council and board chairman, the Austrian mayor is also directly charged with certain functions by the central government. In the less populous municipalities he is usually the only full-time board member and is generally the dominant one; in the more populous municipalities the other board members have more important duties and the role of the mayor is nearer to that of a *primus inter pares*.

In Germany many of the municipalities, especially the larger ones, have gone back to the council-board form of government with a strong chief executive. In other municipalities, there is a council and strong chief executive, but no board. Most chief executives are council elected, some are council appointed, a few are popularly elected.

Most of the Swiss municipalities have a popular assembly in addition to a council. A few others, generally the larger ones, do not have a popular assembly but they do have a board. In either case the smaller organ has the central co-ordinating role for directing the activities of the staff organs and for taking the initiative in the discussions in the larger one.

In the Benelux countries, the Netherlands, Belgium and Luxembourg, the authority of the municipality is divided among three organs: the council, the board, and the mayor who is the chairman of both the other organs. In all three countries the mayor is centrally appointed, but whereas in the Netherlands this official is an experienced public administrator, in Belgium the appointee is almost invariably a councilman who has been recommended by the majority, or majority coalition, of the local council. The Luxembourg local government code is almost identical to the Belgian; both local governments operate in many respects like the French.

4. *The East Europe group*

The East Europe group includes the Soviet Union, Poland, Bulgaria and Yugoslavia. In each of these countries a Slavic tongue is the leading language. More important, in each of these countries Communism is the official ideology, which forms the philosophical basis of all society, including government structure. Communism first developed its governmental institutions in Russia. Since the end of World War II the other East Europe countries became People's Democracies and their local governments, not surprisingly, have taken on a remarkable resemblance to the Soviet model. There are probably no countries included in this survey in which the extra-structural aspects of local government, namely the party, play a more important role.

The local councils in each of these countries have a relatively large number of members. Nominees for the council seats are mostly selected by the various factory and other local vocational associations, after which they are approved by the party, and are then presented for election to the voters. In the U.S.S.R. there are only as many candidates on the ballot as there are seats to be filled.

In each of these countries the local council makes extensive use of committees which play an active role in administering the local public activities. Many of these committees undertake duties which in other countries would be functions of private enterprise, or other non-governmental institutions. Most of the members of these committees are appointed from outside the council, thus increasing the participation of the local residents in local government. Committees are responsible for their duties not only to the local council and board, but also to the parallel committees in the next higher units.

The actual direction and control of the public business in Russian, Bulgarian, and Polish local units is centralized in the board, which in rural municipalities may consist only of the chairman, vice-chairman, and secretary.[1] This body conducts the day-to-day business and passes ordinances in the name of the council. Among the East European countries in this survey, only the Yugoslav municipalities do not have boards; there the mayor and secretary alone perform the over-all directing role. The Yugoslav municipalities are unique in that they have bicameral councils.

One interesting feature of the Russian local government system is that the secretary is chosen from the ranks of the council members, thus he is an elected official rather than a career officer. This is a carry-over from the original revolutionary ideas of government by the workers. Usually these elected officers are re-elected for many terms.

Perhaps the best summary of Russian local government is that the underlying principle appears to be "the encouragement of the interest, participation and initiative of the citizens while retaining complete central control and central direction of general policy in all respects."[2] Although one finds many close resemblances between the formal structures of the East European and North European local governments, actually they operate in far

---

[1] Note, though, the role of the chairman of the popular assembly in the Polish rural municipalities; see page 115.
[2] Barfivala, C. D., *Local Government in the U.S.S.R.* (Bombay 1958), p. 5.

different ways. In the East European countries the forms of local representative government are present, but the important decisions are in many cases made by the party organs outside of the formal government structure.

5. *The South Europe group*

The South Europe group includes France, Italy and Greece as well as Spain and Portugal. Except for Greece the major religious faith in each of the South European countries is Roman Catholic and the major tongue a Latin one. Compared to the other European countries the competence of the municipalities is generally limited and the effect of the powers of the central government to review is more severe. In all of these countries the mayor is the dominant force and he has a large measure of authority directly devolved by the central government. There is, however, a sharp contrast between the French and Spanish mayors. Whereas the former is council-elected and depends on the support of the council for continuing in office, the latter is appointed by the central government or other higher units and is not dependent upon a representative organ.

France and Spain have had a particularly noticeable role in influencing the development of forms of government in other countries. During the French Revolution there were several experiments with a comprehensive system of uniform municipalities. Later, under Napoleon the local government system was re-drafted and given the foundation of its present form. Since that time no country has had its local government institutions so widely and so closely copied as has France. They have been imitated not only in countries which have been part of the French Empire, but also in many others. During the course of the nineteenth century several South European countries, and to a more limited extent other European countries, set up over-all systems of local government and adopted many of the features of the French system. Since the late nineteenth century local government along French lines has appeared to be particularly well adapted to the less-developed countries as they have begun setting up over-all systems of local representative government, partially because local representative government as it is known in the South European countries combines a relatively large degree of the structural characteristics of local representative government with a minimum opportunity to make what the central government organs would consider to be wrong decisions. In fact, in many cases local government in these countries has developed with many of the same steps as it did in France.

Under the French municipal system as it was set up under Napoleon, all of France was divided into municipalities (*communes*) each of which had the same legal status and the same form of government. Originally each municipality was administered by a chief executive (*maire*) aided by an advisory council, both of which were appointed. By 1831, the council was elected. The basic law on municipal administration passed in 1884, provided for a mayor elected by the council. Furthermore, the council was no longer only advisory. Thus is traced the development of a system of local government from one of local agencies of the central government to local units with a measured degree of representative government.

The power in the French municipality remains, however, focused in the local chief executive, who is accountable not only to the council for carrying out its decisions but also to the central government for the functions which are directly devolved to him. The mayor in France also has a stronger position in regard to his fellow board members (assistant mayors or *adjoints*) than does his counterpart in such countries as Germany or Sweden. One might contrast the north Europe board members and the French *adjoints* by calling the former colleagues and the latter assistants. The principal administrative collaborator of the mayor is the secretary or secretary-general who is the hierarchical superior of the department heads.

The remarkable similarity between French and Italian local government is the result of a conscious and virtually complete imitation by Italy of the French system. By the latter part of the nineteenth century, when Italy emerged as a unified nation and was interested in creating order out of the chaos of local government institutions, the system of local government in France was fully developed. The relatively minor differences which one finds between the two systems today are almost entirely a result of changes made since that time.

Greek local government has also been closely modelled along the French pattern. It does not, however, have a uniform municipal system. In the urban municipalities the popularly-elected mayor is aided by a board; in the rural municipalities the council-elected mayor is not.

There is a marked contrast between the institutions of local government in Spain and Portugal and those in the other European countries. These co-inhabitants of the Iberian peninsula speak similar languages and have similar cultural institutions. Most of both countries was under Arab domination from the eighth to the thirteenth century and this fact still appears to be reflected in some respects in their cultural and political tone. Local government institutions in these countries tend to resemble the earlier less representative eighteenth century French institutions rather than the forms which were developed later. In fact there appears to be a close inter-relationship between the type of government at the local level and that of the national. The local power is to a very great extent focused in the mayor (*alcalde*) who is a political appointee of the central government and is the head of the local branch of the sole political party. In Portugal, whose municipalities are fairly large, the local councils are elected by vocational groups, but only the boards and the chief executives have any significant authority. The Spanish municipal councils, which are elected in part by the heads of families and in part by the various trade and vocational groups, have only a limited authority. There are "boards" in some of the more populous municipalities; however, the board members (other than the chief executive) are not elected by the council but appointed by the chief executive, albeit from among the members of the council.

The role of Spain as a colonial power during the sixteenth to the eighteenth century did much to prepare the way for the spread of an Iberian-type of local government to Latin America and the Philippines. Likewise Portugal played an important role in Brazil.

6. *The South and Central America group*

The South and Central America countries included in the survey are Brazil, Ecuador, Colombia and El Salvador. Each of these countries, except Brazil, was a part of the colonial empire of Spain. In Brazil, which was a colonial possession of Portugal, Portuguese is the major tongue. Spanish is the major tongue in the other countries; Roman Catholicism is the major religious faith in all of these countries.

The local government institutions of South and Central America are partially influenced by three different factors. First of all each country has an Iberian heritage, which is still deeply ingrained in the Latin American way of life. Secondly, the underdeveloped condition of a large part of these countries has retarded the growth of responsible units of local representative government.

The third influence is that of the United States. Many of the South and Central American governmental institutions, both central as well as local, have been more recently, in some cases strongly and in other cases only superficially, influenced by the example of their North American neighbour. The formal framework of the national government of many of the Latin American republics is similar to the United States presidential system. The extent to which this influence extends to the local government institutions varies in the different countries.

Brazilian local government is one of the most interesting examples of how characteristics of the Iberian and North American government have been synthesized. Brazil has a federal constitutional system, and it has a mayor-council form of local government in which the mayor is directly elected, similar to that in the U. S. cities with a strong mayor-council form of local government. Like Portugal, though, Brazil has a uniform system of municipalities, which are generally quite large, and rather populous, and which are divided into sub-municipal units.

In El Salvador, too, one finds an interesting combination of features of local government. Each municipality in this uniform system has an elected council and a popularly elected mayor who is automatically a member and the chairman of the council. Usually he dominates the council but his role in the staff activities depends on the influence of the chief administrative officer.

In Ecuador and Colombia the forms of local government are not as similar to the North American models. Although each of the municipalities has a council, the local chief executive, who is not the council chairman, is centrally appointed. The Ecuador basic units are divided into sub-municipal units and in a few of the larger cities, the locally elected council chairman has some executive duties.

7. *The West Asia and North Africa group*

The West Asia and North Africa group, often called the Near and Middle East, includes Tunisia, Turkey, the Lebanon, and Iran. All are Islamic countries, most countries are Arab or Arab-influenced, much of the area of all five countries is barren. The influence of French local government in this area is pointed out by W. Hardy Wickwar:

> "All countries of the Near and Middle East ... have a hierarchy of administrative sub-divisions reaching from the centre to the field. Systematized in France and other parts of Continental Europe during the generation of the Revolution and Bonaparte, this pattern has spread over the Near and Middle East reaching Mohammed Ali's Egypt in 1826, Rashid Pasha's Ottoman Empire by the 1840's and Riza shah Pahlevi's Iran in 1937."[1]

In each of these countries there is a large degree of centralized authority. The local power is mostly focused in the local mayor or headman who almost invariably dominates the council, where one exists. Many local units, however, have no representative government in any form.

The forms of government at the basic level in Turkey and the Lebanon are very similar. The urban municipal governments of both countries are modelled after that of France. In both countries, too, the urban municipalities are geographically divided into sub-municipal units, which, however, are general-purpose administrative sub-divisions of the intermediate units, not of the municipalities. The rural units in each country are administered by a locally selected headman (*Mukhtar* or *Muhtar*) whose ap-

[1] Wickwar, *Revue Internationale des Sciences Administratives*, Vol. XXIV, No. 2 (1958), 148.

pointment is officially made by the higher units. He is assisted by a locally selected council with traditional duties. A large part of the work of the local executive in both the urban and rural units is carrying out duties which are directly devolved to him by the central government.

In Tunisia, which just recently won its independence from France, the urban municipal structure and councils are modelled closely after their French counterparts. There are, however, no councils in the rural areas. The rural basic units are directly administered by one man, who is recommended by the leading persons of the area and appointed by the provincial officials.

In Iran local representative government is just beginning. The national statute authorizing its establishment in the urban basic units was passed in 1955; it is not yet possible, however, to foresee how it will operate. At present the majority of municipalities have few functions; the central government still directly administers most activities through the intermediate units.

8. *The South Asia and East Africa group*

The South Asia and East Africa group includes India, Ceylon, Malaya, and Burma, as well as the Sudan and Ethiopia. With the exception of Ethiopia, these countries are former parts of the British Empire which have achieved independence since World War II. In each of them the British influence has had a telling effect on the development of institutions of local representative government, especially in the urban areas.

In India contact with the West has undermined and at least partially destroyed the indigenous local representative governing institutions. The Indian village councils began to decline in power soon after the Muslim conquest of India. They did not wholly die out, however, and were still functioning when the British conquered India several centuries later. It was the nineteenth century extension of the modern central government control even to the remote villages that finally led to their disappearance. The servants of the village community such as the headman and the watchman became the servants, and often the nominees, of the faraway central government carrying out its orders. The judicial, revenue, and police functions of the villages were taken over, often completely, by government officials. In the absence of any important functions formal local representative government by a council of elders trying disputes, collecting revenues and coordinating public works projects virtually ceased.[1] Impelled by new legislation the number of formally constituted local councils with governing powers has greatly increased since India's independence. There are over 100,000 rural councils and the plan is eventually to cover all of rural India with such bodies.

It is in the urban units that the similarity of the Indian forms of local government to the U. K. ones is most pronounced. While still under British rule the urban municipalities already had a council with a typically English maze of committees. Now, though, there is usually an official in whom some degree of executive power is focused. In many cases he is an elected mayor who may be described as a quasi-chief executive. In many of the larger urban municipalities the chief executive is an official appointed by higher units, usually called "commissioner."

In Ceylon units of local representative government cover almost all the island. As in India the form of government is the council-committee one in which the council-elected mayor generally plays a more influential role than does his English counterpart. Furthermore, the chief administrative officer, who is appointed by a centrally organized Local Government Service Commission, has a relatively stronger role than the English clerk.

In Malaya, too, the urban municipalities have the English council-committee form of government. The chief executive is generally appointed by the state government and is therefore in a strong position. Much of the rural area in Malaya is directly administered by the centrally appointed district heads.

Burmese local government has also developed along British lines. The urban municipalities have the council-committee form of government, but until recently there was no local representative government in the rural areas. A program to develop these rural units, however, has recently been commenced; it has yet to be seen how successful the program will be. In many of the South Asian as well as East African countries, traditions of authority and paternalism, the illiteracy and passivity of the

[1] Srinivasan, *FEQ*, XV, No. 2. (Feb. 1956), 204–5.

people, the lack of trained cadres and financial stringency have combined to perpetuate the *status quo*. The local organs have been regarded almost wholly as agents for the central government which has insured their docility by keeping the local unit in a state of chronic financial dependence.[1]

Sudanese local government presents a varied picture. Large areas of the country, particularly in the southern parts, have not been organized into municipalities and are directly administered by district-heads in many cases working through local chiefs and headmen. Over fifty municipalities, which cover a large area and have consequently large populations, are organized. They are set up along the lines of the British local councils, with a committee form of government. The mayor, however, plays a relatively more important role as the focus of political power.

In Coptic Christian Ethiopia, most of the urban councils have only limited powers and the chief executives are central government appointees. There are no local representative organs at all in the rural areas.

9. *The East Asia group*

The East Asia group includes Thailand, the Philippines, and Japan. In each of these countries the factors affecting the development of local government have been quite different.

The over-all system of local government in Thailand is modelled after the French hierarchy and the urban municipal structure is a copy of the French municipalities. In the rural areas a pattern of rural municipalities is being developed from a system of administration by headmen.

Superficially the Philippine municipal structure closely resembles the American strong mayor-council form. The role of the popularly elected mayor, however, is limited. Each of the municipal department heads is appointed by and is responsible to the head of the parallel department at the provincial or nation-

---

[1] Thompson, Virginia, "Rural and Urban Self-Government in South-East Asia," Emerson, Rupert, *Representative Government in South East Asia* (Cambridge, Mass. 1955), pp. 118–9.

al level. The mayor's effective power depends almost solely upon his relationship with the department heads, and this in turn depends on his political connections with the provincial or national political leaders.

Japan's local government structure, like the country, is more fully developed than that of most of the other Asian countries. Before the last war the local government system was similar in many respects to the French. As a result of the American occupation, however, many changes were forced on the system to make it conform, at least in the more superficial structural aspects, with the American strong mayor-council form of government. Now that the occupation is ended, however, the Japanese are slowly eliminating from the system those post-war non-indigenous aspects which are most inconsistent with the basic tone of their local government system. A high degree of centralization has gradually returned in fact, if not in theory. Most of the local executive power is now centered in the mayor, who is still popularly elected.

(I)

THE ANGLO SAXON GROUP

THE UNITED KINGDOM*

IN England and Wales local government began in the small Anglo-Saxon townships where rights and privileges, which ultimately became charters of incorporation, were given first by the local feudal lords and subsequently by the King. Towards the end of the 11th century the shires, which formed the bases of the present counties, came into existence as military units and in the 13th century Justices of the Peace, who gradually came to possess a variety of administrative duties, were first commissioned by the Crown to keep the peace. Under the Municipal Corporations Acts of 1835 and 1882 the constitution of the ancient municipal corporations was made uniform and those that had lost their mediaeval importance were abolished; since then many additional boroughs have been created by royal charter.

In 1888 the county councils were created and given the administrative functions formerly exercised in the counties by the Justices of the Peace. At the same time the larger boroughs were called county boroughs because in their areas the county councils have no concern with local administration. Shortly afterwards, in 1894, urban and rural district councils were set up to provide services in the remainder of the county outside the boroughs, in what were formerly the urban and rural sanitary districts, and

---

* This summary on local government in the United Kingdom is somewhat different from the set-up and wording of the other summaries. This was done at the request of the British Section of the International Union of Local Authorities which felt that a description on the basis of the other country summaries might give a mis-representation.

UNITED KINGDOM

PATTERN OF GOVERNMENT UNITS

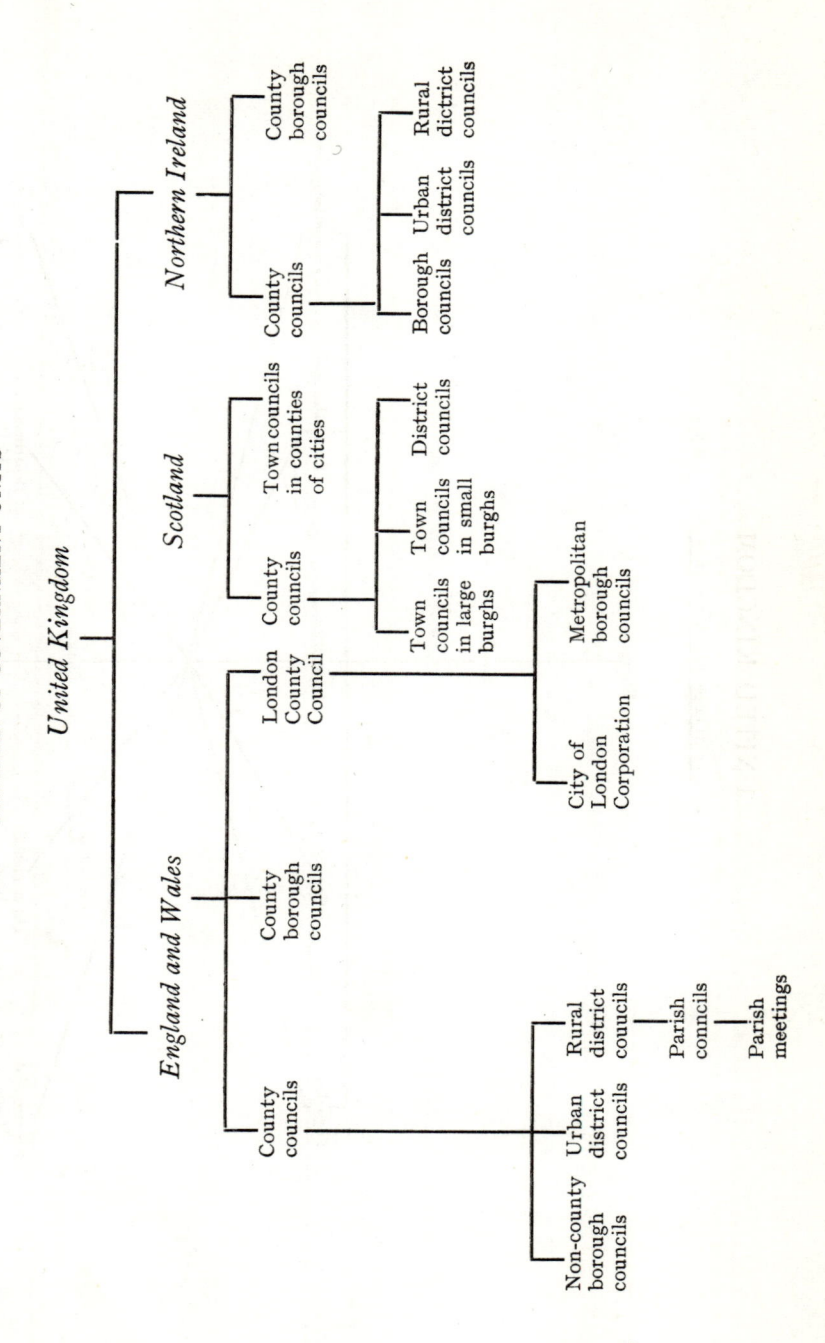

United Kingdom

- *England and Wales*
  - County councils
    - Rural district councils
      - Parish councils
        - Parish meetings
    - Urban district councils
    - Non-county borough councils
  - County borough councils
  - London County Council
    - Metropolitan borough councils
    - City of London Corporation
- *Scotland*
  - County councils
    - Town councils in large burghs
    - Town councils in small burghs
    - District councils
  - Town councils in counties of cities
- *Northern Ireland*
  - County councils
    - Borough councils
    - Urban district councils
    - Rural district councils
  - County borough councils

UNITED KINGDOM

STRUCTURE OF LOCAL AUTHORITIES

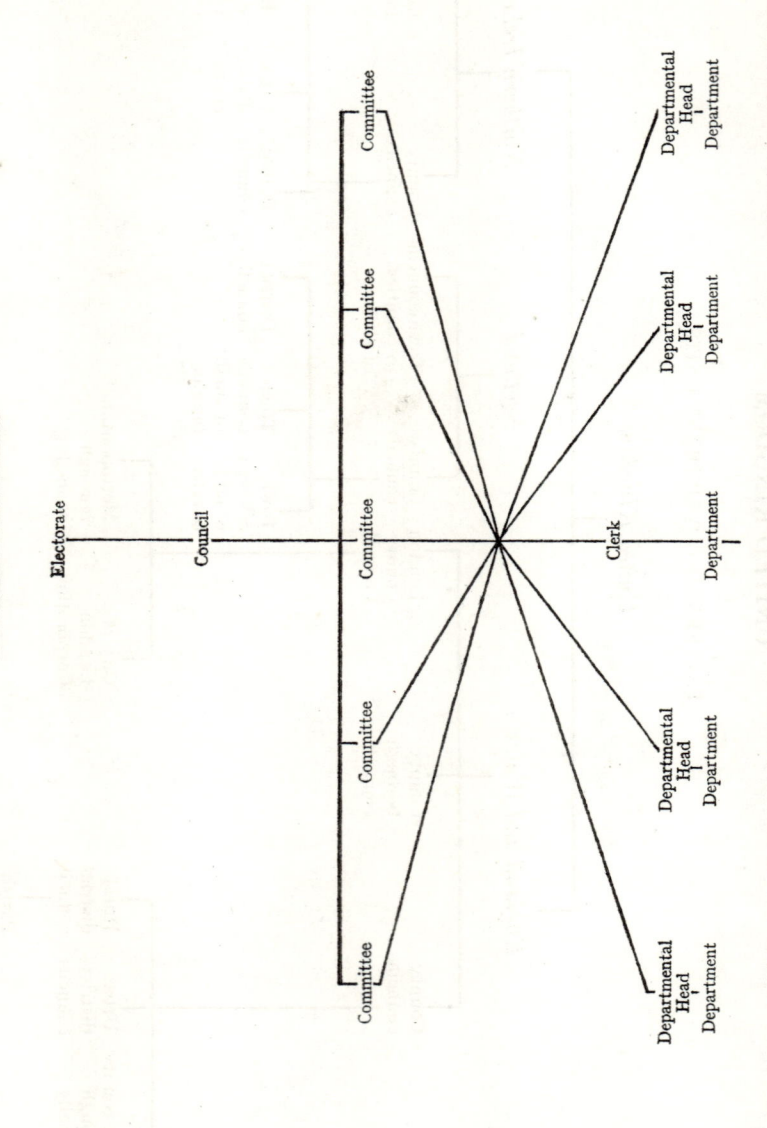

Electorate

Council

Committee — Committee — Committee — Committee — Committee

Clerk

Department

Departmental Head — Department

Departmental Head — Department

Departmental Head — Department

Departmental Head — Department

parish councils were created in the majority of the parishes into which the rural districts were divided.

The earliest known exercise of local management of local affairs in Scotland was that practised in the burghs established as trading communities in the early part of the 12th century. During the 15th and 16th centuries numerous merchant guilds and councils of burgesses took upon themselves the ordering of local affairs and it was this tradition of local self-rule that afforded the framework on which local government in Scotland was built.

In the 19th century many local separate bodies were established in Scotland to provide individual services but were later merged into authorities responsible for a number of services, including the county councils which were created in 1889 in the mediaeval sheriffdoms. The abolition in 1929 of many of the smaller units of administration further simplified the structure of local government in Scotland.

Local government was first introduced in Northern Ireland in 1835 by the Municipal Corporations Act, and since 1898 the development of local government there has been on similar lines to that in England and Wales.

ENGLAND AND WALES

Counties, Urban Municipalities and Rural Local Authorities[1]

England and Wales are divided into administrative counties and county boroughs. Each county borough has a single council responsible for all services within its area but the counties contain non-county boroughs (metropolitan boroughs in the area of the London County Council), urban districts and, generally, rural districts; and the rural districts are further divided into parishes. The county council is responsible for certain services over the whole administrative county (i.e., the geographical county excluding the county boroughs), and the non-county and metropolitan borough councils, the urban district councils, and the rural district councils are responsible for other services within their own areas. All these authorities are independent of each other.

---

[1] The rural local authorities in the United Kingdom correspond to the rural municipalities in other countries and as defined in Part 1.

COUNTY COUNCILS – Three-quarters of the members of a county council (six-sevenths of the members of the London County Council) are directly elected for a term of office of three years. The remainder are aldermen who are elected by the councillors from among themselves or other persons qualified to be councillors – generally those who have given distinguished service to the locality. The aldermen serve for six years, half their number retiring every three years with the councillors. There is no distinction between the duties of aldermen and councillors.

The chairman of the council is elected by the councillors, generally from among themselves although the chairman may be some other person who is qualified to be a member. He serves for one year, during which he is ex officio a Justice of the Peace. The council also appoints a vice-chairman from among the members. The number of members of the council varies from 28 to 162.

The services for which county councils are normally responsible are education, the personal health services, the care of old people and of children deprived of a normal home life, libraries (except in London and in some boroughs and urban districts), town and country planning, main roads (and all roads in rural districts) and the fire service. In London the County Council's powers also include main drainage and housing. County councils may be required to delegate the maintenance, repair and improvement of main roads to non-county boroughs and urban district councils with a population of 20,000 or over. Under legislation passed in 1958 they may also be required to delegate various education, local health and welfare functions to non-county boroughs and urban district councils with a population of 60,000 or over. In addition, outside London and Middlesex and parts of the adjoining counties which make up the Metropolitan Police District, the authority responsible for the police service in a county is the standing joint committee comprised of equal numbers of members of the county council and of the Justices of the Peace for the county.

COUNTY BOROUGH, NON-COUNTY AND METROPOLITAN BOROUGH COUNCILS[1] – County boroughs are the larger boroughs which usually, but not always, have a population of 75,000 or

[1] There are 28 metropolitan boroughs and the City of London within the County of London. The City of London Corporation has a constitution distinct from all other local authorities in the United Kingdom and is not described here.

more; boroughs can become county boroughs only by special Act of Parliament. Although having different powers and duties the county and non-county borough councils are identical in structure. The former have from 48 to 160 council members and the latter from 12 to 48; three-quarters of those council members are directly elected for a term of office of three years, one-third retiring each year. The other quarter of the members are aldermen who are elected by the councillors from among themselves or from among persons qualified to be councillors, for a term of six years, one-half of the aldermen retiring every three years. In the metropolitan boroughs, where the number of members varies from 30 to 60, only one-seventh of the members of the council are aldermen. There is no distinction between the powers and duties of aldermen and councillors.

The Mayor, or Lord Mayor as he is called in some boroughs (generally those which have been designated for historical or other reasons as cities), is elected by the members of the council from among themselves or from among persons qualified to be councillors. He generally serves a term of office of one year but is eligible for re-election. He takes precedence over all other persons, with the exception of the Sovereign or his representatives, within the borough and is ex officio a Justice of the Peace. If he wishes, the mayor may appoint a deputy from among the members who may carry out any of the mayor's duties, except that he may not preside at council meetings unless he is specifically authorised to do so.

The county borough councils are all-purpose authorities and have all the powers and duties of a non-county borough council and of a county council. In addition, all the county borough councils, except the three in the London Metropolitan Police District (and also a few of the larger non-county borough councils) are responsible for the police service within their territory. The non-county borough, metropolitan borough, urban district and rural district councils share responsibility for services in their area with the county council.

The services for which non-county borough councils are responsible include housing, the supply of water, the provision of sewers, the suppression of nuisances, minor roads and bridges, supervision of buildings, parks and open spaces, baths and washhouses, museums and libraries.

URBAN AND RURAL DISTRICT COUNCILS – All the members of both the urban and rural district councils are directly elected for a term of three years and, unless the county council at the request of the district council directs otherwise, one third of the councillors retire every year. The chairman of the council is elected each year by the members of the council from among themselves or from persons qualified to be council members. He is eligible for re-election, and is ex officio a Justice of the Peace. The services provided by the urban and rural district councils are similar to those provided by the non-county borough councils, except that the rural district councils are not responsible for highways, bridges or libraries.

Sub-Municipal Units

PARISH COUNCILS AND PARISH MEETINGS – In every rural parish there is a popular assembly called the parish meeting; where there are 300 or more residents a parish council is elected every three years. If the population is below 300 a parish council can be elected if called for by the parish meeting, but the county council may decline to arrange this if the population is below 200. The parish council has from 5 to 21 members, and the chairman is elected by the council members from among themselves or from those qualified to be council members. Where there is no parish council the parish meeting is held twice a year and has some of the powers of a parish council. The parish council is able to provide local amenities, including the provision of allotments, village halls, playing fields, public seats and bus shelters, street lighting and the upkeep of footpaths, but has a very limited power to spend money.

SCOTLAND

Counties, Urban Municipalities and Rural Local Authorities[1]

In Scotland there are four burghs which are called counties of cities, whose town councils are all-purpose authorities analogous to the county borough councils in England and Wales. The re-

[1] See footnote on p. 209.

mainder of Scotland is divided into counties which contain burghs, generally both large and small, and districts. The county council is responsible for most services throughout the county; the town councils of the large and small burghs are responsible for some services within their own area; and the district councils carry out certain limited functions similar to those of the parish councils in England and Wales.

COUNTY COUNCILS – The county councils consist of from 20 to 95 members, some of whom are directly elected to represent the landward areas (i.e., those portions of the county not included in a burgh) and some represent the burghs. The latter councillors are elected by the town councils from among their own members and they participate in matters affecting the burghs which come under the administration of the county council. Presiding over the county council is the Convener who is elected from among the councillors to serve for three years and is ex officio a Justice of the Peace. There is also a vice-convener who is appointed by the council from among the members.

The services for which the county council is responsible include (1) in the large burghs – education, rating valuation and in some instances police; (2) in the small burghs – education, town and country planning, the personal health services, the care of old people and of children deprived of a normal home life, the fire service, rating valuation, classified roads and police. In the landward areas the county council is responsible for all the services except those which are entrusted by Parliament to the district councils, which may also be appointed by the county council as its agents in carrying out certain of its functions in their districts.

TOWN COUNCILS IN COUNTIES OF CITIES AND LARGE AND SMALL BURGHS – Elections are held annually, one-third of the members retiring every year. The council (which has from 8 to 113 members) is presided over by the Lord Provost or Provost, elected by the members from among themselves for a term of three years. The members of the council also elect a number of bailies, and the Lord Provost, or Provost, and the bailies are the magistrates concerned with the administration of justice of the county of city, or the burgh, during their term of office. With one exception the large burghs are those with a population of 20,000 or over, and their services include housing, the personal health services, the care of children deprived of a normal home life and of old people, the supply of water, the provision of sewers, the suppression of nuisances, town planning, and classified roads. The small burghs are responsible for housing, unclassified roads, the supply of water, the provision of sewers, the suppression of nuisances, and the provision of local amenities.

DISTRICT COUNCILS – The district councils are composed of the county councillors representing the area of the district, who are ex officio members of the council, and other district councillors who are directly elected for a term of three years. The total number of members of the council varies from 7 to 33. The chairman and the vice-chairman are elected by the members of the council from among themselves, and the chairman is ex officio a Justice of the Peace. The district council is responsible for services connected with social and physical recreation, such as the provision of playing fields, open spaces and village halls, and for the upkeep of footpaths. It may also provide places of public entertainment. In addition, the district council may be appointed as the agent of the county council to provide any of that council's services within the district, with the exception of education and police.

NORTHERN IRELAND

The structure of local government in Northern Ireland is similar to that in England and Wales, except that there are no *parish councils*. For all councils elections are held every three years; the aldermen are directly elected and hold office for three years like the councillors; and the mayor or chairman is always elected from among the members of the council, and is not ex-officio a Justice of the Peace.

General

As a general rule all local authorities in the United Kingdom have only the powers which have been granted to them by an Act of Parliament; such powers may be granted by ordinary statutes (general Acts) or by local Acts which apply only to a particular local authority. Anything that is then done outside these stated powers is beyond the competence of the local authorities and is thus *ultra vires*.

One of the outstanding features of local government in the United Kingdom is the appointment of statutory and permissive committees which administer the various services. In addition to councillors, members of the statutory committees often must include persons from the community with special knowledge of the work of the committees, e.g., education. Although the other committees too may have co-opted members up to not more than one-third of the total number of members, relatively little use is made of this power to include persons who are not members of the council.

Both the method of selecting councillors and co-opted members to serve on committees and the degree to which the committees have delegated functions vary between local authorities. Some committees have very extensive powers, although none may borrow money nor levy a rate. In general the work of the committees is to examine in detail specific proposals and to consider the advice of the staff on these matters. Although it is not always done, it is customary for the committees' minutes to be submitted to the next meeting of the council for information or approval, depending on the degree of delegation.

The committee chairman has considerable importance and is generally given authority to make decisions on urgent matters which arise between the committee meetings. Sometimes he is selected by the committee because he is a senior member of the council or because he is an alderman, or he may be chosen by the major political group. In some councils the chairmen of the committees form an unofficial policy committee within the major political group. Although the mayor or other chairman of the council is generally not a committee chairman, he is usually ex-officio a member of all committees.

All local authorities have the power to appoint such staff as are necessary to carry out their work and they have a statutory obligation to appoint such officers as the clerk of the council (or similar officer) who is the chief administrative officer of the local authority and is responsible for the conduct of council business.

The clerk is often a solicitor, in which case he is also the council's chief legal officer. The council's financial officer is the treasurer (or similar officer); he advises on the financial implication of proposals, collates the annual estimates and acts as chief accountant and internal auditor. Appointment and dismissal of some chief officers are subject to the approval of the central government.

Whereas no local council is supervised by another local council, there is nevertheless considerable co-operation between them and many schemes exist for services to be carried out jointly by two or more councils. Furthermore, some members serve concurrently on the county council and on a borough or district council and are thus fully informed on the problems and needs of both.

As for the relationship between local and central government authorities, a considerable proportion of expenditure by local councils comes from grants by the central government. Moreover, money needed for the purchase of land or for capital building works can be borrowed only with the consent of the central government or of Parliament. Other money needed which is not covered by the grants, borrowing, or income from municipal housing, etc., is raised by means of rates on the occupiers of property which are fixed by central government valuers in England, Wales and Northern Ireland (in Scotland the basis is established by lands valuation assessors appointed by county councils and town councils of counties of cities). Appeals from the assessment of rateable value may be made to a special tribunal and ultimately to the courts.

The accounts of all councils, with the exception of certain accounts of most borough councils in England and Wales, are audited annually by auditors appointed by the central government. The residents have an opportunity to inspect the accounts and to raise objections which the auditor must consider; any item of expenditure disallowed as being not authorised by law is surcharged on the members or officers responsible for incurring it. These members or officers can then appeal to the central government, or, in respect of large amounts, to the courts.

Further local-central government relationships concern the making of statutory rules and orders pertaining to certain services by the central authorities, where such action is authorised by Act of Parliament, and the issue of explanatory circulars and memoranda of guidance. The latter are to insure that a service is maintained at the desired standard. In addition, some councils must have schemes for the general administration of a service approved, as is also the case for town planning schemes and by-laws. In some instances local governments may be required to submit reports and undergo periodic inspections for certain of their services. Should a local council default in the execution of a statutory duty the central government may carry it out itself by appointing commissioners or direct that it be undertaken by some other council; this power, however, is very rarely exercised.

AUSTRALIA

Australia, the smallest continent and the largest island in the world, was discovered by a Dutch explorer in the early 17th century. The nearby island of Tasmania, now one of the federated states, was discovered some 14 years later. It was not until after Captain Cook landed on the east coast of the mainland in 1770, however, that colonisation was begun in Sydney with the transportation to the new territory of English convicts. These settlers' numbers were rapidly increased by the immigration of free men who sought their fortunes in growing wool, and in the 1850's, in the search for gold. At this time, too, limited governmental responsibility was granted the colony by the mother country. In 1901 the Australian territories were federated and became a member nation in the British Commonwealth. As such the country is a sovereign self-governing parliamentary democracy based on the British model with the Queen as head of State. She, in turn, acts through her representatives, the Governor-General on the federal level, and the individual governors on the state level.

The Commonwealth of Australia, between one-half and two-thirds of whose territory is sparsely populated, is divided into six states and two territories. The latter are under the direct control of the central government, whereas the former are self-governing within the framework of the Commonwealth Constitution. Each state thus creates its own local government structure, which is a single-tier system in all but New South Wales; in this state there is, in addition, a number of county districts. The further subdivision of the urban local government units into *wards* and the rural areas into *ridings*, primarily for electoral purposes, is optional in some states and compulsory in others.

Urban and Rural Municipalities

Although there is no single system of local government throughout the Commonwealth of Australia, there is considerable similarity in structure and in character between the urban (variously called *municipality, municipal corporation area, borough, town* and *city*) and the rural units (called *shire, district, council district* and *road district*). In general, the former perform more diverse functions while the latter are primarily concerned with the construction and maintenance of roads and such additional services as are determined by the needs of the respective communities.

Local government functions cover the provision of such services as water supply, sewerage, gas and electricity, garbage collection and disposal, construction and maintenance of roads, control of land subdivision and erection of buildings, parks and recreation areas, libraries, mother and baby health centres and youth and cultural centres. Other services such as education, police, hospitals and with two exceptions housing, are provided by the state. Public transportation is also a function of the central government in each state, although Melbourne and Brisbane now manage their own tramway systems.

Each of the municipalities has a council ranging in size from five to a maximum of 24 members in the urban areas and 13 in the rural areas, who usually serve three-year terms of office with one-third retiring each year. In New South Wales and Queensland, however, all members of the councils retire at one time. Election is usually by plural-member and sometimes by single-member wards or ridings; in areas where these sub-divisions do not exist elections are at-large. In South Australian cities a combination of methods is used with the councilmen (*councillors*) being elected by wards and the aldermen being elected at-large. Councilmen are elected by simple majority in South Australia and Tasmania and in the rural areas of Western Australia. In all other instances the alternate vote system of election is used, an exception being in New South Wales when there are three or more vacancies to be filled. In these cases the list system of proportional representation is in effect.

Heading the council in all mainland municipalities is a chairman or mayor (*warden* in Tasmania) who may be either elected at-large or by the council from among its own members. In the rural areas the chairman or president is, with the exception of Queensland where he is elected at-large, selected by the council. The Lord Mayors of Sydney and Brisbane hold office for three years; the term of office of the chairmen of all other areas is one year.

The duties and functions of the chairman follow a similar pattern in each state as far as they relate to presiding at and conducting council meetings, giving effect to the resolutions of the council and carrying on the regular services of the council and authorising the payment of salaries and wages. In these respects the chairman is regarded as the chief executive and administrative functions repose in the town clerk. In other respects the duties and functions of the chairman vary from state to state and include the authorisation of urgent minor works within the limits of expenditure prescribed, the control, direction and suspension of municipal employees and, in Tasmania, the remission of rates, as established by the council. In New South Wales and in municipalities in Western Australia the mayor is ex-officio a member and chairman of each committee of the council. In Tasmania he is chairman of those committees of which he is a member; in other states he may be a member ex-officio of committees, but not necessarily the chairman.

In some of the more densely populated areas councils use standing or special committees to investigate problems relating to and to supervise the carrying out of such municipal activities as finance, public works, town planning, libraries and health. In New South Wales it is compulsory for a council to elect or appoint each year two standing committees, namely, the finance committee and the works committee. Unlike the British system, Australian committee members are not usually co-opted, although this is possible in certain cases in New South Wales and South Australia. In most other respects, however, there is great similarity between the committee systems of the two countries.

Acting as general administrative officer of the municipality and co-ordinator of its activities is a full-time clerk. Not a lawyer but an administrator, the clerk also acts as secretary of the council and is responsible to that body for the carrying out of its decisions. Other basic staff include the engineer (civil and electrical or gas if these two services are provided), health inspector and, in New South Wales, town and country planner.

On the whole, the sphere of competence of the Australian municipalities is limited in scope. Because they are creatures of the respective states their relationship with these and the central government is determined by the legislation which create them. It is unusual for the municipality to be used as an administrative agent of the state; for the most part the municipalities are charged with establishing and administering policy in those matters specifically delegated to them.

In the metropolises of the state capitals, with the exception of Brisbane, special boards and commissions undertake the management of port and harbour facilities, fire protection, public transportation and water and sewerage services and, over the whole of the state, the construction and maintenance of main arterial roads (as distinct from local roads) and the generation of electricity. Outside the areas controlled by these authorities councils own and operate many of the public utilities mentioned. Such authorities then act through commissions or boards which may be appointed by Parliament, elected by users of the services, or may be composed of a combination of appointed and elected members.

Within the limits of their respective charters local authorities in Australia are, in general, autonomous bodies subject to a varying degree of supervision of their activities by the respective state departments of local government. These departments make regulations governing such matters as municipal organisation, procedure at council meetings, qualifications and status of local officials, maintenance of accounts, general standards of administration, public health, control of building and many other activities. Moreover, all ordinances and regulations must have the governor's approval before they can be put into effect as must also all constitutional alterations, loans and certain other matters pertaining to finance. In addition, audits of accounts are made at least once each year and departmental inspectors of accounts carry out periodic inspections of accounts and internal municipal organisation and management. If justifiable circumstances arise from such inspections or for any other good reason the governor may dismiss the council concerned and provide substitute administration.

Counties

Unique to New South Wales under the Local Government Act of 1919 is the provision that groups of urban and rural municipalities, in whole or in part, may be constituted as county districts for the purpose of undertaking local government services or functions which, for technical or other reasons, must in many cases be carried out on a district or regional basis. Among these delegated functions are the supply of electricity, gas and water, town planning, flood control, the destruction of harmful weeds and the provision of abattoirs.

Each county district has a council composed of delegates who are elected by the municipal councils in the smaller counties and at-large in the larger county districts. Members' terms of office are three years and the councilmen elect one of their members as chairman each year. The chairman has responsibilities and functions similar to those of the municipal mayor. Considered an outstanding success, the 52 county districts in New South Wales now cover most of the state.

Still in the early stage of consideration is the establishment of regional councils to promote the interests of natural regions, although realisation of such a scheme can be seen only in the far future.

SOUTH AFRICA*

The Cape of Good Hope, the southern tip of Africa, was first used by Europeans as a refreshment stop for English and Dutch

* Information on local government structure and activities was received from only two of the four provinces of South Africa (Natal and the Orange Free State). However, Mr. D. P. Strydom, Secretary, United Municipal Executive of South Africa, stated in a letter of May 9, 1958, "I may state that although the local authorities in the Union are governed by separate ordinances in each of the 4 provinces, these ordinances are much the same in principle...."

ships going to and from the East. In 1652 the Dutch East India Co. established a permanent station at the Cape with trade as its main purpose, and ruled there until 1795, at which time Great Britain occupied the Cape for a three-year period and then three years later came to occupy it permanently. The 19th century in South Africa was one of expansion for the Cape Colony by means of annexation; in the early 20th century expansion resulted from war between Great Britain and the two republics which had been established by colonists who had moved out of the Cape Colony. This resulted in the establishment in 1910 of a Union whose boundaries remained the same to the present time.

The Union of South Africa is composed of five provinces (including South West Africa), each of which consists of urban and rural municipalities and territory that is directly administered by the province. In some provinces certain areas not within the municipalities may be designated as Health or Malaria Committees. Such areas then establish a government-type structure to carry on various health and public works activities.

Urban Municipalities (Boroughs)

South African municipalities are created by and responsible to the provincial governments, although certain activities such as public health, control of natives, housing, segregation, control of illegal squatting on land, and the equality of use of the Afrikaans and English languages by local authorities are regulated by acts of the Union parliament.

All urban municipalities have a council whose members are elected by majority vote from each of the *wards* into which the municipality may be divided. In most municipalities the maximum representation on the council for each of these wards is three councilmen. All serve a three-year term of office, with 1/3 being elected each year. Under provincial law a municipal councilman may be removed from office if he fails to attend two consecutive council meetings without reason or if he fails to attend two or three consecutive meetings of any committee of which he is a member. In some provinces, too, the law provides that whenever a council is below the number necessary for a quorum, through deaths, resignations or other reason, the chief executive officer of the province, the governor, may appoint persons to serve until a new council is elected or until the number of councilmen required for a quorum is elected.

In general, the powers of the council concern such matters as establishing a budget; acquiring and disposing of municipal property; constructing and maintaining roads, bridges, dams, irrigation works, pure water supply and drainage works, markets, cemeteries, abattoirs; and libraries, public parks, museums and art galleries. The council may also establish electricity and gas works, town planning and housing schemes, airports, hospitals, transport services and fire brigades, as well as erect, purchase or lease houses for municipal employees.

To help carry out its responsibilities the committee system is used by the municipal council. Usually members are appointed by the council from among its own members to serve on general or special purpose committees. Terms of office are, for the most part, one year and each committee elects its own chairman and vice-chairman to serve during this time. Among the most important of the committees is that of finance, which may control municipal expenditures through its power of approval. Usually, the committees investigate and present their findings to the council for its action, unless the larger body has delegated power to the committee to manage, regulate or conclude a matter itself.

One of the responsibilities of the municipal council is to elect a mayor who serves a one-year term of office. In addition to presiding over council meetings the mayor may also cast the deciding vote in case of a tie, call municipal-wide meetings to discuss important matters that may arise, act as the legal representative of the municipality, be ex-officio member of all council appointed committees, and serve as the municipality's ceremonial head. Usually he is assisted in his tasks by a deputy-mayor who is also elected by the council from among its own members.

To serve as the chief administrative officer of the municipality the council selects a Town Clerk to serve at its pleasure. He coordinates municipal activities and directly supervises daily administration. Other municipal officers appointed by the council may include a Treasurer, an Engineer, a Medical Officer and a Sanitary Inspector. In all provinces the dismissal of the Town Clerk and sometimes other officials is subject to the approval of the provincial governor (Administrator).

Control over urban municipalities by the provincial governments is extensive, and is exercised through the governor. Almost every action of the local governmental units must be approved, sometimes before it is put into effect and sometimes after according to the law. Any changes in municipal property, for example, must receive prior approval. In some provinces the governor may refer a resolution concerning such changes back to the council with instructions to submit it to a meeting of registered owners of property for further consideration, or he may refuse to grant permission, for a change, in which case council action is null and void. Also requiring approval prior to being put into effect are the by-laws pertaining to public health, native administration, building, traffic, and those governing the various municipal services. In most instances the governor may alter the council proposal in consultation with that body, as well as approve or reject it. In addition, municipal accounts are checked by a provincial auditor, as well as expenditures scrutinized for legality.

Upon the basis of a report from a mayor, town clerk or any citizen the governor may also investigate illegal actions of a municipal councilman during which time the councilman may be suspended from office. Upon completion of the investigation and the report of its findings, the governor may disqualify the councilman from sitting on the council or he may re-instate him. As was mentioned earlier, the governor may also appoint persons to serve on a municipal council that does not have a quorum, until such time as that quorum may be established. A further control in some provinces is the issuance of "standard by-laws" by the governor in any matter in which the council has authority, which may then be adopted by the council. These by-laws may be amended or rescinded by the governor at any time.

Rural Municipalities (Townships, Villages)

The provincial governor may declare any area which is not part of an urban municipality a rural municipality (or *township* or *village* as it is variously called). This unit has a governing board or council consisting of five, seven, or nine members who are elected by the qualified voters, often at a town meeting, to serve a one- or two- year term of office. Some provinces provide that in the event the voters fail to elect a total board of the required number of board members, the governor may appoint local property owners to serve in this capacity. In Natal board members may be elected by wards into which the rural municipality is divided, in which case each ward may elect a maximum of two members, with total board membership limited to nine. In other areas board members are elected at-large.

A chairman and deputy-chairman, if necessary, is elected by each board from among its own members to serve a one- or two-year term of office. The board also appoints a town clerk or secretary to supervise daily administration of rural municipal affairs.

For the most part the powers of the rural municipality are similar to those of its urban counterpart, with chief limitations being those of finance. The role of the board chairman is also similar to that of the mayor, for he must preside at board meetings and serve as the ceremonial head of the rural municipality. If needed, the board may also use committees to investigate and report to the larger group which may then take indicated action. In addition, like the urban areas, the rural municipalities may also call together qualified voters to consider regulations made by the board or to discuss any other important matters which may arise.

Again, control over the rural municipalities by the provincial government, through the governor, is virtually complete. All regulations and by-laws must be approved before being put into effect. In some provinces, would the board fail to enforce regulations or to carry out any health work it is empowered to and should carry out, the governor may require that such action be undertaken. Should the board fail to act, the governor may then issue regulations which shall have the force of law or he may authorize a person of his own choosing to carry out the necessary measures.

In the case of defaulting in financial matters, some provinces provide that the governor shall appoint an investigator who will also control revenue and expenditures. At such times a special rate is then levied on the property owners by the investigator, with the approval of the governor, to take care of the deficit. And finally, the governor may dissolve a board for failure to meet and then appoint others to act in its place until a new election is held, or he may institute investigations of the exercise of its powers by a board or of the conduct of individual board members. On the completion of such an investigation the governor may then act as he deems just or expedient and the board must comply with his orders.

Health and Malaria Committees

In some South African provinces the provincial governor may declare any area which is not already part of an urban or rural municipality a Health or Malaria Committee and establish its boundaries and jurisdiction. Just as he may create such committees, the governor may also abolish them at any time. To supervise the carrying out of necessary duties the governor may, from time to time, appoint a varying number of people to serve as a board, or in the case of Health Committees, he may declare that such people shall be elected by the qualified voters of the area.

The powers and duties of the Health Committees are those conferred by the Public Health Act of 1919, and chiefly concern supply of good water, construction of streets, and regulation and control of buildings and premises. The powers of the Malaria Committees concern the prevention of the spread of and the eradication of malaria. The governor may make regulations for any Health or Malaria Committee concerning the carrying out of its work, meetings and proceedings of its board, conduct of board members and finances. He may also require that reports, statistics and documents be furnished as required. In addition, the governor may investigate any matter concerned with the exercise of its powers by a Health or Malaria Committee as well as any matter concerning board members, and on the basis of this investigation issue such orders as he may consider just or expedient.

Provinces

Each of the South African provinces has a council composed of 25 to 68 members who are elected for a five-year term of office. In addition to its white members the council in the Cape Province only may have an additional two members who are natives elected by natives to also serve a five-year term. This council deals with such provincial matters as finances; primary and secondary education; construction and maintenance of roads and bridges; establishment of hospitals; supervision of horse racing and betting; and game and fish preservation. All ordinances are subject to the veto of the Governor-General-in-council.

The executive head of the provincial government is the governor (Administrator) who is appointed by the Cabinet (although officially by the Governor General) to serve a five-year term of office. This official sees to daily provincial administration, closely supervises urban and rural municipalities and serves as the chief provincial representative of the Union government.

CANADA

Canada is a young nation with the relatively small population in 1957 of 17,000,000 inhabitants in an area of some 3,845,800 square miles. Thus, the density of population is approximately 4.42 persons per square mile, with almost three-quarters of the inhabitants living within 100 miles of the Canadian-United States border.

The country's political institutions are an amalgamation of several influences: the inherited British parliamentary system, close proximity to the United States, the distinct French-Latin culture in the province of Quebec, and the great distances separating the several economic and cultural regions.

There are three levels of government in Canada: federal, provincial and local. The intermediate level, the provinces, have their own provincial laws and are self-governing through their elected legislatures. Eight of the ten provinces have only a single tier of local units, called by a variety of names, into which the more populated areas are divided. A second level of local government, the county, occurs only in the more populated areas of Quebec and Ontario. Large sparsely inhabited areas of the provinces are directly administered by the provincial governments.

Urban Municipalities (Cities, Towns, and Villages)

The Canadian provinces have complete authority over the creation, supervision and control of municipal government. Their structure, organization and powers are based on provincial statutes which may be general for all municipalities or special for each category. Most of the larger cities, however, have their own charters, although they are still subject to the general laws applying to all municipalities within their province.

The incorporated Canadian municipalities have complete legislative authority within the limits of their competence and defined powers. Each is governed by an elected council which has, in addition to its legislative power, administrative authority as well. In size, these councils vary from three members in British Columbia villages to a 100 member council in Montreal. For the most part, they number between five and twenty members, and are elected either at large from the municipality or by districts or wards. Terms of office range from one to three years, with overlapping terms frequently being used in the councils with three-year terms.

In addition to the council, each municipality has a popularly elected mayor (sometimes called a *reeve*), who is a member of the council and presides over it. His term is usually the same as that of the other council members, but may be for a shorter length of time. The responsibilities of both the mayor and the council are determined by the organizational structure which the municipality adopts. In general, this structure falls into one of four main categories.

The most common structure used in municipal government in Canada is that of *council-committee*. Here the council, which is elected by wards, appoints its members to serve on the various standing committees whose primary functions are to supervise one or more departments, or one or more functions of the municipal government. Thus the committees consult with department officials and report their findings and recommendations to the council for action. Their role is to initiate policy, as they cannot act except with the approval of the council as a whole. The number of standing committees varies with the size of the municipality and of the council, and may range from three to eight, with six or seven being an average number. In this system the mayor, who is elected at large, serves as an ex-officio member of each committee. His chief functions are to provide political leadership, to initiate recommendations, to co-ordinate administration and to carry out ceremonial functions. In addition to the standing committees, special committees may also be used to investigate and report on a particular municipal problem, with the result that each councilman usually serves on two or three committees at one time.

In some municipalities an administrative board appointed by the council and composed of such officials as the treasurer, engineer and clerk review municipal matters before they are forwarded to the standing committees for their study and recommendations. Thus, this board serves as a co-ordinating body, as well as an advisory group to the council through its committees, to which it reports rather than to the council as a whole.

Exclusively used in the provinces of Saskatchewan and Alberta is another form of local government in which the council (which is elected by wards), appoints one or more *commissioners*, outside its own group, to hold office at its pleasure. The popularly elected mayor may then serve as a *commissioner* either in an ex-officio or an active capacity. The functions of the paid *commissioner(s)* are to exercise broad powers of supervision over all city departments, as well as administer the budget, co-ordinate the work of departments and advise council on over-all policy. Where he serves as an ex-officio *commissioner*, the mayor then assumes the same role that he has in the council-committee form of government.

In some municipalities the council appoints two full-time *commissioners* to serve as advisers to the mayor. One of these commissioners co-ordinates financial, administrative, organizational and management activities and the other is responsible for the management of engineering, public utilities and other public works functions. This board of three then serves as the city's executive body and is responsible to the council for the administration of all services and activities. The mayor is the chief advocate of recommendations presented to council, with the two *commissioners* attending council and standing committee meetings to provide technical information and advice on request. Standing committees exist in this as well as the previous forms of government.

A growing number of municipalities throughout the country

use the *council-manager* form of government whose aim is to separate to some extent municipal policy and administration. Such cities feature a small council, ranging in size from six to ten members who are generally elected at large on a non-partisan ballot. The main functions of the council are to adopt by-laws, vote appropriations and appoint the manager, who serves at its pleasure. The manager, in turn, is charged with the administration of council policy. He thus prepares the budget which he submits to the council for review and adoption; administers the use of funds; supervises municipal departments, whose officials he appoints according to civil service regulations; makes recommendations to the council, and prepares and submits to that body whatever reports they may require. A variation on this form of government occurs in smaller municipalities where one or more officials, such as the clerk-treasurer and others, may informally emerge as an effective administrative co-ordinator or co-ordinating group by virtue of his or their positions and general knowledge of municipal problems and policies.

Mandatory structure for Ontario Province municipalities with over 100,000 population and optional for smaller municipalities in this province and in British Columbia, is that of *council-board of control*. Under this system four board-members plus the mayor, who serves as chairman, are elected at large to serve in the role of formulators of policy which is then reviewed and voted on by a council which is elected by wards, of which the board members are also members. The powers and responsibilities of the board, which are extensive, are not delegated by the council, but are specifically stated in a provincial act. Certain recommendations of the board, such as those pertaining to the budget and the appointment or dismissal of department heads, can only be reversed by a 2/3 vote of the total council. The responsibility of the board extends to the whole field of administrative co-ordination and supervision of departmental operations. Here, as in the other forms of local government used in Canada, standing committees are an integral part of the council structure and close relationships exist between the civic departments and the committees. Those departments not under the control of a standing committee come under the direct administrative jurisdiction of the Board of Control.

In many Canadian cities, special-purpose authorities for such municipal functions as education, police and public utilities are used. For the most part, these bodies have a relatively independent status in municipal government.

Within the provinces various departments exercise a degree of authority over the activities of municipal governments, although this is mostly nominal in actual practice. Each of the provincial governments has a department devoted only to municipal affairs, whose duties are of general oversight, standardizing accounting procedures, compiling statistical information, conducting special investigations, offering advice when requested, and promoting municipal administrative education by courses and memoranda. Control by the provincial departments of municipal affairs may take several forms. Certain types of by-laws, such as for zoning, and certain expenditures may require approval before being passed by the council, or in two provinces, the department may null a by-law already passed. The provinces may also require certain qualifications for such officials as doctors and auditors. In unusual circumstances, such as a default on municipal bond obligations or gross local maladministration, a local council may be dismissed from office and replaced by a provincial or appointed administrative body.

Rural Municipalities

Like their urban counterparts, Canadian rural municipalities are called by a variety of names, ranging from rural district, to parish, township and district municipality. They exist primarily in the more densely populated areas of Ontario (*township*), Quebec (*parish*), British Columbia (*district municipality*) and the prairie provinces (*municipal district*).

In general, the function of the rural municipality is to maintain public roads and to keep the public peace and order. Each of the rural municipalities has a popularly elected council, which ranges in size from four to twelve members, although the average size is six to eight councilmen. The term of office is usually one year. Executive functions of the rural municipality are entrusted to an officer (*reeve*) who carries out the decisions of the council and assumes various ceremonial functions. He may or may not have an assistant (*deputy reeve*).

Like its urban counterpart, the rural municipality is delegated its power and duties by law and is fairly autonomous within this delegated sphere. Moreover, as is the case with the urban municipalities, the rural municipalities are also subject to limited supervision by the province.

In Nova Scotia and New Brunswick the county, into which all the territory of the province is divided, is the basic unit of rural government and is known as the *county municipality*. Governmentally it may include, as in New Brunswick, the cities and towns within its territory, each of which has representation on the county council; or it may exclude all incorporated municipalities from its jurisdiction, as do the counties of Nova Scotia. In general the county municipality has the same governmental structure and performs the same functions as do the rural municipalities in the other provinces.

Counties

In the southern parts of Ontario and Quebec the county is the secondary level of local government and consists of all territory within its boundaries which is not included within the limits of an urban municipality. This territory is then divided into incorporated rural municipalities, called *parishes* or *townships*, whose structure and functions are described above. Within the sphere assigned to them by provincial statute these rural municipalities are not subject to the direction or control of the county.

There are, however, in these two provinces county municipalities, similar to those in Nova Scotia and New Brunswick, which include all the territory within the county area except that within the limits of any large urban municipality or, in Ontario, of any "separated" town lying within the county. Like the other counties in Ontario and Quebec, the county municipalities are responsible for the upkeep of roads, the maintenance of jails, and any other matters of common county interests. These county municipalities, however, do not have the power to levy taxes, and their funds, therefore, come from the requisitions they make to each of the municipalities within the county. These municipalities, in turn, raise the needed money by adding a levy for county funds to their own local levy.

The county councils of Ontario consist of the executive officer (*reeve*) and his assistant (*deputy reeve*) of each municipality within its jurisdiction. If such municipalities have more than 1,000 electors, moreover, their respective representatives on the county council are allotted two votes in the making of council decisions. In Quebec the county councils are composed of only one person from each member municipality, which is that municipality's executive officer. Thus, the councils range in size according to the number of member municipalities, with the range being from six to 20 councilmen. The term of office is one year. Serving as the executive officer of county government is a *warden* who is elected each year by the councilmen from among their own members.

A unique feature of the Quebec county council system is the *Board of Delegates*, which consists of the delegates (*warden* and two other county councilmen) from each of two adjoining counties who may be called together at any time to decide on matters of common interest to adjoining local munipalities in different counties. In Ontario, contiguous counties with small populations may be combined under one council, called the county's council, which is similar in structure and duties to that of the regular county councils.

THE UNITED STATES OF AMERICA

Despite early colonization by a variety of nationality groups the basic structure of local government in the original 13 colonies of what is now the United States of America was British in origin. This basic structure, however, was adapted to local conditions, with the result that the importance given to one local governmental unit, such as the county, over another, such as the rural municipality (*township*), varied throughout the colonial territory and this is still true today. As the population expanded westward in the 19th century new living conditions were encountered and variations on the old forms of government evolved to meet these changes. Reaction to the form of government which provoked the War of Independence in 1776 led to the opposite extreme of the

Jacksonian period. Under this philosophy any man was considered capable of participating in governmental affairs. In addition, the office of the chief executive was de-emphasized by its subordination to an elected council and by the election of most other local officials. Such a system in turn gave rise to the growth of political parties and with them, especially in the rapidly growing cities, the rule of the boss, with its accompanying graft and corruption.

The period of reform in American local government began with the late 1800's and extended into the first decades of this century. Not only were existing systems improved upon but whole new approaches to urban municipal government were developed. Chief among these were the "commission" form of municipal government, which is of decreasing importance today, and the council-manager form, variations of which are being applied to both urban and, to a very limited extent, rural local government throughout the country.

The United States is a federation of 48 quasi-sovereign states,[1] all the territory of which is divided into further units. The largest of these units is the county (known as *parish* in Louisiana) which exists in all states but Rhode Island and which in about half the states is further subdivided into rural municipalities (*townships* or *towns*). In some states the boundary of the county may also be coterminous with that of a municipality, with the result that city-counties can exist. These, however, are very small in number. Government in the urbanized areas is carried on by incorporated units variously called cities, boroughs, villages and incorporated towns. Further local governmental units are the school districts and the special districts which provide such services as fire protection, soil conservation, water and other utilities.

Urban Municipalities (Cities, Boroughs, Villages, Incorporated Towns)

Because the American urban municipality is a creature of its individual state government there is a wide difference in the pre-

---

[1] This report was written before Alaska officially became the 49th and Hawaii the 50th state of the Union.

UNITED STATES OF AMERICA

PATTERN OF GOVERNMENT UNITS

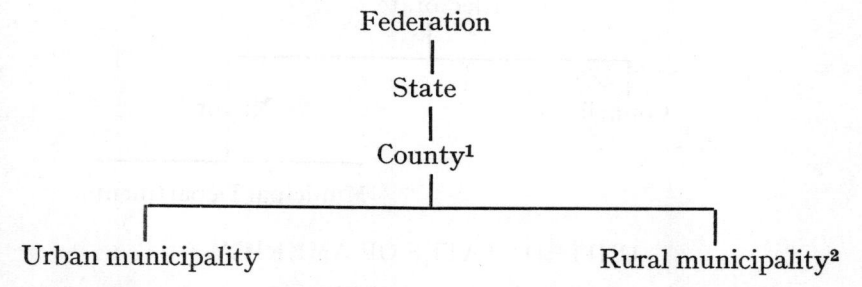

Federation
|
State
|
County[1]
|
Urban municipality   Rural municipality[2]

[1] With only a few exceptions all the U.S. is included in one of the 3,049 counties. One should remember, however, that although the municipalities are geographically included within the county they are not administratively subordinate to the county government. The county government has, in general, no power of review or any other control over the municipal government activities.

[2] In 26 states there are no rural municipalities, the county being the basic local unit in the areas that do not have urban municipal government.

UNITED STATES OF AMERICA
STRUCTURE OF MUNICIPAL GOVERNMENT

so-called strong mayor system

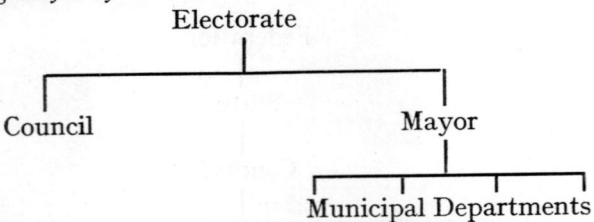

```
            Electorate
           /         \
       Council      Mayor
                      |
              Municipal Departments
```

UNITED STATES OF AMERICA

so-called weak mayor system

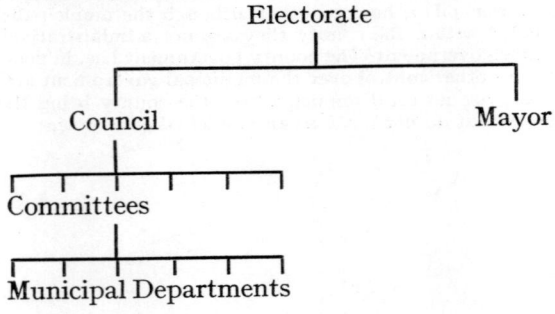

```
            Electorate
           /         \
       Council       Mayor
          |
       Committees
          |
    Municipal Departments
```

UNITED STATES OF AMERICA

council manager system

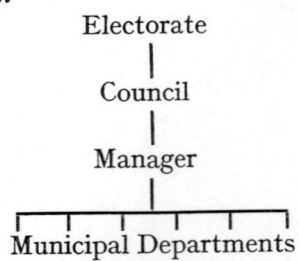

```
    Electorate
        |
     Council
        |
     Manager
        |
  Municipal Departments
```

UNITED STATES OF AMERICA

commission system

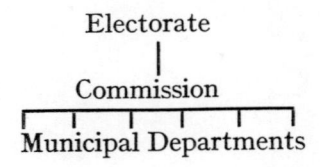

```
    Electorate
        |
    Commission
        |
  Municipal Departments
```

requisites for its establishment throughout the country. All, however, are incorporated through one of the following methods: special charter, whereby each municipality is established by a separate and distinct action of the state legislature; general law, under which system charters are granted to municipalities according to their classification as to population, geographical location or assessed valuation; optional charter, whereby local voters may choose which one of several forms of municipal government they would like to have; or home rule, through which method the citizens of a municipality may elect a charter commission which will draw up and submit to the state legislature and to a vote of the people a document setting up the form of government. Despite their differences in size and method of incorporation American municipalities have the same general functions, which include police and fire protection; public works; libraries; parks and recreation; public utilities; zoning and city planning and sometimes public health, airports, harbours and housing. The three major forms of municipal government in the United States are (1) mayor-council, further subdivided into weak mayor-council (or council-committee) and strong mayor-council; (2) commission and (3) council-manager.

The council in the *mayor-council* form of government varies in size from three to fifty members (seven is the median number) who are elected most frequently by wards. They may also, however, be elected from the municipality at-large or through a combination of ward and at-large elections. Terms of the councilmen, who are selected through the simple majority or proportional representation method of voting, vary from two to four years and are often staggered so that only part of the council goes out of office at one time. In addition to its general ordinance-making powers, which include all activities in which the municipality is legally empowered to act, the council also adopts the annual budget; authorizes loans; establishes taxes and fees; and in the weak mayor-council municipalities approves certain appointments and dismissals of the mayor. In many of the smaller municipalities the council must also issue liquor licences; make assessments for such services as water mains, curbs and gutters and new thoroughfares; and approve contracts. The presiding officer of the council generally is the mayor.

Many of the mayor-council municipalities make use of council committees, the complexity of which system varies from place to place. In the weak mayor form of government these committees, in addition to studying and making recommendations on various municipal activities, may also directly supervise the daily administration of the municipal departments.

The executive of the mayor-council municipality is the popularly elected mayor who serves a two to four year term of office and whose designation as weak or strong depends on the amount of power granted him by law. In the so-called weak mayor municipalities the mayor is greatly limited, not only in the number of appointments he may make but also in having to submit such appointments as well as dismissals to the approval of council; by the "long ballot" whereby many of the other city officials, such as the clerk, treasurer, engineer, etc. are elected by the people and therefore responsible to them rather than to the municipal executive; and by direct supervision of municipal departments by committees of council.

Such limitations on executive authority do not exist in the strong mayor municipality which is the form used in most of the large metropolitan areas. Under this type of charter the mayor exercises leadership over the departments by his ability to appoint and dismiss department heads and by his issuance of directives and instructions. In all mayor-council forms of government the mayor may also be allowed to propose ordinances and resolutions, to prepare a budget and to veto all or selected measures passed by the council. Such a veto may then be over-ridden by a majority, 2/3 or 3/4 vote of the council. The mayor may also be given the power to investigate any phase of municipal administration and to take then the necessary action called for.

In addition to policy and investigative powers both the strong and the weak mayor is the ceremonial head of the municipality and its official representative to visitors and on festive occasions. In many of the larger municipalities the mayor may appoint an administrator to help him supervise daily activities. Such an administrator then is directly responsible to the mayor, whose assistant he is, and not to the council or the electorate.

Under the *commission* form of government, which came in with the reform period in American local government and is now used in about 13% of all American municipalities over 5,000 population, a small council of from three to seven members is elected, usually at-large, to direct municipal activities for a four-year term. This form of government also brought with it the *initiative*, where legislation is initiated by the citizens upon presentation to the council of a petition signed by a legally established percentage of the voters; the *referendum*, whereby measures are submitted to the public for their approval or disapproval; and *recall*, the device used to allow citizens to remove dishonest or incompetent officials from office by circulating a petition to be signed by a fixed percentage of the population, followed by an election to determine whether or not the official should continue in office. Although not as frequently incorporated into new charters today as in the early part of this century, these devices are still available to the citizens of many municipalities and are considered an important adjunct of local self-government.

The council (*commission*) as a whole passes ordinances, fixes tax rates, makes appointments and dismissals, determines the annual budget and adopts general policy concerning municipal administration. It may also appoint various boards and committees to work with and be directly responsible to it in such fields as health, libraries and recreation. Individually, members supervise the daily administration of municipal departments, the number of which is usually equal to the number of commissioners.

Among the council members is a mayor, who usually is elected to this office by the voters, or who may be so chosen by his fellow commissioners. The mayor is not the municipal executive as in the mayor-council form of government, but is rather *primus inter pares* in regard to policy and administrative leadership. In most municipalities he does not have a veto and it is only in the ceremonial functions that he is distinguished from his fellow commissioners.

The reform period in local government also introduced, coinciding with municipal home rule, *the council-manager* form of government, which is at present used in over 1500 cities. The policy-making body is still the council which is limited in size from three to nine members, generally elected at large in nonpartisan elections. This group passes ordinances; sets tax rates within the limitations of state and charter provisions; determines the budget and hires the manager who serves at its pleasure. In slightly more than half of the council-manager municipalities the mayor is selected by the council from among its own members; in the remainder of the municipalities he is directly elected by the voters. His role is chiefly that of ceremonial leader of the community in addition to presiding over council meetings, although the municipal charter may give him other responsibilities such as designating local citizens to serve on advisory boards and committees.

The chief executive is the manager who directly supervises municipal affairs. He appoints all or nearly all the department heads, whom he may also dismiss, and is the general co-ordinator of all governmental activity. His activities are defined by the charter and for his actions he is directly responsible to the council who may dismiss him at any time. In addition to his supervisory role the manager serves as adviser to the council in the formulation and revision of policy. He also prepares the annual budget (in the large cities in conjunction with a budget director), which budget he submits to the council for review and adoption. The manager, too, prepares special studies, makes reports to the council and presents an annual report to the electorate on general municipal conditions.

Control over municipalities by state governments includes, in addition to granting charters which establish structure and range of powers, direct and indirect supervision. Direct supervision may involve prior approval before an action can be carried out, particularly in the fields of finance and public works. Thus, in many states approval of plans for municipal water works or sewerage systems must be obtained before work can commence, or local bond issues and increases in tax rates must be submitted to the proper state department. States may also issue orders and regulations which establish uniform procedure in regard to financial, public health and public education matters. Inspections and audits are then carried out to see that these orders and regulations are put into effect, with prosecution sometimes following where local action is not forthcoming.

Municipal functions may also be transferred temporarily or permanently to state agencies, as in the case of assessment of public utilities, the provision of roads or the establishment of a municipality on a sound financial basis. In some states certain local officials must be approved before they can be employed; in others the state makes actual appointments, as is the case where local officials are negligent in their duty to appoint such officials themselves. More common, however, is the power of the state governor to remove local officials for neglect of duty or certain types of misconduct.

Indirect control of state over municipal governments includes giving advice and assistance when requested on matters covering the whole range of municipal functions. States may also require various reports, particularly in the field of financial and public health affairs. In addition, many states review such local actions as assessment of property and, upon petition, of tax levies and local bond issues. Finally, through the system of grants-in-aid to municipalities the states may establish broad standards of administration and personnel which must be met as well as follow through with periodic inspections. Grants-in-aid from the federal government may also be made to municipalities in the field of slum clearance and housing, construction of airports and highways, and civil defence. Like the state grants, those of the federal government also involve setting standards of administration and personnel, as well as require many kinds of reports and statistics. In many fields of municipal government the local units may also obtain advice and assistance from the federal government, such as in police administration, public health and welfare, juvenile delinquency and public education.

Counties

The American counties are agencies of the state government which also may abolish them, and thus their nature and functions vary from place to place. In the New England states this unit of government is primarily a judicial district; in the southern and far western states it serves as the primary rural local unit controlling courts, education, health, public welfare, public works and roads. In all but two states[1] urban municipalities are within the

[1] Virginia and Rhode Island. The latter is not divided into counties.

county and their residents pay taxes to support the county government as well as that of their municipality.

The principal governing organ of a county is a council, generally known as the Board of Supervisors, Commissioners or Freeholders, or the Police Jury in Louisiana. Its composition varies widely throughout the country and may consist of the township supervisors of all townships within the county; the judicial officials within the county; a popularly elected member from each district into which the county is divided for this purpose; the commissioner of roads and revenue within the county; commissioners chosen by the state legislature plus one or two elected officials, etc. Just as the composition varies, so does the size with large organs existing where township supervisors serve (Wayne County, where Detroit, Michigan is located, has a membership of 114 members) to just three members in those counties whose board members are popularly elected, which is the case in over half the 3,049 counties throughout the country. Terms of office are usually two to four years.

In general this organ may levy taxes, appropriate money, issue bonds, maintain law and order, care for prisoners, conduct elections, maintain roads, record deeds and vital statistics, supervise weights and measures, settle estates, care for dependent and neglected children, advance agriculture and assume certain public education responsibilities. It may also exercise optional powers granted to it by the state, such as county planning and zoning, various public health and recreation activities and housing. In 11 states the fiscal powers of the council are assumed by another organ which may consist of members of the state legislature from that county, the county Justices of Peace, or a separate popularly elected council. This body then adopts the county budget, fixes the tax levy and authorizes bond issues, among other responsibilities.

Most county governments are characterized by a large number of officials who share governmental responsibility with the board. Such officials may include the recorder of deeds, treasurer, county clerk, sheriff, prosecuting attorney, coroner, county surveyor and probate judge. Most of these are popularly elected and there is therefore little integration of activity as the county has no single official who serves as chief executive. However, in the interest of better government some counties have elected chief executives or presidents whose duties are similar to those of the strong mayor. In six states *home rule* has been granted to some counties and other states have optional charters which may be adopted. Progress has been slow to come to the county, however, and it is only in recent years that the council-manager form of government has begun to be applied to county government. A small number of other counties, particularly in California and North Carolina, have a county administrator, appointed by the county council, whose duties are similar to those of the manager.

Rural Municipalities (Townships or Towns)

The *township* or *town* exists in about half the 48 American states, although in only 11 of these does township government cover all rural areas. Generally, large densely populated areas are not included within township government although the smaller ones may be and their residents then pay township taxes and vote in township elections.

In six states having township government that unit is charged only with assessing and collecting taxes and acting as a judicial and election area. In other states the townships have large urban areas and must thus provide many of the services of the incorporated municipality. In general the township assumes such functions as maintaining roads and administering certain health and public welfare services. The recent trend, however, is to transfer these functions from the township to the county.

The general representative organ of the township or town is the town meeting in the New England and eight other states, although only in the former has this kind of assembly proved consistently effective. Other states have no general meeting but instead elect one to three township officers who then submit some questions for popular referendum. In these states the form of government closely follows that of the county, with the supervisor or trustee or chairman, as he is variously called, serving as the head official. This official is popularly elected, usually serves a two- or three-year term of office and is primarily concerned with co-ordinating township activities. In New England the town meeting elects three persons (selectmen) to serve as the governing organ. Other officials who share governmental responsibility for the township or town may be a clerk, assessor, justices of the peace, constable, treasurer and tax collector.

(2)

THE NORTH EUROPE GROUP

SWEDEN

SWEDEN'S history is closely linked with that of Norway and Denmark with whom it has had close ties for many centuries, varying from unions for trade to centralized rule. In this country, as in Norway and Denmark, local government has ancient roots. The old form of local government, however, gave way in the 16th and 17th centuries to organs established by the central government. At the same time the ecclesiastical parish, which originally dealt with matters of the church, came to assume gradually care of the poor and public health and education functions.

Under the Municipal Acts of 1862 ecclesiastical and civil duties were separated, with the result that governmental affairs are now carried out by urban and rural municipalities and provinces, and ecclesiastical affairs by the original parishes. Important recent developments in the field of local government in Sweden are uniform legislation for the urban and rural municipalities, the latter of which have also been greatly affected by large-scale amalgamation measures.

Municipalities (Urban and Rural)

The new Swedish Local Government Act of 1953, which was put into effect in 1955, gives urban and rural municipalities approximately the same structure and powers. The governing body of the Swedish municipalities is a council whose members are elected by proportional representation to serve four-year terms of office. In size these bodies range from a minimum of 15 members to a maximum of 100 members in Stockholm. The council is competent to act in all matters which are of purely local concern and which have not been delegated to any other body. This is considered the "free" or unregulated part of their field of authority. In addition there are functions which have been turned over to the municipality by the state and which are based on state rules and regulations. Such functions are considered the regulated part of the municipality's competence.

Included in the regulated category of municipal activities are such social welfare services as assistance for people who have no means of support, old age, invalid and survivors' pensions; child welfare and youth protection; care of alcoholics; temporary nursing aid for families; family subsidies for dependents of men in military service; public health provisions including inspection of food and drugs, drains and sewers, and street cleaning and collection of refuse; town planning and building; housing, by subsidy or loans and grants, and by building; protection against fire; police and public order; local courts and juries; and administration of primary schools. The unregulated sphere of activity of the municipality includes the provision of tramways and bus lines, harbours, airfields, gas and electricity works, hotels, baths and laundries, sports and open air grounds, libraries, theatres, concert halls and public meeting places.

The duties of the council thus include adopting a budget; levying taxes; buying and selling real estate; raising loans; appointing municipal officials and delegating their responsibilities; issuing regulations and instructions for the organization of the municipality; and passing local by-laws. The chairman of the council (*ordförande*) who is elected by the council to serve a one-year term of office, presides over council meetings and serves as the official representative of the municipality.

The executive business of the municipal council is carried out by the standing and special committees which meet as frequently as is necessary. The municipal committees have a great deal of power. Before being submitted to the council for final decision every proposal is dealt with in the proper committee which makes a report recommending or disapproving the proposal or making the alterations and amendments the committee thinks fit. As a rule a special committee exists for each of the more important fields of activity of the regulated administration. Many of these committees are statutory. In small municipalities, however, certain functions may be assigned to another appropriate committee, in which case it is often stipulated that some particular member of the designated committee, in addition to his ordinary job, shall have the special duty of carefully following activities within the field in question so that such activities will not be neglected for lack of a special committee.

Committee procedure and activity are regulated by a uniform state code in the case of matters which fall within the regulated sector of municipal functions, or by the new municipal law in those matters which do not. Furthermore, where state interest is paramount, as is the case with elections, pensions and rates, committee chairmen may be appointed by the provincial governor. Otherwise chairmen are selected by the council or by the committee itself.

The committees are composed partly of council members and partly of citizens who are selected by the council or by the committees themselves. For some committees the law requires one or more persons with special qualifications to be appointed; for instance the law requires a medical doctor to be on the temperance committee.

Supervising the activities of the committees, as well as the administration of the affairs of a municipality is a board, or in a few municipalities a finance committee which has in practice the same power as a board without the formal authority. This body administers the municipality's affairs and supervises the activities of the committees. It also sees that the council's decisions are carried out and acts as a general co-ordinating organ, whereby it gives its opinion on all questions before they are introduced in the council. In general, an item cannot be decided upon by the council before the board has had an opportunity to examine it closely.

Chosen by the council, the board numbers at least 5 members who serve a four-year term of office. The term, however, begins one year later and extends one year longer than that of the council; the advantage appears to be that continuity is provided and recently elected councilmen are able to acquire experience and knowledge before the new members to the board are elected. The chairman of the board is appointed by the council from among the board members, and serves a four-year term of office, except in Stockholm where the chairman is newly selected each year. On the whole this post is the most important one within the municipality.

For the most part, the amount of central supervision that is exercised over the municipal governments varies with the activity. For those measures which are designated by law as "free" and unregulated, main responsibility rests with the local government. For those functions in the regulated field of activity, local councils and committees are supervised in various ways by the pertinent central government ministry and by the provincial governor. Thus prior approval is required for council decisions pertaining to public health, fire protection, building and planning and in such financial matters as increase in tax rates, raising loans and issuing bonds. In addition, in some instances the provincial governor may act as a judge in disputes involving interpretations of administrative law. In other instances this official may require a municipality to discuss questions and make certain provisions if he finds that the present arrangements are inadequate. Still again, central departments may have local inspectors, as is the case with the Social Board and the Board of Education.

The system of appeals by local citizens to the central government also provides a measure of control over the municipal governments. Thus anyone may appeal a decision of the municipality in the area of "free" functions, but only on the basis of legality or formal procedure. In these cases the Supreme Administrative Court acts as the final authority. In the area of regulated activities appeals may be made only by citizens affected by the decision and not only may the merits of the decision be challenged by the central government, but a new decision may be forced on the municipality.

Provinces ('Län')

The 24 provinces of Sweden (25 including Stockholm) are administrative units of the central government and as well representative governing units with a governmental structure similar to that of the municipalities.

The representative governing provincial government is entrusted to a popularly elected council (*landsting*) which varies in size from 30 to 70 members. As meetings are usually held but once a year, the carrying out of council decisions is done by various standing and special committees, chief among which are the board and the finance committee.

The task of the landsting is to maintain hospitals for the treatment of physical diseases, but they also deal with district nursing, the national dental service, midwifery and maternity welfare, education for agriculture, handicrafts and industry.

Heading the provincial government is an appointed governor (*landshövding*) who is directly responsible to the central government. His office is responsible for police protection within the province and for the maintenance of public order and safety. In addition, it supervises the activities of the municipalities in those fields mentioned above. The provincial staff is responsible not only to the governor but also to the central ministries concerned with such functions as health, education, labour, housing, town planning and social affairs.

The five largest urban municipalities in Sweden are not part of the governmental structure of the provinces in which they are located. Consequently they assume the duties of both municipalities and provinces. In addition Stockholm has the status of a province.

FINLAND

Finland was an integral part of the Kingdom of Sweden from the late 12th and early 13th centuries until 1809 when it was attached to the Russian Empire as an autonomous Grand-Duchy. One hundred and eight years later, on December 6, 1917, Finland declared herself an independent and sovereign state and has remained so until the present time.

Geographically Finland is divided into 10[1] provinces, which are further subdivided into urban municipalities (cities and towns) and rural municipalities. Further divisions of the country are

[1] Two more provinces have been established in 1960.

various administrative units which carry out such services as social welfare, public schools and roads, and unions of municipalities which assume responsibility for services which cannot be provided by individual municipalities.

Urban and Rural Municipalities

The development of cities and towns in Finland dates back to the Middle Ages, whereas the rural municipalities have evolved out of the ecclesiastical parishes from which the civil administration was separated under the local government acts of 1863. Regardless of this historical circumstance, however, under the Municipal Law of 1948 today's urban and rural municipalities have almost the same structure and similar functions. The main distinction is that the urban municipalities assume greater responsibilities in town planning, building and other related activities, maintenance of courts of justice and police forces and powers of distraint. In addition the government subsidy received by the urban municipalities is smaller than that received by their rural counterparts.

In general, the Finnish municipalities assume all functions which are of joint concern to the local inhabitants. These include provision of a safe and adequate supply of water; disposal of sewage; protection against fire; oftentimes provision of electricity, gas and public transport services; educational, social welfare and public health services; medical care; libraries, museums, sport halls and fields; and sometimes municipal theatres and orchestras. If they so desire, municipalities may also provide public baths and swimming halls, laundries, saw mills, and kitchen gardens or a forest farm.

The representative organ of the municipality is the council, which varies in size from 13 tot 77 members, according to population, who are elected by proportional representation to serve four-year terms of office. The presiding officer is a council-elected chairman who serves a one-year term of office, or in his absence, the vice-chairman, who is similarly selected.

The executive body of the council is a board which consists of at least four members in the urban municipalities and at least five in the rural municipalities. Members are elected by the council either from within or outside council membership, and terms of office are one year in the urban municipalities and two years in the rural ones. Serving as chairman of the board in all the urban municipalities and some of the rural ones is the municipal manager, in the other rural municipalities a chairman is selected by the municipal council from among its members to serve in this capacity for four years. Wherever there are assistant managers in a municipality, these also serve as permanent board members. In addition, the council chairman and vice-chairman may attend board meetings at which they have the right to speak, but not to vote.

The duties of the municipal board include preparing a budget and other matters to be put before the council and effectuating that body's decisions. A special feature of this latter responsibility is that the board has the power to decide whether council decisions are legal or have been passed in the required manner. If such is found not to be the case the board may then refuse to put the decision into effect, at which point it returns the matter to the council for further consideration. Should the council still adhere to its original decision, however, the matter is than handed over to the provincial administration for a final decision.

A further important responsibility of the board is to supervise the activities of the municipal committees in matters relating to general administration and economy. It also administers public property, where this responsibility has not been assigned to a special committee; keeps the financial accounts of the municipality and presents them once a year to the council; and provides information to provincial and central government authorities on certain required matters. In addition, all motions and statements to be presented to the higher authorities by the council or the committees must be transmitted by the board, provided it has not been stipulated otherwise.

Sharing executive functions with the board are various council committees about 10 of which, not including those pertaining to public schools, are statutory and from five to 20 or more of which may be optional and are created to perform specific tasks. Committee members are selected by the council, usually from citizens outside the council membership, to serve one- to four-year terms of office.

Only to the extent to which a committee has been granted independent powers by law may it function uncontrolled by the municipal board. Otherwise its activities are closely supervised by that body, mainly through a board representative who is appointed annually to serve in that capacity. The responsibility of this representative is to present the views of the board to the committee and to keep the municipal board informed of committee decisions. In addition, any decision of a committee which is not within its specifically delegated independent powers must be submitted for board approval upon request. Such decisions may be vetoed by the board with the power of appeal to the municipal council being granted to the committee. A further control of the committees by the board is the requirement of a yearly account of its activities.

Under the terms of the Municipal Law an urban municipality must have as its chief executive a professional administrator and assistant(s), if necessary, who are appointed by the municipal council and serve at its pleasure. In the rural municipalities the appointment of a manager is not compulsory, although the continual growth of municipal duties is making such action increasingly essential. At the present time such officials have been appointed in about one tenth of the rural municipalities. The primary duties of the manager are to co-ordinate and supervise daily municipal administration and to preside over board meetings.

Managers and their assistants may be dismissed by the municipal council without the approval of the higher authorities only in the event that they are unable to perform their duties due to prolonged illness. In all other cases dismissal must first receive the prior approval of the provincial administration. In those rural municipalities that do not have managers, co-ordination and supervision of daily affairs are performed by a municipal secretary.

Control of municipal activities by the higher authorities is mainly in the field of fiscal affairs and those functions which are performed by the statutory committees. Thus, prior approval must be received from the Ministry of the Interior or from the provincial administration for the granting of sureties or contracting of loans which extend over a five-year period. Also, certain welfare, nursing and other institutional matters must be approved by provincial or central government authorities, as well as regulations pertaining to town planning, harbours, fire protection and health service. Control over activities of the committees is through the competent central ministry or district officers or inspectors by means of inspections, executive advice, prior approval and reports, especially in regard to the use of state grants and loans.

Finally, control is exercised over the actions of the municipal authorities by the right of appeal granted to citizens from the decisions, other than those of an executive nature, of a municipal council or board. Such appeals are made first to the provincial administration, with final recourse to the Supreme Administrative Court. The municipality, in turn, can also appeal to this court decisions of the provincial administration or other state authorities, including ministries and the Cabinet.

Provinces

Finnish provinces serve only as administrative areas of the state and are under the supervision of the Ministry of the Interior. With the exception of Åland, the smallest province, which mainly consists of islands and which has a kind of provincial self-government, all are directly administered by a governor without the aid of a council. This official is appointed by the President and is directly subordinate to the Ministry of the Interior. However, in matters relating to other ministries the governor is responsible to the respective ministry. In practice the provincial administration is the most important branch office of the central government.

NORWAY

The unification of Norway took place during the Viking period from approximately 800 to 1050 A. D., following which was a long period of intermittent warfare, widespread trade and Scandinavian unions. Toward the end of the 14th century the three northern kingdoms became united under a centralized rule, from which Sweden broke away in the middle of the 15th century. In 1660 a joint central administration was established between Norway and Denmark which was finally dissolved as a result of the Danish alliance with France in the time of Napoleon. Following this Norway was ceded to Sweden in 1814 which union, in turn, was declared dissolved by Norway in 1905. Neutral during World War I, Norway was occupied by Germany during the second world war, at the conclusion of which it resumed its former form of government.

Local autonomy was established in Norway by the Act of 1837, which was revised following full independence from Sweden in 1905. The present local government law was enacted in 1954 and incorporates important reforms designed to bring the functions and duties of Norwegian local government up to date. Administratively the country consists of provinces and urban and rural municipalities.

Urban and Rural Municipalities

Under the 1954 Act concerning local government in the municipalities there is no basic difference in structure and competence between the Norwegian urban and rural municipalities. All have a council (*kommunestyre*) whose members are elected by the list method of proportional representation except in the smaller municipalities where there is either no list or only one list, in which case election is then by simple majority. The term of office is four years and the size of the council, which must always be an uneven number, varies from 13 to 85 members, as determined by the council itself, according to a scale established by law.

The competence of the municipal council includes adopting a budget; levying taxes, licences and fees; making expenditures from municipal funds; raising loans; acquiring and disposing of real estate; providing housing facilities; administering roads and thoroughfares; establishing a town plan; providing various social, sanitation and public health services; affording protection against fire; establishing various public utilities and municipal enterprises; providing educational facilities and such cultural services as libraries, theatres and sport stadia. In addition, the

NORWAY

PATTERN OF GOVERNMENT UNITS

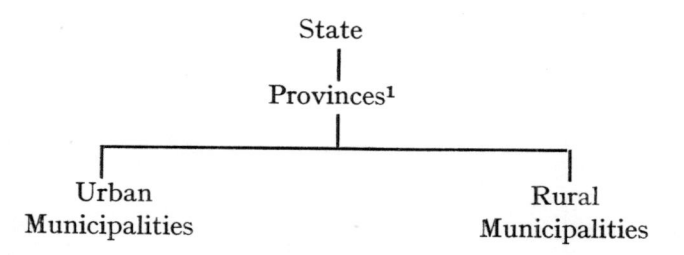

```
            State
              |
          Provinces¹
              |
    ┌─────────┴─────────┐
   Urban              Rural
Municipalities    Municipalities
```

[1] The provincial council has representatives from, and discusses matters pertaining to, the rural municipalities only. The provincial governor, however, has jurisdiction governing both types of municipalities.

THE STRUCTURE OF AN URBAN AND RURAL MUNICIPAL GOVERNMENT

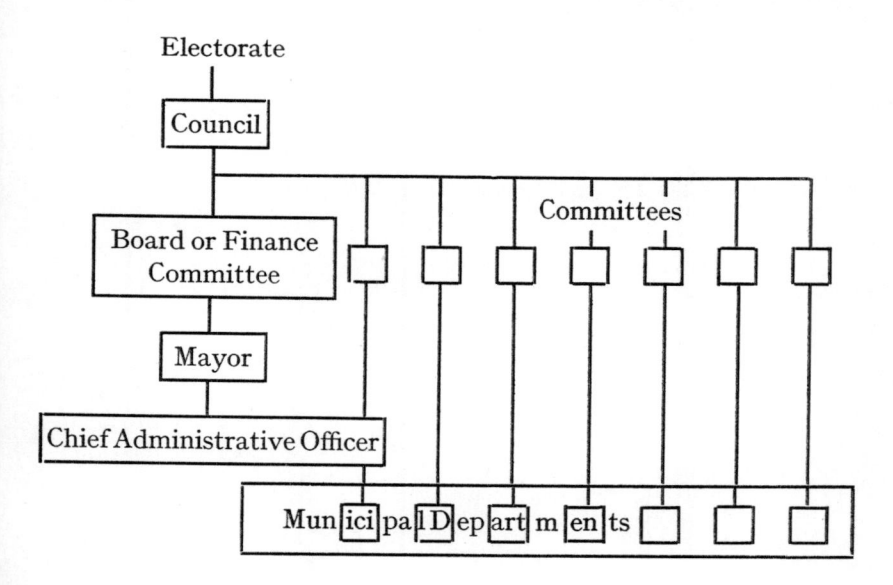

Electorate
|
Council
|
Board or Finance Committee — Committees
|
Mayor
|
Chief Administrative Officer
|
Municipal Departments

council appoints a chairman and vice-chairman, a board, a municipal treasurer and where one exists, a municipal chief administrative officer, and municipal committees.

One-quarter of their members are elected by the council to serve as a board (*formannskapet*), also for a four-year term of office. This body is presided over by the council chairman. In general, the duty of the board is to supervise the finances and administration of the municipality. It thus presents the budget to the council for its discussion and approval; supervises municipal accounts and presents a yearly report on them to the council; sees that council decisions are put into effect; and assumes any responsibilities which are delegated to it by the municipal council. In these matters, which may not involve acquisition and disposal of real estate, beginning of new projects or extension of earlier projects, granting concessions, raising loans, issuing guarantees and appointing a municipal treasurer and administrator, the board may pass resolutions and in other prescribed ways act on behalf of the municipality. In times of emergency the board may also make decisions which normally should be made by the council, following which it must inform the council of such action as soon as possible.

To help carry out the varied functions of municipal government the Norwegian councils establish standing and special-purpose committees and determine by general regulations their sphere of action. Usually this involves the preparation of matters to be considered by the council, the performance of special functions, and serving as a consultative authority. The sphere of action of the committees may also be extended to include functions which might also be delegated to the board, although this delegation can never include those functions mentioned above which can only be assumed by the municipal council itself. The size of the committees is determined by the council, although individual chairmen and vice-chairmen are named by the board unless otherwise provided. Membership mainly consists of councilmen, with municipal officials included only in exceptional cases. No member of the board, however, can be appointed to participate in any committee dealing with accounting matters and the appointment of an auditor.

The chairman of the council and the executive committee

(*ordförer*) is elected by the council to serve a two-year term of office. He is the legal representative of the municipality and signs on behalf of the municipality in all instances where such authority has not been delegated to others. In conducting council and board meetings the chairman enforces the rules of procedure and the provisions of law concerning the requirement of a valid decision. He makes sure that matters under consideration have been properly prepared and superintends the recording of proceedings. In addition to his ordinary right to vote in the meetings of the council and the board the chairman also casts the deciding vote in case of an equal division of opinion, except in the instance of an election or the appointment of an official.

The chairman is responsible for the proper keeping of municipal books and documents. He must see that extracts of council and other municipal authority decisions are sent to the provincial governor and that required information is submitted to the proper authorities. He also sees that decisions and communications from the higher authorities are transmitted to the proper municipal person or body. And finally, insofar as the power to authorize payments has not been delegated to others, such as a chief administrative officer, the chairman has such power.

In municipalities with a minimum of 10,000 inhabitants the administrative head of local government is a council-appointed chief administrative officer who serves at the council's pleasure. It is the responsibility of this official to carry out the decisions of the council and to provide immediate supervision of the entire administration of the municipality, particularly in its financial and accounting responsibilities. He submits a budget proposal to the board and states his opinion on the financial aspects of matters under consideration. The chief administrative officer also has the power to authorize payments, or if this power has been granted by the council to other officials as well, supervision of this delegated power is exercised by the administrator. The chief administrative officer must attend meetings of the municipal council and board, but he cannot be elected a member of them. He can also attend meetings of committees and boards of municipal enterprises, to which he may be elected a member and thus have the right to vote.

Although Norwegian municipalities have much local autonomy,

close supervision over their actions is exercised by the central government through the provincial governor. Thus, all decisions of the council and many of those of the board must be submitted to the governor. Those pertaining to loans, guarantees, long-term economic commitments and sale of public property must receive prior approval by the Ministry of Municipal Affairs and Labour or by the governor before they can be put into effect. The governor shall declare any decision invalid which is in contravention of an act or a provision issued in pursuance of an act or which has been made by an authority not legally empowered to make the decision. In these instances the provincial governor immediately informs the council chairman of his action and the municipal board may, within a period of six weeks, appeal the governor's decision to the Crown, or bring the matter before the courts, if this is the required remedy. Until the decision of the governor has been reversed or upheld no action may thenceforth be taken by the municipal authorities.

If a decision of the municipal council does not obtain a two-thirds majority at the final vote, the matter shall be reconsidered by the municipal council at a later meeting. If again the two-thirds majority required for a positive decision does not result, the matter shall be submitted to the King, if the minority – at the meeting – so requests by a majority vote among themselves. The King may confirm or reject the decision.

Province ('Fylket')

Government functions which must be carried out on a broader basis than the municipal unit are the responsibility of the province. These include special schools, health service, communications and roads. The representative body (*fylkestinget*) of the province is composed of the chairmen of the rural municipalities within the province. The council, which meets once a year, elects four of its members to serve with the governor as the provincial board (*fylkesutvalget*). The term of office of the elected board members is two years.

The provincial governor is appointed by the Crown upon the recommendation of the Ministry of Justice and Police. His is a dual role, to serve as legal representative and executive officer of local provincial affairs, and to act also as the representative of the central government in the administration of national laws. In his former role the governor serves as chairman of the provincial board and attends council meetings where he is allowed to discuss and recommend but not to vote. A further responsibility of this official is to prepare the budget, which is then discussed and approved by the council. The governor may only declare a council decision invalid if it is contrary to the law. The King (the Ministry of Municipal Affairs and Labour), on the other hand, may refuse to approve a decision made by either the municipal council or the representative body of the province (*fylkestinget*).

DENMARK

The history of Denmark, like that of many other countries, has consisted of periods of greatness and prosperity alternating with times of civil and foreign war and economic disasters. Especially close have been its relationships with the other Scandinavian countries. These have ranged from war to unions for trade and common government, the latter of which existed with Norway from 1380 to 1814. The present form of government is a limited monarchy which operates under the Constitution of 1915, as amended in 1920. It has also been amended in the 1950's.

Governmentally Denmark is divided into 25 districts which comprise some 1300 rural municipalities; outside the jurisdiction of the districts are the 85 urban municipalities. This division of local government units can be carried far back into history. The oldest urban municipalities were mentioned in historical accounts from the ninth century and the boundaries of the rural municipalities coincide with those of the historic ecclesiastic parishes. Finally, the district originates from the division of the country into feudal estates in the middle ages.

Urban Municipalities

The Danish Constitution guarantees to all urban municipalities the right to manage their own affairs under the supervision of the state. General provisions for administration are established in the Act of March 25, 1933 although Copenhagen, the capital, has its own municipal law which dates back to 1857, and was amended in 1938.

In addition to carrying out matters of purely local interest, Danish municipalities are also delegated tasks by the state. It is not always possible, however, to classify tasks as clearly state or municipal, for many are of highly mixed interest. In general, municipal functions include: adoption of a budget; assessment of rates, by a special assessment committee; planning and carrying out public works, including road construction, housing and development of a town plan; ownership or financial support of local railways, buses, tramways and harbours; and administration and financial support of such social services as public assistance, pensions, homes for the aged, maternity homes, workhouses, and almshouses. Urban municipalities also provide primary and usually secondary schools, youth education, protection against fire, civil defense, and such public utilities as gasworks, waterworks, power stations, heating stations, public baths and slaughter-houses. Further, the municipalities provide libraries and sports grounds and may also support public theatres and orchestras.

The representative organ of the 85 urban municipalities is the council (byråd) which is composed of seven to 25 members who are elected for four-year terms of office by proportional representation. The council, in turn, elects a chairman (borgmester), in whom is vested the executive power. In practice, however, the chairman shares this executive power with a number of statutory and other committees which are appointed by the council to prepare matters for submission to the council and to carry out then the decisions of the council in their respective spheres of interest.

Of particular importance is the Treasury and Accounts (finance) Committee, over which the council chairman presides. This acts in the same capacity as a board through its controlling influence on all other committees. Some of the larger municipalities, however, have an official board which consists of the council chairman and from two to four other members elected by the council from among its own membership. On the whole, these boards are vested with the same power as are the Treasury and Accounts Committees and the board members have no special functions. Only in Århus, the largest provincial town, do the board members have executive responsibility over a particular department.

In most of the urban municipalities there is an appointed chief administrative officer, called the director (*kommunaldirektør* or *kaemner*) who works closely with the heads of municipal departments and aids the council chairman, the board, where one exists, and the committees in carrying out their assigned duties and responsibilities.

General provisions for the administration of urban municipalities are established by law. Specific rules are laid down in a set of local government regulations adopted by each individual town council and ratified by the Minister of the Interior. Under particularly close supervision by the state are the financial activities of the municipal government, whereby prior approval must be received before the contracting of loans; the purchase, sale and mortgage of property; the expenditure of certain capital funds; and the imposition of taxes over a certain limit. Furthermore, all town plans must be approved by the Ministry of Housing, as must the appointment of teachers by the Ministry of Education. School superintendents and principals are nominated by the King. A final control over urban municipal activities is the general power of the central government to nullify any unlawful council decisions.

Rural Municipalities ('Sogne Kommuner')

Outside the urban municipalities Denmark is divided into approximately 1300 rural municipalities which differ widely in area and population. These municipalities are established by, and function according to, the terms of the Act of March 25, 1933, as amended in 1950, which pertains to districts and rural municipalities. In general, the functions of these municipalities include: levying taxes on income and real estate; adopting a budget; providing schools; constructing and maintaining minor roads; providing such social services, often in conjunction with neighbouring municipalities, as homes for the aged, housing for the homeless, maternity homes and hospitals.

The representative organ of the municipality is the council (*sogneråd*) which consists of an odd number of members, varying between five and 19, who are elected by proportional representation to serve four-year terms of office. The council, which meets once a month, elects its own chairman (*formand*) who serves as the municipality's chief executive, a deputy chairman and a treasurer, who is usually selected from outside the council membership. At the present time the larger rural municipalities have a salaried official in this position. By virtue of his position the treasurer usually serves as the chief administrative officer of the municipality.

Like their urban counterparts the rural municipal councils function through statutory and other committees, the most important of which is the financial one.

Supervision of the activities of rural municipal councils is by the district councils which have the power to nullify any action taken which is considered by them to be beyond the legal competence of the rural municipality. In addition, prior approval must be received by the rural municipality from the district council in order to contract loans, adopt a budget, buy or sell real estate, make an unusual increase in the tax rate or to establish a joint committee with other municipalities to provide such services as schools, hospitals etc.

Districts ('Amter')

The governor (*amtmand*) of the district is appointed by the Crown at the suggestion of the Minister of the Interior. He thus serves not only as the chief representative of the national government in the district, but also as chairman of the district council (*amtsråd*). This organ is composed of nine to 15 members who are elected by proportional representation for four-year terms of office, at the same time as representatives are elected to the rural municipal councils.

At their meetings the councils have decision-making responsibilities for the district, such as the approval of district tax rates on real property and the budget, building and maintenance of highways, the operation of hospitals, and the supervision of the rural municipalities within their territorial limits.

Most of the same restrictions which are imposed by the Minister of the Interior on the urban municipalities are also imposed by that official on the districts. As in the case of the former, although budgets do not require prior approval, usually large tax increases do. In addition, uniform accounting systems are obligatory for all district governments. Besides the Minister of the Interior, various other central government ministries work closely with the district governments.

ICELAND*

Local government in Iceland had, as its basis and mainspring, even before the days of recorded history, the systematization of the maintenance of the poor. Gradually, under the rule of first Norway, then Denmark, other services were added, until today, as a sovereign republic, Iceland performs the same range of governmental functions as do the other countries of the world.

Under the Act of 1872, the rural municipality (*parish* or *hreppar*) was established as the basic unit of local government in Iceland. As an intermediate level of power, districts (*sýslur*) consisting of several rural municipalities, were retained to perform certain central governmental tasks, as well as to supervise the rural municipal activities. A third unit of local government, the urban municipality, had not developed at the time of the Act, and until today each urban municipality has existed under its own charters and by-laws. Efforts are made to arrive at a national Municipality Act, but they have not been realized as yet.

Urban Municipalities

There are altogether 13 chartered municipalities in Iceland, including the capital. Each is governed by a popularly elected council, varying in size from seven to 21 members, and elected for four-year terms. Each council selects its own chairman, who

* not checked

presides over meetings, as well as various committees, which help carry out the duties and responsibilities of the council. Executive responsibilities are assumed by a mayor, also elected by the council, either from its own membership, or from the community at large. Unless he is a councilman, the mayor is not entitled to vote at the meetings of the council, although he may take part in its deliberations and offer his advice.

The mayor receives regular compensation for his activities, whereas the councilman may or may not be given per diem remuneration. In the larger municipalities, a separate body, called the town board, handles administrative duties. This body is elected by proportional representation by the council from among its own members, and serves as its executive committee.

The principal services provided by the urban municipalities, some of which are statutory, include poor relief, the building and maintenance of local roads, water supply, the building and maintenance of sanitation, housing and public health, police, fire defence, electricity and some cultural activities. The principal tasks of the municipalities are defined in their charters and by-laws and subject to the direct supervision of the Supervisor of Local Government in the Ministry handling local governmental affairs. It is the duty of the Supervisor to give advice to the municipalities, as well as approval for such matters as long-term loans, sale and acquisition of real estate, and the levying of communal taxes beyond a specific amount. In such cases, the Minister's veto is absolute, and there can be no appeal from his decision.

Rural Municipalities

The rural municipalities, for the most part, consist of only scattered farmsteads and villages. Each is governed by a council of three to seven members, who are elected for four-year terms. The chairman, who is chosen by the council from among its own members, is responsible for the executive work of the council and represents the parish on ceremonial occasions. In the more densely populated rural municipalities the council may also elect a paid special chief administrative officer, who may or may not be a member of the council. These officers, plus council-elected committees, are responsible for carrying out the duties and responsibilities of the parish government.

It is the task of the rural municipal council to provide such services as public roads, waterworks, control of housing, aid to the poor, assistance to farmers, sanitation control and public health, and education. Direct supervision of this service is given by the district council in such areas as annual audit of accounts, prior approval of loans, disposition of municipal real estate, and the increase of taxes beyond a specific limit. In these matters the veto of the district council has only deferring power, for if approval is withheld, the rural municipal council may refer the matter to a competent meeting of all taxpayers in the rural municipality, where it may become valid by a 2/3 vote, notwithstanding the refusal of the district council. In addition, should the district council deem a measure adopted by a rural municipal council illegal or contrary to its duties as prescribed by law, or harmful to its residents, it may annul that measure. Disputes on such matters may, however, be referred for decision to the Minister in charge of local government affairs.

Districts

Each of the 21 districts of Iceland covers a varying number of rural municipalities, ranging from a minimum of six to a maximum of 18. Each has a council composed of one representative from each of the rural municipalities, plus a government appointed chairman (*sýslumenn*) who presides over meetings and is the chief district executive officer. As a rule, the council, which is elected for a four-year term, meets only once a year, at which time it discusses not only district business, but rural municipal affairs, as enumerated above, as well. Just as the district council must approve certain measures pertaining to rural municipal government, so must the Minister of Local Government give prior approval to district decisions; he may also annul measures which he considers illegal, or not in the best interests of the citizens.

(3)

CENTRAL AND NORTH-WEST EUROPE

THE GERMAN FEDERAL REPUBLIC

THE structure of local government in Germany is based on the division of the country into two separate and distinct zones. In the Eastern Zone, the German Democratic Republic, local government is fashioned after the Soviet model. In the western part of Germany, the German Federal Republic, local self-government has been established according to western democratic principles.

The German Federal Republic is composed of 10 states (*Länder*), three of which, Bremen, Hamburg and West Berlin[1], have dual status as both municipalities and states. The states in turn are divided into districts (*Landkreise*) and these are sub-divided into municipalities. Some municipalities (*kreisfreie Städte*) are governmentally detached from the district and have a status in this respect which is comparable to that of the city states on the federal level. All other municipalities are within the district administration. In some states the municipalities may join together to form unions (*Aemter*) to perform one or more joint governmental duties. In a few states a further division of territory is the province which serves only in the capacity, however, of an administrative arm of the central government.

---

[1] The status of West Berlin is similar to that of a state, although according to the four power occupation agreements it is not legally incorporated in West Germany.

Urban and Rural Municipalities ('Gemeinden')

All German municipalities are creatures of their respective states, with the result that there are considerable differences in municipal constitutional law throughout the Federal Republic. Common to all states, however, is the obligation established in the Bonn Constitution that the representative organs of the municipalities be selected by means of universal, direct, free, equal and secret ballot, and that the municipalities be guaranteed the right to regulate and assume responsibility for all local affairs within the framework of the laws.

In addition, there are certain principles which are the same for all municipalities. They are as follows: the representative, elected council is the supreme and most important organ in the municipality. The chief executives are either selected by the citizenry or by the council. In the small municipalities these are usually honorary positions; in the larger municipalities, however, these positions are professional and the terms of office of the incumbents are usually longer than are those of the council members. Basically, the municipalities have the authority to carry out all public tasks which are not assigned by law to other authorities. Such tasks may be *a.* voluntary representative governing tasks which are carried out according to the independent decisions of the municipalities as based on local needs and in accordance with the law; *b.* representative governing tasks which the municipalities are obliged to carry out by law; *c.* tasks which are delegated by the central government.

Finally, the municipalities are subject to central government supervision. In the execution of the representative governing tasks (*a.* and *b.*) this is limited to the observance of the laws. In the execution of those tasks delegated by the central government (*c*) the municipalities are also subject, according to the law, to pertinent instructions. The municipalities are also supervised by the state governments. In the case of those municipalities which are not administratively part of the district (*kreisfreie Städte*), state supervision is done through the provinces; in all other municipalities (*kreisangehörige*) state supervision is carried out by the districts. When measures of the supervisory authorities violate self-government laws they may be contested by the municipality before administrative courts.

As for the differences among the municipalities in the German Federal Republic, these relate primarily to structure, of which four constitutional types can be distinguished:

Strong mayor-council system. The main representative organ of the municipality is the council (*Gemeindevertretung*) composed of five to 51 members who are elected for a period of four years. The council, in turn, elects a mayor (*Bürgermeister*) who serves as chairman of the council, in which body he has the right to vote, and as chief executive officer of the municipality. The mayor is the public representative of the municipality, is responsible for day-to-day administration, prepares matters for council decision and carries them out, and has the right and duty to contest decisions of the council when they contravene the law. He is also responsible for the execution of whatever tasks may be delegated to him by the central government. This system is used primarily in Rhineland-Pfalz.

South German council system. In this system which is used in Bavaria and Baden-Würtemberg, the municipal council (*Gemeinderat*) is the main representative organ. The council consists of the mayor and from six to 60 councilmen, all of whom serve four-year terms of office. In addition to serving as chairman of the council the mayor who is directly elected by the population is the official representative of the municipality, prepares and carries out the decisions of the municipal council, supervises the day-to-day administration and has the duty of contesting those decisions of the council which contravene the law.

Council-board system. Again the main representative organ of the municipality is the council whose members (varying in number from 5 to 80) are elected for a four year period. The council elects its own chairman (*Ratsvorsitzender*) to preside over meetings as well as a board (*Magistrat*) consisting of six to 12 members, to serve as the executive organ of the municipality, and designates one of the board members to act as chairman of the board and mayor of the municipality. Tasks of the board include day-to-day administration of the municipality and preparation and execution of council decisions and the contesting of decisions of the council as provided by law. The board chairman, in turn, who in relation to the other members is fundamentally *primus inter pares*, has the right to contest decisions of the board. This is the form of local government used in Hamburg and Bremen and usually in Hesse and Schleswig-Holstein.

Council-mayor-director system. The council, which is responsible for municipal administration, elects from among its own number a chairman who also acts as mayor. The mayor is the political head of the municipality while the administrative work is the responsibility of the chief executive officer (*Gemeindedirektor*). This official, who is selected by the council for a 8–12 year period, prepares and carries out the decisions of the council and also has the duty to contest those decisions which contravene the law. This form of government is used primarily in Nordrhein-Westfalen and Lower Saxony.

For the most part the councils of the municipalities establish general principles according to which administration is to be carried out; make by-laws pertaining to purely local matters; pursue such financial matters as adopting a budget, approving yearly accounts, arranging for loans and making financial and policy decisions on municipal enterprises; and delegate functions to the executive organ and to the committees of council. A few municipalities which have fewer than 200 residents have popular assemblies in addition to the council.

The boards and the executive officers have various individual powers of decision as established by law. On the whole they are responsible for drawing up a budget, executing council decisions, discharging municipal business, defining the duties of municipal departments and officials, appealing decisions of the council which are contrary to law, discharging obligatory tasks described by the state government and seeing to the general administration of public institutions and enterprises.

Among the voluntary tasks of municipalities are: institutions for the general benefit of the people such as theaters, libraries, museums, hospitals, homes for the aged, cemeteries, as well as refuse disposal and sewerage; and public utilities such as gas and electric works, and transport. The obligatory tasks which are prescribed by law include: social welfare services, fire service, primary schools, road construction and maintenance, etc. Besides there are numerous functions which are delegated by the states to the municipalities such as: maintenance of public security, matters concerning trade, civil defense, care of refugees, regulation of traffic.

Districts ('Landkreise')

Like the municipalities the German districts are creations of the individual state governments and the general principles which apply to the municipalities also apply to them, unless special conditions are stated as applicable only to the districts. Comprising the area of the municipalities belonging to it, the district is, in general, responsible for those tasks which are necessary for the district as a whole or the execution of which exceeds the capability of the individual municipalities. These may include: hospital, road maintenance, social welfare, such as youth homes, homes for the aged, schools especially for vocational and agricultural education as well as secondary schools, water supply. In addition, the district is responsible for encouraging representative government in its municipalities. In several states the district is also a province and thus an administrative division of the central government.

The governmental organs of the district are the council (*Kreistag*), the board (*Kreisausschuss*) and the chief executive officer (*Landrat* or *Oberkreisdirektor*). The council is popularly elected, usually for a four-year term of office, and may have 21 to 47 members. It is the supreme organ of the district and makes fundamental decisions on all important matters. Among its tasks is to elect a board, usually from among its own members, which prepares the meetings of the council and carries out those tasks allotted to it by the council. The district board may have 5 to 12 members; the term of office of its members is the same as of the members of the district board.

The chief executive officer of the district (in Nordrhein-Westfalen *Oberkreisdirektor*, term of office 12 years; in other states *Landrat*, term of office from 6 to 12 years) is sometimes elected by popular vote and sometimes by the council. In the southern German states he is, at the same time, chairman of the district council.

Intermunicipal unions ('Aemter')

In three states so-called *Aemter* serve as administrative unions of several municipalities, especially in the rural districts, to carry out tasks of a general nature which are delegated to them by the state government and also to carry out self-government tasks for the member municipalities. Administration of the unions is entrusted to a council and a director. In two states (North-Rhine–Westphalia and Rhineland–Pfalz) the council of the *"Amt"* is elected in general elections by the inhabitants of the constituent municipalities, in Schleswig–Holstein the council is composed of the chairman of the councils of the constituent municipalities plus some members elected by these councils.

AUSTRIA

In 1945 Austria became a free country after seven years of German occupation. At that time it again put into effect its 1920 Constitution, revised in 1929, which provides for a federal form of government, with duties and responsibilities being divided between the central and state governments in such a way that everything that is not expressly assigned to the federal government falls within the independent sphere of action of the states (*Länder*). The basic unit in the Austrian governmental structure is the municipality (*Ortsgemeinde*) which is still functioning to a certain extent under the Imperial Municipal Law of 1862 whose essential regulations were incorporated in the Constitution in 1925. At the present time a move is being made to modernize the municipal law and thus make it more flexible.

Between the municipality and the state is an administrative branch of the state, known as the district, which has no legal identity of its own. In addition, there are 14 municipalities with special charters from state governments. These corporations not only assume municipal responsibilities but district ones as well, and are thus directly supervised by the state governments in the carrying out of the latter duties. Vienna, the capital of the country, holds a special position constitutionally, as it is not only a municipality, but a district and state as well. All three governmental areas are thus united into one organization.

Municipalities ('Ortsgemeinden')

Austrian municipalities (*Ortsgemeinden*) are legal creatures of their respective states and as such have responsibility for carrying out certain duties delegated to them by that government, plus duties delegated to them by the central government. In addition, they must carry out those responsibilities which fall within their own autonomous sphere of action. Regardless of their size all, with the exception of the municipalities which have received special charters from the states and thus have a superior status, are legally equal within each state.

Each municipality has a council which is popularly elected through the system of proportional representation to serve four- to six-year terms of office. The councils vary in size according to population, the usual range being from eight to 39 members, although Vienna's council numbers 100 councilmen. The council is responsible for such activities that fall within the municipality's autonomous sphere of power as the administration of municipal property; contracting loans; approving the budget; making changes in the tax rate, within limits prescribed by law; examining and approving municipal accounts; maintaining municipal roads and bridges; fire protection; building and maintaining primary schools; promulgating police ordinances; appointing certain of the municipal employees; guaranteeing the security of individuals and private property; and providing local police. The law can, however, provide that tasks of the local police can be assumed entirely or partially by special police authorities of the central government.

The council also elects a mayor (*Bürgermeister*), usually from among its own members, and a board which consists of the mayor, from one to three deputy-mayors as decided by the council, and a varying number of other members who are from within or outside the council. As is the case with the council, the number of board members varies according to the state, some of which specifically provide by law that the board may not exceed 1/3 or 1/4 the number of members of the council. In other instances, the 14 municipalities with special charters for example, the charters may specifically establish the maximum and minimum size of the board. In all states the board members serve the same four-to six-year term of office as do the mayor and council.

The board is the executive agency of the municipal government. It effectuates the policy decisions of the council; is responsible for the spending of municipal funds; supervises the construction and maintenance of public works; directs the activities of the local police and supervises public institutions. In some municipalities each member of the board also heads one of the municipal departments.

Chairman of both the council and the board, the Austrian mayor usually possesses the right to veto council decisions. In such an event the council can subsequently pass another resolution effecting a "state of no change" and thereby dispose of the veto's effect. In some states the mayor may then appeal such a matter to the municipal supervisory authority, which is usually the district commissioner. In the 14 municipalities which have their own charters and thus serve also as districts, the mayor, in addition to his municipal duties, also acts as district commissioner in that area, and must carry out the additional state activities which this involves.

A further responsibility of the mayor in all municipalities is to see that those functions and activities which are assigned to the municipality by the federal and state governments are carried out in compliance with regulations and directives handed down by the respective higher authority. In the case of the federal government these assigned functions include such matters as: application of the electoral laws, the taking of the census and of vital statistics, registration of foreigners, preparing rolls for military conscription, aid in administering social security and providing various reports. The functions assigned by the state governments vary, but may include the provision of municipal courts, aid in the field of education and the administration of hunting and fishing acts.

And finally, in one state, a further duty of the mayor is to preside over a yearly assembly of all the voters to inform them of future plans and to then allow for general discussion of these plans.

Within their sphere of inherent authority the municipalities are virtually independent. Certain actions, however, such as the contracting of loans, must receive prior approval. Also, uniform instructions drawn up by the Federal Ministry of Finance must be followed by the municipalities in the compilation of budgets and in the drawing up of accounts. Although no prior approval is required for either of these documents, in municipalities with at least 20,000 inhabitants the mayor must submit copies of the budget and of the accounts to both the Accounting Court and the state government each year. Accounts in these same municipalities are also audited each year by the Accounting Court which operates on behalf of the various state governments. This same Court also audits the accounts of institutes, funds and organizations for whose administration the municipality is directly or indirectly responsible and does test-checks in those municipalities with less than 20,000 inhabitants if a well-founded request to do so is received from the state government concerned.

In some states control is also exercised over local governments by the right of referendum, by which a fixed minimum number of voters can ask for a vote on questions concerning municipal affairs. The results of such a referendum, however, are not binding on the municipal government.

In the field of delegated functions, local municipalities are directed and closely supervised by the state and central government authorities to see that they do not exceed their legal powers and do not infringe upon the laws of the higher governmental units. When this is found to be so, the municipal legislation is then annulled. Additional supervision is given by the various central ministries in those municipal fields with which they are particularly concerned.

Districts

The Austrian districts have no legal personality and exist only as administrative divisions of the state government. An exception to this are the 14 municipalities with special charters which serve as both municipal and district units of government. The districts have no representative body which serves in a legislative capacity, but do have a commissioner who is appointed by the state to serve as the district's chief executive. A major part of his responsibility is to supervise the activities assigned to the municipalities by the state or national government, as well as to carry out any state and central government responsibilities specifically delegated to him. In all matters regarding strictly state matters the commissioner is responsible to that government; for matters pertaining to the federal government he is responsible to the state governor and to the various governmental bodies of the federal government.

SWITZERLAND

Until the middle of the 19th century Switzerland was a confederation whose member states, the cantons, were completely sovereign. With the Constitution of 1848, revised in 1874, she became a federal state in which the sovereignty was in theory divided between the central state and the 22 cantons, three of which are subdivided into two demi-cantons with equal sovereignty. The cantons and demi-cantons are sovereign in all fields where the Constitution does not expressly provide for the jurisdictional competence of the Confederation, and are therefore not comparable to the provinces of a unitary state. Such a strongly decentralized organization finds its *raison d'être* in the extreme diversity of Switzerland which includes a population having four different languages and two different religions.

Within the framework of their sovereignty the cantons determine for themselves their own internal organization. Seven of them have decentralized their administration by dividing their territory into districts or circles (*Bezirke* or *Kreise*) which have at their head a prefect or commissioner who represents the cantonal government.

Municipalities ('Communes')

The territory of the cantons and of the districts is divided into municipalities, known in Switzerland as *communes*. They are not, however, administrative divisions as are the districts, but are autonomous units with the right of representative government within the framework fixed by the Constitution and by cantonal laws. The Confederation, including as it does 25 cantons and demi-cantons, has 25 different systems of local administration

SWITZERLAND

PATTERN OF GOVERNMENT UNITS

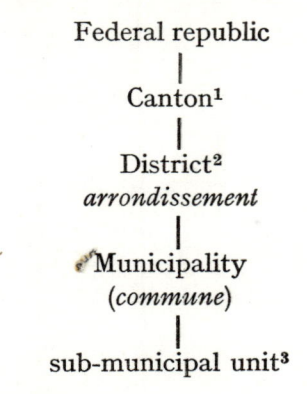

Federal republic
|
Canton[1]
|
District[2]
arrondissement
|
Municipality
(*commune*)
|
sub-municipal unit[3]

[1] Including the 6 demi-cantons
[2] In all but 8 cantons
[3] In a few communes

STRUCTURE OF A MUNICIPAL GOVERNMENT
WITH A REPRESENTATIVE COUNCIL

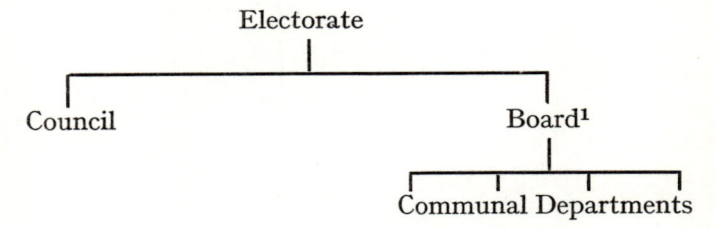

Electorate
├── Council
└── Board[1]
    └── Communal Departments

[1] In the canton of Vaud the representative councils elect the boards

STRUCTURE OF A MUNICIPAL GOVERNMENT
WITHOUT A REPRESENTATIVE COUNCIL

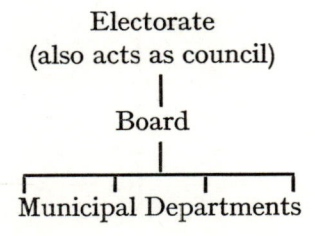

Electorate
(also acts as council)
|
Board
|
Municipal Departments

and the extent of autonomy allotted to the municipalities varies from canton to canton. In a general way this autonomy is more extensive in German Switzerland and in the Grisons than in cantons where French and Italian are spoken.

Until the 19th century Swiss communes were political or economic corporations composed of people who were citizens of the commune, the rights of this communal citizenship being hereditary. The development of industry involved important migrations within the country and part of the population could not henceforth participate in the life of the commune of residence, since this no longer co-incided with the commune of birth. The Constitution of 1874 remedied this situation by providing that all active citizens could take part in the political life of a commune, if they were residents of it for at least three months. Thus the political commune, called municipality (*Einwohnergemeinde, municipalité*), which includes all the population residing in one commune became the most important organ of local administration. The burgher commune (*Bürgergemeinde, commune bourgeoise*), composed of persons who originate from the commune, continues, however, to co-exist with the political commune for the same territory in the majority of the cantons.

A distinction is still made in several cantons between the parish commune (*Kirchgemeinde, commune paroissiale*), which groups the inhabitants of a commune of the same religious denomination and ensures the practice of religion; the school commune (*Schulgemeinde, commune scolaire*), which provides for education; and the public assistance commune (*Armengemeinde, commune d'assistance*). This co-existence of several types of commune is peculiar to Switzerland.

Switzerland has 3,101 political communes, or municipalities, whose administration is generally entrusted to two main organs, a deliberative authority with legislative powers, and an executive authority entrusted with administering and directing municipal services. In 2,795 municipalities (generally those which are not densely populated) the deliberative body is an assembly of electors (*Gemeindeversammlung, assemblée communale*) which meets periodically and which is the supreme communal organ. By this typically Swiss system, which is that of *direct democracy*, the people are called upon to deliberate as a whole on such communal affairs as approval of municipal regulations, the budget, accounts and the issuing of loans; the acquisition and disposal of real estate; and the nomination of members of the executive authority.

In municipalities which are more densely populated, especially in towns, the communal assembly can, or must be replaced, depending on the canton, by an elected council (*grosser Gemeinderat, conseil communal, consiglio comunale*). Election may be either by proportional representation or by a simple majority. In this connection, some cantons impose a system which is uniform for all their municipalities while other cantons leave the choice to the municipalities.

In the municipalities that do not have a council there exists the institution of the *referendum*, by which the municipal council submits certain of its decisions to a vote of the people. The conditions under which these referenda take place are regulated by cantonal law. Sometimes the referendum is mandatory for important communal affairs or for decisions which involve expenditures over and above a fixed amount, in which case the people must automatically be called upon to vote on the decisions of the municipal council. Sometimes the referendum is optional, which means that a vote of the people takes place only if a certain amount of electors request such a vote within a period of time determined by law. Only the optional referendum is required by some of the cantons.

Furthermore, in municipalities having a people's assembly each citizen has the right of *initiative* which enables him to make proposals for municipal action. Such a request is made by a petition which must be signed by a certain number of electors. In most of the cantons this right of initiative also exists in those municipalities which do not have a council.

In general, Swiss municipalities are administered by a board or college which has a number of names: *Gemeinderat*, or *Stadtrat* in German Switzerland; *municipalité, conseil communal, conseil municipal*, or *conseil administratif* in French Switzerland; and *municipio* in the Ticino. This body, which directs various municipal activities and services, is composed of from three to nine members who are popularly elected usually for a four-year term of office. The president of the board (*Gemeindepräsident, Stadtprä-*

sident, Stadtammann or *Gemeindeammann, maire, syndic* or *sindaco*) is either designated by that body from among its own members, or is named by the communal assembly or the municipal council. Usually the president has special powers which distinguish him from the other members of the board; sometimes he is only the *primus inter pares*.

For the most part municipalities assume functions in the following fields: local police, which includes security, control of morals, control of foreigners, etc.; in many cases also the organization of education; the construction and maintenance of public buildings, highways, museums, theatres and slaughter-houses; and the provision of funeral services and of public assistance.

Municipal authorities are subject to supervision by the cantonal authorities which is more or less strict according to the canton and the degree of autonomy allotted the municipality. This control is to ensure above all the legality of municipal decisions and the avoidance of municipal debt. It is exerted in the following ways: periodic inspections; the possibility of a representative of the cantonal government participating in the deliberations of communal bodies; and the mandatory ratification of such municipal decisions by cantonal authorities as the adoption of municipal regulations, the budget and the accounts of the municipalities, transactions in real estate and the issuing of loans.

When the cantonal government notes that there are irregularities, abuses or bad management within the administration of the municipality it can take various measures, ranging from a simple warning to the municipal authorities in question, to annulment of decisions and even to the revocation or dissolution of the municipal body. Such measures must sometimes be ratified by the cantonal parliament, to which the municipalities may have recourse in certain cases.

In addition, several cantonal laws enable the canton to appoint an administrator to directly manage the affairs of a municipality which is in particularly grave circumstances. Such a measure, which must be decided upon and approved by the cantonal parliament, is rarely taken for it implies putting the municipality under tutelage and thus attacks the very principle of municipal autonomy.

The autonomy of the municipalities is protected by law in that they have recourse to the highest court of the country, the Federal Tribunal (*Tribunal fédéral*), when the municipalities feel that the cantonal authorities are exceeding their powers of supervision or are making arbitrary decisions.

THE NETHERLANDS

The territory that is now The Netherlands, Belgium and Luxembourg was greatly influenced first by the Romans and then by the Franks. Following the death of Charlemagne and the disintegration of his realm there developed in this area numerous local aristocracies who formed a number of countries, marquisates and duchies which were then acquired by the Duke of Burgundy, subsequently passed on to the house of Habsburg by marriage, and eventually were passed to Philip II of Spain in 1555. Under his rule the territory revolted and there followed an 80 years war ending with freedom from Spain for the northern provinces in 1648; the southern provinces, however, alternated between the control of Spain and Austria. Finally all were incorporated into the French Empire under Napoleon.

In 1814 the Treaty of Paris formed the provinces of Holland and Belgium into the Kingdom of the Netherlands, but 16 years later the southern provinces broke away and formed the Kingdom of Belgium and in 1890 the union with Luxembourg came to an end. Thus was formed the present Kingdom of the Netherlands which has existed until the present time.

Governmentally, the country is divided into 11 provinces and 994 municipalities. In addition to these there are the territories of the IJsselmeer polders, which are now in a transitional period and therefore cannot be classified as either provincial or municipal.

Municipalities ('Gemeenten')

All Dutch municipalities, into which the entire country has been divided, have been accorded the same powers and legal status under the Municipal Act of 1851. Duties and responsibilities for

THE NETHERLANDS

PATTERN OF GOVERNMENT UNITS

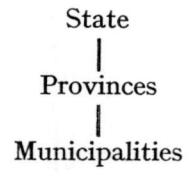

State
|
Provinces
|
Municipalities

STRUCTURE OF MUNICIPAL GOVERNMENT

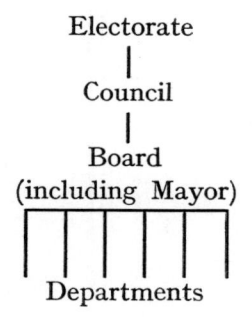

Electorate
|
Council
|
Board
(including Mayor)
Departments

formulating and executing municipal policy are divided among the council (*gemeenteraad*), the board (*burgemeester en wethouders*), and the mayor (*burgemeester*) alone, although ultimately the power rests with the council.

Composed of seven to 45 members who are popularly elected by proportional representation for four-year terms of office, the council makes decisions on all affairs of municipal interest that are not otherwise delegated to the board or to the mayor. These include the fixing of tax rates; the formulation of regulations for the maintenance of public order, morals and health; and the construction of roads, bridges, airports, tramways, etc. The council also prepares the municipal budget, contracts loans, purchases and sells municipal property and appoints certain officials. Finally, the municipal council may be called upon to execute central government laws and decrees in such fields as building and housing and the control of the sale of alcoholic beverages. Any subsequent central government law that is enacted, which deals with a matter on which the municipality has already legislated, invalidates the local regulation. In many cases, however, the central government laws establish only broad outlines and the municipality makes supplementary regulations which thus allow for differences in execution according to the character of the municipality.

Responsibility for carrying out daily governmental tasks such as executing council decisions, preparing matters to be submitted to council and supervising municipal affairs lies with the board. This body consists of the mayor and from two to six other members who are elected by the council from among their own number to serve four-year terms of office. In the larger municipalities the individual board members (*wethouders*) are responsible for supervising the execution of council policy by one or more municipal departments and therefore work closely with the respective department heads. Over-all co-ordination, however, is exercised by the board as a whole, with the mayor playing a leading role. A final duty of the board is to carry out functions delegated to it by the state and provincial governments.

In the larger municipalities, at the request of the board, the council may appoint three to five member Committees of Assistance from among its own members to aid and advise the council in the execution of its duties. Such Committees of Assistance, the total number of which varies according to the size of the council, may be concerned with such fields as finance, municipal enterprises, sea and air ports, housing, traffic, public health, public works and education. Members are selected according to their knowledge of the various aspects of municipal government and it sometimes happens that proposals rejected by the Committees of Assistance are then withdrawn by the board and not presented to the total council for discussion and action. Conversely, suggestions from the Committees of Assistance are often adopted by the board and are either put into effect by that body or are presented for approval to the council as a whole.

The chief executive of the municipality is the Crown appointed mayor (*burgemeester*) who serves a six-year term of office. Unless he has been nominated in another municipality, moreover, the mayor is almost automatically re-nominated after his term of office has expired. The role of the mayor is two-fold: to fulfil his responsibilities to the municipal council and to serve as the local representative of the central government. In his municipal functions he serves as chairman of both the council, in which he has no vote, and the board, in which he does. In his latter role he may also cast the deciding vote in case of an even division of opinion. Primarily his duties involve co-ordinating daily administration; signing, with the municipal secretary, all correspondence and official documents assigned to his authority; representing the municipality in all litigations to which it is a party; and performing many ceremonial functions.

The mayor is also responsible for protection against fire and for the maintenance of public order. In the larger municipalities which have their own police force the mayor is their direct supervisor. In those municipalities where order is maintained by the state police, although the mayor may request their use, he has no direct or absolute command over them. In case of public disturbances the mayor may draw up and proclaim "police regulations" which must be made known to the provincial governor and to the municipal council as soon as possible. Such regulations remain in force only after ratification by the council at its next meeting, providing that their execution has not meanwhile been suspended by the provincial governor.

As an agent of the central government the mayor's chief responsibility is to guard against municipal violations of the national laws and encroachments upon the national interest. Therefore, he may hold up, for 30 days at the most, the execution of a decision of the council or of the board which in his opinion is contrary to the law or to the general interest and should be suspended or annulled by the Crown. Many mayors also consult their councils on the performance of functions which the central government has delegated to them or to the board, solicit their advice and subsequently explain their course of action, although they are not legally obliged to do so.

Responsibility for the daily work of municipal employees rests with the municipal secretary (*secretaris*), which position in some of the smaller municipalities may be combined with that of mayor. The financial affairs of the municipality are partly in charge of the receiver (*ontvanger*) who serves as bookkeeper, treasurer and tax collector.

Dutch municipalities are responsible in many realms to the provincial and central governments. All important resolutions of the municipal council, especially the budget, accounts, loans, purchase and disposal of property, lease of buildings, contracts for execution of work, and institution of legal proceedings, must be approved by the provincial board before they can be put into effect. All by-laws concerning municipal taxes must be approved by the central government (the Crown).

The Crown may also nullify any municipal resolution that conflicts with a law or with the public interest; this power, however, is exercised with the utmost reserve and care. In addition, all by-laws with penal sanctions must be submitted to the provincial board. If such by-laws are contrary to the law the provincial board will so advise the Crown, who may then nullify the by-laws. Finally, where the central government finds that a municipal government neglects its tasks or in general acts contrary to the public interest, Parliament can by a special act remove the municipal council in office and replace it with a special delegate of the national government. However, this has happened only three times and then for a relatively short period.

Provinces ('Provincies')

Like the municipalities, each of the 11 Netherlands provinces has a popularly elected council, which varies in size from 35 to 82 members, and whose term of office is four years. The function of the council is to legislate in those fields with which the province is charged, such as public health, social and cultural work, agriculture and public enterprises, providing such regulations are not contrary to the acts of the central government or to the general interest. They also levy taxes and set fees for provincial services and may be required to execute acts and decrees of the central government. A special function of the council which is shared with the provincial board is to establish and regulate the *"waterschappen"* or boards which are responsible for the maintenance of dry land and for the level and quality of the water; the care of drinking water, however, lies outside their competence.

Daily oversight of provincial affairs is entrusted to a board (*Gedeputeerde Staten*), consisting of the governor and six members elected by the council from among their own number to serve four-year terms of office. Whereas the main task of the board is to execute the ordinances, regulations and resolutions of the provincial council, they also are charged with certain tasks by the central government, as well as certain responsibilities concerning the supervision of the *"waterschappen."* Furthermore, they are charged with the supervision of the municipalities and have the semi-judicial function of making a decision in those cases where there is a right of appeal.

At the head of the provincial government is the governor (*Commissaris der Koningin*) who is appointed by the Crown for an indefinite period. Like the municipal mayor the governor may only give advice in regard to matters which come before the council, of which he is chairman, but he has a full vote in decisions of the board, of which he is also chairman. Like his municipal counterpart, too, the governor may suspend execution for 30 days of a provincial council or board resolution if, in his opinion, it is contrary to the law or to the general interest, and should be suspended or annulled by the Crown.

In his role as agent of the central government, which is a more important aspect of his position than is the case of the mayor, the governor may advise the Crown on the appointment and reappointment of mayors, and he may receive various instructions from the Crown which he is compelled by law to carry out. To a certain extent, too, the governor is responsible for the maintenance of public order in the province.

Control over provincial government by the Crown is similar to that of the provinces over the municipalities, although stricter in some respects. All provincial ordinances, for example, must be approved by the Crown. The provinces are political units of a different character than are the municipalities; they are more important in guidance and control than in direct action.

BELGIUM

Belgium, essentially a route of passage between northern and southern Europe and between England and the Continent, has a continuous history of domination by first one and then another of the great European powers, either by conquest, treaty or marriage. Fifteen years after being re-united with Holland the Belgians revolted, and in 1830 established a constitutional monarchy, which has existed until the present time. From its domination by France Belgium received its administrative organization of nine provinces, which are subdivided into 26 districts (*arrondissements*), which are, in turn, further composed of some 2,660 municipalities (*communes*).

Municipalities ('Communes')

The large amount of autonomy which Belgian municipalities enjoy today is rooted in feudal times when it was difficult for governments located in distant countries to organize strong central agencies in their provinces. Thus, the Constitution of 1831 continued this tradition by delegating to the local governments the right to regulate all that is within their exclusive interest and which is not otherwise delegated to a higher governmental unit. To carry out this task the Communal Law of 1836 provided for a popularly elected council (*conseil communal*), a board (*collège des bourgmestre et échevins*), and a mayor (*bourgmestre*). The council is selected by proportional representation for six-year terms, and varies in size from seven to 45 members, depending on the population of the municipality. Its competence includes adopting the municipal budget, establishing taxes and fees, regulating municipal enterprises and making ordinances concerning the entire range of local government services. In this respect its competence is limited only by that which is given by law to the board, and in case of any doubt, competence automatically goes to the council.

From among its members the council, in turn, elects by proportional representation from two to eight councilmen who serve, with the mayor, a six-year term as the municipal board. As such their duties consist of publishing and putting into effect the regulations passed by the council; authorizing expenditures from public funds; collecting revenues; administering public property; supervising municipal employees other than the police; representing the municipality in judicial matters; approving building by both private citizens and business enterprises; and supervising the development of the municipality in accordance with a master plan, where this exists. In the last two instances, appeals may be made from the decisions of the municipal board to the board of the provincial council or to the courts when it involves a question of ownership of property. The board is also responsible for the supervision of commissions of public assistance and care of the insane, and for the carrying out of any duties delegated to it by the provincial or central governments, such as the application of the electoral laws. Individually, board members are responsible for the supervision of one or more municipal departments.

Serving as chief executive of the municipality for a six-year term is the Crown-appointed mayor (*bourgmestre*), who is recommended by the municipal council from among its members. Although the council may, if it so desires, submit a name from outside its membership, this is rarely done and first requires the approval of the board of the provincial council. In effect, the mayor is a political choice and as such represents the strongest party or party coalition on the local political scene. In addition to answering the local correspondence and serving as the ceremonial head of the municipality, the mayor presides over both the council, and the board. For the municipality itself, his principal duty is to see that the laws and regulations of the council and the board are executed. For the central government he acts as an agent for the carrying out of provincial and central laws and regulations and the supervision of certain services. The foremost of these is the maintenance of good order and public security through direct supervision of the police force, and the issuing of directives for its work, although general police regulations are legislated by the council. Other responsibilities may be assigned to him from time to time and for these he is responsible to the provincial governor or to the central government ministries.

Supervision of day-to-day municipal administration may be entrusted to a municipal secretary who serves at the pleasure of the council, and whose nomination, suspension and dismissal must be approved by the higher authorities.

Although the local authorities enjoy much discretion in the regulation of purely municipal matters, all laws and ordinances are nevertheless subject to examination by the provincial board. This is to ascertain that the legislation is within the law as well as within the delegated sphere of action of the council. Financial matters must be submitted to the provincial board or to the King, who acts on the advice of the former, for prior approval. Thus, the annual budget, in which the provincial board may write items which are required by law or may remove non-essentials in order to attain equilibrium, must be approved. The provincial board must also approve annual accounts of receipts and expenditures; transfer, sale or exchange of public real estate; long-term leases, loans and mortgages; partition of real estate if this has not been done by the court; levying of taxes, tolls and fees; acceptance of donations and legacies to the community in excess of a certain minimum; and the setting or changing of the salaries of the mayor and the board. Prior approval must also be obtained from the provincial authorities for all decisions regarding the use of public lands for pasturage; right to cut firewood; location and use of halls, markets, slaughter-houses and fairs; and construction projects or major repairs or demolition. In addition, certain social service activities must be approved by the King, who also sees that no religious discrimination is made in the granting of such aid.

Where action is taken by municipal authorities which is considered contrary to the law or not in the general interest, the provincial governor may suspend the law or regulation, and the provincial board may decide whether or not to uphold his decision. If they do not, the governor may then appeal the adverse decision of the board to the Crown, which must annul the legislation within 40 days of the receipt of the governor's communication concerning the suspension. If annulment is not made within this time, the local legislation may then be put into effect. In addition, the governor or provincial board may directly interfere in the affairs of a municipality where it is considered that there is neglect of duty. This may be based on negligence to perform tasks prescribed by law or to carry out orders or instructions issued by higher authorities. In such cases one or more commissioners may be sent to the municipality to take appropriate action, at the personal expense of the municipal official who is at fault, and the local authorities may be ordered to act themselves or a task may be directly carried out by the governor's office. The necessity for such action on the part of the governor and the provincial board, however, is rare.

Districts ('Arrondissements')

The districts in Belgium exist to aid the provincial governments in carrying out their responsibilities. They do not have a legal personality of their own nor any kind of legislative body. The chief executive in the district is the commissioner (*commissaire*), who is appointed by the Crown, and whose main responsibility is to supervise the activities of municipalities under 5,000 population, unless they are the capitals of the district, in which case they are then directly supervised by the provincial authorities. Supervised himself by the provincial governor and the board of the provincial council, the commissioner watches to see that local authorities execute the general laws and maintain public order. He also may give advice and information on request and serves as the liaison between the provincial and the local governmental units.

Provinces

Like the municipality, the Belgian province has a council (*conseil provincial*), popularly elected by proportional representation, but in this case, for a term of four years. In size the council ranges from a minimum of 50 to a maximum of 90 members, and it is charged in its yearly sessions, or in those which are specially called, with legislating on all matters which concern the interests of the province and which are not otherwise delegated to other governmental bodies. These include adopting a provincial budget, approving yearly accounts, levying fees and taxes, making nominations and presentations, and discussing any matters presented to it by the board or the governor. It also elects a president every four years who presides over the council sessions.

Between sessions the work of council is carried out by a board (*Députation permanente du Conseil Provincial*) whose six members, also serving four-year terms, are elected by majority vote and by separate lists for each seat. Such a system results in a coalition of the majority parties, with no representation of the opposition. The board supervises the execution of council legislation and the day-to-day administration of provincial affairs. The governor can question the right of the board to raise matters for investigation by the council, from which decision the board can then appeal to the Crown, with the approval of the governor. Where approval is not granted, the matter cannot then be pursued further.

Primarily, the work of the board is to administer the goods and finances of the province. An important task is to prepare the budget, which must then be adopted by the council. It may also exercise all the powers of the provincial council when it is not in session, with the exception of passing the budget, accepting the accounts and making nominations and presentations. The board also plays an important role in the supervision of municipal administration, especially in the area of prior approval or advice before approval. More and more, the board is acquiring special functions which it carries out not only as "deputy" of the council, but directly by virtue of the law. In this way its importance is considerably increasing and its work-load becoming greater.

Presiding over the board, in which he has a vote, is the Crown-appointed governor. As an agent of the central government his task is to execute state laws and supervise the general administration of central regulations and ordinances; maintain public order, which includes the power to enact police regulations; make a preliminary examination of and supervise the execution of the decisions of the provincial council and its board; and to generally supervise the actions of the province and of the municipalities and sub-provinces within his area. When a council decision is considered by the governor to be against the public interest, the governor may suspend its execution or take whatever other measures that are provided by law, and refer the matter to the King whose decision is final.

Just as the provincial authorities supervise the legislation and activities of the municipal governments, so does the central government supervise the activities of the province. All legislation is examined by the Minister of the Interior and, where pertinent, by any other minister, to see that it conforms to the law and that it is in the general interest and without prejudice, excess or encroachment on other governmental bodies. Further control is maintained through the appointment and removal of the governor, the chief agent of the central government in the province.

LUXEMBOURG

Until 1868 the history of Luxembourg is a series of foreign rules over this small country strategically located between the major powers of Europe. Burgundy, Spain, France, Holland and Belgium at various times were in control of the country until the Congress of Vienna met in the last half of the 19th century and certified the country's freedom, this time from the neighbouring state of Belgium. At that time the Grand Duchy of Luxembourg, a constitutional monarchy, was established, which form of government remains to the present time.

Administratively the country is divided into districts and municipalities (*communes*).

Municipalities ('Communes')

The law governing the Luxembourg municipalities is inspired to a large extent by its Belgian counterpart; organization and powers of the local governments are based on both the Constitution and on a number of ordinary laws.

The main organs of municipal government are the council (*conseil communal*), the board (*collège des bourgmestre et échevins*), and the mayor (*bourgmestre*). The council is popularly elected for a six-year term of office by absolute majority in municipalities with less than 3,500 inhabitants and by proportional representation in those exceeding this population figure, and varies in size according to the population of the municipality. Regular council meetings are called by the board as needed or, in case of emergency, by the mayor or by a majority of the council members; all meetings are presided over by the mayor. Any councilman who is not at three consecutive meetings without a good excuse can be declared decommissioned by the Minister of the Interior on the request of the other council members.

The competence of the council includes adopting a budget and voting taxes and fees; organizing such public services as water supply and fire protection; passing rules concerning the administration of the goods and property of the municipality and the regulation of building, sanitation matters, traffic, health and safety and public order, naming various municipal officials, such as the treasurer and the municipal secretary, where one exists, and setting their salaries; and approving the budgets and accounts of almshouses run by the Bureau of Social Aid, as well as approving certain other public welfare decisions.

To help it with its work each council can establish various committees (*commissions*) composed of council members. These committees study such matters as finance and the regulation of municipal affairs and give advise to the council in their field of interest and prepare proposals for council decision. With the exception of the school committee, of which the mayor or a person delegated by him is chairman, all committee chairmen are named by the council.

The execution of council decisions is the responsibility of the board whose members in the larger municipalities are appointed by the Grand Duke (Duchess) from among the council members; the mayor, however, may be appointed either from within or outside the council membership. In the smaller municipalities the board is appointed by the Minister of the Interior from among the council members. For the most part these appointments are based on recommendations of the municipal councils themselves.

During its six-year term of office the board serves as both an agent of the state and an agent of the municipality. In its former role it sees to the execution and decisions of the central government ministries and of the Grand Duke (Duchess), oversees the keeping of the civil register and archives and takes inventory of public property; and supervises the public almshouses and the Bureau of Social Aid, certain of whose decisions it must approve.

As an agent of the municipality the board sees that council decisions are put into effect; publishes council and board regulations; decides what activities the municipality will undertake and appoints municipal employees; supervises municipal expenditures and accounts; administers municipal property and the collection of municipal revenues; and undertakes legal actions in the name of the municipality. Although the board cannot delegate its power of decision to anyone else it can designate one of its members to investigate a matter and then prepare a proposal for submission to the council. In certain cases, however, such as when inaction would cause prejudice or inconvenience, the mayor can act alone; he must then report his action to the other members of the board at its next meeting. Also in cases of emergency the mayor has the casting vote; otherwise the matter is discussed again in the next meeting of the board.

Like the other members of the board the Luxembourg mayor has a dual responsibility, to the state and to the municipality. As an agent of the central government the mayor executes the decisions of ministers or of the Grand Duke (Duchess) in police matters and serves as an officer of the police judiciary. Thus, in the smaller municipalities where there is no police commissioner the mayor has the power to investigate and draw up information against any contraventions of the law, which power may also be delegated to a member of the board with the consent of the state prosecutor. He must also attend certain meetings of the administrative board of the public almshouses and the Bureau of Social Aid at which he is allowed to vote.

As an agent of the municipal government the mayor is charged with the execution of municipal by-laws and regulations; serves as president of the council and of the board; and signs the municipal correspondence. In case he is unable to fulfil his duties, because of illness or for other reasons, the mayor may be replaced by the first member of the board.

Of importance among municipal officials is the treasurer (*receveur*) who is responsible for collecting the municipal taxes and fees and for making payments in accordance with the budget or with special provisions. In only one municipality there is also a secretary who is appointed by the council with the approval of the Minister of the Interior. The secretary takes minutes at council and board meetings, works with the council committees, and countersigns by-laws and regulations of the council and the board, public acts, municipal correspondence and demands for payment.

Although the authority of the central government extends to all matters throughout the country, the municipality has a certain amount of autonomy within its legal sphere of competence. Matters which must receive the approval of the central government are the municipal budget and accounts, the establishment and abolition of taxes, the acquisition and transfer of real estate mortgages, the construction of municipal buildings and the issuance of municipal bonds. In addition, certain other municipal matters must receive prior approval from the central government, through the district commissioner, the Minister of the Interior or the Grand Duke (Duchess) before they can be effectuated. Any measures taken by the municipality which exceed stated powers or are contrary to the law or the general interest can be suspended or annulled by the Grand Duke (Duchess) who can also suspend the council for good reason.

Districts

The districts of Luxembourg serve only as administrative agencies of the Duchy. They are headed by centrally appointed commissioners who are the intermediate authorities between the central and the local governments. In certain cases the commissioners exercise a power of supervision over the communes; generally they only transmit the decisions of the local authorities to the central authority and annex their advice. In principle the commissioners have no regulative power.

(4)

THE EAST EUROPE GROUP

THE UNION OF SOVIET SOCIALIST REPUBLICS

THE beginning of the modern phase of Russia's history can be dated back to the revolution of 1917. It was not until 1923, however, that a federal union was established and the basis for the present governmental structure was laid. At the present time the structure of the USSR consists of 15 states (republics), 142 provinces (territories, autonomous regions and national areas), 3,980 districts, 5,024 urban municipalities and 46,675 rural municipalities.

Each of the governmental units in the USSR, regardless of size, has a similar structure and comparable functions. The result is the unified system of government for the entire country which is described below.

Urban and Rural Municipalities, Districts and Provinces

The representative organ of each of the units of government in the country is the council (Soviet of Working People's Deputies), which is considered a local organ of the state. The members are popularly elected by secret ballot to serve two-year terms of office. The size of the council depends on the population and area of the respective governmental unit and may vary from 20 to over 100 members (deputies).

Under article 97 of the Constitution of the USSR and the respective constitutions of the republics and provinces, each local council is a legal entity whose function is: to direct the work of the local staff, to ensure the maintenance of public order and the observance of the laws, to protect the rights and interests of the citizens, to settle their requests and complaints, to draw up the budget and to direct economic and cultural affairs.

In carrying out these functions the councils consider and approve the current and long-range plans for the development of the economy and culture within their area and see to their fulfilment. They co-ordinate the drafting, and control the carrying out of housing and municipal development plans, social and cultural development and local improvement work, adopt the budget and approve the report on its execution during the preceding year and see to the financing of local industry and social and cultural measures. Furthermore, the councils direct the development of local industry, supervise the work of the enterprises subordinate to the higher state organs, direct the development of agriculture and take the necessary measures to promote bigger crops and higher productivity of livestock. The councils also administer the municipal services, housing and trade, enforce the law on universal compulsory education and take the necessary measures to develop health services, cultural activities and social insurance.

Council sessions, which may be called by the board on its own initiative or if demanded by no less than 1/3 of the councilmen, are conducted by a chairman assisted by a secretary. They are elected for each session by the council from among its own members. Questions for discussion by the council are submitted by its board, standing committees and individual councilmen. The latter also have the right to submit questions to heads of offices, enterprises and organisations which individuals are obliged to make replies in a period specified by the respective council. Councilmen may also make inquiries on any question within the competence of the council to the board and the heads of its departments and divisions, regardless of the session agenda. The group or individuals to whom these inquiries are addressed are then obliged to reply to the inquiries during the given session or, in exceptional cases and by permission of the council, at some later date set by the council.

Council decisions are adopted by a majority vote and are signed by the chairman and secretary of the board while the records of each session are signed by the session chairman and secretary. Meetings of the councils may be attended, in a consultative capacity, by members of the councils of the higher governmental units as well as by representatives of central government offices, factories, collective farms, co-operatives and other public organisations, workers, collective farmers and office employees.

The executive organ of the council is the board which is elected for a two-year period of office by the council from among its own members. The board consists of a chairman, vice-chairman, secretary and several members, as decided by the council. The board has a dual responsibility, to the council which elected it and to which it reports on all its work and to the board of the next higher unit of government.

The board exercises control over the economic, cultural and political development of its territory on the basis of the decisions of its council and the organs of the higher units. It thus passes decisions and issues orders which may be revoked, however, both by the council which elected it and by the board of the higher unit. Upon expiration of the term of office of a council the board retains its powers pending the formation of a new board by the newly elected council. The newly elected council is convened by the board of the outgoing council not later than 15 days after the election.

The boards of the provincial, district and urban municipal councils have departments and divisions which are formed by the respective council; these are not established in the rural municipalities. Such departments and divisions exercise direct control over all governmental activity in the area such as health, education, general affairs, building and architecture, social insurance, finance, motor transport and highways, local industry, agriculture, planning and personnel, the latter of which is under the chairman of the board. Other departments and divisions may be set up under the law in accordance with the particular needs of the respective area; all have a dual responsibility, to the local council and its board and to the respective organ of the board of the higher council.

To deal with the main fields of governmental activity during its term of office each council sets up standing committees which vary from council to council. For the most part the committees are set up in accordance with the basic branches of economic, social and cultural activities and are auxiliary organs of the council. Thus they participate in the preparation of the questions submitted to the council or its board, make proposals, appoint members to report on questions and help supervise the carrying out of the decisions and orders of the council and its board, as well as the decisions of the higher state organs. The committees also organise the population for the practical implementation of the decisions and orders of the council and its board and the higher state organs, in addition to which they supervise the work of the respective departments of the board and the enterprises, offices and institutions subordinate to them. The committees, in turn, are subordinate to the council which establishes them and to whom they report on their work.

Each council is guided in its work by the Constitution and laws of the USSR and the respective province, the decrees of the supreme executive organs of the Union and the ordinances and orders of the higher councils and their boards. Decisions of a council may be suspended by the executive organ of a higher unit and annulled by the council of a higher unit. Furthermore, each councilman is responsible to the electors, both on the work of the council as a whole and on his own work, and may be recalled from the council at any time by a decision of these electors, as prescribed by law. Finally, in the event of a council vacancy the board of the higher council calls for new elections in the respective constituency within two months of the vacancy.

POLAND

In 1919 the independence of Poland was officially recognized after many years of partition among Austria, Prussia and Russia. In 1939, however, Poland again lost its independence and until 1944 was occupied by Germany. When Poland regained its independence a provisional government was established which became generally recognized in 1945. The new Constitution was adopted in 1952.

The state of Poland is divided into 17 provinces (*voïvodies*), plus five cities with provincial status; some 400 districts, of which 75 have the status of municipality and district; and, at the base, the urban and rural municipalities. The larger municipalities are divided into sub-municipal units.

Urban Municipalities

The present system of local government in Poland was established in 1950, and further legislation was passed in January, 1958. Whether large or small all municipalities have similar structure and basic competence and the same organs of government, which are the council, the committees and the board. The board, in turn, directly supervises the departments.

The urban municipal councils are elected by all citizens over 18 years of age to serve three-year terms of office. Candidates are nominated by political and economic organizations, unions and youth organizations which are united in Committees of National Unity. The elected council ranges in size from 16 to 50 members for the average municipality, up to more than 100 members in the large municipalities that also have the status of province. All councilmen may be recalled on the demand of the electors.

In their meetings, which take place at least once a month, the urban municipal councils discuss and make decisions on those matters of local interest which are delegated to them by the state, usually on the basis of the size of the municipality, its degree of urbanization and the rights of the municipality, the district or the province. In general, however, the competence of the council includes primary schools for which the council constructs and maintains buildings and engages teachers, as well as supervises the course of study. The council also has responsibility for secondary schools as well as for the supervision or establishment of various professional schools. In the field of public health the council sees that medical assistance is organized and establishes and maintains hospitals and special dispensaries and clinics for mothers and babies, as well as crèches for children and nursery schools. It is also responsible for protecting the individual farmer and the co-operatives and helping fight plant and animal diseases, maintaining public order and security, which includes supervising the

POLAND
PATTERN OF GOVERNMENT UNITS

```
                State
                  |
               Provinces
                  |
               Districts
        _____|_____
       |           |           |
     Rural       Urban       Urban
 Municipalities Municipalities Municipalities
                                |
                         Sub-Municipal Units
```

STRUCTURE OF AN URBAN MUNICIPAL GOVERNMENT

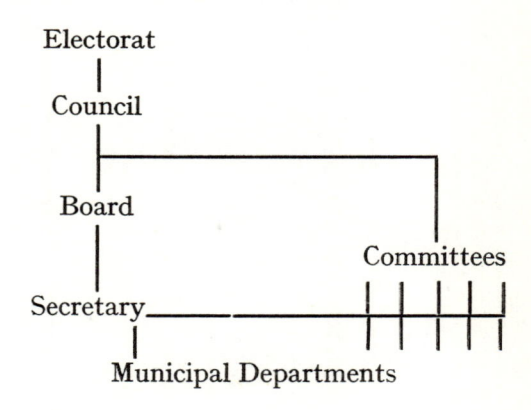

```
            Electorat
               |
            Council
          _____|_____
         |                     |
       Board                   |
         |               Committees
     Secretary_____  | | | |
         |                | | | |
   Municipal Departments
```

POLAND
PATTERN OF GOVERNMENT UNITS
State

Province

Districts

| Urban | Rural |
| Landau Municipalities | Staedtgach | Municipalities |

Sub-Municipalities

STRUCTURE OF AN URBAN MUNICIPAL GOVERNMENT

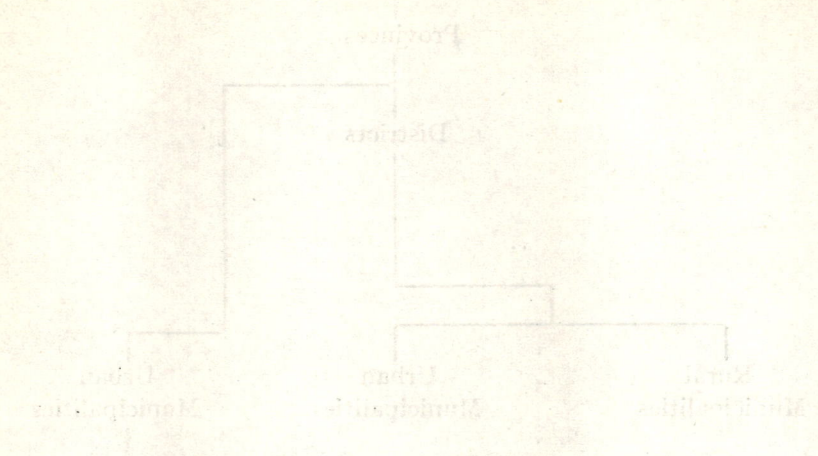

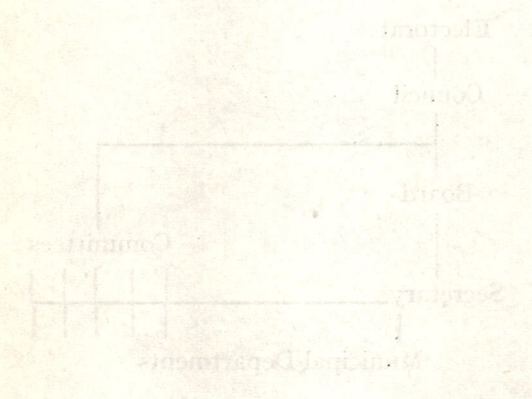

Electorate

Council

Board

Committees

Secretary

Municipal Departments

activities of the militia, providing leadership in the time of natural disasters, and promulgating local and state regulations aiding and controlling the activities of individual artisans and private commerce; and supervising the organization of national commerce and industries in the municipality. Finally, the council administers such municipal enterprises as transportation, street cleaning, water supply, housing projects and construction.

To see to the execution of their decisions and the fulfilment of administrative tasks the urban municipal councils elect a board and various administering committees, and one of the council's main responsibilities is to carefully supervise their activities. The council may also, through its committees, question the activities of any municipal or state department or institution located in the municipality and these, in turn, are required by law to give explanations. They must also co-ordinate their activities with those of other such organizations and institutions in the municipality, at the request of the council.

The number of standing and special purpose committees, used by the Polish urban municipality as well as their range of power is individually determined by the council and thus varies from municipality to municipality. Membership, which usually consists of five to 15 persons, includes both council and non-council members and the main "raison d'être" of the committees is to involve the greatest possible number of citizens in the government of the country. The activities of the committees include preparing matters for discussion by council, in which instance they may give advice on the way in which a matter should be handled, and promoting activities which the committee feels should be carried out. They also supervise the various fields of activity of the council and exercise those measures of control delegated to them by the council, although the committees themselves do not have the right of decision or of rule making. Responsibility of the committees is directly to the municipal council.

In addition to the administering committees, the urban municipalities organize various other committees, such as those of parents, youth, neighbourhoods, etc. Considered auxiliary organs of the council these latter committees have the right to make proposals to the council about matters concerning them specifically as well as about financial and economic plans of the municipality in general. The competence of committees elected by tenants, which exist in the various neighbourhoods of the municipality, includes supervising the sanitary conditions of dwellings, the maintenance of lawns and the lighting of streets, as well as providing cultural activities for the local residents.

Selected by the council from among its own members, the board of the Polish municipalities consists of four to nine members who can also be dismissed by the council at any time. Otherwise the board serves the same term of office as does the council, which is three years. The composition of the board is a president and from one to three deputies, depending on the size and importance of the municipality, the secretary and a varying number of other members. Its main functions are to determine such matters which have been delegated to it by the state, as drawing up a projected budget and economic plan for the municipality, as well as to prepare the agendas for council meetings and report to that body on its activities, execute the decisions of the council, and direct all municipal activities under its supervision, which includes most of the municipal departments and institutions whose officials it may also engage.

The president of the board organizes that body's work, supervises daily administration of municipal affairs, executes board and council decisions, assumes leadership in the case of an emergency when the total board is not available, and serves as the chief representative of the urban municipality. He is assisted by a secretary of the board who prepares documentation for the council and co-ordinates the work between the board and the committees.

All municipalities with over 200,000 population have sub-municipal units, each of which has its own popularly elected council, committees and board. Besides acting as an electoral unit, the sub-municipal units also carry out any administrative duty assigned to them by the municipal council.

Control over the activities of the urban municipalities is exercised both horizontally and vertically. Municipal councils supervise the activities of their boards, committees and departments. The counterpart local government organs at the next highest level, be they district or province, closely control the work of those directly below them in the hierarchy. The Council of State, which is subordinated to the Parliament (*Sejm*), supervises the work of the councils and the Council of Ministers supervises the work of the boards. They give directives and instructions to the local councils and boards, examine reports of their activities and guide their work in general.

The law provides that decisions of local bodies (councils, boards and municipal departments) may be annulled or execution suspended where such decisions or actions are against the law or do not conform with the fundamental policies of the state. Such annulment or suspension may be done by counterpart organs at the next highest or at any other higher level.

In 1954 a new unit of administration, the settlement, was created to help accelerate the work of urbanization in residential suburbs of factory workers, colonies of fishermen or resort areas. The settlements have their own councils which have the same rights as do those of the municipalities.

Rural Municipalities

Contrary to the practice in many other countries throughout the world, the trend in rural government in Poland has been to create more, rather than fewer, rural units with the purpose of thus increasing citizen participation in the municipal government of the country. The result is that there are now approximately 8,100 rural municipalities with an average population of 1,800 inhabitants.

Like the urban municipalities, those in the rural areas have a popularly elected council consisting of from 11 to 27 members who are elected to serve three-year terms of office. They deliberate and make decisions on those matters which are delegated to them by law. They also select from among their own membership a board composed of from three to four persons which assumes the executive duties of the rural municipality and such committees (which usually number from four to six), as they may need.

In addition, the council appoints a secretary who is responsible for the co-ordination and supervision of the daily administration of rural municipal government. This secretary may be neither a member of the council nor of the board.

In addition to the council rural municipalities have popular assemblies which are organized at the initiative of the council or of the inhabitants to discuss such local questions as the betterment of economic and cultural conditions, increases in rural production, innovations in agriculture and various hygienic services. Assemblies can decide to carry out certain works and to impose a levy on the local inhabitants to cover the cost of such works. Aid, however, is given by the state in such fields as construction and repair of roads, electrification and land improvement.

Another responsibility of the assembly is to elect a liaison officer (*zoltys*) who serves as the link between the municipal council and the people. The *zoltys* also convokes the general assemblies and presides over them, keeps the board informed of current happenings, sees that decisions of the council are carried out and presents to the council the complaints and suggestions of the citizens.

As with the municipal units of government in the urban areas, control exercised over the rural municipalities by the district and the other higher units of local government is extensive and is exercised horizontally as well as vertically.

Districts and Provinces

The structure of government for both the districts and the provinces is comparable to that of the municipalities. The councils are popularly elected and in the districts vary in size from 50 to 60 members who meet at least once every two months. In the provinces the councils consist of 80 to 120 members and meet at least once every three months. Elected by the councils from among their own members are the boards, which vary in size from four to six members for the district and somewhat larger for the province, and the committees, whose number varies from six to eight members. In addition to carrying out those tasks delegated to them or which come within their sphere of competence by law, the districts and the provinces directly supervise the activities of the governmental units below them in size. Control, like that in the urban and rural municipalities, is both horizontal and vertical.

BULGARIA

In 1908 Bulgaria declared its independence after many years under Turkish suzerainty and established its own government headed by a Tsar. This form of government continued until 1946 when a country-wide referendum called for its replacement by a republic. The People's Republic of Bulgaria was then established under the Constitution of 1947. The present governmental structure has been strongly influenced by that of the Soviet Union.

Bulgaria is a unitary government which, as of January 23, 1959, has been divided for administrative purposes into 30 provinces, three of which are cities including Sofia, the capital. The provinces, in turn, are subdivided into some 108 urban municipalities and 882 rural municipalities. This new partition of territory is based on economic units which have been formed, with the provinces corresponding to economic regions and the municipalities corresponding to the territories of the unified agricultural co-operatives.

Municipalities

Bulgarian municipalities, both urban and rural, are based on the Constitution and the People's Councils Law of 1948. Regardless of size, all have the same structure and functions, which vary slightly according to the size and needs of the population. The organs of municipal government are the council, the board and the permanent committees (or commissions). Also, as in the other People's Republics, the Communist Party has an important role in all governmental affairs. Daily administration of urban municipal affairs is carried out by various divisions, bureaus, sections or services, such as those for commerce, rural economy, and recruitment of men for military service. In the rural municipalities these functions are assumed by the board.

Municipal councilmen are popularly elected from single-member wards to serve a three-year term of office. The councils meet in regular sessions once a month and in extraordinary sessions when the need arises. The presiding officer of the council is newly elected at each meeting and serves only for the duration of that meeting. In general, the responsibility of the council is to perform both the local and the state tasks which are delegated to it by law. Specifically, the council passes ordinances in regard to, as well as sets fines for the infraction of, the following matters: maintenance of public order; assessment of taxes and duties; direction of all sanitary, public health, lodging, social welfare and cultural enterprises; control of the forests; method of work in the industrial enterprises and the public utility establishments within the municipality; betterment of the local economy; administration of farmers' and workers' co-operatives; fight against plant diseases; and the obligatory course of school study. Tasks performed directly for the state are public transportation, communications and national defence.

The council also selects a board from among its own members, and various permanent committees (or commissions), all of whom also serve three-year terms of office. In addition, the council closely supervises the work of the board, by accepting the budget and the accounts and by checking on the legality and regularity of its decisions, which may be annulled if they are not in order. At their meetings the councilmen may also question the president or any members of the board or the head of any service, bureau, or division in the municipal government. Finally, the council may demand information on the activities of any establishment, organization or enterprise within the municipality, which demand must be answered within five days.

The council-elected board is the executive agency of the municipal government. It consists of a president; vice-presidents, the number of which is determined by law, according to the population of the municipality and the size of the council; a secretary; and a varying number of members, again depending on the population of the municipality and the size of the council. Its responsibility is to set up a budget, keep the municipal accounts, create needed local enterprises, with the approval of the respective state minister, execute the decisions of the municipal council and fulfil any other responsibilities which are specifically assigned to it by law. The president of the board co-ordinates its work as well as the activities of the various municipal services. He also represents the council in legal matters, signs correspondence, and performs ceremonial functions.

Each of the permanent committees established by the council has a chairman and from two to 10 members who serve for the council tenure. They may call in workers, artisans and representatives of the various economic, social and cultural activities of the municipality as specialists. The number of committees and the activities they encompass vary with the municipality and may include such matters as finance, municipal economy and public works, public instruction, public health, social welfare, agriculture, forests, local industry, commerce and food control.

Control over municipal activities is both horizontal and vertical. The council closely supervises the activities of the board and the board, in turn, supervises the activities of the council. Either may annul the decisions of the other which are considered illegal or irregular. In addition, the counterpart of the council, the board and the municipal bureaus, divisions, sections or services on the next higher, or provincial, level supervise the activities of those below them. Especially important is financial control, which is continuous. The Minister of Finance must approve budgets before they can be put into effect, as well as closely supervise the expenditure of municipal funds. In addition, councils may be dissolved by the provincial counterpart as well as by the President of the National Assembly, in which case the dissolving authority then names a provisional board to function until the newly-elected council elects its own board. Functions of the state government which are performed by the municipality are directly supervised by the respective state ministry.

Provinces

The popularly elected provincial councils closely resemble in structure their urban and rural municipal counterparts. By virtue of a recent law the former competence of the councils, which included public instruction, public works, industry and commerce, protection of water supplies and means of production, public health and social welfare, cultural activities, sports, and supervision of the activities of the lower governmental units, has been enlarged. Thus, in line with the acceleration of the development of the national economy and the bettering of the material and cultural conditions of the people, the provincial councils have now become the centre of the economic, cultural and state life in their territory and are the local organs of the state, both economically and administratively.

As in the municipalities, the execution of council decisions is carried out by the provincial board and by the various divisions and services and permanent committees which give aid and advice on request. Furthermore, control over provincial activities is also exercised both horizontally and vertically by the National Assembly, the Presidium and the President of the Presidium. In addition, with the abolition of those ministries whose tasks were recently entrusted to the provinces, the Council of Ministers has created special committees, such as those for industry and technical progress, construction and architecture, work and prizes and for control by the state, to supervise the principal branches of the economic and cultural life of the country and to assure the realization of the national tasks which have been established.

YUGOSLAVIA

The first common state of the Yugoslav people was created after the first World War through the union of the two independent states of Serbia and Montenegro with the Croats, Slovenes and those segments of the Serbs who had lived under the Austro-Hungarian Monarchy before its collapse. Between the two wars the Yugoslav Kingdom was a highly centralized state with poorly developed forms of local government.

In 1941, Yugoslavia was invaded and occupied by German forces. A short time later the first uprising of the Yugoslav people took place and wherever territory was liberated local organs called People's Liberation Committees were established. Although government was highly centralized immediately after the war, functions were rapidly delegated to the local organs of government by the laws of 1946, 1949 and 1952. The present local government law was passed in 1955 and new additions made in 1957.

Yugoslavia is a federal country which is divided into six states (*republics*) which are in turn, with the exception of Montenegro, the smallest state, subdivided into districts. The districts are composed of municipalities (*communes*) and all, irrespective of size and whether urban or rural, have the same legal status. Following reorganization in 1955 the number of Yugoslav municipalities was reduced by approximately one-quarter with the result that they have thus become economically stronger and better able to perform the many tasks required of them.

Municipalities ('Communes')

Almost every Yugoslav municipality has a bicameral municipal council, called the *People's Committee*, which is composed of a political chamber (*Municipal Council*) and an economic chamber (*Council of Producers*). The former is a general representative body elected by all adult citizens by direct, equal and general ballot. The economic chamber, on the other hand, is composed of representatives of industry, transport, commerce and agriculture and the number of councilmen from each of these groups is based on the proportion of that group's contribution in the municipality to the total economy. The economic chamber comprises two basic producer groups. The first are workers and various office employees engaged in industry, mining, forestry, construction work, transport, the post, telegraph and telephone service, commerce, municipal services and those in the handicraft trades, both members of the handicraft co-operatives and independent craftsmen who are members of their respective trade associations. The second basic group is composed of agricultural workers and represents the various farm co-operatives composed of farmers who own their own land, and the employees of co-operatives or state farms.

Members of the political chamber of the municipal council are elected by electoral units, each of which, as a rule, comprises one village or settlement. The more densely populated areas, however, consist of several such electoral units. The range in size of the council is from 15 to 70 members, and all are elected for a four-year term of office. The electoral units for members of the economic chamber (*Council of Producers*) are the organizations of workers and such like in the various branches of the economy and the term of office is also four years. In size this chamber ranges from 75 to 100% of the number of members of the political chamber. Any member of the economic chamber ceases to serve when he is no longer employed in the organization, co-operative or association in which he was elected.

Although the economic chamber of the municipal council is not completely equal in power to the political chamber, neither is it an advisory body. Both chambers participate, at separate meetings, in the enactment of the economic plan, in the adoption of the municipal budget and the approval of the annual financial report, in the founding of enterprises and institutions, in the adoption of municipal pay scales, in the distribution of funds and the disposal of public property, and in all other decisions concerning the economy, finances, social insurance and labour relations in the municipality. No decisions or acts of the council in regard to these matters may be put into effect unless both chambers, at their separate meetings, have voted on identical texts. Should any disputes arise the matters are settled by arbitration committees selected jointly by the two chambers.

At a joint meeting the two chambers of the municipal council elect from among their own membership a council president or mayor, and vice-president, the president of each chamber, and members of the joint committees. They also appoint the municipal secretary and his aides, municipal court judges and other municipal officials, and appoint and dismiss the directors of municipal enterprises in accordance with the proposals of the joint committee (*commission*) of the two chambers concerned with such matters.

All other business of the council is discharged by the political chamber. This includes social welfare and public health matters, various communal services, education, cultural activities and daily administration. The economic chamber, on the other hand, is responsible for sanctioning the decisions of management, handling any questions that arise in regard to labour-management relations, and seeing that the economic enterprises fulfil such obligations as paying taxes, etc. Permanent committees (*commissions*) composed of members of both chambers of the municipal council examine and make proposals to the respective chambers or to the council as a whole on such matters as elections and nominations, petitions and complaints, regulations and or-

YUGOSLAVIA
PATTERN OF GOVERNMENT UNITS

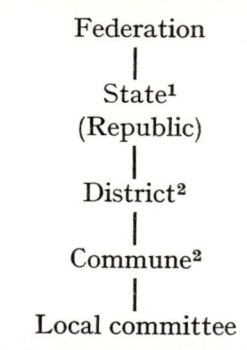

Federation
|
State[1]
(Republic)
|
District[2]
|
Commune[2]
|
Local committee

[1] called Republics; one has two semi-autonomous provinces within it
[2] some communes in urban areas are associated together in urban committees.

STRUCTURE OF MUNICIPAL GOVERNMENT

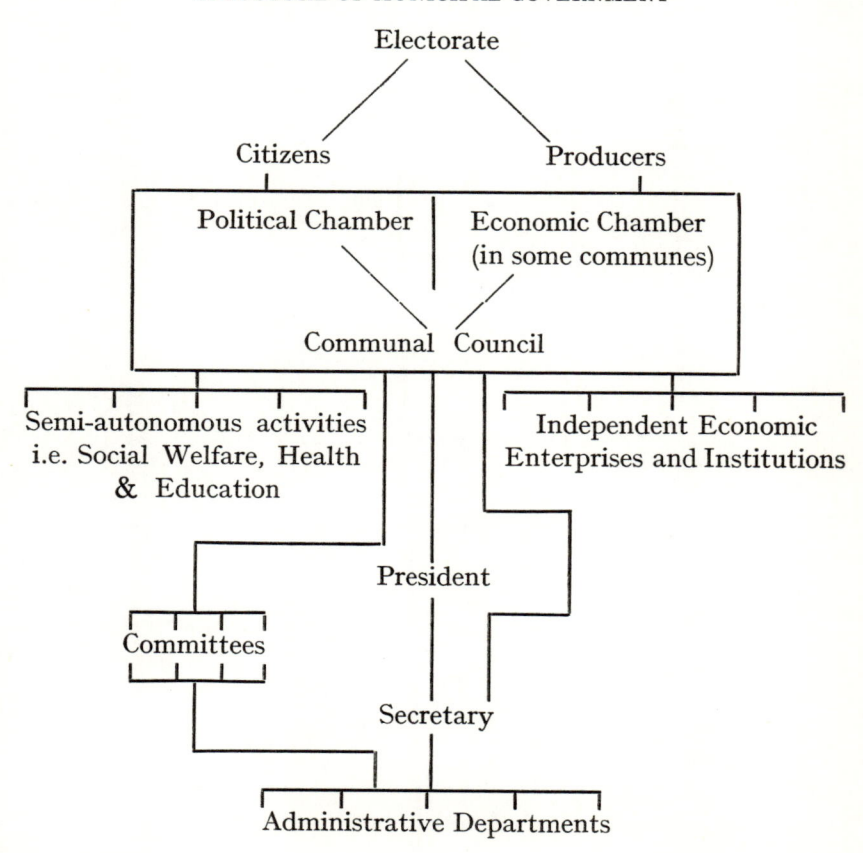

Electorate
/   \
Citizens   Producers

Political Chamber | Economic Chamber (in some communes)

Communal Council

Semi-autonomous activities i.e. Social Welfare, Health & Education

Independent Economic Enterprises and Institutions

President

Committees

Secretary

Administrative Departments

ganizational matters, general economy, and credentials and immunity. Joint special committees are also established to deal with specific problems as they arise. As a rule, no matter which is in the jurisdiction of one of the joint committees may be discussed by the council as a whole, until the responsible committee has first examined the matter.

A large amount of the council's work is delegated to functional committees (*boards*) which are concerned with such matters as town planning, finance, housing, education, cultural activities, public health, social welfare, mother and child welfare, labour relations, agriculture, forestry, general administration, sports, tourism and commerce. Associated organs of the council, each of these committees has from 5 to 13 members, at least 2 of which must also be members of the council. By far the largest number of committee members, however, are citizens who represent pertinent organizations and groups within the municipality. Committee meetings are devoted to discussing proposals to be recommended to the council, passing by-laws when authorized to do so, supervising the pertinent work of the municipal administration and acting as a link between the local government and the various independent institutions and organizations within the municipality. Clerical and administrative tasks of the committees are performed by the secretariat of the council.

The foremost figure of the council is its president who is elected by that body from among its membership to serve a four-year term of office. His duties involve presiding over the council, for which he also prepares the agendas, acting as the legal representative of the council, and generally co-ordinating the work of the selfgoverning institutions and the government within the municipality. The president may also stay the execution of any decision of a municipal department which has been adopted without the proper administrative procedure, and is thus considered illegal, in which case he must so inform the council of his action at its next meeting.

Serving as co-ordinator of the daily administration is the municipal secretary who is appointed by the council and is directly responsible to the council president. In this capacity the secretary is responsible for the organization and functioning of the administrative organs and assigning personnel to them. The secretary also attends all meetings of the council, in which he has no right to vote, and on invitation meetings of the various committees. To both the council and the committees the secretary gives legal opinions on important matters that arise.

Within the area of competence of the municipality, which covers all local matters except those which are specifically designated to some other level of government or to some self-governing organization or institution, there is a great deal of independence. The district council may supervise the work of the municipal councils within its territory, but only in terms of controlling the legality of municipal council decisions, not their merit. When decisions are found to be outside the law, the district or state council, not the executive or administrative authorities, may annul the local decision. On the other hand, should any regulation or other decision be enacted by a superior governmental authority which infringes a legally determined municipal right, the municipality may file an appeal with the designated authority.

Sub-Municipal Units (Local Committees)

Those municipalities which include several villages or settlements may, if they desire, form local committees in order to discharge business of direct interest to the local population. This usually occurs when the size of the municipal territory and the dispersion of the settlements is such as to allow no direct participation of the citizens in municipal government, or when the formation of a committee is requested by the local population.

Committee members consist of the municipal councilmen who have been elected from the territory of the local committee and a number of members elected by the voters at their meetings. Funds required by the local committee to carry out its tasks are obtained from the municipal budget and administrative work is often done in conjunction with the local office of the municipal government, as the local committees do not have administrative employees of their own. Supervision of the work of the local committee is undertaken by the municipal council which may annul any decisions which are illegal.[1]

[1] A recent Act on community settlements, dating from 22 April, 1959, provides for the establishment on a large scale of community councils in municipalities.

Intermunicipal Units (Town Councils)

Some of the densely populated areas of Yugoslavia are composed of several municipalities, each of which has the same status as that of all other municipalities throughout the country. Many matters, such as a water system, sewage disposal, public transportation and general area planning, can best be handled for the area as a whole. In these instances, the law empowers the district council to unite the work of the component municipal councils.

In other densely populated areas which also include several municipalities, the district council may, when desirable or necessary, organize a special intermediary council (*town council*) to assume certain municipal and district functions. Such is the case in districts which are predominantly agricultural and where the district council cannot therefore devote sufficient attention to the problems of the urbanized area. The intermediary council thus formed may consist of members of the district council who are elected from the municipalities within the populated area, members of the municipal councils involved, or a combination of the two, as determined by the district statute.

The intermunicipal council is not an organ of government, nor does it have committees or special administrative organs; it works merely as a representative co-ordinating body. Accordingly, it enacts no administrative decisions, but may make decisions on matters of a general nature, which are then binding on the component municipal councils, organizations, self-governing institutions and inhabitants. The intermunicipal council may also decide that certain of its decisions be enforced by the administrative authorities of the district council, which is under obligation to do so.

District

The second tier in the fundamentally two-tier local government system of Yugoslavia is the district, which closely resembles the municipality in structure. One major difference, however, is that the district council, which also consists of two chambers, is not elected directly by the people of the district, but is elected instead from among members of the component municipal councils, according to a determined procedure.

The district looks after the work and checks on the legality of actions of institutions and organizations which have a broader character, scope and interest than do the individual municipalities, such as the district hospital and the secondary and higher schools. The district is also in charge of various economic, cultural and social affairs of general interest to the municipalities in its territory. Of greatest importance, however, is its co-ordination and channeling of economic development within the district territory. In this regard, one of its significant tasks is to give assistance to underdeveloped municipalities.

Supervision of district activities by the state is similar to that exercised over the municipalities by the district, with state organs having the same power of review, especially as regards legality of decisions and actions.

(5)

THE SOUTH EUROPE GROUP

FRANCE[1]

IT is under the laws passed by the Constituent Assembly at the time of the revolution in 1789 that the present territorial and administrative divisions of France were established. The historical provinces which had previously existed were abolished and the new system was marked by a strong trend toward decentralization. This structure has undergone further changes since then, particularly in 1800 when Napoleon Bonaparte re-drafted the whole system of local government and gave it the basic foundation it has today.

Territorially, the country is divided into 90 provinces (*départements*) which comprise over 300 sub-provinces (*arrondissements*). The latter consist of some 3,000 cantons, which in turn include approximately 38,000 municipalities (*communes*), the basic French local government unit.

Municipalities ('Communes')

The Communal Charter of April 5, 1884, as amended, is the legal basis for municipal government today. Its most prominent feature is that all communes, with the exception of Paris, the capital, have the same system of government. All, too, have a dual function as autonomous local governmental units and as local

---

[1] Revisions of the legislation promulgated in 1959 have been incorporated.

units for certain parts of the central government administration.

The representative body of the municipality is the municipal council (*conseil municipal*) whose members, in communes with over 120,000 inhabitants, are popularly elected by proportional representation. In municipalities less than this size election is by simple majority vote. In size the councils vary from nine to 37 members, and all councilmen serve a six-year term of office. Each council, in turn, elects from its membership the municipal mayor (*maire*), who is a deliberate political choice, and from one to 12 assistant mayors (*adjoints*), depending on the size of the commune. These together form the corporation or *municipalité* and serve in this capacity, unless removed for some reason, for the term of the council. Although the mayor is legally the only official charged with municipal administration, he may delegate part of his functions to his deputies or, in certain cases, to a member of the municipal council. Thus, in the larger municipalities, the deputies may be charged with the supervision of one or more municipal functions or departments, for which they are directly responsible to the mayor. He, in turn, is responsible to the council.

At its regular meetings held four times a year, or at special sessions called by the mayor, 1/3 of the council, or the provincial governor (*préfet*), the municipal council carries out its general grant of power to provide for all matters of municipal interest. Among those duties specifically defined by law are adoption of a budget, approval of the yearly financial accounts, maintenance of public property, buildings and roads, and the provision of public education, health, sanitation, and assistance services. Other matters of municipal interest vary from commune to commune and within their broad grant of power the councils may initiate, control and administer a variety of services, as well as grant leases and make proposals to join a "*syndicat intercommunal.*"[1]

---

[1] Such "*syndicats*" are public bodies with the status of corporate body and a budget of their own. They can be established for the carrying out of works or management of services which are of an intermunicipal interest. Although municipalities used to be free to join such syndicates, as a result of recent legislation affiliation can be made compulsory for certain municipalities if a legally defined majority of the municipalities concerned have approved the establishment of the syndicate in question. Recent legislation also provides for the possibility for municipalities situated in a metropolitan area to form an "urban district" for the accomplishment of common services.

FRANCE

PATTERN OF GOVERNMENT UNITS

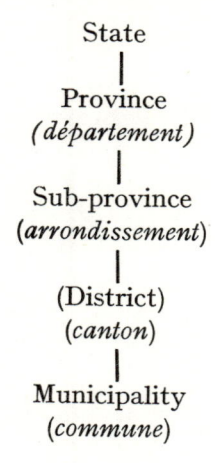

State
|
Province
(*département*)
|
Sub-province
(*arrondissement*)
|
(District)
(*canton*)
|
Municipality
(*commune*)

STRUCTURE OF MUNICIPAL GOVERNMENT

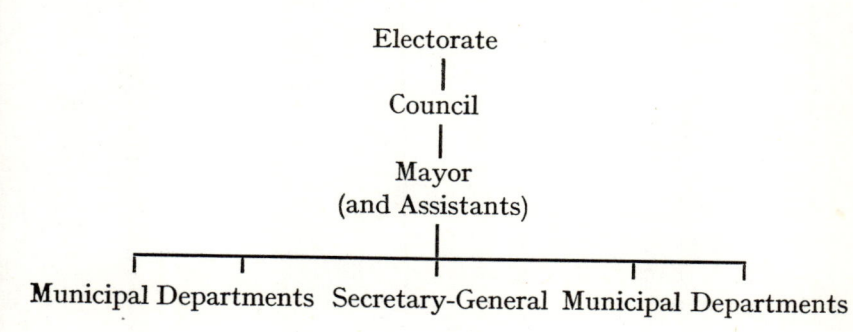

Electorate
|
Council
|
Mayor
(and Assistants)

Municipal Departments — Secretary-General — Municipal Departments

To aid it in its work the council may appoint from its membership standing and special committees, varying in size and number with the municipality. The former provide continuity in government when the council itself is not in session, while the latter may be used to investigate and make recommendations on specific problems which have come before the representative body.

As chief executive of the municipal government, the French mayor puts into effect the decisions of the council, over which he presides; he is responsible to this body for his actions in these matters. He also represents the municipality in legal matters and in dealings with the central government, and serves as the commune's first citizen. By virtue of his office the mayor draws up the agenda for council meetings, initiates measures for consideration by the council, and acts as the overall supervisor of municipal personnel. He alone, with the aid of his deputies, can draw up the municipal budget, although items may be amended or rejected by the council. Once the budget has been accepted, however, only the mayor can authorize expenditures from municipal funds and ensure the legality of the financial accounts. Thus, he may decide in what order work will be carried out and although the total sum under each budget heading may not be changed, the mayor may reallocate funds within these headings and thus determine, to a great extent, just how the available community funds will be spent. The only check the council has on these actions is to make a yearly examination of the accounts and to question the mayor on any entries in the municipal books. This is the only session of council over which the mayor is expressly forbidden by law to preside.

Just as the mayor has a great deal of initiative in matters of expenditures, so does he in other matters of administration. Not infrequently, however, a municipal council questions whether or not a mayor has overstepped his legal subordination to them. In such cases the council may appeal directly to the provincial governor to order the mayor to carry out orders they find he has neglected, or they may appeal to an administrative court to annul decisions they claim to have been enacted outside the spirit and intent of the law. In cases where neglect is charged the governor may order the mayor to act, and refusal to do so is then considered breach of duty and is followed by suspension from functions or, as a last resort, dismissal from office by the Minister of the Interior. Where appeal has been made to an administrative court on the legality of a mayor's decision, such a decision may be annulled. If, however, the council claims compensation and its appeal is granted by the court, the mayor may be held personally liable for the cost of work done or damage suffered. For the most part, the quality of the relationships between the mayor and the municipal council is determined by the former's personality and personal prestige, and to some extent by the balance of political forces in the council. Where friction exists that cannot be resolved the mayor may resign or if he does not, all his proposed measures, especially acceptance of a budget, may be opposed by the council, with the result that the Minister of the Interior may be forced to call for its dissolution, followed by new elections, at which time the mayor may or may not be re-elected.

In many of the larger municipalities day-to-day administration is often under the supervision of a secretary-general. He is directly responsible to the mayor and it is to him that the department heads report, although the mayor and his deputies may have general oversight of one or more communal departments. In these municipalities the mayor serves mainly as a policy maker and political leader.

In addition to his purely municipal duties, for which he is responsible to the council, the mayor also serves over half the time as an agent of the central government, and in this role he collects statistical information, registers births and deaths, compiles military conscription lists and agricultural statistics, issues certificates and references, publishes the laws and provides any other information requested. For these duties he is directly responsible to the provincial governor or to the sub-governor.

A third area of responsibility of the mayor is that of protecting and maintaining the public security, morality and hygiene (*police municipale*), under the control of the prefect or sub-prefect. His powers here vary according to the size of his municipality, for in communes with over 10,000 inhabitants police are under state control. In this case the chief executive is only vested with powers of restraint and may issue decrees pertaining to security of the highways, decent burials, sale of pure foods, safety of public and private buildings, control of stray dogs, and order and safety in markets, fairs, and other places of public gathering. In the smaller municipalities, in addition to the above mentioned duties, the mayor must also appoint and supervise the local police force, which may be supplemented by state personnel in times of emergency. General control over the ordinances issued by the mayor in pursuing these police functions is exercised by the *Conseil d'Etat*. At the provincial level, the governor may request certain policing action which, if refused or neglected, may result in the governor or the sub-governor personally issuing orders for the municipality. The governor may also make a general provincial ordinance which then supersedes those of the individual communes.

Control over municipal government by the higher authorities is extensive. Although, by virtue of the principle of local autonomy, decisions of municipal councils are self-executory, certain action must receive prior approval by a higher authority, be it sub-governor, governor or Minister of the Interior, depending on the size of the commune.[2] All ordinances and decisions must be transmitted to the prefect or sub-prefect for examination as to legality before it can be put into effect. Where municipal legislation conflicts with a national law or an administrative regulation, or where certain conditions for the time and attendance of the council meeting were not met, the higher authority may state his objections to the legislation and request that the mayor resubmit it to the council, or he may annul the legislation. When the latter occurs, the municipality then has the right of appeal to an administrative court for a final decision. In addition, certain defined legislation must receive prior approval of a higher authority before a decision may be made at all. This includes certain ways of handling loans, imposition of extraordinary taxes and acceptance of conditional bequests.

Further control is exercised over municipalities through such provincial and state financial bodies and officials as the *trésorier payeur général*, the *inspection des finances* and the *Cour des Comptes*. Thus, the local governments are subject to audits of their

[2] A distinction is made between municipalities with more and those with less than 9,000 inhabitants. In the latter category no control is carried out over the budget and the contracting of loans (except under certain conditions); in the smaller municipalities a more extensive control is carried out.

books at any time by the first two bodies and a procedure has been established for the yearly examination of all municipal accounts by the latter (*Cour des Comptes*), at which time the mayor may be questioned on any item of expenditure. Municipal personnel, too, come under close supervision, through nationally determined examination requirements for certain salaried personnel, and suspension and dismissal of mayors, individual councilmen and the council as a whole, for sufficient cause. At such times the supervisory authority may then appoint an interim governing body or official until new elections have been held. In other areas of administration, uniform procedure is required, as established by the Minister of the Interior or the provincial governor, and the use of draft or model contracts requires less delay in action than is otherwise the case. On the whole, the municipality's autonomy is severely limited in scope by control of the higher authorities.

Canton and Sub-Province ('Arrondissement')

Between the basic unit of French government, the municipality, and the provinces, lie the *"canton"* and the sub-province (*arrondissement*). The former is a collection of communes formed for army, judicial and electoral administration, and for the collection of taxes and the registration of various kinds of required information. Like the former, the latter is a purely administrative division which has no corporate personality and no elected council, but which serves the important function of easing the burden on departmental administration. Its chief official is the sub-governor (*sous-préfet*) who is appointed by the central government. By virtue of his position, the sub-governor receives and passes on official papers, documents and orders from the governor to the municipalities, approves the appointment of certain officials, including the local police where they exist, and arranges the details of elections. Although he also has certain supervisory powers over municipal mayors within his territory, particularly in regard to the budget and police ordinances, his main function is to give advice and technical assistance to these officials and to serve as a liaison between the local and provincial governments. As an agent of the central government, his main role is to serve as adviser on conditions within the sub-province and to put into effect state or provincial policy within his area. Like the governor, the sub-governor is a member of the *"corps préfectoral"*.

Province ('Département')

The organization of the province is characterized by the fact that it constitutes at the same time a subdivision for the administration of services in the general interest and as the center of the administration of provincial affairs. Like the municipality, the province has a popularly elected council (*Conseil Général*), consisting of one representative from each canton. In size the councils range from 20 to 68 members who are elected for six-year terms, with 1/2 going out of office every three years. Just as many members of the municipal councils also serve on the provincial council or in Parliament, so do provincial councilmen serve as national assembly members or in some other central government role. Provincial councilmen also form the Electoral College, whose function is to elect members of the *Conseil de la République*, with the result that the office carries much prestige and is highly desired by those with political aspirations.

At the second of its two yearly meetings the provincial council elects its own president who presides over regular and special meetings, a vice-president and one or more secretaries, all of whom serve a one-year term of office. At the same time it also elects four to seven of its members to serve for one year on the council's standing committee (*Commission Départementale*), whose main function is to keep watch over the actions of the governor during the times the council is not in session. To prevent it from rivalling or hampering the governor, deputies, senators and the mayor of the provincial capital are legally ineligible for election to the standing committee.

In the area of provincial affairs, the function of the council is to adopt a budget (which is presented by the governor, but which may be amended or altered by the council and which must eventually be approved by that body), dispose of provincial property and estates, build and maintain highways, decide on expenditures from provincial funds, provide public assistance institutions and welfare services, initiate litigation on behalf of the province and provide for certain aspects of public education. At its second session each year the council also hears a summary of provincial affairs for the past year and recommendations for the coming year given by the governor, and examines in detail the yearly accounts, on which they may question the chief executive at length.[3]

The relationship of the provincial council to the central government includes providing and maintaining certain public buildings, such as those used by the governor and sub-governor, the offices of educational authorities, teachers' training colleges, barracks of the state police, courts, and certain detention quarters. Although the province is required by law to accept this responsibility, the amounts to be spent and the order in which repairs will take place are its sole decision. In addition, individual councilmen serve on such state bodies as military tribunals for exemption from national service and various boards for a variety of social welfare services. Moreover, no Minister can make grants within a province for the upkeep of churches, charitable institutions, kindergartens or agricultural associations without the approval of the council, which also can decide in what order the work will be done. Through its president the council can also propose matters of special interest to the Ministers and pass motions on economic policy and general administration.

Over matters of municipal interest the provincial council also has certain jurisdiction. In this area it can set rates to be charged by hospitals and allowances to be made to indigents. Its main influence, however, is in the area of intermunicipal relations, where its decisions on almost all matters are final. Thus, it can apportion the cost of intercommunal works between municipalities when there is a dispute, can designate the sections of main highways for which each municipality is responsible, apportion taxes raised by the municipalities for provincial use to the municipalities, and make the actual grants.

As was mentioned previously, between its sessions the council

[3] Recent legislation has simplified the control over the provincial council. In most cases the Ministry of the Interior needs no more to approve the budget or loans contracted from certain public banks. Moreover, there is a provision for tacit approval by the governor or Minister of the Interior.

may delegate responsibility to its standing committee (*Commission Départementale*). Mainly this involves examining the monthly accounts of the governor to check his expenditures against authorizations voted in the provincial budget. This body also examines the chief executive's budget before it is presented to the full council, and draws up recommendations on it, examines and makes recommendations on the agenda prior to council meetings, decides how and when the governor may spend money provided in the budget for unforeseen expenditures, authorizes payments from funds accrued from police fines and from loans, and fixes the priority of order in which provincial work will be done, unless the council retains this function for itself. Where there is a disagreement with the governor on such priorities, the latter may refuse to act until the matter has been discussed by the council as a whole. If this body then upholds the governor the standing committee may be dismissed and a new one elected. For the most part, the standing committee undertakes small but necessary administrative jobs which would constitute a burden on the council as a whole to discuss and decide upon. Although, in addition, it serves as a watchdog on the activities of the governor, its role is a subordinate one, and the latter is, in fact, the chief executive of the provincial administration.

A member of the *corps préfectoral*, the governor (préfet) is appointed by the Minister of the Interior and serves at his pleasure. His essential role is that of representative of the Government in his province, moreover, he is chief administrator of purely provincial matters. In his former responsibilities the governor is the official through whom all ministerial directions and requests are given to the provinces. The departmental chiefs of various central government technical and administrative services may propose measures, but only the governor can make the final decision. Through his police powers he is responsible for maintaining public order, morality and hygiene, maintaining the security of the state and executing its laws (*police générale*). In these matters he can issue ordinances for the province and serves as the provincial chief of police. He directs all administrative and technical services of the state in his area, and may thus appoint many junior officials to their posts and supervise their activities. Only he can authorize payment from state funds in the province, serve as its representative in all litigations except that between the province and the state, and sign state contracts for work within his territory. He also is responsible for collecting and transmitting information required by the Ministries. In addition, he supervises the subgovernors within the province, arbitrates between the service of various ministries within his territory and last, but certainly not least, he is the chief executive of the provincial council, whose decisions he must put into effect.

In his relationship with the municipalities the governor can suspend mayors for a month for grave breaches of conduct, approves budgets, into which he may write any obligatory expenditures that have been omitted, and approves or annuls all mayor's police ordinances. He is the supervisor of all provincial departments, and it is only with his approval that officials may furnish reports on their administration or answer questions at the council meetings. He, too, reports to the provincial council and may be questioned on any aspect of organization and administration or any branch of the state's services working within the province. In turn, the governor supervises the activities of the council through his power to pass on the legality of its decisions. Thus, no decision may be fully put into effect until 10 days after the end of the council session, during which time the governor may challenge it before the *Conseil d'Etat*. If that body, in turn, has not annulled the decision within six weeks, it then becomes effective.

The Minister of the Interior has many of the same powers of supervision over the province which the provincial governor has over the municipality. Thus, he approves the provincial budget, which he may alter or amend, especially in the case of obligatory expenditures. Where such action involves a point of law, appeal can be made to the *Conseil d'Etat*, otherwise political pressure is the only recourse open to the council. Prior approval of the Minister must be received to raise revenue or borrow money by certain means or to levy extraordinary local taxes. Control over the council involves its possible dissolution by a decree of the president of the Republic, although this has not occurred since 1874, and approval of appointments of certain provincial employees and members of certain boards. The main control, however, is through the appointment or removal of the governor who plays the pivotal role in provincial administration. Thus, all his actions and decisions are liable to examination and reversal by the Minister of the Interior. As long as the governor remains in his position, therefore, he can be considered to have the support and confidence of his superiors.

ITALY

From the downfall of the Roman Empire until political unity the Italian states suffered centuries of war and foreign domination, although this period also saw the rise of cities whose culture and ideology extend to the present time. In 1870, however, the culmination of the uprising against Austria and various small states was the unification of the country into the Italy of today. At that time the Constitution established a highly centralized government whose local units were the 92 provinces and over 7,000 communes. In 1948 the new Constitution established a third level of government, the region, whose boundaries were determined on the basis of the historic, geographic and ethnic divisions of the Italian Peninsula. On the whole, these regions were to function as administrative subdivisions of the central government, although a law of 1953 provided local autonomy for the 19 areas. So far, only four regions have put this law into effect, although projected plans are to extend decentralization to the other 15 in the near future.

Municipalities ('Comuni')

Municipal units have been traditional in Italy since pre-Roman days. Under the administrative regulations of the last century all were given a uniform structure and duties, although in practice these have been somewhat modified to take into account variations in size and importance. In general, the functions of the municipalities are: to provide sanitary and health services, public lighting and public transportation; to construct and maintain roads and schools; to control traffic and the construction of buildings; to provide various kinds of assistance; and to keep a civil register.

Each municipality has three organs of government, the council (*Consiglio Comunale*), the board (*Giunta Comunale*) and the mayor (*Sindaco*). The councils are popularly elected and vary in size from 15 to 80 members who serve four-year terms of office. In its two regular sessions each year and in any special sessions which may be called by the mayor, the board or 1/3 of the councilmen, the council adopts the municipal budget and accounts and deliberates concerning municipal finance matters; public works, health, hygiene, assistance, education, and public enterprises; municipal streets and traffic; acceptance of inheritances; and the supervision of the municipal police force.

The council also elects from among its own number from four to 15 people to serve a four-year term of office as the municipal board. This board is responsible for supervising the day-to-day administration, for initiating recommendations to the council and for putting into effect the council's decisions. Furthermore, the board represents the council when it is not in session and may undertake certain of its responsibilities during this time. Such actions, however, must be reported to the council at its next session, and ratification obtained. Additional responsibilities include various ceremonial functions, making an annual report to the council on board activities and primary authority in dealing with certain financial matters as well as in dealing with municipal personnel. Individually, each board member may be assigned general oversight of one or more municipal departments.

The mayor is the chief executive officer of the municipality and a representative of the central government. In his former capacity he draws up the agendas for, presides over and executes the decisions of the council and the board; signs correspondence, contracts and other municipal documents; takes care that municipal regulations are observed; represents the municipality in any legal litigations and supervises all municipal offices and institutions. As an officer of the central government the mayor must publish the laws, regulations, decrees and announcements of the state; maintain public law and order; supervise the recording of vital statistics, the electoral rolls and the conscription lists; and assume certain functions in regard to public works and public health.

In addition to the elected officials, each municipality has a secretary(-general) who is appointed by the central government and who directly supervises and co-ordinates daily administration. It is therefore to the secretary(-general) that the municipal department heads are directly responsible. Although his primary responsibility is to the council, the secretary(-general) may nevertheless refuse to implement any illegal acts of that body or of any municipal officer, thereby guaranteeing impartiality of administration by the elected and appointed officials. The secretary(-general) also provides continuity during change-overs in administration and in many cases serves as the local expert in public administration and administrative law.

The Italian municipalities are subject to strict controls by the provincial and central governments. All decisions of both the council and the board must be submitted within eight days of their passage to the provincial governor (*Prefetto*) for examination of their legality. If the governor does not annul the decisions within 20 days they may be considered approved and may be put into effect. Moreover, such financial matters as the municipal budget, expenditures covering more than a five-year period, the levying of taxes and contracting of loans, and certain types of investments; litigations; expropriations of property and matters pertaining to the direct administration of public services must be approved by the provincial administrative committee (*Giunta Provinciale Amministrativa*) for legality and merit before they can become effective. Provision is also made for putting a law into immediate effect on a simple majority vote of the council, although if it is subsequently found that the legislation is illegal, it then becomes void. Annulment of municipal legislation can only be done by the governor when the law has been violated or when municipal competence and powers have been exceeded and appeals from the governor's decision may be made by the municipality to the Minister of the Interior.

Additional control over municipalities is exercised through the provincial inspectors who check on municipal organization and administration to see that it is efficient and adequate. If an inspector finds that a municipal administration is grossly neglectful he may so inform the governor who will then send a commissioner to either take over one particular function or the total direction of municipal affairs, at which time the council is dissolved. Appeal to the Council of State from such action of the governor is permitted to the municipality. Furthermore, the governor can suspend a mayor, who may then be dismissed by the President of the Republic, for grave neglect of duty or violation of the law. The number of dissolutions of council and dismissals of mayor, however, is small.

A commissioner is also appointed if a mayor resigns as a result of a vote of no-confidence of the council in which case the council may be dissolved making new elections necessary; the commissioner holds office until a new mayor is elected. This situation recently occurred in a number of large cities.

Provinces ('Provincie')

The territory of each Italian province contains two separate administrations. One is a local representative government with certain functions which have been entrusted to it by law and the other is an administrative arm of the central government.

Among the activities of the representative provincial government are the drawing up and administering of a budget, construction and maintenance of roads, bridges and dikes, anti-rabies control, provision of hygiene and prophylaxis laboratories, secondary schools, and the improvement of agricultural methods. These are effectuated through a popularly elected council (*Consiglio Provinciale*) which ranges in size from 24 to 45 members, according to population, and which serves a four-year term of office. From their membership the council, in turn, elects a board (*Giunta Provinciale*) and a chairman (*Presidente*) who presides over both the council and the board.

The co-ordinator of the non-representative administration of the province is a centrally appointed governor (*Prefetto*). Essentially an expert in administration the governor, who is responsible to the Minister of the Interior, is charged with maintaining public security and order, publishing and carrying out national laws and supervising certain public health functions. He also is responsible for deciding on the legality of municipal and provincial by-laws, in which work he is aided by various advisory groups, such as his own cabinet, a council of health and hygiene, etc.

In addition the governor shares responsibilities with the Provincial Administrative Committee (*Giunta Provinciale Amministrativa*) which is composed of central government officials, members elected by the provincial council, and the provincial inspectors. The administrative committee is mainly charged with exercising supervisory control over the activities of the province, the municipalities and certain intermunicipal associations for hydraulic works, land improvement, drainage, dike building and protective works against the water. The provincial inspectors check periodically on the efficiency and effectiveness of municipal government administration and make recommendations to the governor, to whom they are directly responsible, for appropriate action.

Regions ('Regioni')

As was stated above, only four of the 19 regions provided for in the 1948 Constitution have been established. The structure of the government of these four regions, which are among the less developed areas of the country, however, parallels that of the municipalities and the representative provincial units, having a popularly elected council (*Consiglio Regionale*), an executive committee (*Giunta Regionale*) and a president who promulgates the regional laws and regulations, directs its activities, and serves as its chief representative. The field of competence of the region includes regional finances, police, public assistance, public health and hospitals, vocational training, assistance to schools, establishment and maintenance of libraries and museums, tramways and buses, facilities for navigation, stimulation of the tourist, hotel and handicraft industries, and control of hunting, fishing, agriculture and forests.

Under the Constitution the chief central government agent in the region is a commissioner (*commissario*) who co-ordinates regional and central government functions. He can also propose to the central government the dissolution of the regional council when it is not able to function or when legislation passed by the council is contrary to the Constitution. In addition, the commissioner is assigned some of the supervisory powers over the municipalities that were formerly exercised by the provincial governor.

GREECE

Greek local government has deep roots in the past. From the city-state (*polis*) of classical Greece came the concept of citizens (*politae*) deriving the right to govern their own affairs by contributing money and military service to the community. This practice, in turn, led to the recognition of citizens as a whole as a sovereign unit, called *demos*, from whence comes the word "democracy" or regime of the people.

The classical period of Greece was followed by centuries of successive domination by the Macedonians, Romans, Byzantines and finally by the Turks, against whom the Greeks waged a successful war for independence in 1833. The present century has also been turbulent for Greece as it has experienced long years of war, occupation by foreign powers and other unfavourable conditions. It is only since 1950 that the country has had real peace.

Administratively Greece is divided into 50 provinces (*nomoi*), which contain some 146 districts. These districts, which are headed by a director (*eparch*), do not have any representative organs and serve primarily as electoral units. Only in the remote and mountainous regions do they assume any further importance as administrative agencies of the provinces. Each province is further composed of urban and rural municipalities, the former (*demes*) having 10,000 or more inhabitants or being capitals of a province, and the latter (*communes*) consisting of villages or settlements, or groups of more than one village or settlement, having 500 or more inhabitants and an elementary school, as well as adequate revenue to carry on necessary local government activities.

Urban Municipalities ('Demes')

Under the Municipal and Communal Code of 1954 urban municipalities are delegated specific power to: construct, maintain and operate waterworks, irrigation and reclamation projects; provide sewage disposal, street cleaning and garbage disposal services; and construct and maintain roads, bridges, electricity projects, kindergartens and seaside facilities. They may also establish various charitable and cultural institutions, such as orphanages, hospitals, nurseries and theatres.

Action on these matters and supervision of their administration is undertaken by a locally elected mayor and council. The latter is elected for four-year terms of office and varies in size from nine to 31 members. Among its specific duties are to approve an annual budget and the yearly accounts; decide upon a yearly public works programme and establish priorities; levy taxes, dues and fees; administer municipal property; contract loans; establish municipal enterprises; act upon inheritances and donations to the municipality; and appoint, dismiss, promote and take disciplinary measures against municipal employees.

Presiding over the municipal council is a chairman who is elected by the council from among its own members. He is aided by a vice-chairman and a secretary who are elected in the same way. There is, in addition, a board consisting of the mayor as ex-officio member and from two to four other members, who are elected by the council from among its own members to serve a one-year term of office. Presided over by the mayor, who also has a vote in board decisions, this body draws up the yearly budget; decides on the disposal of amounts listed in the budget for unpredicted expenses; contracts loans; calls for and decides upon bids, unless the council reserves this right for itself; pre-audits the annual accounts and appoints certain municipal employees.

The municipal mayor (*demarch*), like the council members, is popularly elected for a four-year term of office. His is a position with dual responsibility, to the municipality and to the state. In the latter role the mayor informs the citizens of national laws and regulations and compiles lists of military eligibles and vital statistics. His responsibility to the municipality is to serve as its chief executive officer; put into effect council and board decisions; act as legal and official representative of the municipality; authorize expenditures from municipal funds and issue citizens' certificates of personal and family status.

The mayor also acts as ex-officio chairman of the boards of

such institutions established by the council as orphanages, hospitals, nurseries and old people's homes and of such enterprises as water supply, irrigation and land reclamation projects and other public utilities. Each board further consists of one or two members elected by the council from its own membership and three to four members selected by the council from the citizens at large. The municipal council must approve such matters of the institutions and enterprises as the budgets, the annual reports, the sale or exchange of real estate and the acceptance of donations or inheritances.

In municipalities whose populations exceed 20,000 or in those which are provincial seats or seats of a court of first instance, a secretary-general may be appointed by the mayor to serve as his assistant for an indefinite period of time. In this capacity the secretary-general is usually responsible for daily administration, including supervision of department heads, issuance of citizen certificates, etc. The secretary-general may be dismissed at any time by the mayor, who is not obliged to justify his actions.

It may at first seem that control over urban municipalities by the province is unduly strict, as every piece of local legislation must be sent to the governor (*nomarch*) for his perusal. Such perusal under the new Code, however, is for legality and not for content. Therefore, unless a resolution cancelling local decisions is received from the governor within 10 days of his receipt of the legislation, the municipal council may put it into effect at that time. Emergency decisions involving small appropriations and legislation which is not financial in nature are exceptions and may have immediate effect.

Certain council decisions require the governor's approval, such as long-term property leases; the annual budget and accounts; sale of property and construction of important public works; and any others involving considerable expense to the municipality. However, if approval has not been received within 30 days, and there has also been no resolution cancelling the legislation, the local council may put it into effect after that time. Finally, the governor may temporarily suspend municipal mayors and councilmen from office for good reason.

Every citizen has the right to appeal decisions of the council to the governor on the basis of legality, which appeal may be accepted or rejected by that official. Adverse decisions of the governor, on the other hand, may be appealed by the municipality or by private individuals to the Council of State.

Control over certain municipal matters, primarily in the financial area, is exercised by the Ministry of the Interior. Thus, that agency must approve loans; the acquisition and disposal of municipal property; expropriation of private real estate, etc., when sums over a certain minimum are involved. It may also request the dismissal of municipal mayors and councilmen through established legal channels in severe cases of fraud, neglect or action harmful to public order and interest.

Rural Municipalities ('Communes')

The difference in structure and activities between Greek urban and rural municipalities is one of degree, based on the smaller size and more limited resources of the latter. Like the urban municipality the rural one has a popularly elected council which serves a four-year term of office and varies in size from five to 15 members. Its presiding officer is a chairman who is elected by the council from among its own members for a two-year term of office. He is assisted by a council elected vice-president in performing his duties as chief executive of the commune.

In addition to calling council meetings, preparing their agendas and presiding over them, the chairman also enforces council decisions; signs contracts; supervises daily administration of municipal activities; approves payments from municipal funds; issues citizen's certificates; and in case of emergency can take any proper measures to protect the interests of the community. Such action is immediately afterwards brought to the council for its approval. The chairman also serves as ex-officio chairman of any municipal enterprises or institutions.

Supervision of rural municipal activities, including suspension and/or dismissal of chairman and councilmen, by the governor and the state is the same as that exercised over its urban counterpart. In addition, the governor must approve the establishment of all unions of rural or urban municipalities which may be proposed for the purpose of undertaking such common projects as roads, irrigation, reclamation, promotion of tourism, etc. Such unions form councils of representatives from each of the member municipalities, elect officers and proceed in much the same manner as do the municipal councils. When a project is completed the union can then be dissolved by decision of the respective councils and upon the issuance of a resolution to that effect by the governor.

Provinces ('Nomoi')

The province (*nomos*) is an administrative arm of the national government. To the governor (*nomarch*) authority is transferred by the central ministries to make decisions on all provincial matters, especially those which require immediate action. In remote and mountainous regions where the governor's supervision is not readily available, provincial offices have been established under a district director (*eparch*) who is subordinate to the governor and who acts upon the authority granted him by that official.

In addition to the governor, who is appointed by the central government, each province has a council composed of both elected and appointed members. The former include one or two representatives from each district within the province who serve two-year terms of office. Although the council serves primarily in a planning, study and advisory capacity, it is able to vote on matters coming before it. These decisions, however, may be overridden (without the possibility of appeal) by the governor. For the most part the council advises the governor on the provincial budget, the scope and priority of the public works programme, and studies local administration and the necessity for various social service programmes.

A recent development is the establishment in each province of a Provincial Fund to finance projects of provincial interest. These funds are used for construction and maintenance of public works aimed at increasing productivity in the territory; projects pertaining to public health, social welfare, education, tourism and athletics; construction and maintenance of government buildings and installations; and acquisition, maintenance and management of technical and mechanical equipment necessary to carry out local projects.

Financed by special appropriations from the national budget and granted special revenues, the Provincial Funds are administered by six-member boards composed of the governor as chairman, two representatives of the local union of urban or rural municipalities and three officials from the provincial agencies of the national government.

SPAIN

Spain was one of the earliest countries to be colonized by the Romans whose influence continued until the end of the second century A. D. and the invasion of the Moors. When the latter conquerors were finally driven from the country 13 centuries later, small and independent kingdoms were established which again were combined during the 16th century when the power and influence of Spain in Europe was at its height. Then followed a series of disastrous wars, first in defence of Roman Catholicism, then against England, Napoleon and the United States and ending with two wars within the country itself. In 1931, a Republic was established and this, in turn, was overthrown toward the end of the decade following a violent Civil War. The Republic was succeeded by the National Syndicalist regime of General Franco which has been in existence up to the present time.

A highly centralized country politically and administratively, Spain is divided for the latter purpose into 50 provinces, which in turn comprise some 9,212 municipalities. Some of the larger ones again, may be divided into sub-municipal units, upon the decision of the municipal councils and with the approval of the central government.

Urban and Rural Municipalities ('Municipios')

The Spanish municipal law, part of which was based on legislation from the 19th century and part of which had been modernized in 1924 and 1925, was brought up to date in 1950, reformed in 1953 and superseded by the new Local Government Act in 1955. The latter act continued the traditional system of dividing the country into municipalities, but provided that each municipality should have its own locally adopted charter as approved by the central government. Thus far, however, only a very small number of charters have been granted and these provide only minor changes in structure and powers from the standard Spanish municipality. As a result there is, in general, a uniform type of local government throughout the country although the organization and powers of municipalities with more than 2,000 inhabitants differ somewhat from the less populated ones.

In theory the municipalities have a wide range of powers to exercise. These include raising revenue by the establishment of taxes, fees and fines; borrowing funds for special projects and activities; constructing and maintaining such public properties as bridges, roads, museums, libraries, schools, markets, recreational areas, woodland and pastureland, and slaughter-houses; providing fire and limited police protection; establishing various public utility monopolies such as water, gas, electricity, and transportation; drawing up a master plan and inspecting buildings; regulating such public health services as the purification of water, inspection of food handlers, slaughter-houses and markets, collection and disposal of refuse, establishment of first aid posts, laboratories and hospitals; and performing such social services as protecting minors, controlling begging and establishing hostels for visitors. In practice, the municipalities are hampered by severe lack of funds and by rigid control over their activities by the central government. Thus, in those municipalities with a smaller population only the essential services are provided by the municipalities; the larger units are financially able to do more for their citizens.

The representative organ of the municipality is the council. In a few local units with less than 2000 inhabitants this has traditionally been a popular assembly of all adult citizens (*Consejo abierto*). As of today, however, such popular assemblies no longer exist. Thus, all municipalities have a representative council (*Ayuntamiento*) which varies in size from three to 24 members, according to the Local Government Act, and whose members, according to the Constitution, have a six-year term of office, with half of them retiring every three years. Elections, however, are held on the issuance of a decree of the Minister of the Interior, which in turn is based on a decision of the Council of Ministers, and so the terms of office may be shorter or longer than the six-year period. One-third of the council members are directly elected by the registered heads of families and one-third are selected by representatives chosen by syndical councils which represent the various professional and trade groups within the municipality. Such members are always among the syndical officers. The last third represents those economic, cultural and professional groups which are not integrated in the syndical organization and these councilmen are selected by the other two thirds.

To facilitate its work the Spanish council may use committees to investigate and make recommendations on various matters of public interest. Final decisions, however, lay with the council as a whole. Like the committees, the council itself is limited in power, for although it discusses all municipal problems and projects and makes resolutions pertaining thereto, all its decisions depend for implementation on the mayor.

The mayor (*Alcalde*) serves as the chief executive of the municipality. In those governmental units which serve as provincial capitals or where the municipal population exceeds 10,000 people, this official is appointed for an indefinite term by the Minister of the Interior. All other mayors, who also serve indefinite terms, are appointed by the Civil Governor of the province.

The duties of the mayor include convening the council, over which he presides, whose agenda he prepares, and whose decisions he may veto. In case of an even division of opinion on a question, he may also cast the deciding vote. The mayor also prepares the budget, authorizes expenditures and presents the final accounts. He represents the municipality in all legal matters; executes council decisions; supervises daily municipal administration, concerning which he may issue special regulations; supervises municipal personnel; and performs any other duties which are not reserved to the council or to the board. As a representative of the central government the mayor must publish and administer national laws; maintain public order and security; co-ordinate all municipal and central government activities in times of disaster; and perform any other tasks assigned to him.

To aid him in performing his administering duties, municipalities with over 2,000 population may have a board (*Comisión Permanente*), composed of the mayor and one or more deputy mayors

(*Teniente de Alcalde*). The deputies are selected by the mayor from among the council members, each may serve as the head of one or more municipal departments.

Co-ordinating daily administration, and acting as an assistant to the mayor is the municipal secretary. Although he, the municipal auditor and the municipal treasurer are the top ranking civil servants in the municipality, they are completely subordinate to the mayor and serve at his pleasure. The mayor may also appoint an "*Alcalde de Barrio*" for certain sections of the town or for centres of population outside the main area of a municipality. The "*Alcalde de Barrio*" assists the mayor.

As has been previously stated, the Spanish municipalities are strictly controlled by the central government authorities. In the financial area all by-laws concerning taxes must be submitted, along with any objections from private citizens or public or private establishments, to the Ministry of Finance representative in the province, within 30 days of their passage by the council. This official may approve, modify or reject the tax if the local authorities have exceeded their power, have violated any central government law or regulation, or have not clearly defined the basis of the tax or the obligation to pay. This same official must also approve municipal budgets, which he examines for legality and for the inclusion of compulsory items. Appeals from the budget decisions of the provincial representative of the Ministry of Finance can be made by the municipality to the Provincial Economic and Administrative Tribunal.

A further control exercised by the central government is that all municipal loans must have the prior approval of the Ministry of Finance, as should any borrowing and transactions involving municipal property. In addition, all municipal accounts must be submitted to the inspectorate of the Ministry of the Interior (Central and Provincial Accounts Committee), along with any objections from private citizens or corporate bodies. The accounts are examined for legality of items and must be approved by the inspectorate. And finally, the yearly audit of the municipal auditor must be approved by the National Inspectorate of Local Authorities.

Aside from financial matters, all other regulations passed by the municipal council must be approved by the proper department of the central government. In addition, any municipal programme that concerns a central government ministry must take its directions from that ministry. Finally, the local mayor is a central government appointee, and his is the dominant voice in all municipal affairs.

A somewhat different kind of sub-municipal units of which there exist only a small number, especially in the province of Castilla, are the *Entidades locales menores*. They are governed by a mayor (*Alcalde pedáneo*), who is appointed by the provincial Civil Governor from among the local citizens, and a board (*Junta vecinal*). The main function of the sub-municipal units, which have their own budgets which are different and independent from those of the municipalities to which they belong, is to preserve and supervise the use of the property of the sub-municipal unit.

Provinces ('Provincias')

Like the municipality, the Spanish province is a corporate body. It has as its chief functions the provision of various services to the municipalities and the carrying out of certain central government responsibilities.

The council (*Diputación provincial*) of the province consists of the President and the members (*Diputados provinciales*). The members, in turn, are composed of two groups: those representing the municipalities in the province and those representing the various cultural, economic and professional groups in the province. The number of members of the first group equals the number of judicial districts in the province, and the number of the second group is half or less than the number of the members of the first group. Like the municipal councils, the provincial bodies have elections upon decree of the Minister of the Interior, as based on the decision of the Council of Ministers.

Presiding over the council is a president (*Presidente Diputación provincial*) who is appointed for an indefinite term of office by the Minister of the Interior and whose duties resemble those of the municipal mayor. Thus, he assembles the council, prepares its agenda, vetoes any of its actions, and casts the deciding vote in case of an even division of opinion; he prepares the provincial budget, makes contracts, approves expenditures, is responsible for collecting taxes, fines and fees, and presents the final accounts. In addition, the president acts as the legal representative of the provincial council; presides over any special committees which are formed; supervises provincial personnel, and performs any other duties which are attributed to him by law. In all matters the council president must act in accordance with directives given him by the Civil Governor of the Province, who is overall supervisor of its activities.

The Civil Governor (*Gobernador*) of each province is appointed for an indefinite term of office by the Minister of the Interior. The Governor is the chief official in the province by virtue of being the representative of the central government, as well as the chief of provincial police and security functions. In addition, he heads all provincial commissions which are created by the central government. These bodies are set up to administer such services as education, social services and public works for any municipality which desires their aid. They also have close contacts with the corresponding central government ministries, who first approve the proposals for service to the municipalities.

As in the case of the municipalities, control over the activities of the province is comprehensive and ranges from the approval of budgets, contracts, taxes and other financial matters to examination of all other legislation before it can be put into effect. Control over council actions is also exercised through the centrally appointed council president who is directly responsible to the Minister of the Interior, and the centrally appointed provincial Governor.

PORTUGAL

Portugal's history is closely associated with that of Spain. It obtained its full independence in the 18th century. During the 19th century there were a number of internal political disturbances as a result of liberal movements against absolute royal power. The Republic was established in 1910, followed by the imposition of a military dictatorship and then, in 1933, by the establishment of the Republic which exists at the present time.

A unitary country, Portugal is divided for administrative purposes into 11 provinces with representative organs. These provinces are, in turn, subdivided into municipalities. These, again, comprise sub-municipal units. In addition to the provinces as intermediate units there are the 18 districts into which the total country is divided for central government administrative purposes.

Municipalities ('Concelho' or 'Municipio')

Portuguese municipalities are of two types, urban and rural. Urban municipalities are: (a) those in which the chief centre of population situated within the municipality's boundaries has a population of more than 25,000; (b) those in which the chief centre of population is the capital of a province or of an autonomous district and has a population of more than 20,000 inhabitants, providing this population accounts for at least 25% of the municipality's total population; (c) municipalities federated with Lisbon and Oporto. All other municipalities are classified as rural and they are subdivided, as are those in the urban classification, into three categories which are based on population and revenue. On the basis of this classification obligatory duties are assigned to the municipalities, according to their ability to carry them out.

All Portuguese municipalities have a common structure, the essential governing organs being the council (*conselho municipal*), the board (*câmara municipal*), and the mayor (*presidente da câmara municipal*). With the exception of the mayor, who is appointed by the central government, council members are indirectly elected by various groups in the municipality, such as the sub-municipal boards; the beneficence or assistance associations known as *Misericórdias*; the doctors', lawyers' and engineers' organizations; the local branches of national trade unions; and the corporate organizations of employers or producers. Where the latter organizations do not exist, representation of local industrialists and farmers is vested in the civil governor of the district, who may appoint up to two spokesmen to represent him. In size, the councils range from six to 14 members, all of whom serve a four-year term of office.

The duty of the council is to moderate and guide the actions of the board which it elects and whose members it may dismiss in certain circumstances. It thus passes judgment on the board's yearly plan of activity and on the fixing of the percentages to be added to state taxes, this constituting one of the principal sources of municipal revenue; accepts the yearly budget and the plans relating to town planning and expansion; and gives approval to those decisions of the board which are required by the Administrative Code. The council also accepts a yearly report of board activities and in addition, may ask the central government to make an enquiry into the actions of the mayor.

The board is an executive organ of the municipality and is elected by the council from among its own membership. It is composed of the mayor and six, four, or two other members (*vereadores*), depending on the category to which the municipality belongs. All serve four-year terms of office, with the exception of the mayor, who remains in office eight years, although he may be released from his duties at any time by the Minister of the Interior. The task of the board is to draw up regulations and by-laws and take decisions pertaining to the following matters: administration of public property; municipal improvement or development, which includes the construction and maintenance of roads, bridges, viaducts, parks, gardens and airports, provision of public transport systems, and the distribution of water and electrical power; culture and assistance, which comprises the building and maintenance of hospitals, primary and secondary schools, libraries, archives, museums, gymnasiums, swimming pools and playing fields; public health, under which is included the treatment of drinking water, the establishment of laboratories, drainage facilities, cemeteries, abattoirs, fish markets, rat and mosquito control and the provision of public housing; police services, such as traffic control and inspection of buildings; and public supplies, which includes water, fairs and markets, and centres for the treatment, distribution and sale of milk.

Collaborating with the municipal authorities in such specialized matters as hygiene and art are committees appointed by the mayor and presided over by members of the board. In Lisbon and Oporto, these committees are headed, not by board members, but by the directors of the municipal services, who are responsible to the board.

Both the mayor and his deputy are appointed by the central government, usually from among persons resident in the municipality, for a term of eight years, with re-appointment being possible. The mayor presides at meetings of the board and the council, for both of which bodies he plans the agenda and presents matters for discussion. He also prepares the annual budget and authorizes payments from municipal funds, prepares a yearly report on municipal finance and activities and submits the board's accounts to the Accounts Tribunal. As the legal representative of the municipality the mayor can make contracts and represent the municipality at law and elsewhere. He publishes the regulations and by-laws approved by the board, superintends municipal services and their staffs, deals with all correspondence and, in general, co-ordinates all municipal activity.

As the representative of the central government the mayor sees to the carrying out of that government's laws and regulations, replies to enquiries on economic or administrative matters and superintends parish administration. As the police authority of the municipality the mayor deals with local police activities including the registration of foreigners, order at public performances and meetings, the enforcement of sanitary and health regulations and the granting of various licences. In exceptional circumstances the mayor may make decisions which are within the competence of the board, providing that he submits such decisions to the board for its ratification. It should be noted, however, that in municipalities which are the chief town of a district or where the chief town has especial importance, police functions are not handled by the mayor, but by the district or section commander of the Public Safety Police.

Supervision of the activities of municipal boards as to legality and general interest are exercised by the Ministries of the Interior and Finance. The former is primarily concerned with the administrative aspects of the activities and the latter with the inspection and control of taxation and financial operations. When it is found that serious irregularities or omissions have occurred the Ministry of the Interior may use such measures of discipline as the dissolution of the municipal organs, which may or may not involve the dismissal of the mayor, in which case these organs are replaced by committees appointed by the central government.

Such occurrences, however, are rare. Some of the board's deliberations, namely those pertaining to health, traffic and loans, must receive prior approval of the central government before they can be put into effect. All others may be revoked, altered or declared null and void on the grounds of illegality within a certain time specified by the Administrative Code. Appeals from these decisions by the central government may be made by the municipality to administrative legal disputes tribunals whose decisions are final. In certain cases also appeals against the decisions of the mayor may be made to the civil governor when such decisions have been taken in the mayor's capacity as police authority. Finally, all municipal accounts must be submitted to the Accounts Tribunal which must verify their legality.

Sub-Municipal Units ('Frequesias')

All Portuguese municipalities are divided into sub-municipal units. The executive organ of the parish is the board which is composed of three members who are elected at four year intervals by the heads of the families registered in the parish. This group, in turn, appoints its own chairman, secretary and treasurer. Its powers consist of the following: establishing rates and taxes, approving a yearly budget prepared by the chairman, authorizing expenses from local funds, requesting financial help from the state in regard to water supply, cemeteries and highways, acquiring the necessary property and goods, and making contracts.

Certain of the board's deliberations must be submitted to the approval of the mayor for legality and conformance with the interests of the municipality. In the case of an adverse decision by the mayor on the legality of a matter, appeal may be made by the sub-municipal board to the district governor, and against that official's decision, to the competent administrative tribunal. In addition, sub-municipal accounts are also subject to the approval of the mayor.

In each sub-municipal unit there is an official who represents the municipality and who is directly responsible to the chairman of the municipal board by whom he is appointed and dismissed. His chief duties are to carry out those municipal orders and decisions which are communicated to him by the chairman of the municipal board; inform that same official of any irregularities he may discover in the administration of the parish; collaborate with legal, police and health authorities; do all in his power to maintain order and safety, in regard to which he is empowered to take suitable measures on his own initiative in case of emergency; and to exercise any other functions which are entrusted to him by the chairman of the municipal board or which are conferred on him by law.

Province

The representative organs of the province, the provincial council (*conselho provincial*) and the board (*junta de província*), are similar to those of the Portuguese municipality. The council consists of indirectly elected members who represent each of the municipal boards in the province; each federation of associations of landowners or producers, as well as each federation of national trade unions existing in the province; collective bodies of public utilities; the senate of each university, grammar, secondary and technical schools in the province; and the directors of the provincial school districts. Like the council in the municipality, that in the province serves a four-year term of office. Its functions are limited to electing members of the provincial board and its chairman, discussing plans of the provincial board, discussing and voting on the provincial budget presented to them by the board chairman, and approving certain deliberations of the provincial board before they may be put into effect.

Elected by the provincial council from among its own membership, the provincial board consists of a chairman, a vice-chairman and three other members. This body is concerned with matters in the following fields: economic development and co-ordination, culture and social assistance. It thus draws up regulations; votes on the imposition of taxes or rates; approves the budget drawn up by the chairman; signs contracts; acquires goods and property; carries out public works. All deliberations relating to the carrying out of public works above a certain amount, the imposition of new taxes or rates and the acceptance of loans must be approved by the provincial council and the central government before they can be put into effect.

The chairman of the provincial board is elected by the council and presides over meetings of both bodies, for which he prepares the agendas. He also prepares the provincial budget, draws up plans for future activities, reports on past activities, represents the province in legal matters and signs all correspondence. Appeals against the actions of the chairman in carrying out the decisions of the provincial board or council may be made to the body which passed the original resolution.

As is the case with the municipality, the activities of the provincial administration are subject to the superv sion of the central government, with the result that some decisions must be submitted for prior approval, and yearly accounts must be accepted by the Accounts Tribunal. Under certain circumstances the organs of provincial administration may be dissolved and replaced, should the necessity arise, by committees appointed by the central government.

District

Not a legal personality, the Portuguese district is an administrative branch of the central government. It is directed by the civil governor who is appointed by the Minister of the Interior, and to whom he is immediately subordinate. His principal administrative duties are: to send to the respective ministries the requests, expositions and petitions handed into the governor's office; to transmit orders and instructions from the central government to the mayors; to help and to co-operate with the officials appointed to inspect the various administrative organs having their headquarters in the district; to approve the statutes of public utilities, cultural and recreational associations, etc. not approved by other authorities. As the police authority, the civil governor is responsible for the maintenance of order and public safety.

In cases of extreme urgency the civil governor may take all necessary administrative steps. All acts, however, which go beyond his normal powers must be submitted to the central government for confirmation. The governor may also be appointed to inspect and supervise any public service in the district regardless of under which ministry it operates. He then corresponds directly with the appropriate minister and carries out the transmitted orders and instructions.

(6)

THE SOUTH AND CENTRAL AMERICA GROUP

BRAZIL

Settled by the Portuguese in the early part of the 16th century, Brazil gained its independence from the mother country in 1822 and adopted its first Constitution two years later. This Constitution established a highly centralized form of government headed by a monarch and remained in force until 1889, at which time the old system of government was replaced by a federal system based on that of the United States of America. The new government, however, was short lived, for in 1930 it was overthrown and successively replaced by a dictatorship, a republican government and another dictatorship. Finally, in 1946 the present Constitution was adopted. This again established a federal system with a representative form of government.

Today governmental power is distributed among the national government, the 20 states and five federal territories, and the basic unit into which all the country is divided, the municipalities. These, in turn, may be divided into sub-municipal units, although on the average there are less than three of these per municipality and those that do exist lack any administrative organization.

Municipalities ('Municípios')

Although the Brazilian municipalities are creatures of their respective states and territories, the principle of municipal autonomy (or inherent competence) is established in the country's

BRAZIL

PATTERN OF GOVERNMENT UNITS

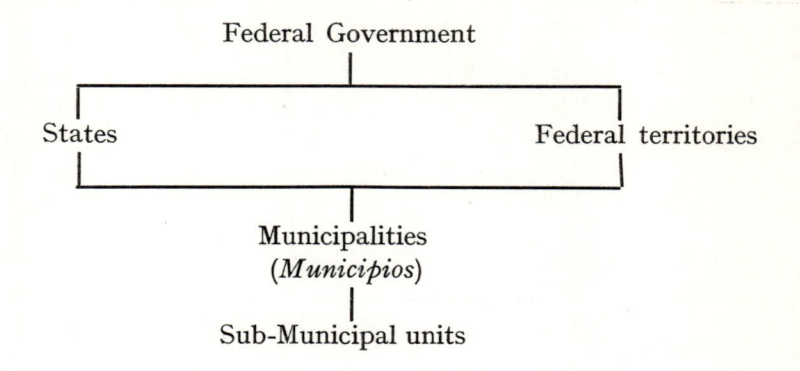

Federal Government
- States
- Federal territories

Municipalities (*Municipios*)

Sub-Municipal units

STRUCTURE OF A MUNICIPAL GOVERNMENT

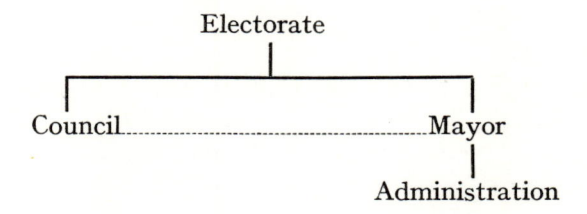

Electorate
- Council
- Mayor

Administration

Constitution, as is the guarantee that the federal government will intervene in any case where this autonomy is abrogated by the state. For the most part, state constitutional provisions of autonomy for their municipalities are repetitions of the federal, with the result that both they and the detailed municipal charters bear striking resemblances to one another and thus provide a uniform municipal system throughout the country. Even in the one state which allows municipalities to formulate their own charters the resemblance is maintained through conformity of these charters to the constitutional principles of the state and of the federation.

Each municipality contains both urban and rural areas, with the seat of government being located in one of the former, called a city. The rural areas are usually divided into sub-municipal units and the centre for each sub-municipal unit is located in a centre of population called a village. Sub-municipal organization, however, as was mentioned above, lacks any real importance and serves mostly as a ramification of the municipal government. Its chief administrator, also known as the sub-mayor, is appointed by the municipal mayor, with the approval of council. In one state, however, the sub-mayor is popularly elected in all sub-municipal units whose population exceeds 5,000 inhabitants.

With the exception of the five federal territories, whose basic units are governed by mayors appointed by the territorial governor, Brazilian municipalities have the strong-mayor council form of government. The council is elected by the list system of proportional representation and varies in size from five to 50 members, all of whom serve a four-year term of office. The council elects a president from among its own members to preside over meetings, and a small executive committee which directs the council's work and its internal administration. The council president also presides over this committee.

The council has no administrative functions. In each state it has the power to legislate on all matters of purely local interest. These include adopting a budget; establishing taxes, fees and fines; adopting a city plan, including zoning and regulations on building inspection; construction, maintenance and cleaning of streets and parks; construction and maintenance of water and sewer facilities; collection of garbage; establishment and supervision of markets, slaughter-houses and fairs; inspection of the opening and closing hours of business and industry; and the establishment and maintenance of various public utilities. In addition, the municipal councils are responsible for certain aspects of education, public health, sanitation and social services, in conjunction with the federal and state governments. Furthermore, although police, in the strict sense, is a state function, the municipal councils can maintain a police force to see that ordinances pertaining to building, sanitary and tax codes, etc. are enforced, and to provide night guards for the protection of persons and property.

Another responsibility of the council is to exercise control over the mayor. This is done through its power of impeachment, through the annual audit of accounts, and in a few states only, through the power of review of fiscal and personnel decisions of the mayor which are appealed by citizens on the grounds of illegality. Finally, because the Brazilian municipality also contains large rural areas, the councils provide such services as distribution of seeds, fertilizers, agricultural tools, chemicals and medicinal products for use against animal and plant diseases and pests.

The chief executive of the municipality is the mayor (*prefeito*). He is popularly elected for a four-year term of office in 15 states and for a five-year term in the remainder. An exception to this rule are the approximately 25 municipalities which are the federal, state and territorial capitals, have natural hydro-mineral projects developed by the state or federal government or have been declared by the federal government to be bases or ports of exceptional importance to the defence of the country. In these the federal law provides that the mayor shall be appointed by the state or territorial governor.

Mayoral duties include preparation and execution of the budget; publication and enforcement of ordinances and resolutions; appointment and removal, according to the civil services laws, of all department heads and other municipal employees; direct supervision of departmental administration; serving as legal representative of the municipality; and imposing fines for the violation of municipal ordinances, resolutions and contracts. The mayor alone can initiate ordinances relating to such matters as salary scales and the creation of new positions in existing municipal services. He also has the power to veto council decisions. Finally, the mayor also serves as the political leader of the municipality and his strength in this connection may determine whether or not the municipality receives requested subsidies for such matters as public works, preparation of a master plan, or various technical and professional services on a short or long term basis.

Control over the municipalities by federal and state governments is primarily in the realm of financial matters. Thus, the federal Constitution restricts the use of municipal funds by providing that 20% of the municipal income from taxes be used for education. It also allows the states to inspect the municipalities' financial administration, especially the execution of the budget. The states, however, in keeping with this power, as well as acting within the spirit of the Federal Constitution, have limited their inspection rights solely to the legal aspects of financial administration and not to convenience or opportunity. They have thus set general legal prerequisites for financial transactions, but have left control over budget execution to the municipal councils themselves, to whom the mayor must submit his annual reports, including a financial statement. If the accounts are unsatisfactory the mayor can be impeached by the council or he may be subject to such criminal proceedings as are provided by law. In some states, in addition to the annual audit by the council, there is also an audit by the State Tribunal of Accounting.

Further limitations set by the states concern the granting of fiscal exemptions and favours by the municipalities; establishing ceilings on the percentage of municipal income that can be used for personnel expenditures; restrictions on excessive taxation and borrowing; and the sale, mortgage or leasing of municipal property. Finally, a few states have made certain services, such as provision of public housing, scholarships and libraries, compulsory.

Lack of compliance to legal provisions must be determined in a court of law, but proof of the lack has no penalties attached. Instead the court has the power only to void the municipal legislation involved. A former power of the state legislatures, that of annulling or suspending local ordinances other than those pertaining to financial matters, has recently been declared unconstitutional by the federal Supreme Court.

In a positive vein, some states have created a department of municipal affairs whose function is to give various kinds of technical assistance to the local government upon their request. Such services include lending road construction equipment; drafting engineering projects; giving advice on legal, accounting and other technical matters; and training municipal personnel.

As for federal control of municipal administration, this occurs only in regard to federal funds and various grants to the municipalities which are given in accordance with federal laws and require reports on their use by the municipal government. For the most part, however, such control is left up to the council and is exercised through that body's audit of the mayor's accounts.

ECUADOR

The Kingdom of Quito was more than 2,000 years old when it was conquered by the Incas in 1470. Sixty years later these conquerors were overthrown by one Atahualpa who, in turn, was defeated by Pizarro following his discovery of the country. Ecuador then became an important part of the Spanish possessions in the New World. In 1809, however, rebellion began against Spain, although it was not until 1822 that the country liberated itself and joined the present countries of Colombia and Venezuela to form Greater Colombia under the leadership of Simon Bolivar. Eight years later this unity was dissolved and Ecuador became an independent republic. Then followed a turbulent century for the republic in which constitutional presidents alternated with dictators and in which there were more than a dozen constitutions which were adopted for a few years and then discarded. The present constitution under which the country is governed was adopted in 1946–47.

The Republic of Ecuador consists of 18 provinces which are divided into 95 municipalities. These, in turn, comprise some 767 sub-municipal units. In addition, there is the territory comprising the archipelago of Colon, or the Galapagos Islands, which are over 600 sea miles from the continent and which have a special form of administration.

Municipalities ('*Municipios*')

The country of Ecuador is divided into municipalities (*municipios*) whose boundaries exactly coincide with those of the *cantons* into which the country is also divided. The municipalities are units of local representative government whose chief executive, however, is appointed by the central government. This same official is, in addition, head of the staff of the unit of local non-representative government, the *canton*.

As set forth in the Political Constitution of the Republic, all Ecuadoran municipalities have a uniform structure, organization and powers. Each has a council (*Concejo Municipal* or *Concejo Cantonal*) which is popularly elected by proportional representation and which varies in size from seven in most municipalities to nine in those which are capitals of the provinces and to a maximum of 11 in the three largest population centres. The task of councilman is obligatory and citizens cannot refuse to serve the two-year term of office except in certain cases which are described in the law. Part of the council members go out of office each year.

The municipal council is charged with establishing a budget, imposing taxes, and passing ordinances pertaining to the following municipal services: town planning; construction and maintenance of roads; establishment of systems of transportation; construction and maintenance of prisons; provision of various social and public health services; establishment of schools and colleges, although the physical facilities, courses of study and appointment of teachers must be in conformance with nationally established standards; establishment of a police force to enforce health measures, building codes, rent controls and care of public property. It may also create new sub-municipal units within its territory, with the approval of the central government, and provide such cultural facilities as museums, libraries, archives and art exhibits. Although protection against fire is a responsibility of the national government, various municipalities can establish volunteer departments which raise their own income and establish their own organizational structure. In such cases the chief of the department is named by the President of the Republic, although there is little, if any, intervention in the department's administration.

The councils have no judicial powers, but they may designate commissioners (*Commissarios Municipales*) who pass judgement on infractions of ordinances pertaining to matters of hygiene, rents for lodgings and construction of buildings. They may also convene an Extended Municipal Council (*Cabildos Ampliados*) which offers advice on matters put before it by the regular council. This group consists of, besides the incumbent council members, the last five mayors or presidents of the council, councilmen who have served during the previous two years, a delegate of the provincial council, directors of periodicals published within the municipalities and national senators and deputies of the respective provinces. Finally, the municipal council may contract loans with international financial organizations, with the guarantee of the Republic, through the intermediary of the Ministry of Foreign Affairs.

In the provincial capitals, with the exception of those three located in the sparsely populated forest region in the east, the presiding officer of the council, in which he can vote only in case of an even division of opinion, is the mayor (*Alcalde*). He is popularly elected and serves a two-year term of office. In the other municipalities each council elects a president from among its own members. For the most part, these officers have limited administrative functions, those of the president being even less than those of the mayor. One duty with which they are charged is to serve as functionaries to whom appeals for writs of *habeas corpus* are made.

The real executive authority of the muncipality is vested in the political chief (*Jefe Político*) who is appointed by the central government on the recommendation of the provincial governor. He must sanction all municipal ordinances, and can refuse to do so when he finds such ordinances contrary to the constitution or the laws of the Republic. As an official of the central government he is charged with keeping the civil register and may perform civil marriages. He is directly responsible to the provincial governor and serves at his pleasure, although dismissal comes through the central government.

In addition to scrutiny and approval of all ordinances by the political chief, the Ecuadoran municipalities are supervised in their administrative activities by the provincial council and by the Ministry of Government and Municipalities. The latter is required by law to safeguard the efficiency and good faith of the municipalities. Its specific responsibilities include attending to complaints against municipal governments, after having first informed the provincial council of the complaints, deciding on all questions concerning the execution of municipal government acts; and establishing a maximum on municipal taxation. The provincial council invests the municipal councils with office; calls forth substitute councilmen when there is not a legal quorum in the council or, should there be none available, names the needed substitutes; receives declarations on the incapability of mayors; and decides on appeals concerning qualifications of municipal councilmen, in which cases the provincial council can also fine those who act in bad faith in questioning the qualifications.

Judicial control of municipal acts is through the Supreme Court of Justice to which any citizen may appeal on the basis that he was unfavourably affected by the ordinance or resolution, or on the basis that the legislation is in violation of the constitution or laws. Members of the municipal government are responsible for any abuses they are adjudged to have committed, either individually or collectively.

Sub-Municipal Units ('Parroquias')

The sub-municipal units into which all Ecuador municipalities are divided serve merely as administrative sub-divisions of the local non-representative government or *canton*; its officials are responsible only to the centrally appointed municipal chief executive. Only in the sub-municipal units in rural areas is there any kind of representative organ; this is in the form of a three-member board (*Junta Parroquiale*) whose members are elected by the municipal council and serve at its pleasure. The functions of the board are confined to looking after minor matters concerned with the well-being of the unit, suggesting general improvements and doing whatever else the municipality, through ordinances, determines.

The chief executive officer of both the urban and the rural sub-municipal units is the political deputy (*Teniente Político*) who is an immediate agent of the municipal chief executive, to whom he is subordinate. He is appointed by the central government on the recommendation of the provincial governor who, in turn, receives recommendations of names from the respective municipal political chief executives. Just as he is appointed by the central government, the political deputy may also be dismissed at its pleasure. In addition to carrying out those responsibilities delegated to him by the municipal political chief, the political deputy has the judicial function of settling minor cases of civil law and acting as judge of instruction in penal law. In general, his duties include publishing the orders of the municipal political chief and seeing that they are complied with; looking after public security, public hygiene and health; protecting the Indians; seeing that public roads are maintained; and informing the municipal council of any irregularities or incorrect actions.

Provinces ('Provincias')

With the exception of the forest regions in the east and the province in which the national capital is located, all Ecuador provinces have a council (*Consejo Provincial*), the number of whose members varies from province to province, according to the Election Law, and whose terms of office throughout the country are two years. Provincial councilmen are elected at the same time as are those of the municipalities and also by proportional representation. Their presiding officer is a president who is elected each year from among the council membership. One of the president's main tasks, in addition to presiding over council meetings, is to approve the annual budget which is prepared and presented to him by the council.

Charged with the over-all task of promoting the progress of the province and maintaining contact with the central government, the council passes ordinances relating to the construction of roads and schools; authorizes certain acts of municipal councils, whose over-all activities it also tries to co-ordinate; presents an annual report of its activities to the Ministry of Government and Municipalities; and acts as the organ of appeal by citizens against the resolutions of the municipal councils. The mayors and councilmen, in turn, can appeal to the Council of State adverse resolutions of the provincial council in such cases.

Serving as the chief executive of the province and agent of the President of the Republic is the governor (*Gobernador*) who is appointed by the Minister of Government and Municipalities (full title: Minister of Government, Police, Municipalities and Religion – *Ministro de Gobierno, Policía, Municipalidades y Culto*) and serves at his pleasure. This official controls all authorities within his territory and serves as the co-ordinator of governmental activity in the province. In general, he sees that what happens in the province complies with the constitution and the laws, keeps order, and sees that there are free elections.

In the province containing the national capital, where there is no governor, his functions are exercised by the Ministry of Government. The archipelago of Colon is under the executive power of a Maritime Governor (*Gobernador Marítimo*) and of various military authorities.

COLOMBIA

The coast of Colombia was one of the first parts of the American continent that was visited by the Spanish navigators and it was here, too, that in 1510 the first permanent European settlement on the American mainland was made. New Granada, as the country was known until 1861, rebelled against Spain in the early part of the 19th century and in 1831 it became an independent republic whose territory included what is now the country of Panama. From the time of its independence until 1903 Colombia experienced intermittent civil war, but at that time peace was attained which has proved to be lasting. In the same year Panama seceded and the present boundaries of the country were formed.

A centralized country, Colombia is divided into provinces (*Departamentos*) and municipalities or municipal districts. The latter, in turn, may contain sub-municipal units (*Corregimientos*) which are created by the individual municipality; this, however, has not been common practice. Within the territorial division of the province but directly responsible to the central government are districts (*Intendencias*), sub-districts (*Comisarías*) and national territories. The districts and sub-districts are found in economically and culturally low developed areas. They, too, may be sub-divided into municipalities and sub-municipalities.

Municipalities

Provisions concerning the Colombian municipalities are contained in both the constitution of the country and in the ordinary laws. The former permits the establishment of different categories of municipalities according to population, fiscal resources and economic importance, and outlines the overall structure of municipal government. The ordinary laws do not constitute a complete set of rules on the organization and administration of the municipalities, but regulate instead individual matters such as management of property, collection of taxes, etc. Bogotá, the capital, is a special district which was established by a decree of the national executive power.

Each municipality has a representative organ known as the council (*Consejo Municipal*) which is popularly elected for a two-year term. It varies in size from 5 members in those municipalities with less than 5.000 inhabitants to 15 members in municipalities with a population of more than 50.000. The councilmen are elected for a two-year term. The council selects from among its own membership a president, vice-president and a secretary.

Included in the council's competence are such public works as construction and maintenance of roads, water mains, aqueducts and public buildings other than schools; public education matters, including obtaining sites for schools; establishment of municipal courts and prisons; and various public welfare and health measures. The council is responsible for examining the accounts of the municipal treasury and for then presenting them to the provincial controller and for deciding on all resolutions (*acuerdos*) which are presented to it by the mayor, treasurer, inspectors of public instruction, municipal engineers, official doctors, presidents of charitable organizations, etc. concerning their particular field of interest. Such resolutions must be debated on two different days in all municipalities except those which are the capitals of the provinces and others especially enumerated by law. If the plan is approved by the council following the second debate, it is then given to the mayor for his approval. This official, in turn, may veto the resolution within two days, on the basis of unconstitutionality, irrelevancy and inconvenience. In provincial capitals, however, and those municipalities with more than 300,000 inhabitants, lack of approval by both the mayor and the governor can only be on the basis of unconstitutionality or illegality. Rather than veto the resolution the mayor may instead indicate his objections to it and extend the time limit for its approval. Should the council recess during this extended period the mayor must publish the resolution in a public place for a specified length of time. On the other hand, should a recess not occur and the mayor not publish or sanction the resolution before the time limit is up, the council may then declare his objections unfounded.

The real decision on such resolutions, however, rests with the provincial governor to whom the mayor must send copies; from an adverse decision of this official the council may appeal to the attorney general who debates the claim of nullity before the proper authority. Once a resolution is approved it becomes effective unless otherwise provided, and must be published in a form that will be understood by the inhabitants of the municipality.

The executive power of the municipality is vested in the mayor (*Alcalde*) who is appointed by the provincial governor for a one-year term of office, although this is usually extended by re-appointment for indefinite periods of time. He has a dual role, to serve as chief of the municipal administration and as agent of the central government. The mayor is a functionary of much importance, especially in view of the geography of the country whereby, in some isolated regions, the mayor has virtually absolute control of all municipal affairs.

The mayor is the executive head of the municipality, in which capacity he supervises its daily governmental operations, executor of council resolutions and immediate agent of the governor. He is, furthermore, chief of police in his territory. His responsibilities include calling the council meetings and seeing that the council meets at the proper times and discharges its assigned duties. The mayor may present resolutions to the council for its approval in all matters of general interest, as well as those pertaining to the giving of municipal services and the maintenance of public order, safety and security. Such resolutions may be general or need apply to only one person. Finally, as was mentioned previously, the mayor must approve or disapprove all acts of the municipal council, in addition to performing whatever additional duties are delegated to him by the provincial governor and the central government.

Strict control over the municipalities is exercised by the central government in the administrative, financial and judicial areas. As regards administrative matters, the governor approves all actions of the council and the mayor and may revise those he considers unconstitutional or illegal. In addition the mayor is subject to dismissal at the pleasure of the governor as well as being subject to his corrections, revocations and directions concerning any municipal matter. In fiscal matters the municipalities are subordinate to the province although control is also exercised by the General Controller's Office which sees that no expenditure is made unless it is specifically authorized by law, establishes rigid rules for bookkeeping, classification of accounts, etc., it audits accounts and determines any responsibility on the part of municipal employees in the discharge of their work.

In the judicial area there are special courts, headed by a supreme administrative court, which adjust differences between administrators and the citizens, between councils and citizens or among the various governmental units, as well as provisionally suspend administrative acts on the grounds of unconstitutionality, illegality, being contrary to provincial ordinances and executive orders of the governor and the central government and being expedited in an irregular or abusive manner.

Sub-Municipal Units ('Corregimientos')

By law municipal councils in Colombia are empowered to create, in important villages, sub-municipal units with a special administration headed by a deputy (*Corregidor*). Actually, these are embryonic municipalities which are able to assume municipal status under certain conditions of population, income, etc.

The sub-municipal deputy is an agent of the municipal mayor by whom he is appointed and to whom he is responsible. In his territory the deputy has corresponding functions to those of the mayor in the municipality. In addition, he must also perform those duties which are delegated to him by his immediate superior. All regulations made by the deputy must be approved by the mayor, who may also modify or improve upon them.

Districts ('Intendencias') and Sub-Districts ('Comisarías')

The district and sub-district have a special system of government, although they are assimilated into the administration of the province to as great an extent as is possible. Their direct responsibility, however, is to the central government. Like the sub-municipal unit the district signifies a preparatory state – in this instance for becoming a province, with the result that these units have a greater participation in the administration of their own affairs than is the case with the sub-districts.

Provinces ('Departamentos')

The Colombian provinces are administrative sub-divisions of the central government and have independence of action, through a provincial council, in those fields assigned to them by the constitution or the law. Their chief function is to act, through the governor, as the link between local and central government and to co-ordinate in a limited fashion municipal activities throughout their territory.

The chief official of the province is the governor (*Gobernador*) who serves as head of the provincial administration as well as agent of the central government. He is appointed by the central government to whom he is responsible, and serves an indefinite term of office. Among his duties are to supervise the smooth functioning of municipal activities, which he controls through decrees, resolutions and orders to the municipal councils and mayors, as well as by approval of all municipal acts. The governor may be removed at any time. Each province has a provincial council whose members are elected every two years. The council has a limited authority to make ordinances.

EL SALVADOR

What is now the present Republic of El Salvador was invaded and conquered by the Spanish in the early 16th century and remained under its rule until 1821 when, along with the other countries of Central America, it declared its independence. The Central American Federation which resulted lasted until 1839, at which time the federation was dissolved and El Salvador became an independent republic. Until the 1930's the history of the country was one of numerous revolutions and wars against other Central American countries. Since that time, however, a large measure of stability has come to El Salvador, the smallest and most densely populated of the Central American states.

For administrative purposes El Salvador is divided into 14 provinces (*departamentos*), which are composed of some 39 districts (*distritos*). The basic unit, into which the entire country is divided, is the municipality, of which there are 260 in El Salvador.

Municipalities

The existence and powers of the municipalities in El Salvador are established by the constitution which in broad terms also prescribes their structure and general duties. Specific details are contained in the Municipal Law of 1908, amended in 1952, which is very similar to the basic compilation of laws relating to municipalities which was enacted in 1879.

As in the past, El Salvador municipalities are now divided into three classes (*ciudad, villa* and *pueblo*) although such division is mainly for honorary and ceremonial purposes. This division is increased to five, thereby including provincial and district capitals, for the purpose of establishing limits on municipal expenditures, and further expanded to six for the fixing of the number of municipal council members. Beyond this, classification is of little importance.

As for the functions and duties of the municipalities, it must first be noted that there is a high degree of centralization of all types of governmental services. In general, the central government provides the basic services and the municipalities supply such supplementary services as their resources permit. Primarily these supplementary services include: public education, for which 5–10% of local revenues must be used for whatever purpose the municipalities wish, which varies from providing school supplies to establishing adult education programmes and additional schools; recreation and cultural affairs; police protection, which mainly consists of guarding public property in the urban areas and collecting taxes and service charges; public health and sanitation, for which 5% of local revenue must also be used; public works and utilities, in which field the municipalities are primarily responsible for routine operation and maintenance; municipal markets and cemeteries; control of livestock; keeping vital statistics records; and such special services as providing an irrigation system, ambulance service, etc.

Each municipality has a council (*concejo*) composed of a popularly elected mayor (*Alcalde*), legal advisor (*Síndico*) and from 2 to 12 councilmen (*Regidores*), who serve four-year terms of office. This is the agency through which the municipality acts and little can be done unless action is initiated or approved by this body. In its monthly and special meetings the council enacts resolutions governing local affairs within its jurisdiction or those which must be approved by the central government. It also is responsible for many administrative duties such as preparing an annual budget; appointing and dismissing the municipal secretary, treasurer and the chiefs of major municipal departments and approving their leaves; also approving the payroll.

In addition, each council is required by law to create four permanent committees from among its own membership. These are: Public Schools, Police, Jails and Public Works; Roads, Streets, Plazas and Sanitation; Water Service; and Weights, Money and Measures. In theory, each of these fields of service is under the absolute charge of its respective committee although in practice many municipalities have established fewer or more committees or have grouped the activities in a different way than is prescribed by law. Only in the smaller municipalities where there are few, if any, departmental employees and where individual council members assume direct responsibility for seeing that services are provided, does the committee system work as envisaged by law.

Legally the mayor is the chief executive officer of the municipality. He serves also as council chairman, in which position he may cast the deciding vote in case the council is unable to come to a majority decision. Furthermore, the mayor is responsible for executing the decisions of the council, for appointing and dismissing minor municipal employees, and for providing over-all supervision of municipal activities, especially where council committees are not active. In practice, his two principal tasks are signing various routine records and documents and talking with people who have specific questions and problems. The relative importance of the mayor varies greatly among incumbents according to individual interests and abilities; in some municipalities the mayor dominates the council and the administration and in others he merely signs documents, attends council meetings and assumes ceremonial functions.

In addition to serving as a councilman, the legal adviser (*Síndico*) has the tasks of representing the municipality in all legal proceedings in which it becomes involved, prosecuting tax delinquents, auditing municipal accounts, enforcing the law and providing general legal and business advice and assistance to the municipality. As is the case with the mayor, however, the effectiveness of this municipal officer varies with the individual. For the most part, the *Síndico*, who often has no particular training for the job, performs only such routine duties as examining and signing various documents, in addition to his duties as councilman.

The municipal secretary is assigned general responsibility for the recording and clerical activities connected with the functioning of the council and its committees and is also custodian of the official documents and records of the municipality. In addition, he attends council meetings as an advisory and non-voting member and assumes joint responsibility with the mayor for certain prescribed acts. Frequently, moreover, he assumes in fact the functions of the chief executive. According to the law the position of municipal secretary has become that of a career municipal employee, for there are specific provisions for transfers of secretaries between municipalities and it is common practice for municipal secretaries to be promoted from small to succeedingly larger municipalities, frequently upon recommendation of the Governor or Minister of Interior.

Central supervision and control over the municipalities of El Salvador is virtually complete. The Court of Accounts, an agency of the national Legislative Assembly, exercises a broad pre-audit and post-audit review of municipalities through its fiscal supervision and control and prescribes in detail municipal accounting records and procedures. Furthermore, the law prescribes that certain percentages of municipal revenues must be used for specific purposes, and the constitution states that local tax measures are to be approved, rejected or revised by the Legislative Assembly, thus taking away from the municipalities control over their incomes as well as much of their expenditures. Inspectors of the Division of Municipal Inspection and Administrative Control of the Ministry of the Interior review all council minutes and make annual inspection visits at which time they observe municipal operations, audit municipal records and discuss local practices and problems with the mayor. When a municipality is found to be violating a law or order of the national government, this is reported to the appropriate authority for corrective action.

The provincial governor also assumes broad supervisory control over the municipality. He is authorized to make annual visits; to decide on appeals from the acts of councilmen, against whom he also may hear complaints; to impose fines on municipalities and their officers for improper actions or non-performance of duties, as well as to discharge them from office; and to determine the need for such facilities as sewers and pavements and to notify then the municipality of the action it should take.

Provinces ('Departamentos')

The provinces are the principal geographic sub-divisions of the national government, both for the local administration of its programmes and for the supervision of municipalities. Several national government agencies use the province as the basic service area for administration of their local programmes, with a field office in each capital city, although others have developed different patterns for service areas.

Heading the province is the governor who, along with a substitute, is appointed by the President of the Republic and is responsible to the Minister of the Interior for the carrying out of his responsibilities. The law assigns functions to the governor as a public official rather than to the province itself and these include: publishing and enforcing all national government laws and decrees; maintaining public order; observing and reporting on the activities of all national government agencies in the province; informing the central government of local needs and problems; inspecting educational, welfare and penal institutions and giving assistance to postal authorities. The responsibility of the governor in exercising supervision and control over the municipalities in his jurisdiction include in addition to those mentioned previously: seeing that municipalities properly carry out all of their functions, without infringing on their autonomy, and submitting comments and reports on municipal plans and proposals to the central government.

To carry out his responsibilities each governor has only a small secretarial and office staff. On the whole, his main task is to encourage local co-operation with and observance of national government laws, programmes and policies and to preside over various fiestas and ceremonial affairs as the official representative of the President. In addition, legislation defining the functions of various ministries have reduced the position of the governor, in regard to the supervision and co-ordination of national government service programmes at the local level, to that of observing and reporting.

An additional level of supervision and control over local government activities is the district (*distrito*) which has been introduced by a legislative act. The chief executive officer of the district is the mayor of the municipality designated as the capital city of the district, who assumes the additional title of district chief (*Jefe del Distrito*). Theoretically the district chief is an assistant governor in his area and has such responsibilities as disseminating information on central government laws and decrees, maintaining public peace and co-operating with the military forces in the area. He is also expected to consult with municipal officials, advise them on local problems, and inform the governor on all matters requiring his attention. Furthermore, he may fine municipal mayors up to a certain amount if they are negligent in their duties and may discharge municipal secretaries and other municipal employees for improper conduct or negligent performance of duty.

In practice, the district has little or no significance. The district chief, moreover, rarely has any official contacts outside his own municipality and leaves the problems of intermunicipal relationships to the provincial governor.

(7)

THE WEST ASIA AND NORTH AFRICA GROUP

TUNISIA

ON 20th March 1956 Tunisia became an independent country after several centuries of foreign domination. The rule of the Turks, which was absolute in the 16th century, became only nominal in the early 18th century when a monarchy was established under the Bey. This ruler completely centralized all governmental activities, even to the extent of placing strangers, rather than the traditional headmen, in charge of tribal affairs. The dissension and warfare that resulted from this action led to the establishment of a French protectorate in 1881 which re-established the ancient system by making the tribal headman the indispensable link between the central and the basic governmental units. Under the present constitution the tribe as the basic governmental unit has been replaced by a larger territorial division, and the function of the tribal headman has been reduced to that of a local chief.

Administratively Tunisia is divided into 14 provinces, each of which contains from 4 to 10 districts. The 83 districts, in turn, comprise some 743 rural basic units, in addition to approximately 112 municipalities.

Municipalities

About 40% of the Tunisian population lives in urban municipalities which, according to the Municipal Law of 14th March 1957, have a similar system of government and similar functions varying only with the size and revenue of the municipality.

The representative organ of the municipality is the council, the number of whose members depends on the municipal population, the importance of the municipality and its tax base. In general, however, the range is from 6 to 30 members, elected by majority vote of all citizens over 20 years of age, to serve three-year terms of office. Under an optional clause of the law the Secretary of the Interior, on the request of the provincial governor, may also name as councilmen foreigners who have lived in the municipality for two years or who have paid municipal fees and taxes for three consecutive years, although this option has not as yet been implemented.

Ordinary council sessions take place four times a year for a period of 10 days each, except in November when the budget is adopted. At that time the session may last up to one month. In addition, special sessions may be called by the mayor at his own desire, at the demand of one-third of the council members or at the request of the governor. Matters discussed at the meetings include all affairs of the community. Specifically, the council adopts a budget, acts as the municipality's legal representative, levies taxes and fees, considers loans, buys and sells municipal property, organizes municipal services and makes rules regarding the status of municipal personnel. It also keeps the central government informed of local conditions and matters. The council, too, may appoint committees whose task between council sessions is to study and make recommendations to the council on various municipal matters that may arise. The chairman of these committees is the mayor, although each such group elects a vice-chairman to convene the meetings and preside over them in the mayor's absence.

Serving as the executive of the municipality is the mayor who is aided by 2 to 6 deputies serving as a board. All are elected by the council from among its own members and serve the same term of office as do the other council members. Like his counterpart in many other countries, the Tunisian mayor has the dual role of acting as an organ of the municipality as well as agent of the central government. In carrying out his former duties the mayor is charged with the execution of municipal decisions, preparation of the budget and contracts, representing the municipality in legal proceedings, hiring municipal employees and supervising daily administration. In addition, he is responsible for the public order and security and it is he alone who is responsible for police functions in the broadest sense. Police personnel, however, are central government employees, and in his capacity of Chief of the police the mayor is directly responsible to the Secretary of the Interior. As an agent of the central government the mayor must publish new laws and regulations, establish electoral lists, register births, deaths and marriages and assume various public order responsibilitities.

The board takes over the mayor's functions in his absence. In addition, it may perform any tasks which may be legally assigned to it by the chief executive. The board members act in most respects like their French counterparts.

Extensive control is exercised over the Tunisian municipalities by the central government, through the Minister of the Interior, the provincial governor and the Secretary of Finance. All legislation must be examined for legality and merit and may be declared null and void if it does not meet these tests. In addition, certain legislation, such as that pertaining to financial matters, municipal property, employees and enterprises, and public health and welfare matters, must receive prior approval. The central government may also require a municipality to act in instances where it finds failure to do so harmful to the public welfare.

Further control is exercised by the power of the central government to suspend or dissolve municipal councils. In the latter case a commission of three members, one of whom is designated as president, is appointed to carry on purely administrative work concerning daily affairs until a new council is elected. Such a commission may not undertake any financial duties, such as drawing up a budget, or those concerning buying or selling of municipal property, nor change any statutes dealing with municipal personnel. Just as is the case with councilmen, mayors and boards may also be suspended or dismissed for failure to act in cases where public well-being is concerned, or in cases where instructions have been issued by the various central government ministries, or for illegal or irresponsible activities.

Rural Basic Units ('Cheikhats')

As was mentioned earlier, the ancient basic division of Tunisian territory by tribes has been replaced with that of division into rural basic units called *Cheikhats*. Unlike the municipalities these divisions have no legal personality nor financial autonomy. Their populations range from 700 to 9,000 and comprise about 60% of the total population of the country.

The chief official of the rural basic unit is the headman or *Cheikh* who is named by the Secretary of the Interior from among a list of three candidates presented to him by the assembly of electors, which consists of all adults over 20 years of age. His duties fall into three main categories: financial, judicial and administrative. In the financial realm the headman helps the central government assess taxes and is responsible for their collection. His judicial functions include issuing summonses to appear before the court, helping enforce court sentences passed and preparing notes on the opinions and procedures taking place in real estate court, as well as being present during investigations carried on in this respect. The *Cheikh* also has somewhat the same function as a rural policeman in regard to the minor offences. For other infractions of the law which come to his attention through complaints or through direct knowledge, the *Cheikh* must report directly to the Public Attorney who then takes action.

In his administrative role the *Cheik* serves as the liaison between the local citizens and the central government. He also helps with any public services within his jurisdiction; reports to the central government on security conditions in his territory; prepares reports on agriculture, livestock, sowing and harvesting; issues certificates of indigence; assists the central government in marking out property and in verifying weights and measures; aids in agricultural demonstrations; assists central government agents in regard to vaccinations and fights against epidemics; registers births, deaths and marriages; and draws up recruiting lists for the army.

To aid him in his work the *Cheikh* may appoint 2 or 3 agents who are then paid in the same manner as he, either on the basis of services rendered or by a general fee. In some districts it is the secretary of the *Cheikh* who is the true rural basic unit leader.

Control over rural affairs by the central government is complete. In addition the Cheikh can be suspended or dismissed at any time if he commits an infraction of the penal or administrative codes.

Provinces and Districts

Directly below the central government are the 14 provinces, each of which comprises from 4 to 10 districts. The chief executive of this unit is the governor who is an agent of the central government. His responsibility is to co-ordinate the work of the various national ministries within the province, exercise certain defined supervision over the municipalities, maintain public order, and assure representation in the province of the national interest. He also presides over an administrative council whose members are named by the central government for three-year terms. In size these councils vary from 10 to 29 members. Their primary function is to give advice to the governor.

Administration of daily affairs is placed in the hands of a secretary and a varying number of deputies. Two or three of these deputies remain at the seat of provincial government to assist the governor, while the others are placed at the head of the districts into which the province is divided, where they exercise the powers of the governor as delegated by him.

IRAN

Iran has a continuous history as a political entity over the past 2,500 years in spite of many fluctuations in size and power. A victim of numerous invasions by foreign people, during one of which the country was converted to Islam, unity was re-established in the country in the late 1700's. The dynasty founded at that time remained in power until 1928, when it was replaced by the absolute rule of Riza Shah until the Second World War. The following years have seen more liberal regimes in Iran, accompanied by increased economic and political development.

For administrative purposes, the country is divided into 10

provinces (*ostans*), 102 districts (*sharetans*) and 356 sub-districts (*dehestans*). In addition, there are 241 municipalities. New municipalities may be created by an official decree of the Minister of the Interior.

Municipalities

The Municipal Law of 1955 removed local government from under the jurisdiction of the Minister of the Interior, except in cases of gross misuse of authority by local officials. At the present time, the change-over from complete responsibility to the central government to that of some degree of local representative government is in process. Under the new law, each municipality is entitled to a popularly elected (only males have the franchise) council, elected for a four-year term. Four cities have councils of 15 members, the rest have councils of five or seven members. Execution of council decisions is through a mayor, also chosen by the electorate. The council is responsible for making policy decisions. The transmittal of these policy decisions into action depends upon the relationship between the mayor, who is the chief executive, and the council.

The municipal officials have wide jurisdiction over public works within their corporate limits, although streets and traffic control are a joint function with the Minister of Roads and the State Police. Authorization is also given them by the central government to establish local planning commissions, adopt zoning ordinances, provide social services and fire, sanitation and public health services. The latter responsibility is shared with the Ministry of Health, to which all municipalities must contribute 10% of their income for public health activities. In addition, the municipalities have partial jurisdiction over water works and electric utilities, operation of which is entrusted to a board appointed by the mayor and council.

Municipalities are directly responsible to the central government, through the Minister of the Interior. The latter may exercise complete control over municipal finance, although this is not done as long as the local government uses the shared taxes for the purpose allocated in the budget, which must be approved by the central government. In most instances, however, the council's decisions are not subject to approval by higher authorities. In the case of difficult political decisions the council is apt to consult with the governor general of the province or with the Ministry of the Interior.

The Minister of the Interior also has the authority to dissolve a municipality or a municipal council. In practice the former is never done.

Provinces, Districts, Sub-Districts

These three administrative sub-divisions of the central government are under the complete jurisdiction of the Minister of the Interior. The heads (supervisor for the sub-district or *dehestan*, commissioner for the district or *sharetan*, and governor for the province or *ostan*) of these units are appointed by the official directly above them at the next highest level, and may also be removed by the same authority. Ultimate authority is to the Minister of the Interior, and also to the other ministries responsible for specific functions, such as health, education and social services. These are no councils, and all policy directives are handed down by the central government, as are detailed instructions for their administration. There is no representative government for any of these administrative units.

LEBANON*

Lebanon was part of the Ottoman Empire until World War I, after which it became a French mandate for 20 years. Today, under a republican constitution, the country has established a unitary government structure administered through its five provinces (*mohafazats*), one of which is the capital city of Beirut, which are divided into districts (*cazas*). These districts, in turn, are composed of municipalities and villages. The executive officer of each of these governmental units is directly responsible to his immediate counterpart at the next higher level, with all responsi-

* This summary has not been checked by an expert from the country.

bility being ultimately vested in the national government through the Director-General of the Ministry of the Interior.

Municipalities

Whatever municipal powers exist in Lebanon are strictly localized and are granted by the district head, to whom municipal officials are responsible. These officials consist of a popularly elected council which, in turn, elects its own president. Their main function is to carry out the responsibilities handed down to them by the district, provincial and central authorities.

As an agent of the central government the municipality must have prior approval for putting into effect any of the resolutions it passes. Especially controlled is the levying and collection of taxes and other revenue by the provincial governor. The latter is also ex-officio president of each municipal council within his area and can dismiss any councilman for failure to attend three meetings of the Council.

The sub-municipal units are geographical sub-divisions but not administrative sub-divisions of the towns. A popularly elected *mukhtar* carries out the administrative responsibilities under the direct supervision of the district head.

Villages

Heading village government in Lebanon is a popularly elected headman (*mukhtar*) and Council of Elders who serve a four-year term of office. The function of the headman is similar, at the village level, to that of the governor at the provincial level. Thus, it is his responsibility to inform the citizens of laws and regulations handed down by the central government, to compile a civil register, supervise the collection of taxes and fees, supervise forests, and encourage school attendance and public health measures.

Provinces and Districts

As administrative sub-divisions of the central government, the provinces (*mohafazats*) and districts (*cazas*) are headed by centrally appointed officials, the governor (*mohafez*) and district head (*caïmacam*) respectively. The governor's primary responsibility is to act as the representative of the central government and to serve as the liaison between it and the citizens of his province. He is responsible for maintaining law and order, collecting taxes and improving the education, social, economic and sanitary conditions of his area. He is advised in the tasks of improvement of local conditions by a council of professional people, business men, industrialists, landowners and trade unionists.

The main function of the district head is to supervise the municipalities and villages within his territory. In this he is closely supervised by the provincial governor who, in turn, is closely controlled by the Director-General of the Ministry of the Interior.

TURKEY

The structure of rural government in Turkey is the result of a long historical evolution under the old regime. Government of urban municipalities, on the other hand, has been strongly influenced by French municipal organization and has its origin in the mid 1850's.

A unitary republic, Turkey is divided for administrative purposes into 66 provinces (*vilâyets*) which, in turn, comprise approximately 493 sub-provinces (*kazas*). The latter are composed of districts (*nahiyes*). The basic level consists of urban municipalities (*belediye*, or basic units with a population over 2,000) and rural municipalities (*köy*, or basic units with populations under 2,000 inhabitants). The urban municipalities contain within their boundaries sub-municipal units called *mahalles*.

Urban Municipalities

Urban municipalities are corporate bodies which have either more than 2,000 inhabitants or are the seats of provinces or districts. Their function is to provide certain required services stated in the Municipal Law of 1930 and any other optional ones. which can be financed from municipal funds. The plural representative organ

(*Belediye Meclisi*), which is popularly elected by majority vote for a four-year term of office, varies in size from minimum 12 members for a population up to 3,000, to an indefinite number based on the population of the municipality. At the present time Istanbul has the largest municipal council which numbers 71 members. The functions of the council include adopting an annual budget, assessing taxes and fees, raising loans, accepting the yearly accounts and passing legislation relating to controlling order in public places, providing sewage systems, taking certain public health measures in regard to slaughter of livestock and supervision of food handlers, fire protection, fixing maximum prices and charges for certain foods and services, town planning and reconstruction and the establishment of public libraries, playgrounds and squares. It also may undertake optional services, such as establishment of museums, zoos, low cost housing projects and such municipal enterprises as water, electricity, gas and transportation. And finally the council may provide vocational evening courses and establish various charity, savings and mortgage establishments.

When the council is not in session, it has as its representative a board (*Belediye Encumeni*) composed of the mayor, who is its chairman, the heads of various municipal departments, who are ex-officio members; plus members elected by the council. The latter must number not more than half the number of the ex-officio members, but can be not less than a total of two. In addition to supervising municipal activities, the board also prepares matters for the consideration of council and is an advisory body to the mayor. It also examines the budget prior to its presentation to the council as a whole, makes rules for the maintenance of law and order, fixes fares and market prices, examines the monthly expense accounts, imposes fines and makes decisions on expropriations.

The executive head of the municipality is the mayor (*Belediye Reisi*) who is elected by the council, either from among its own members or from outside its membership, and may be assisted in his duties by aides. All serve a four-year term of office. Like the French mayor, the Turkish one has a dual role – to serve as the chief executive of local administration, and as a representative of the national government in the municipality. In his former role the mayor prepares the budget, which is then examined and approved by the council, enforces municipal ordinances and regulations, manages public properties, and carries out any other duties which are assigned to him by the council. His power, however, is limited by an elaborate appeal machinery, whereby any disputes with the board are decided upon by the council, which decision may in turn be appealed to the State Council (*Devlet Surasi*) if the municipality is a provincial centre, and in other cases to the provincial administrative council. As a representative of the national government the mayor is responsible for providing certain records, such as those of births and deaths, and any other reports and information which may be requested of him.

Since 1863 the Turkish urban municipalities have been geographically divided into small sub-municipal units called *mahalles*. Each has a popularly elected chairman (*mukhtar*) and a four member "Council of Elders," all of whom serve a two-year term of office. For the most part, this group carries out central government functions such as issuing certificates of birth, death, marriage and change of residence; furnishing information to army recruitment authorities and notifying conscripts; aiding police in the inspection of buildings, providing death reports to taxation officers; preparing yearly lists of children of primary school age and informing parents of compulsory education; informing the government of all human, animal and plant diseases; certifying status of poor people; issuing certificates of good conduct and residence and informing police of suspect persons. Although located within the municipality, the *mahalle* is subject to provincial or sub-provincial governments for any change in name, area, function or status. There is no formal relationship between the *mahalle* and the municipal government.

Control of the actions of municipalities by higher authorities is extensive. According to what is its immediate superior authority – the sub-province, province or central government – a municipality must have that unit's prior approval before it can put into effect a budget, close the annual accounts, raise loans and set tariffs for municipal services. If such approval is not forthcoming within a week of its submission to the proper authority, the municipality may then submit the matter to arbitration by the Council of State which has the final authority in this respect. Other council decisions must be submitted to the proper higher authorities and may be annulled within a given length of time if they are outside the letter or intent of the law.

In the area of personnel, the mayor of a provincial capital must be approved by the Minister of the Interior before he can take office. Once in office, he may be questioned by the council on any of his actions, and where these are deemed insufficient or unacceptable to that body, the verbal proceedings of the session may then be submitted to the provincial governor or to the Minister of the Interior for approval and arbitration. Should the higher authority support the council, the mayor may then be decommissioned. The council, too, is subject to strict supervision as to the legality of its actions, and where these are found wanting, this body may be dissolved by the Council of Ministers on the proposal of the Minister of the Interior. Such action, however, is not frequently taken.

Rural Municipalities ('Köy')

Under the Village Law of 1924 Turkish rural municipalities (*köy* or *villages*) were established as legal corporate units and given detailed functions and duties. The population of the village is known as the village association (*Köy Dernegi*) and it elects, for a four-year term of office, a "Council of Elders" (*Köy Ihtiyar Meclisi*), composed of eight to 12 members, depending on whether the village has a population over or under 1,000 inhabitants. This council is the chief policy making body of the rural municipality and its functions include arranging the priority in which local work is to be done, deciding on the work the villagers must undertake without payment, purchasing or expropriating land to build schools and other public buildings, and levying taxes. It also makes decisions in regard to such mandatory village responsibilities as building water channels and roads, draining swamps and preventing disease, and optional services such as the building of public baths, markets, laundry houses, stables, cemeteries and nurseries, and the provision of books and other publications for public use. The council also has the power to settle disputes between citizens and impose fines on those who do not participate in compulsory services or who do not pay their share of the costs involved. Many of the decisions of the council are subject to appeal to the sub-provincial administrative council or its executive, who then makes a final decision.

As chief executive of the rural municipality, the popularly elected chairman, who also serves a four-year term of office, acts, in addition to his local duties, as a representative of the central government. In his role as head of the rural municipal administration the chairman represents the municipality in courts and on other occasions, carries out the decisions of the "Council of Elders," collects taxes and pays expenses, makes monthly reports of his activities to the council and guides the village in all its various activities. As representative of the central government the chairman announces the laws and instructions issued by the state, maintains security and order, keeps records of births, marriages and deaths, recruits men for the army and notifies the authorities of suspect people. For the most part, his purely local activities are subject to the approval of the sub-province executive, who may annul those he considers outside the letter or intent of the law.

In general, there are four other regular officials of the Turkish rural municipality – a guard and a clerk, both of whom are appointed by the village president; a religious official, who is chosen by the village at-large and approved by the district religious officer; and a teacher, who is an official of the Ministry of Education.

Like the urban municipality, the rural municipality is subject to close supervision by higher authorities, particularly by the sub-province executive and council. Prior approval is required for most decisions in the financial area and for the execution of optional services. In addition, although not provided in the law, it is customary for the election of the village president to be approved by the sub-province executive or the provincial governor before he can assume his duties.

Provinces, Sub-Provinces, and Districts ('Vilâyets,' 'Kazas,' 'Nahiyes')

The Turkish province has two major sub-divisions, the smallest of which is the district (*nahiye*). Although it is not a legal personality, has no property and adopts no budget, the district does have an advisory council (*Nahiye Meclisi*), which is composed of both administrative officers ex-officio; the district chairman (*Nahiye Mürüdü*) and one elected representative from each village Council of Elders and each municipal council in the district. The elected members serve four-year terms of office and represent their areas on the council. This council, which meets once a year, is presided over by the district head, who also is chairman of the council's four member executive committee (*Nahiye Encümeni*). The latter body meets monthly and acts as adviser to the district chairman and to the council as a whole.

The head of the district is selected by the Minister of the Interior and assigned to a provincial governor who, in turn, assigns him to a district post. The direct responsibility of the district head, however, is to the chief executive of the sub-province, who is his immediate superior in the chain of command. As the official representative of the central government in his area the district head supervises, inspects and reports on all local services, except military and judicial. His main function, however, is to serve as the liaison between the central and rural municipal governments. He also, despite an inadequate staff, acts as adviser to the basic units in road and school building and in providing water supplies. He inspects municipal records of income and expenditures, the findings of which he reports to the sub-governor, and has the power to approve municipal budgets. In addition, he may decide land disputes between rural municipalities or their residents; in the latter case, however, only where the local chairman may not be considered as impartial. At election time he prepares the electoral lists and assists in the electoral process. On the whole, his role is a limited one and subject to complete supervision by the sub-province executive.

The sub-province (*Kaza*), which is not a corporate body and has no elected assembly, is headed by a sub-governor (*Kaymakam*) who has many of the same responsibilities for his area as the governor has for the province. The sub-governor, a career government officer, is appointed upon the collective decision of the Minister of the Interior and the Prime Minister and the approval of the President of the Republic. He is directly responsible to the provincial governor. The duties of the sub-governor include supervising the central government agencies located in the *Kaza*; he represents the State in complaints of citizens against each other, settles land disputes, authorizes benefits for aid to families of soldiers, and makes periodic inspection trips to the districts within his jurisdiction, from whose chairmen he also receives monthly reports. To advise and assist him in his work the sub-governor has an administrative council, which is composed of the sub-governor as chairman, his secretary, the sub-provincial finance officer, medical doctor, and heads of the education, agriculture and veterinary services. This council also hears appeals from the sub-governor's decisions, as well as from the decisions of the municipal officials.

As in France, the provincial government of Turkey has a representative organ although it largely acts as an administrative subdivision of the central government. The province has a council (*Vilâyet Umumi Meclisi*), whose members are elected for four-year terms of office. Members are elected from each district and the size of the council thus varies according to the district population. Although the usual session of the council, which is presided over by the governor, is 40 days per year, it may have special sessions by the decision of the central government, the governor, or the council itself, upon approval of the Minister of the Interior. The main function of the council is to examine and approve the provincial budget, which is presented to it by the governor, examine the yearly accounts and make policy for those public services offered by the province. These include public works activities, such as the building, maintenance and repair of roads; drainage of lakes and swamp lands; issuance of licences for such public utilities as electricity, gas, tramways and buses; establishing model farms and plant improvement stations; establishing schools in cities and arranging the courses of instruction; and such social welfare services as the establishment of hospitals, and the provision of assistance to the indigent and disabled. All the decisions of the council are subject to the approval of the governor; where this is not forthcoming the council has the right of appeal to the State Council, whose decision is final.

To carry out the work of the council when it is not in session, to advise the governor on the budget before it is submitted to the council and on any other matters he may put before it, the council elects four of its members to serve on the provincial executive committee (*Vilâyet Daimî Encümeni*). This body, which is presided over by the governor, serves a one-year term and elections attempt to select members from various regions, where this is possible. In addition to those duties mentioned above, the executive committee also audits and approves monthly expense accounts submitted by the governor and prepares an annual report of the provincial activities.

As chief political and administrative officer of the province, the centrally appointed governor serves in the dual role of executing the decisions of the council in their limited area of decision-making, and acting as the provincial representative of the central government. In carrying out the latter duties the governor is the representative of all ministries within his territory and serves as co-ordinator of their work and the provincial superior of all their representatives. Thus, although each agency has direct contacts with its central government ministry, all requests for technical and accounting information must go through the governor, who, in turn, decides what are technical and accounting matters. Those requests which he considers to be within these categories are forwarded to the central agencies; others are not, and his control thus lies in this power of decision. In addition, all budget requests from the agencies must go to the governor and are sent on by him. However, this is of limited value to the governor because each central ministry then makes its own decision, with the result that there is little, if any, co-ordination of proposed expenditures in the province. A further power of supervision possessed by the governor is the making of efficiency reports on provincial employees of the central agencies, which reports help influence the career development of the employees. He is often consulted, too, when promotions or transfers are to be made. Finally, the governor supervises the work of all sub-governors within his territory, and is the representative of the province in its relationships with all other levels or agencies of government. In his relationship with the representative organs, the governor prepares and submits a budget, first to the executive committee and then to the council as a whole, disburses all public funds and approves all expenditures before they can be made. He also has the power to appoint minor officials in the lower governmental units.

As an arm of the central government, the province is directly under the supervision of the Minister of the Interior. Just as all decisions of the council must be acceptable to him, so must all the governor's decisions be approved by his central government superior. As in France the faith and confidence of that superior in his local representative is evidenced by the governor's continuance in office.

(8)

THE SOUTH ASIA AND EAST AFRICA GROUP

INDIA

IN 1947 India obtained its independence after many centuries of foreign domination. Between the breakdown of Mughul rule and the extension of control by the English East India Co. in the 17th century, the country suffered a period of anarchy or military despotism resulting in a breakdown of the former social framework and local institutions. This was followed by many years of highly centralized administration, first by the East India Co. and then by the Crown. Gradually, however, the growing demand for participation in government by the educated Indians and the great need for local services led to reforms which granted first urban municipalities and later rural areas limited control over their own affairs through wholly or partially elected local councils. Thus was created a totally new structure of local government whose only comparable antecedent, as far as citizen participation was concerned, was the former village council (*panchayat*) which acted mainly, however, in the settlement of personal local disputes. Under the 1950 constitution the concept of local representative government was further affirmed through the directive that rural municipal councils were to be organized and endowed with sufficient powers and authority to enable them to administer and control their own local affairs.

The Union of India is composed of 14 states (plus 6 territories). The states are divided into provinces, which geographically are further sub-divided into districts. Some districts comprise a varying number of sub-districts (*tahsils* or *talukas*). Both the provinces and the sub-districts are units of local non-representative government. The basic units of local government are the urban and rural municipalities, in the latter of which live 80% of the Indian population.

Urban Municipalities (Corporations, Municipalities or Borough Municipalities, Towns, Notified Areas)

All units of local government are creatures of the various states and possess those powers and functions which are specifically granted to them by law. These vary with the size of the municipality and thus its classification as a corporation, a borough, a town or a notified area.

Corporations are large urban centers whose special acts give them more extensive powers than have the others and a large measure of freedom from the control of the state. The borough has over 10,000 population and is governed by an act based on general law which allows more limited functions than are possessed by the corporations and a greater degree of control. Fast disappearing, through being absorbed into the larger population centers of which they are suburbs, are the notified areas, which exist for the most part in only one of the 14 states. The status of the town, a population center situated in the midst of a rural area, has changed little in the past few years.

Under their special and general state laws, all Indian urban municipalities have such obligatory functions as construction, maintenance and lighting of roads; regulation of trades; water supply and drainage; abatement of public nuisances; maintenance of hospitals, dispensaries, maternity centers and child welfare clinics; construction and maintenance of public markets and slaughter-houses; education, particularly primary; and fire protection. Other duties are optional and may include housing and city planning schemes; reclamation projects; acquisition of land and the construction and maintenance of parks, libraries, museums and mental hospitals; the taking of census and other surveys; giving relief grants; and establishing, managing or subsidizing municipal enterprises.

On the whole, however, although state legislation is fairly

complete in many respects, it leaves a wide range of rule-making, as well as details and application of the law, to the state governor. Therefore, in practice, the degree of local control depends on his policies. It is the governor, for example, who has the discretion of granting a charter which may change the status of a town to that of borough and which fixes its boundaries, divides it into wards, establishes the size of its council and the number of reserved seats, where these exist, and provides for its dissolution and supersession and the abolition of the municipality itself.

Regardless of size and classification, however, all urban municipalities have a representative organ (called *council*, *board* or *committee*) which is responsible for the discharge of all municipal functions. For the most part these councils are elected from wards, either by universal adult or limited suffrage and they vary in size from 16 to 80 members. Terms of office vary from three to four years (5 in one state). The system of council members being nominated by the state government, which was in force during the days of British rule, has largely disappeared and is provided for in some states only when the local electorate fails to fulfil its obligations. In other states this practice has been replaced by co-option of local citizens by the elected council members themselves. Also, separate electorates for minority groups have been abolished, although some states have, in its stead, reservation of seats in proportion to population, co-option, or provision of minority contest for unreserved seats.

As in the English system of local government, the municipal council has both representative and administrative functions. The former include making by-laws, voting taxes and a budget, sanctioning contracts above a certain amount, and making the higher municipal employee appointments. The administrative functions are chiefly carried out through various statutory and other administering committees which closely supervise the day-to-day functioning of the municipal departments.

Although each municipality has a chairman, or president, or mayor, who is elected by the council for a term of office varying from three to five years, and serves as the municipality's ceremonial figurehead, he is not really a chief executive officer. Instead, executive functions are shared by the mayor with the council, the various committees and the municipal secretary. In his duty of general supervision of council administration, however, the mayor closely approaches the role of that body's executive and every item of executive power which is not vested in any other authority belongs to him. In some states the mayor may also preside over council meetings; in others this responsibility is entrusted to a separately elected chairman. In municipalities where the chairman is elected by the voters, provision is also made for his removal by a no-confidence vote of council, or, in certain cases, through action by the state government. In some states the chairman may appeal to the state government for the dissolution of council at the time of a no-confidence motion, and the final decision between the chairman and the council is then left to the higher authority. In other states a no-confidence motion may be met with a request by the chairman to dissolve the council, which request is automatically granted. Provision is also made for the resignation of a chairman, with the permission of the state government, where a council is obstructive. At such a time the council is dissolved and new elections are held for both the representative organ and the office of chairman.

Serving as the chief administrator of day-to-day administration in the municipality is a paid secretary (also called *commissioner*). He may be elected by the council, especially in those states which also elect a municipal chairman who has executive powers, and serves at their pleasure. The state government, however, prescribes the qualifications for the post and may also require confirmation of appointment or dismissal. Appeal from the latter may be made by the chief executive officer to the state government, whose decision is final. In increasingly more municipalities, however, the chief administrator is appointed by the state government for a definite period of time, often three years, which time may be extended. He is a professional administrator and, in most instances, may be removed by the council only on the vote of a large majority of its members. In addition to coordinating and supervising daily functions of government, the chief administrator may also prepare the budget, which must be accepted by council, assess and collect taxes, and exercise disciplinary control over municipal employees.

Indian municipalities are subject to statutorily defined supervision and control by the state government through the Ministry of Local Self-Government. This department has the authority to make regulations; obtaining information; inspection; sanctioning taxation and loans; approving budgets of indebted municipalities; auditing accounts; establishing qualifications and salaries of staff; sanctioning higher appointments and hearing appeals against punishment; suspension of local resolutions where they are likely to affect peace and order; action in default; hearing appeals in specified matters from citizens aggrieved by local decisions; and deciding disputes between municipalities. In addition, the state can remove members of local councils and municipal chairmen and supersede or dissolve the former when it is guilty of abuse of power or persistent neglect of duty. Decisions as to the legality of local legislation are left to interpretation by the courts which may null any acts considered *ultra vires* unless their jurisdiction has been specifically barred in a particular sphere or class of matters. And finally, control over the various technical activities of the municipality, such as education, health, public works, etc. is exercised by the appropriate technical department of the state government.

Rural Municipalities ('Gram')

As in the case of the urban municipalities, the structure and powers of the Indian rural municipalities are established by general laws of state-wide application, which were first developed in the 1930's. Rural municipalities may be villages or groups of villages. Such laws permit a wide range of activities, although, owing to a serious lack of finances as well as lack of experience and sometimes interest, it often results that such activities are exercised at a minimum level. In many areas, too, rural municipal governments are still in the process of being organized, so that the concept of representative government is one which is unfamiliar to a large number of rural people.

Under most state laws each rural municipality has a council (*panchayat*) with representative and sometimes judicial functions as well. The representative duties concern the areas of such obligatory functions as maintenance and lighting of village streets and paths; sanitation; education; markets and fairs; maintenance of wells and grazing grounds; fire protection; and such state government functions as registration of births, deaths and marriages. Permissive functions include distribution and sale of seeds and agricultural equipment and establishment of libraries, reading rooms and various social services facilities. Judicial functions exercised by the councils in some states are limited to petty cases, such as cattle trespass, theft, simple hurt, gambling etc. In other states, this function is entrusted to a special judicial *panchayat*.

In some states the basic plural representative organ is an assembly of all the adult residents (*goan sabhs*) who meet twice a year or more and who elect a council, which in these cases is the executive organ and manages the day-to-day administration of the village. This assembly may then elect the chairman and vice-chairman of the smaller organ, or these officers may be nominated by the organ itself. The chairman is also the executive officer when there is no specially appointed Executive Officer (which is true for many states). In other states the basic plural representative organ is a council which meets at least once a month and usually ranges in size from three to 25 members. Its term of office, as well as that of its officers, is usually three years. As in the municipalities, elected chairmen can be removed by a vote of no confidence and, in addition, council members can be removed for absence from three consecutive meetings. One state is unique in providing for recall votes for individual council members by the general electorate.

Because of their lack of financial resources, the Indian villages are often unable to hire full-time employees, especially those to serve in a co-ordinating and day-to-day supervisory role of village activities. Thus the state often appoints, controls and pays for such officials in the larger villages and in groups of villages. These officials then advise the local authorities, serve as their secretary and act as the liaison between the state and the local governmental units in collection of revenue, maintaining records and in other specified duties.

Control by the state over village activities is very extensive, and is exercised through a *"village officer"* of the Ministry of Local Government or the Deputy District Commissioner who is the principal officer of the State administration, stationed in the district.

The Village Officer has no power of supervision or veto. This power is exercised by the Ministry of Local Government in some states and by the Deputy Commissioner in others. The Executive Officer of the panchayat, where he exists, can only report to the Government on *ultra vires* actions of legislature of the panchayat, and the State Government exercises the function of veto through its officers. In a few states this power is also exercised by the District Collector.

All village budgets and accounts as well as all expenditures above a certain amount must be approved. The state may also have the power to cancel, reverse or change resolutions of local boards, suspend the carrying out of works and orders of that body, demand explanations for any defaults, and even dissolve the local representative organ and take over its functions. The latter happens fairly frequently, and is thus an important power of the state official to possess. Further control is exercised through the grants-in-aid, whereby various state departments closely supervise the use of funds by local village governments.

Districts

Originally created by the British to aid in the maintenance of law and order and to collect revenue, the Indian districts still retain these functions as well as supervise those areas within their boundaries which are not included within municipal areas. Their principal activities, however, are the construction and maintenance of roads and bridges and education, chiefly elementary. The district is also responsible for certain medical and public health services and the provision of ferries, rest-houses and markets, where these are not already provided for by village units. Permissive functions relate to reclamation schemes, prevention of river pollution and registration of vital statistics.

The district has a dual function – as a unit of the state government and as a unit of local self-government. To aid in its latter role each district has a popularly elected council, consisting of 20 to 40 members, who meet once a month. This council, in turn, elects a president and vice-president, and to a limited extent, standing and special committees. The president serves as chief executive of the council, although supervision of day-to-day administration is done by a council-appointed secretary. This offfficial also is responsible for the preparation of council agendas, maintenance of records, and execution of decisions of the deliberative body. Depending on his experience and personality, he may or may not exercise much influence on the district government.

The amount of control over district councils which is exercised by the state government is similar to that it also exercises over municipal governments. Thus, district councils must submit reports and budgets and are liable to having their legislation nulled by the state government. In only extreme cases, however, are they dissolved or their presidents dismissed. Again, the courts have the power of declaring acts outside the law, and further supervision is exercised through the system of grants-in-aid, where certain requirements and standards of personnel and efficiency must be maintained.

CEYLON

In 1948 Ceylon became an independent country within the British Commonwealth of Nations. It had previously been a part of the British colonial empire since 1796 when the British seized the area from the Dutch who, in turn, had previously taken it from the Portuguese. The local government system of Ceylon reflects a strong degree of British influence which has been adapted, however, to the Ceylonese environment. The history of local government in the country goes back to the 4th century B. C. and written records and rock inscriptions of the period show that there was a well developed system of local councils prevailing at that time.

Today 97% of Ceylon is covered by one of four types of municipal governing bodies. The other 3% of the land is within the jurisdiction of the Gal Oya Development Board whose responsibility is to develop the area's agriculture, industry and general economy. In those parts of this area which are "developed" the usual forms of local self government are in existence. Over and above the division of the country into municipalities is its administrative division into 12 districts. The primary purpose of these units is to supervise the rural municipalities within their jurisdiction.

Urban Municipalities (Municipalities, Urban Councils and Town Councils)

Urban municipalities in Ceylon are divided into three categories, *Municipalities, Urban Councils* and *Town Councils*, according to their population and degree of urbanization. All, however, are independent statutory corporations and their structure, powers and duties are established by the respective national ordinances of 1947 which apply to them.

Basically, the functions of the urban municipalities are to promote the comfort and welfare of the people. Specifically this involves drawing up and adopting a budget; levying taxes, rates and fees; issuing various licences; contracting loans; establishing a municipal plan; maintaining thoroughfares; providing and maintaining such public utilities as water, electricity, sewers and whatever other municipal resources permit; establishing cemeteries, public baths, markets and housing facilities; and where possible, providing fire brigades, rest houses, community centres, public libraries, free dispensaries and various other health, recreational and cultural facilities. Education and police, on the other hand, are functions of the Central Government.

The basic representative organ of the urban municipalities is a council which is composed of members who are elected by majority vote from single member wards to serve three-year terms of office. In size the councils vary from three to eight members for the smallest municipalities and from four to 12 or more for the larger municipalities. The presiding officer is a council appointed chairman, called mayor in the larger municipalities, who also serves as the municipality's chief executive in putting council decisions into effect. Although a council may vote a "lack of confidence" in its chairman and replace him, this seldom occurs and the recognized role of the chairman is that of political and policy leader of the council as long as he retains the majority's confidence.

The work of councils in the larger municipalities is carried out through standing and special committees which are selected by the council from among its own members. Of the standing committees, the most important is that of finance, which studies all financial matters before they are presented to the council and makes recommendations on them for action by the council. Other standing committees may be concerned with such fields as law and general subjects, sanitation and markets, housing and town improvement, public works, traffic and transportation. From time to time the council may also appoint from among its own members, special committees to study and make recommendations on some particular phase of municipal administration. It is the special committees which are more likely to be used by the smaller municipalities who do not have a sufficient number of council members to form an adequate number of standing committees and who do not have as complicated problems to handle. In general the council committees exercise such powers, duties and functions as are delegated to them by the council.

Direct supervision of daily administration in Ceylonese urban municipalities is entrusted to a chief administrative officer, called the municipal commissioner, who is directly responsible to the mayor. The post of this officer to whom all municipal employees are responsible, is filled through appointment of the Local Government Service Commission, a central government agency for the recruitment, appointment and transfer of the majority of local government employees. Established in 1946 the Commission is composed of eight members selected by the Minister of Local Government, plus the Commissioner of Local Government who is ex-officio chairman. Of the nominated members, four are the direct choice of the Minister; the other four are selected by him from nominations submitted by various organizations representing the municipalities. In the Commission is vested full power for all personnel measures, including establishment of salary scales and allowances and pension funds. Uniformity in local government service has thus been established and better trained and experienced officials made available to the municipalities.

The kind and degree of control over municipal councils which is exercised by the central government, through the Commissioner of Local Government and his officers, varies according to the size of the urban municipality. All local by-laws, including taxes and rates, must be approved by the Minister of Local Government and confirmed by the two chambers of parliament before they can be put into effect. The Minister of Local Government may also vary the number of councilmen prescribed for municipal councils, may vary the limits or the wards of any municipality, and may dissolve the council and constitute another authority in its place.

Furthermore, the Minister may remove any or all of the council members for refusal to hold or attend meetings, for disobeying or disregarding his directions or recommendations, for neglect to perform duties, or for incompetence, mismanagement or abuse of power. In such a case the Minister may then appoint a Special Commissioner(s) to administer the affairs of the municipality, or he may constitute a new council with a larger or smaller number of members. The Minister may also require various statistics and reports, as well as proceedings of the council or of any committee or sub-committee of council.

Perhaps the most vital forms of control over the municipalities, because many of the above forms of control are seldom invoked, are the annual audit as well as the continuous audit which is carried out by the Auditor-General, and the supervision of grants given by the central government for particular purposes, where specific conditions must be satisfied to qualify for the grant. The Minister of Local Government must also approve loans of a certain maximum and closely supervise the budgets of municipalities that are not in good financial condition. In a more positive vein, the central government also offers information and expert advice to municipalities in such fields as public works, public health, town planning, and valuation and rating.

Rural Municipalities (Villages)

Ceylonese rural municipalities are constituted according to the provisions of the Village Communities Ordinance which establishes councils (committees) to administer areas consisting of one or more villages or groups of villages. The villages are the least developed type of local government authority in the country at the present time.

Some of the important powers of the rural municipality councils are to levy taxes and rates; contract loans; provide various public works and public utilities, such as water and electricity; construct and maintain community centres, reading rooms, playgrounds, maternity and child welfare centres; provide ambulance service, village markets and ferries; and carry out slum clearance and housing schemes. These municipalities may also conduct agricultural experiments and provide aid in the time of famine and epidemics.

Like their urban counterparts, the rural municipalities each have a popularly elected council of three to 15 members who serve three-year terms of office. They also elect one of their members to serve as chairman during this time to see that the decisions of council are put into effect.

The degree of supervision and control exercised over the rural municipality councils by the central government is similar but more strict, particularly in the financial realm, than that exercised over the urban municipalities. Supervision is through the 12 Assistant Commissioners of Local Government, each of whom is assigned to one of the 12 districts into which the country is divided for administrative purposes. Directly responsible to the Commissioner of Local Government, the Assistant Commissioners' main responsibility is to supervise and aid the rural municipalities within their area. They have the power to disapprove tentative by-laws and to direct the undertaking of certain acts. They must approve all loans, contracts, purchase, sale or exchange of any public lands and buildings; the creation of any salaried office; and any plan to relieve distress. The Assistant Commissioners also have the power to inspect books, documents, projects and the detailed operations of the rural municipal councils. As is the case with the urban municipal councils, those in the rural areas may also be dissolved or individual members removed for good reason. And finally, the chairman of the council may be removed from office for misfeasance, malfeasance or nonfeasance.

BURMA

On January 4, 1948, 62 years after the final absorption of Burma into the British-Indian Empire, Burma once more became an independent, sovereign state. Soon after its independence the Burmese government set up a commission to recommend a reorganization of the local government structure. The commission's recommendations were incorporated into the 1949 Democratic Local Government Act which provided for representative organs in the villages, village groups and districts, as well as in the urban municipalities and the wards within the municipalities. The 1949 Act was superseded in 1953 by a revised statute, and only then did implementation of the new programme begin. The democratization programme is still in an experimental stage, however, and many adjustments have yet to be made. Thus, at the present time most local government in the country continues to function under the old arrangements inherited from the days of British rule.

The Union of Burma is made up of Burma proper and five special territorial jurisdictions, each of which has its own government. Almost nowhere in these five areas does government at the local level exist, even in the limited way that it has come into being in Burma proper. Burma proper, on the other hand, which is administered by the Union Government of Burma, is divided into seven provinces (*divisions*), which are in turn sub-divided into 34 districts, one of which is the capital city of Rangoon. The districts are composed of sub-districts (*sub-divisions*), the sub-districts of village groups (*townships*) and the village groups of individual basic rural units. The more densely populated areas are organized into urban municipalities which, in turn, are composed of *wards*.

Urban Municipalities

For the most part, local government in Burma has been local administration by the central government hierarchy. The municipal councils, however, are statutory bodies that have limited discretionary powers, although their functions are mostly confined to operating markets, undertaking minor road repairs, conducting conservancy programmes, and collecting those revenues allocated to them by the central government. In the majority of cases these revenues are derived from the operation of markets and the collection of a property tax, plus additional rates for conservancy, water and street lighting, where provided. Under the Democratic Local Government Act these functions are to be augmented by those currently being performed by various departments of the central government, such as education, health services, construction of roads and buildings and provision of water supply. The limited resources of the municipalities, both in terms of revenue and skilled personnel, have so far precluded embarkation upon a full programme of local services.

Under the provisions of the Democratic Local Government Act members of the municipal councils are selected by the committees of the *wards* into which the municipality is divided. The *ward* committees, on the other hand, consist of from three to five members who are directly elected by the local inhabitants and it is from their own number that the committees select from one to three persons to serve on the municipal council. The *wards* serve primarily as electoral districts, not as administrative or service units.

Administration of municipal affairs is chiefly by committees, to one or more of which each council member belongs. Each of the committees is responsible for one or more municipal functions and matters pertaining to these functions that require executive decision are generally resolved by the committee itself, rather than by the municipal secretary. Under each committee there is usually an appointed engineer, health officer or similar executive who is responsible to the committee, and through it to the council, for the day-to-day work in his field. Such officers, plus the municipal secretary, are appointed with the approval of either the commissioner of the province or the Ministry of Democratization of Local Administration and Local Bodies in the central government, depending on the amount of salary the position carries.

Co-ordination of the work of the municipal officers and committees is essentially the function of the municipal secretary who serves, however, more as a communications centre than as an executive officer.

Representative government of the urban municipalities is virtually non-existent at the present time. The Ministry of Democratization of Local Administration and Local Bodies must approve and confirm all municipal by-laws which, according to the Constitution, must be laid before Parliament for final approval. The central government may also legislate concerning all local matters and issue general orders and regulations directing administrative activities.

On the financial side, the urban municipalities have a limited scope for taxation and consequently are directly dependent on the central government for financial assistance, which is sometimes forthcoming in the form of grants and sometimes in the form of loans. Furthermore, the central government maintains law and order and may act for the municipal authority in case the latter defaults in the administration of certain responsibilities. In more serious cases the council may be superseded, although in practice this drastic authority is seldom used.

Rural Basic Units

By far the greatest portion of the Burmese people live in the rural areas. The rural units, however, may not always be the traditional village community, but may be a more artificial unit. It is never a larger area, however, than can be administered by one headman, and few rural units have more than 1,000 inhabitants.

The chief official of the rural unit, who has direct supervision over the people, is the popularly elected headman. His main duties are to maintain order, to collect taxes, and to perform any other tasks requested of him by the central government, as well as to perform some traditional duties. Although elected by the residents of the village, the headman may be replaced by an appointed headman if he is considered by the higher authorities to be unsuitable for the job.

Under the re-organization plan, which is being put into effect in 10 pilot districts, each rural unit has a popularly elected council headed by a chairman, and an appointed village clerk to perform executive functions.

Village Group, Sub-District, District, Province (township, sub-division, district division)

As administrative divisions of the central government, these units are headed by officials appointed by the central government and form a pyramidal hierarchy with the Minister of Home

Affairs at the top in matters of appointment, transfer and promotion. In the substantive work in their areas these officials are responsible to the various central government departments and ministries. Their principal duties are to maintain order, collect revenues, and co-ordinate the work of the central government units in their respective jurisdictions. Except for the head of the province, these officers also have certain judicial functions which occupy a substantial portion of their time.

Under the reorganization plan the village groups in ten districts will have a council composed of members indirectly elected through the subordinate representative bodies. The official of this unit will then serve as the executive officer of the village group council.

The district councils were largely superseded by District Officers (*Deputy Commissioners*) during the war, and since independence they have continued in obeyance through the "Suspension Act", an interim measure passed in 1947 to maintain the *status quo* pending local government reorganization. As was mentioned above, the councils, which consist of members elected by the subordinate governmental bodies in the district, have been re-instituted in 10 pilot districts up to the present time.

Heading the district is the District Officer who is appointed by and responsible to the central government. This official is the most important executive in local administration, and the village group and sub-district officers are primarily his assistants rather than true executive officers in their respective jurisdictions. Although matters such as education, health, agriculture, forests, roads and irrigation are the responsibility of the various central government ministries, co-ordination of their work is carried out by the District Officer and it is anticipated that these activities will eventually be turned over to the district authorities. In addition, the District Officer supervises those functions specifically allotted to the district, such as operation of markets and minor road repairs, and is responsible for maintaining order, collecting revenue and performing certain judicial functions.

Although the provincial head (*Divisional Commissioner*) is theoretically the liaison officer between the District Officer and the central government, the usual practice is direct communication between the district and central government units. As a unit of the central government hierarchy, the district is completely subject to its authority and control.

Under the reorganization plan the District Officer serves as the chief executive officer of the district council. In addition, such officials of the central government as the district engineer, the district civil surgeon and other technical officers will be available to perform executive functions for the district councils.

MALAYA

The relationship between the Federation of Malaya, a member of the British Commonwealth, and Great Britain dates back to the establishment of trading stations by the East India Co. in the late 18th and early 19th centuries. In 1895 four of the Malayan states became a federation with a British High Commissioner and a system of centralized government. Some 14 years later protection and control of four states in the north and one in the south also was transferred to Great Britain.

The Malayan Union, which included the settlements of Penang and Malacca, was established in 1946 following the second world war and the Japanese occupation. Two years later a new Constitution was adopted which gave each state and settlement the right to retain its own individuality while still being united under a strong federal government. This was replaced, in turn, by the Constitution of 1955 which transferred to the elected representatives of the people most of the responsibility for the internal government of the Federation. Finally, in 1957 the Federation became a member of the British Commonwealth of Nations.

The Federation is divided into nine quasi-sovereign states headed by hereditary rulers and two former British settlements, now called states, headed by appointed governors. The Federation as a whole is headed by a Paramount Ruler who is elected by and from the hereditary rulers of the states. The states, in turn, are divided into districts which further contain urban and rural municipalities. The former are under the direct supervision of the state government while the latter are supervised by the districts through the state-appointed district officer. Those rural areas which are still unorganized are under the direct administration of the districts.

Urban Municipalities

The structure, powers and duties of Malayan urban municipalities are defined in the Municipal Ordinance (Laws of the Straits Settlements), the Town Boards Enactment (Laws of the Federated Malay States) and certain state enactments. The first two are federal laws which are applicable in all states, the Municipal Ordinance applying to the three population centres having over 100,000 inhabitants and the Town Boards Enactment applying to the 78 municipalities (*towns*) which have between 2,000 and 125,000 inhabitants.

In general, the duties of the urban municipalities include public housing, town planning, maintenance of public thoroughfares and roads, maintenance of sanitation, conservancy and certain public health services, provision of public transportation and the provision of such optional facilities as libraries, sports fields, community halls and other cultural facilities.

The plural representative organ of the urban municipality is a council (called *board* where the members are appointed by the state government or are ex-officio, and *council* where a majority of the members are popularly elected). In several of the municipalities all council members are popularly elected; in the three large municipalities and in an ever increasing number of smaller municipalities such is the case for the majority of the council members. In both instances the elected members are chosen from single or plural member *wards* to serve three-year terms of office with one-third going out of office each year.

Council members appointed by the state government serve one-year terms of office and are selected to provide representation for various groups within the municipality. The capital city, Kuala Lumpur, for example, has six members nominated by the state ruler in consultation with his council to represent various minority groups within the municipality. Ex-officio members, who mainly serve on the councils of the smaller municipalities, are such officials as the local health officer, a Public Works Department engineer and sometimes the local police superintendent. Usually these officials and technical officers act in an advisory capacity only and tend to abstain from voting on controversial matters outside their sphere of technical competence. For the most part the municipal boards and councils range in size from seven to 25 members.

Duties of urban municipal councils include accepting a yearly budget and the yearly accounts; assessing rates; setting fees for licensing certain trades, businesses and public services; and making regulations and by-laws governing those subjects within their legal sphere of competence as mentioned above. To aid them in this work the councils have a varying number of administering committees, depending on the size and complexity of the municipality. These committees, in addition to studying various municipal problems and presenting recommendations to the council as a whole, directly supervise the various municipal departments, although the heads of such departments owe their primary responsibility to the chief executive of the municipality rather than to the committee or its chairman. All committee proposals and decisions require ratification of the council as a whole before they can be put into effect.

The chief executive of the urban municipality is the mayor (*president* or *chairman*) who is usually a member of the Malayan Civil Service and is appointed by the state ruler-in-council or governor-in-council. He serves as chairman of the council and is responsible for supervising the day-to-day administration of the municipality and for effectuating the decisions of the council. One of his primary functions is to advise the council on the legality of its decisions and proposed subsidiary legislation. In the unlikely event that the council did not accept his advice the mayor could then refuse to put the council decisions into effect. In the supervision of daily administration the mayor is directly responsible to the municipal council; in advising the council on the legality of its decisions and proposed legislation his immediate supervisor is the state secretary.

In the few municipalities where all council members are elected, these in turn elect their own chairman who serves as the chief executive of the municipality. He presides over the council meetings, assumes various ceremonial functions and often sits as the chairman of one or more committees – particularly those of finance and public works. In these municipalities supervision of day-to-day administration is carried out by a municipal secretary and his assistant(s). The secretary then acts as *primus inter pares* in relation to the department heads. A further duty of the secretary is to advise the council on the legality of its decisions and subsidiary legislation.

At the present time local government in Malaya is in a transitional stage from a system of direct administration by government officers supported by appointed councils to one of representative local government. In many respects the municipalities are closely supervised by the states. Thus, all budgets must be approved and where a council has not yet obtained financial independence control is exercised by the higher authority over the expenditure of the "balancing grant" (subsidy provided by the central government to balance the municipal budget) as well as over the locally raised revenue. Furthermore, loans may only be sought from the federal government and all municipal accounts are subject to audit by the Federal Audit Service. In addition, any change in status or area must receive prior approval. In municipalities which do not have an elected mayor supervision over council actions is maintained by the appointed mayor and by the ex-officio council members who serve in advisory capacities. Finally, the constitution of municipalities or the membership of individual councilmen may in certain circumstances be revoked by the state government, although there is little need for the exercise of this power.

Rural Municipalities (Villages)

The organization of rural municipal government (*villages*) by the Malayan government began in 1949 with a vast programme of resettlement of squatter villages. Prey to terrorism by roving communist bands these communities on the fringes of the jungle were transferred to compact villages where there was economic security as well as easy access to efficient military and police protection. With the emergency not yet passed this work is continuing under the powers of the federal Local Councils Ordinance of 1952.

This ordinance provides for popularly elected councils (*Local Councils*) which vary in size from seven to 15 members who serve three – year terms of office. The council, in turn, elects its own chairman who is responsible for supervising the implementation of the decisions of the council. The powers of the village council are similar to those of its municipal counterpart and thus include such responsibilities as adopting an annual budget; accepting the yearly accounts; assessing rates and levying various fees and fines; maintaining public thoroughfares and roads, as well as sanitation, conservancy and public health services.

Control over the activities of rural municipal governments is fairly extensive and is exercised chiefly through the state appointed district officer who has a number of statutory powers. His main function is to assist the local council in exercising its statutory powers and he approves the council's budget and by-laws. He may also recommend in extreme cases the suspension of a council or certain of its members. The need for such action, however, is rare. As for financial control, this is exercised by the state government which gives annual grants to the village government. Also the Federal Audit Department audits the yearly accounts of the villages.

In the two former British settlements of Malacca and Penang, where local government developed earlier, the rural municipalities (*districts*) are governed by a system of rural councils deriving their powers from the Municipal Ordinance. These are under the general control of the settlement (now state) governments which supervise their budgets and appoint government officers as their chairmen, although some of the rural councils have elected chairmen. The functions and duties of the councils are similar to those of the rural municipal governments in the other states.

Districts

As has been mentioned above, the Malayan states are divided into districts which are purely administrative units of the state government. The chief official in the district is the state appointed district officer who implements state policy and supervises the activitities of the village governments, principally in an advisory capacity, although he has several statutory powers.

THE SUDAN

The *Meglis*, or general assembly of the tribe, is the forerunner of present-day local representative government in the Sudan. Still in existence to a limited extent in the north, this institution has barely survived the penetration of the Arabs into the country in the 13th and 14th centuries, the Turko-Egyptian regime of 1820–1885, and the following revolt which led to a 13-year period of independence. From that time until the first world war direct administration was exercised by the Condominium regime of Great Britain and Egypt. Gradually a progressive policy was adopted by these countries whereby Sudanese were appointed to junior but responsible administrative posts. At the same time, certain judicial powers within their own geographical area were entrusted to a limited number of tribes.

In 1953 the Condominium was abolished by mutual agreement and two years later the Sudanese parliament passed a resolution declaring its sovereignty. This was accepted by Great Britain and Egypt and on January 1, 1956 the independent government of the Sudan officially came into being.

The present administrative division of the country into 9 provinces which are sub-divided into 46 districts, was introduced, first under the Turko-Egyptian regime and later under the Condominium. The municipalities were created later.

Municipalities

Under the Local Government Ordinance of 1951 there is a single tier system of "all purpose" local representative government units with corporate status which serve both urban and rural areas in all of the Northern Sudan and in large areas of the South. The ultimate aim is to have a network of such local units throughout the entire country. Although the name of each municipality distinguishes it as either urban (*"municipal"*) or rural, such a distinction is in name only and no difference of status between the two obtains. Instead, the precise status of each municipality is determined by the powers conferred upon it by its charter or warrant, and these, in turn, depend on local circumstances and the state of development of the municipality. Theoretically, therefore, there is no reason why one type of local council should have greater or lesser power than another.

When, in any area, the central government feels that it is not yet time for the formal establishment of a municipality, powers under the Local Government Ordinance are conferred by order on the district head (District Commissioner). He is then authorized to form an "Advisory Council" which he can allow to exercise some or all of his powers, although he himself remains the statutory local government authority and is personally responsible for the proper exercise of its functions and duties. After a period of tutelage and experiment, councils may then be warranted with full municipal powers under the 1951 law.

The exception to the "single tier" system described above is found in areas where subordinate councils have been set up, as for example in small towns within the area of a rural municipality. The towns may then exercise such powers as are delegated to them by the parent municipality, although subordinate councils are not corporate bodies, nor, with the exception of two such councils, do they have budgets. Some of them, however, are allowed to allocate those funds assigned to them by the parent council, at their own discretion.

Although the composition of the councils of the municipalities are alike in principle, they vary in manner of selection and in size. Thus, the councils which have 20 to 30 members, are elected from single member constituencies either directly or indirectly through electoral colleges, or are nominated. The general policy is that the nominated members, who number one-third of the council membership, are appointed by the provincial governor, unless the municipal charter specifically names another appointing authority. All serve for a three-year term of office with own-third retiring each year. Despite a lack of statutory limitations to the contrary, the nominated members never exceed one-third of the total council membership; they are selected by the provincial governor to represent tribal, economic or other special interests. The general trend is for more and more councilmen to be elected.

All councils have the right to make contracts; sue and be sued; issue occupational licences; own land; levy taxes and various fees, penalties and charges; prepare anual ann budget;

and make by-laws and ordinances pertaining to some or all of the following: education, public health, public order, agriculture, construction of buildings, town planning, and the establishment and administration of public utilities. In addition, the council may be delegated responsibilities by the central government such as the collection of revenue, for which the council receives a commission, and a variety of other duties for the various governmental agencies. The performance of the latter duties is an increasingly important feature of the council's work; in most cases, the council assumes also residual duties previously exercised by the District Commisioner.

Each council has a chairman who is selected according to the terms of the municipality's charter. Thus, he may be annually elected by the councilmen from among their own members, as is most often the case in the larger municipalities, or he may be appointed by the provincial governor or district head, as was formerly the general rule. Often in the past, moreover, it was the District Commissioner himself who served as the municipal council chairman. Today it is only an occasional District Commissioner who also takes on this added responsibility. The administrative officers of the municipalities, chief of whom is the Town Clerk, are most often appointed from a general list made up by the Ministry of Local Government, although a few are still seconded from the central government, as was the former practice.

An important feature of the local government system in the Sudan, as in the United Kingdom, is the use of committees. Some, like the finance and the personnel committee, of which the council chairman is also chairman, are statutory; others are special committees and serve for as long a period as they are needed. The committees in the Sudan tend to be less important than their counterparts in the United Kingdom, although in certain matters they may be delegated full power by the council.

Control over the municipalities by the central government is extensive and is exercised by the provincial Governor and by the Ministry of Local Government. Under the Local Government Ordinance the governor must approve all municipal legislation; he may also suspend for 30 days decisions as are found not to be in the interest of good government and of public security. The decision is then submitted to the Minister of Local Government who either confirms or objects the action of the governor. The governor may also request councils to pass certain acts or orders. If they fail to do so he may then issue such orders or acts on the councils' behalf and transmit this action to the Minister of Local Government for his confirmation.

In addition the Director of Local Government, who is directly responsible to the Minister of Local Government, may, through his power of investigation, suspend, cancel or amend a council's charter or suspend any of its powers. This occurs only when it is found that the council has failed to do what it is required to do by the terms of its charter, or by any other law, or where it has failed to remedy its failure when so ordered. The Minister may also, in extreme cases, provide for a substitute administration for a temporary period of time. However, this is only a legal possibility and has never been effectuated.

All municipal budgets must be submitted for approval to the Ministry's Inspectors stationed at provincial headquarters, and finally to the Director of Local Government. Where circumstances justify, however, a local budget may be passed by the council, and supplementary approval given subsequently by the Director. Control is also exercised over borrowing and capital expenditures. In addition, each municipality must submit a monthly statement of accounts to the Director of Local Government. Where it is found that the standardized accounting system has not been followed, or where any other irregularities are apparent, appropriate action may be taken. Municipalities are also liable to having their accounts inspected at any time by either the provincial Governor or the Director of Local Government. This is in addition to the annual audit which covers the correctness of the accounts, the legality of the items, the evidence of necessary approval for all relevant items, and the conformance of expenditures with existing regulations.

In addition to strict financial supervision, the Minister of Local Government also has wide powers of technical control over the municipalities. Thus, he may make regulations concerning the establishment of local government positions as well as for the recruitment, training, conditions of service and pay for those so employed. He may also issue procedural regulations for conduct of councils and committees, as well as a variety of model laws which may, if desired, be adopted by the council and adapted to its particular circumstances. Finally, control is exercised by the provincial Governor through his right to appoint members of local councils, as well as their chairmen, and by the central government through the seconding of its officials to local councils.

Districts

The functions and responsibilities of the districts, which are headed by centrally appointed civil servants, the district heads *(District Commissioners)*, are the same as those which are conferred on municipalities wherever they are formed. The eventual aim is that these responsibilities will be shared, throughout the country, by the municipalities and special technical officers of the central government. Until this time, however, when the organization of municipalities is complete, the districts will continue to exist and the District Commissioners will perform their assigned functions. At the present time this re-assignment of responsibilities has resulted in the abolition of six district governments.

In those areas, particularly in the south of the country, where municipalities are not yet established, the District Commissioner may continue to perform all or part of his assigned responsibilities. As was mentioned earlier, some Commissioners have formed advisory councils to which various powers have been assigned, although the Commissioner still remains the statutory local government authority and is personally responsible for the proper exercise of the delegated duties. Other Commissioners are still appointed chairmen of local councils, through which position they assume fairly complete authority in those areas as well as act as an intermediary between the local units and the provincial government. Still other commissioners work through organized tribal leadership. The District Commissioner is an assistant of the provincial Governor and is therefore directly responsible to him for his actions.

Provinces

Each of the provinces has an appointed governor who is also a member of the Sudan Civil Service. His chief function is to co-ordinate and supervise all the local governmental units within his area and to perform such central government duties assigned to him as maintenance of public order and security; development of improvement plans for the province; issuance of passports and various permits; protection of the forests and control of plant diseases. For carrying out his supervisory duties over the local governmental units within his province the governor is directly responsible to the minister of local government. For the performance of his other tasks he is responsible to the various central government ministries within whose competence the tasks lie.

ETHIOPIA*

Ethiopia, whose geographical location isolated it from the rest of the world for many centuries, emerged during the first to the ninth centuries A. D. It was the threat of a Muslim invasion and the arrival of the Portuguese in 1520, however, that led to the country being gradually opened to foreigners. Following the victory of the Ethiopians over the Muslims in 1543 there were first many years of rule by strong kings and then, in the 18th and 19th centuries, a series of conspiracies and civil and foreign wars. Following the crowning of Haile Selassie as Emperor in 1930 the reform and modernization was begun which was temporarily interrupted by the Italian occupation of 1936–1941.

The present Constitution of Ethiopia was first given to the country by Emperor Haile Selassie in 1931. It was re-instituted in 1941 and expanded in 1955. Under its provisions the country is divided into 12 provinces and Eritrea. The 12 provinces consist of 74 sub-provinces which, in turn, are further divided into 360 districts. The districts are composed of 1,112 sub-districts for administration purposes and these contain within their area municipalities and rural units. All governmental units are directly responsible to the Emperor, through the Minister of the Interior.

Municipalities

One of the aims of the government of Ethiopia is to encourage municipal government, whose form and structure is established

* Not checked by the country.

by the Municipal Clauses in the 1942 Administrative Decree and enlarged by the Municipalities Proclamation of 1945.

The 1945 document divides municipalities into two categories. Category A consists of the six largest or most important urban areas, and category B of 100 municipalities or towns.

Provision is made for the establishment in each municipality of a council which is composed of two kinds of members, those appointed by the provincial Governor from among the representatives of national ministries located in the municipality, and seven members annually elected from among municipal immovable property owners. (In Addis Ababa, the capital, there are 20 elected members who serve a three-year term of office; one third of these council members are elected each year from among all tax-paying citizens.)

The council's field of competence is limited, although by law it contains setting rates on property and water and on various licences and fees; proposing a budget; authorizing expenditures from municipal funds; town planning; limited welfare functions, including health and hygiene measures not otherwise provided for by the medical department; public order; fire protection; maintenance of roads, lighting and water supply; issuance of licences for privately owned business, vehicles and animal-drawn carts, and the registration of property, births, marriages and deaths. All taxes must be approved by the provincial governor before they can be put into effect and all regulations must be likewise approved by the Minister of the Interior. The provincial governor may also establish municipal water authorities to manage and supervise the local water works and supply and make rules concerning water supply. These decisions, in turn, are subject to the approval of the Minister of the Interior.

The chief executive of the municipality, who is called the mayor (*Kantiba*) in Addis Ababa and in one other city, and the municipal officer or director in all others, is appointed by the Emperor. He is directly responsible to the Minister of the Interior in the capital city and to the respective provincial governors in all other. The duty of the chief executive includes keeping the provincial governor informed of municipal happenings and supervising daily administration, including the activities of the local police force assigned to each municipality by the provincial government. The municipal chief executives are aided by one or more assistants who are also appointed by Royal Decree.

Rural Basic Units

By far the greatest proportion of the Ethiopian people live in villages where authority is vested in a headman (*chiqa-shum*) who serves as leader and representative of his people and agent of the Emperor. Tenure of office of the headman, who may direct the affairs of one or several villages, varies from a definite period to life. In some of the northern provinces this position is rotated yearly among men of a few leading families; in other villages the position is hereditary. The source of this official's appointment also varies, sometimes being a royal decree and sometimes the provincial governor, but the person requested by the villagers is almost invariably selected. The duties of the headman are to preside over any village meetings and to collect local dues, government taxes and customs duties on the roads. He may also settle local disputes, publicize government proclamations and preside at civil marriages.

Sub-Districts and Districts ('Mikitil Weredas' and 'Weredas')

The Ethiopian sub-district is supervised by an executive officer (*Mikitil Wereda-Gedj*) who is appointed by the governor of the province and serves at his pleasure. His direct responsibility, however, is to his next in the chain of command, the district head, who supervises such duties of the *Mikitil Wereda-Gedj* as the making of reports on prevailing conditions in the sub-district and reports on unfavourable personnel conditions. The executive officer also enforces laws through the police force allotted to him, performs any duties assigned to him and approximately twice a week hears petitions and complaints from any member of the general public.

In addition, he supervises the representatives of the various national ministries in the sub-district as they conduct their activities and uses them in a staff capacity. He also acts as president of any sub-district court, in which capacity he is assisted by judges appointed by royal decree upon the recommendation of the Minister of Justice, to the latter of which all are then responsible. Assisting the *Mikitil Wereda-Gedj* in his non-legal duties is a secretary who directs the work of the clerical staff and assumes the duties of the executive officer when the latter is absent.

The district is composed of a number of sub-districts and except for its larger size is the exact replica of the sub-district. The district head is called the *Wereda-Gedj*.

Sub-Province ('Awraja')

Immediately above the district in the administrative hierarchy is the sub-province which has a head (*Awraja-Gedj*), an advisory council and a chief secretary. The head serves as the liaison between the provincial governor and the smaller administrative units of the province and transmits orders and information up and down the line. He is appointed by the Emperor upon the recommendation of the provincial governor and the Minister of the Interior and serves an indefinite term of office.

Like the district *Wereda-Gedj* the sub-provincial head visits and inspects all parts of his territory twice a year and submits reports on his observations to the governor-general of the province. He also sends monthly reports on sub-provincial conditions to his superior and supervises the police force assigned to him. In addition, he supervises the chief secretary and the employees of the various central government ministries whose complaints he may hear. And finally, like his district and sub-district counterparts, the *Awraja-Gedj* serves as president of the sub-provincial court in which capacity he is directly responsible to the Minister of Justice.

Assisting the sub-provincial governor in his work is a chief secretary who is appointed by the Emperor and who does general secretarial work and supervises the clerical staff. Serving in a purely advisory capacity to the *Awraja-Gedj* is a council, presided over by him, which consists of the chief secretary, the municipal officer of the town in which the sub-provincial headquarters are located, the executive officers of all the sub-districts within the sub-province, the officials of the various central ministries in the sub-province and not more than two local elders. No decisions of this council, which meets three times a year in addition to any special sessions called by the sub-provincial governor, may become effective without the approval of the provincial governor-general.

Provinces ('Tekelay-Gizats')

The chief executive and the representative of the central government in the province is the provincial governor who is appointed for an indefinite term by the Emperor, either with or without the recommendation of the Minister of the Interior. This governor supervises all officials in the province who have been appointed by either the Minister of the Interior or any other minister although the latter employees are responsible for their actions to their respective central government ministries. He also supervises all governmental units directly below him in the administrative hierarchy – sub-provinces, districts, sub-districts, municipalities and rural units – and all his orders to these units must be given in accordance with the instruction of the Minister of the Interior. Furthermore, it is only with the designated chief executive of these lower units that the governor may deal.

Still another responsibility of the governor is to preside over a provincial council which has no legislative powers but which serves only in an advisory capacity in matters relating to the welfare of the inhabitants of the province. Membership of the council includes, besides the provincial governor, the provincial director, the principal secretary, the district heads, the provincial representatives of the various central government ministries, the chief police officer and the officer of the municipality of the capital of the province. Any decisions of the council which are not covered by law or custom must be approved by the Ministry of the Interior. Finally, the provincial governor serves as president of the provincial court.

Appointed by the Emperor in each province, on the recommendation of the Minister of the Interior, is a director who is responsible for supervising the daily administration of provincial affairs as well as the expenditure of provincial funds and the forwarding of accounts to the Ministry of Finance. He also presides over the provincial council in the absence of the provincial governor. As in the other units of government, a further provincial official is the principal secretary who is appointed by the Emperor and who supervises correspondence, the archives and general secretarial matters.

(9)

THE EAST ASIA GROUP

THAILAND

Known as Siam until 1939, the kingdom of Thailand is the only South Asian country that was not colonized by western powers. Its first capital was founded in A. D. 575 and its history from that time until the 19th century had been one of intermittent warfare with the surrounding countries of Cambodia, Burma and Pegu. In the 1800's the country came into close contact with Great Britain and France who had interests in the Indo-Chinese Peninsula and despite border disputes with France in particular, a convention of the two western powers concluded in 1896 assured Siam's continued independence. In 1932 a revolution resulted in the overthrow of the absolute monarchy and the establishment of a constitutional kingdom in its place. With the interruption of World War II this form of government has existed until the present time.

Thailand is divided into 71 provinces, which consist of 445 districts. The districts, in turn, are composed of approximately 4,000 rural municipalities, which contain some 39,000 sub-municipal units. The districts also contain sanitary districts and some urban municipalities.

Urban Municipalities ('Nakorn,' 'Muang,' 'Tambol')

Based on its total number and density of population and its political importance, the Thai urban municipalities are classified into three groups: *nakorn*, *muang*, and *tambol*, as defined by the Municipal Act of 1951. The first two are supervised directly by the provinces, the latter by the district. Among the mandatory tasks of the urban municipality are maintenance of public peace, maintenance of roads and waterways, disposal of refuse and garbage, protection against fires, prevention and control of infectious diseases and the provision of local education. As population and revenue increase, the urban municipality must also provide drainage, water and electrical facilities, medical services, slaughter-houses, etc. In addition, each class of municipality may provide such optional services as markets, cemeteries and various public health, hospital and social services.

Legally the Thai urban municipalities are corporations whose main organs are a council and a board. The former are popularly elected and vary in size from 12 members in the *tambol* municipality to 18 in the *muang* and 24 in the *nakorn*. All have a five-year term of office. Presiding over the council meetings is a chairman who, with a vice-chairman, is appointed by the provincial governor from among the council membership. For the most part, such appointments are made only after consultation with the council, and the two officers are therefore, in reality, a local choice. The council, which meets in two to four regular sessions per year as well as in extraordinary sessions as approved by the provincial governor, can debate all matters which are within the council's legal competence. Councilmen may also question any member of the board on matters under council jurisdiction, and the council as a whole may appoint ordinary (composed only of councilmen) and special (consisting of both council and non-council members) committees.

The most important action of the council is to review the annual budget which is presented by the board. Should the council reject this document, the board must then resign. Such action, however, has occurred only rarely in the country's history. In addition, the council may pass by-laws dealing with any subject not contrary to or inconsistent with central government law as long as those subjects are within the competency of the municipality. Once such a by-law is passed it must be sent within 15 days to the provincial governor for his signature. In the *tambol* municipality the by-law must first be sent to the district officer.

Should the governor or district officer not approve the by-law, he returns it to the municipal council for reconsideration. Should that body again pass the original draft by-law, the governor turns it over to the Minister of the Interior for his approval or rejection. If the Minister approves, the by-law is returned to the governor for his signature; if he rejects the by-law, it then lapses.

The executive authority of the municipality is vested in a board consisting of three to five council members, one of whom is the council chairman, all of whom are appointed by the governor. Theirs is a dual function – acting as local government organs and as central government agents as well. In the latter role the board performs both civil and criminal duties, such as keeping census, vital statistics and other records; law enforcement; informing citizens of provincial and national laws and regulations; informing the provincial government of the general welfare of the municipality; and taking leadership in public emergencies. In addition, the chairman, who serves as ceremonial head of the municipality, may also be given power by the Minister of the Interior, to settle offences against by-laws by levying fines.

In its municipal duties the board prepares the budget and presents it to the council; drafts all by-laws for council approval, and supervises the over-all administration of department affairs. For the most part this is done individually, with each board member responsible for one or more departments. Daily administration is in charge of a chief administrative officer who is appointed by the Minister of the Interior through the Governor. This officer is under the constant control and policy guidance of the board, particularly the chairman. As a group the board is responsible to the council, and can be questioned in council meetings on municipal affairs. The board must resign from office in the following events: if the annual budget is rejected by the council, the chairman of the Board resigns, or a dismissal order is issued by the Minister of the Interior. Individual members may leave the board by resigning, by an impeachment resolution of the council, or they may be removed by order of the Minister of the Interior on the grounds that they have direct or indirect financial interest in the municipality, or for unsuitable conduct, misfeasance, malfeasance or non-feasance.

Control of Thai municipalities by the central government is

comprehensive, particularly in the financial area, where budget preparation, revenue administration, expenditures, investments, purchasing, contracting and all other operations must be carried out in accordance with regulations periodically issued by the Ministry of the Interior. In addition, policy and legal advice is given by municipal inspectors attached to each governor's office during their periodic inspection visits to the municipalities. There is also an audit of municipal financial affairs and accounts by the National Audit Council. Although it is intended that such audits should be performed annually, lack of staff has made such a plan impossible up to the present time. The provincial governor has the power to supervise and control the operations of the municipalities in his area to see that they are in accordance with the law. He may examine books and accounts and summon municipal officials, board members and council members to him, to admonish or advise them. The governor, or the district officer in the case of *tambol* municipalities, may also revoke or suspend any act of the council which he finds detrimental to the municipality or the central government. A final decision on such a suspension is then made by the Minister of the Interior. Furthermore, the governor can dissolve a municipal council and order new elections, or he can suspend, for good reason, individual councilmen. Finally when special problems exist in a municipality which require a different kind of organization the municipality can be placed by Royal Decree under the direct supervision and control of the Ministry of the Interior.

Sanitary District Organizations ('Sukhaphibans')

The sanitary district is a transitional organization for rural areas which have certain urban-type problems. Administration is in the hands of a commission which consists of both appointed and elected members. Those appointed by the provincial governor are the district and assistant district officers, the local police chief, the district treasury and health officers, and the headmen of all the villages within the area. Moreover, four members are directly elected by the sanitary district inhabitants for a five-year term of office.

Serving as ex-officio chairman of the commission is the district officer. A vice-chairman is elected by the commission to serve a one-year term of office. Acting as chief administrative officer of the sanitary district is a commission-appointed officer who is aided by a treasurer and clerks in overseeing such public works activities as maintenance of waterways and highways, disposal of refuse and garbage, provision of clean water, water works, market places, electric and other lighting, wharfs and ferries. He also supervises public health functions, such as provision and maintenance of hospitals and nursing homes and protective measures against epidemics, and provides fire fighting equipment and personnel. To aid it in its work, the commission may appoint ordinary or extraordinary committees to consider detailed projects and report back to the total body.

Extensive control over the sanitary district is exercised by the district officer, the governor and the national government. Thus, all procedural rules for the commission are established by the Ministry of the Interior, and all administrative plans and procedures drawn up by the commission, as well as the budget and all other by-laws, require prior approval of the governor before they can be put into effect. Although the 1952 law which established the sanitary districts also provided for their being raised to municipality status on the attainment of a certain amount and density of population, none have so far been changed. Several of these units, however, are ready to assume municipal responsibilities, and it is expected that their status will be changed in the near future.

Rural Municipality ('Tambol')

The recently created rural municipality consists of a number of *Muban* (sub-municipal units or villages). The chief official of the rural municipality is a headman (*Kamnan*) who is elected by the headmen of the various villages within the municipality, from among their own members and for an indeterminate term of office. The *Kamnan* thus serves as headman of his own village, in addition to his duties as headman of the rural municipality. He may be removed from office in case he resigns as headman of his own village, if his resignation is demanded by a majority of the rural municipal council, or the provincial governor considers him unable to carry out the duties and responsibilities as required by law. Because of his many duties the *Kamnan* may have two assistants as inspectors, who are appointed on his recommendation by the Governor; he may also be assigned a medical officer. The plural representative organ of the rural municipality is the council, composed of one popularly elected councilman from each sub-municipal unit for a three-year term. The Council has a chairman and vice-chairman both of whom are appointed from the membership by the district officer. The council meets once annually for not more than fifteen days, but extraordinary meetings may be called by the district officer upon petition from the chairman of the council, the rural municipal headman board, or 1/3 of the council members. Included among their limited decision-making powers is that of passing the annual budget and passing other by-laws consistent with the functions of the *Tambol* administration.

The *Tambol* board is the executive body similar to that found in urban municipal organization. It consists of the *Kamnan*, who is chairman, the *Tambol* physician and a village headman plus others appointed at the discretion of the district officer, for example, the school headmaster and the head of a government production organization (rice, tobacco, gunny bag, sugar, etc.). The board has the power and authority formerly possessed by the *Kamnan* and village headman in carrying on local administration. The actual administration is headed by a chief administrative officer who is responsible to the rural municipal board, but is a civil servant subject to central government direction as well. The functions of *Tambol* administration are similar to those established for urban municipalities, being primarily provision of basic health and welfare services. They are subject to change and limitation by Ministerial notification.

Like the village headman the *Kamnan*, under the supervision of the district officer, must keep records, enforce the law, assist central government officials, provide for the public welfare and assume leadership in cases of emergency. He must present to the district officer and the governor all information about droughts, unemployment, prevention of disease, floods, irrigation, etc.

In the field of public health he is responsible for the inspection and maintenance of such public facilities as ponds, rest houses and cattle pastures. In conjunction with the medical officer the *Kamnan* must also inspect dwellings and other buildings and take appropriate action if they fall into disrepair. His duties in regard to criminal administration are similar to those of the village headman and are primarily concerned with making reports, arresting offenders and serving warrants. In all his duties, the *Kamnan* is assisted by the sub-municipal headman and by the medical officer, who is responsible not only for the public health aspects of the division, but for its general administration as well.

Sub-Municipal Unit ('Muban')

The Thai rural sub-municipal unit (*Muban* or village) has a simple governmental structure headed by a popularly elected headman who serves an indeterminate term of office. He may be removed from office, however, if he: lives outside the village for more than 6 months, is sentenced to a prison term, is appointed to another position which prevents him from carrying out the duties of his office, is found to be dishonest, is considered incapable of performing his job by the governor, or if a majority of the inhabitants demand his removal. When he is temporarily unable to carry out his duties, the headman may authorize a neighbouring headman to act in his stead.

Like the board of the urban municipality the headman has both civil and judicial administration duties. The former include maintenance of the peace, record keeping, taking action in case of public emergencies, and publishing and enforcing central government laws and orders. The judicial duties involve power of arrest, service of warrants, confiscation of evidence and giving information to the division headman on any crimes committed in the village. Informally the headman performs many traditional services for the village inhabitants. He also plays a role in division activities, such as serving as an elector of the rural municipal headman, serving on the division council and assisting the rural municipal headman in his administrative duties.

Basically the rural sub-municipal headman has limited authority and most of his activities are subject to the direction, supervision and control of the central government officials (particularly the district officer) in the area.

District ('Amphur')

The main responsibility for rural administration is focused at the district level. Heading the administration is a district officer *(Nai Amphur)* who is appointed by the Minister of the Interior and is, in turn, responsible to him through the provincial Governor. Within his territory the district officer must help implement the programmes of all central government ministries. He supervises the rural municipalities and some of the smaller urban ones and serves as ex-officio chairman of the sanitary district board. He is directly responsible for the work of the rural municipal headmen and through them for that of the sub-municipal headmen as well.

Province ('Changvad')

Serving as the liaison between central government, district and local units of government is the province, whose governor is appointed by the Under-Secretary of the Interior. Under the Changvad Government Act of 1955 new powers were given to the provincial council, which is composed of both elected and appointed members. The former are popularly elected for a five-year term of office, and the latter are appointed by the Minister of the Interior from among municipal and sanitary district chief executives and other qualified residents of the province.

The council may be invested by Royal Decree with the power to enact ordinances in the same matters as do the municipalities (public order, education, public health and sanitation and public utilities), as well as those pertaining to commercial matters in the province, and those regarding an annual budget. After being passed by the council an ordinance must be submitted for the approval of the governor. If he signs it, it has immediate effect;

if he does not, the ordinance is then sent to the Minister of the Interior who may approve it and return it for the Governor's signature or who may reject it, in which case it does not become effective. Once approved, the ordinances are effective for all areas of the province outside municipal and sanitary district boundaries.

Central government control of the provincial council is concentrated in the hands of the governor who maintains a constant awareness of its activities. He has power to review its ordinances, finances and activities, including the personal qualifications and suitability of the individual members. He must take the necessary steps to investigate and suspend any action which is against the interest of the central government or is *ultra vires*. The final authority of control, however, is the Minister of the Interior who may order the dissolution of the council as well as issue orders and regulations concerning most financial transactions.

THE PHILIPPINES

The Philippine Islands, which were discovered by Magellan in 1520, were conquered by Spain in 1565. They remained under Spanish rule until 1898 when they were ceded to the United States following the Spanish – American war. By an agreement with the American government in 1934 a ten-year transitional period, during which the islands were known as the Philippine Commonwealth, was established, at the end of which time complete independence automatically became effective. Thus, on July 4, 1946, the Republic of the Philippines came into existence with a Constitution which was adopted in 1935 and amended in 1940 and 1946.

The pattern of local government administration in the Philippines blends many of the institutional and other characteristics of the Oriental, Spanish and American. The result is outwardly a governmental structure similar to that of the U.S.A., while in reality the system is highly centralized. Administratively the country is divided into 52 provinces, three of which have sub-provinces, and each province is sub-divided into municipalities. These, in turn, consist of sub-municipal units.

Urban Municipalities (Chartered cities)

Each of the 28 municipalities within this category is a legal personality and operates under a separate charter granted by Congress which defines that municipality's powers, organs of government and the method of selection and the duties of its officials. In general, the competence of these municipalities includes establishing a budget, constructing and maintaining roads, bridges and public buildings, providing social welfare and health services, secondary schools, fire protection, public safety and police services and establishing public utilities and various cultural and recreational centres.

For the most part there is a general over-all structure established for the urban municipalities; details, however, vary from one to another. Although each has a council there is no uniformity in the number, qualifications, manner of selection, tenure or compensation of its members. In number the membership varies from five to 13 councilmen (councillors), an arbitrary matter which has no relationship to the size or importance of the municipality. In five municipalities councilmen are elected at-large; in others they are partly elected and partly appointed by the President of the Republic. Additional members in the latter councils include ex-officio the popularly elected vice-mayor or heads of departments. The usual term of office for councilmen is four years, although those appointed by the President serve at his pleasure and may be removed at any time. All other members, regardless of their method of appointment, may be removed for disloyalty, dishonesty or misconduct by the President.

The main function of the council, whose presiding officer may be the mayor or a council-elected chairman, is to approve the budget, establish salary rates for municipal employees, maintain public safety services and provide other needed public facilities. In all but five or six of the largest municipalities which are divided into districts, each councilman is assigned the general supervision of one or more sub-municipal units (*barrios*) and acts as the medium through which *barrio* problems are brought to the attention of the council as a whole. His contact with the *barrio* is through the *barrio lieutenant* who is elected by the *barrio* residents for a one-year term of office and who presides over an advisory council composed of three councilmen and a *deputy barrio lieutenant*, all of whom generally serve a one-year term of office. Such a structure has as its purpose the two-way exchange of information between the municipal government and the local neighbourhood.

In 14 of the urban municipalities the mayor is popularly elected for a definite term of office. In one he is a provincial governor acting ex-officio as mayor, and in the remaining 13 municipalities he is appointed for either a definite or indefinite term of office, depending on the municipal charter, by the President of the Philippines, with the consent of the Committee on Appointments. This is a joint congressional body composed of twelve members of the House of Representatives and twelve members of the Senate, and is presided over by the President of the latter.

Although theoretically the chief executive of the municipality, the mayor has no power to appoint department heads, who are named instead by the President or by the heads of the corresponding national departments, to whom they are then responsible. The mayor, however, may appoint the subordinate employees of a municipal department, but only upon the recommendation of the department head. For the most part, the responsibility of the mayor is to prepare the municipal budget, which he then submits to the council for comments and approval; to recommend legislation, which may be accepted, rejected or ignored by the council; and to co-ordinate administration wherever possible.

Although he does not have the right to vote in council decisions, the mayor may, however, veto ordinances which the council, in turn, can again pass over his veto. If the same measure is vetoed twice, it is then forwarded to the President for a final decision. The main effectiveness of the mayor is through his political leadership, in which activity he is aided by his secretary, whom he himself appoints. The latter supervises the operations and the personnel of the mayor's office and frequently functions in his place when he is absent. In 22 cities the popularly elected vice-mayor may also assume some of the mayor's responsibilities when the latter is unable to do so.

In practice, the urban municipalities are closely controlled. All local ordinances must be reviewed by the President, through his executive secretary, to see that the local councils do not exceed their legal powers. Those matters pertaining to finance are directly supervised by the central Finance Department, just as other local matters are supervised by the counterpart central department or agency. The President also has the power to appoint and remove many of the councilmen and mayors. In addition, the constant stream of directives and circulars which come from the central government give detailed instructions to the municipalities on carrying out national services assigned to them, so that even in this respect little, if any, discretion is left to the local governmental unit.

Rural Municipalities (Municipalities)[1]

The rural municipality, into which the greater part of the country is divided, comprises both rural and semi-urban areas. It is a corporate body that is very limited in its exercise of authority. Its council, which shares with the mayor the responsibility of governing the municipality, is composed of the mayor as presiding officer, the vice-mayor as an ex-officio member, and from four to eight others elected at large every four years. Like the urban municipal councilmen, each of these councilmen is also assigned an area composed of one or more *barrios*, the residents of which he is to keep informed on municipal happenings and serve as their representative on the council. In general, the council possesses specific power to pass legislation to provide for the well-being of the municipality.

The chief executive of the rural municipality is the mayor who is popularly elected every four years. Although responsible for the general administration of the municipality, the mayor can appoint only the local police. All other municipal officers are named by the corresponding provincial authorities, to whom they are responsible. Thus action on many local affairs cannot be taken until clearance is obtained from these agencies or from the President. The position of the mayor, like that of his counterpart in the charter municipalities, is one of political leadership and of coordination, where possible.

The vice-mayor, who is also popularly elected, serves as an ex-officio member of council and may assume the mayor's

[1] A new Barrio Charter was promulgated in January 1960 giving considerably more powers to the *barrio*.

responsibilities when the latter is unable to do so. One of the most important other officials of the rural municipality is again the secretary, who is appointed by and responsible to the mayor. He serves as both secretary to the mayor and to the council, and may also be responsible for the recording of the municipality's vital statistics.

The Filipino rural municipality is a creation of the central government; its authority is defined and limited by the grant of power conferred upon it. In reality, it has little authority to exercise. All municipal decisions and executive orders must be submitted to the provincial board for approval, and they may be declared null if they do not conform to legal requirements. In addition, the chief executive may be suspended or removed from office, for good reason, pending a hearing by the provincial board. Responsibility of department heads is to their provincial counterparts and ultimately to the central government officials. A chief form of control, moreover, is financial, whereby local authorities are so limited in their powers of taxation that, should they have the power, in many instances they would be unable to use it.

There is a special category consisting of 169 rural municipal units *(municipal districts)* which are vested with less governmental power than the other rural municipalities. However, these automatically assume regular status once their annual receipts exceed a specified sum.

Provinces

The fifty-three provinces and the three sub-provinces located within three of the regular ones are administrative sub-divisions of the central government and perform such functions as are conferred upon them. The provincial board, which has only an advisory role, is composed of a popularly elected governor, two other elected members, and where sub-provinces exist, the heads, or lieutenant governors of these. All serve four-year terms. The main task of this body is to approve the provincial budget, as well as minor appointments of the governor, and to review rural municipal ordinances for their legality. It does not possess the power to pass provincial ordinances.

The governor has little importance as head of the provincial administration, but he is a politically strategic official. Within his office are several "assistants" who are active as political aides. Although the governor also has general supervisory powers over the municipal units within his territory, he seldom finds it necessary to exercise them, as active supervision of administration is done by the provincial department heads over their local counterparts. The governor may be removed for good reason by the President, who also may fill his position with a temporary appointee in case of sickness, absence or other disability.

Like the other units of local government, the province is closely controlled. All department heads are responsible to their central government counterparts; all administrative actions of the governor can be appealed to central agencies. In addition, the province has no power to tax and is dependent for revenue on allotments given to it by the national government. Practically all details of provincial administration are handed down from the central government.

JAPAN

The system of local government that is known in Japan today first came into being in the late 1800's. This pattern, which was modelled mainly on that of Prussia, originally provided for a very strong centralized form of government. In 1947 the provisions of the new Local Autonomy Law decentralized the governmental system, with the result that the local units were virtually autonomous. Since the end of the U. S. occupation, however, the trend has been toward increasing control over local governmental units by the central government. A radical change in local government occurred in 1953 when a law to expedite the merger of municipalities having less than 8,000 population was promulgated, with the result that the number of towns and villages has been reduced by one third (about 3,000).

Administratively, Japan consists of two tiers below the central government, the provinces, of which there are 46, and the municipalities, which are categorized according to their population and commercial and industrial activities into cities (*shi*), towns (*machi*) and rural municipalities (*mura*). All, however, have the same legal structure and status. Tokyo, the capital, ranks as a

JAPAN

PATTERN OF GOVERNMENT UNITS

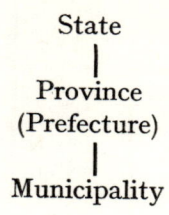

State
|
Province
(Prefecture)
|
Municipality

STRUCTURE OF A MUNICIPAL GOVERNMENT

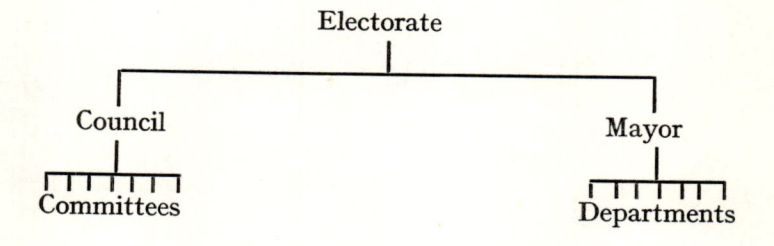

Electorate
├─────────────────────┤
Council   Mayor
| |
Committees   Departments

province and functions under a special charter, although in structure it differs little from the other municipalities in the country; Tokyo and some of the other larger cities are further divided into sub-municipal units or wards.

Municipalities ('Shi,' 'Machi,' and 'Mura')

The structure and functions of present-day Japanese municipalities are regulated by the Local Autonomy Law of 1947 which is based on the provisions of Chapter 8 of the Constitution. Under this law municipalities have a dual role, to handle matters of a purely local nature and to act as an administrative organ of the state, so-called entity delegation. The purely local matters include provision of municipal finances; housing, although city planning is determined by the Minister of Construction; such public works as the construction of roads and bridges which are not undertaken by the provincial or central governments; establishment and administration of hospitals and health centres; disposal of trash; establishment and administration of public pawn shops, employment agencies for women and educational institutions; and various public enterprises. Police matters are attended to by the province except where the central government reserves its rights in this area.

The plural representative organ of the municipality is a popularly elected council which ranges in size from 12 members in the smaller units to 120 councilmen in Tokyo. The term of office of the members, and of the chairman they elect, is four years. Their primary responsibility is to compile the budget; levy and collect taxes, fees and rentals on municipal property; make contracts; acquire and dispose of public property; accept the municipal accounts; control the activities of public organizations within the administrative area of the municipality; and pass and amend by-laws and resolutions pertaining to strictly municipal affairs. For the most part, resolutions and decisions are presented to the council by the mayor. To help them in their work, the municipalities use standing committees to study and prepare for discussion by the council various matters of municipal interest.

The mayor, who is popularly elected as the executive of the municipality, serves as its ceremonial head and as the co-ordinator of municipal administration. He has the power to call the council into session and to bring matters before it. Traditionally he has had a great deal of power in the municipality and an attempt was made under the Local Autonomy Law to reduce his control by giving the council authority to pass a vote of no-confidence, in which case the mayor must either resign or dissolve the council and call for a new election. Although in many instances the chairman of the council or the chairman of the most important standing committee is the chief political rival of the mayor, it is seldom that differences between the plural representative organ and the chief executive reach the breaking point and a confidence vote results.

In addition to serving as executor of council-made policy, the mayor is also responsible for carrying out certain responsibilities entrusted him by the central government and other public organizations (so-called agency delegation). For these tasks direct supervision comes from the state, and the municipal council has no control.

The mayor is aided in the carrying out of his responsibilities by an assistant, a treasurer and committees which handle such functions as education and elections. The five members of the education committee and the three members for the smaller municipalities and five for the largest cities of the election committee are appointed from the citizens of the municipality by the mayor with the approval of the council.

The amount of control over local governments which is exercised by the central government depends on whether a function is being performed by the municipality as an autonomous organization or as an organ of the state. In the former category the central government, through the provincial government, has little control. In such matters, however, as changing the name of the municipality, raising long term loans and forming special purpose associations of municipalities, prior approval must be obtained from the higher authority. Over those functions, moreover, which are performed by the municipality as an organ of the state, direction is given by the provincial government. In addition, the governor has the power to remove a local official for neglect of duty or violation of responsibilities. Again, in the financial realm, there is a great deal of central control. Where municipalities receive subsidies from the central government or perform certain delegated state functions, supervision is given by the provincial governor as well as by the competent State Minister, who has the authority to inspect, instruct and direct according to the provisions of the grant or according to the provisions of the law. The municipality must also submit to an audit by the Central Audit Board and present any reports required of it by either provincial or central government authorities.

Provinces

Like the municipalities, the other tier of government, the provinces, have popularly elected councils and a council-elected chairman, all of whom serve four-year terms of office. The councils vary in size from 40 to 120 members, depending on the provincial population. The chief executive officer, the governor, is also popularly elected for a four-year term. Although directly responsible to the council for the execution of its decisions, the governor is, in addition, closely supervised by the central government in carrying out those responsibilities delegated to him by the state.

A large part of the responsibility of the provincial government is to serve as the local agency of the central government. Thus it directs and supervises the activities of the individual municipalities, co-ordinates their activities on an area-wide level, and serves as liaison between the central and local governmental units. It also handles the establishment of institutions of higher education, the construction and maintenance of second class roads, and provision of police services for the provincial territory, including the municipalities.

As a result of the revisions under the Local Autonomy Law of 1956 the provinces have come to assume strongly the character of a national government agent. Therefore, just as they closely oversee the activities of the municipalities within their boundaries, so does the central government keep close watch over them, particularly in financial matters. In addition, whenever a governor fails to perform adequately the responsibilities delegated to him by the central government, he may be removed from office by the central government through legal proceedings.

PERU[1]

Hundreds of years before Europeans came to South America there were Indian cultures in the land that is now Peru. Most important was that of the Incas who began expanding their empire between 1100 and 1200 A.D. The Incas remained in control over most of what is now Peru and parts of neighboring countries until 1531–33 when the forces of the Spanish conquistadores Pizarro and de Almagro captured the Emperor and occupied Cuzco, capital city in the Andean Mountain, of the Inca Empire. For almost 300 years afterward, Peru remained a center of Spanish power on the South American continent.

Independence from Spain was proclaimed by San Martin in 1821 although not until five years later was it finally accomplished by the forces of Simon Bolivar. Stability, however, has been slow in coming to the country for since independence there have been dictatorships, civil and military rebellions, a successful war with Spain and an unsuccessful one with Chile. Interspersed among these happenings, however, have been periods of calm and improvement, such as the country has experienced during the past decade. At the present time, Peru is governed in accordance with a Constitution adopted in 1933 that provides for a highly centralized government, no doubt influenced by the Inca and Spanish traditions.

Provinces, Sub-Provinces, Districts

Peru is composed of 24 geographical areas called provinces

[1] This survey on local government in Peru is a summary of an article by Mr. Wells M. Allred, at present attached as a visiting professor to the University of the Philippines. Although this summary was received only just before publication date of the book, it was deemed of sufficient importance to include it, although no data on Peru are included in the part I of this book nor in the tables. Also, this summary is not wholly conform the set-up of the other summary descriptions, contained in part II.
As was mentioned in the Introduction to Part II(p. XLI) the report on Peru was received shortly before publication of this book. For this reason no information on Peru was included in the rest of the book nor is any mention made in the index. It will be noted that there are certain omissions in this report, chief of which are the original Spanish names of governmental units and officials for which the standardized English titles have been used. Time, however, has been the major reason for this departure from the general outline.

(Departamentos). These are divided into 124 sub-provinces *(Provincias)* which are in turn subdivided into 1,435 districts *(Distritos)*. The maintenance of internal peace and order is primarily the responsibility of the Ministry of Government and is administered through the provinces, sub-provinces and districts.

Officials, with wide powers, are appointed to administer internal security in these subdivisions. *Prefectos* are appointed heads of the province, *sub-prefectos* are heads of sub-provinces, and governors are appointed heads of districts. Lieutenant governors are appointed assistants to governors to serve in open country and village neighborhoods. Each of these appointed officials is responsible to the one above him. They are considered official representatives of the President and constitute the extension of the President's authority throughout the provinces.

The provincial *prefectos*, sub-provincial *sub-prefectos*, district governors and lieutenant governors not only represent the President of the Republic within their respective areas of jurisdiction but also serve as the chiefs of the national police and thus maintain peace, order and safety of persons and property and enforce laws and ministerial decrees. They hear complaints of individuals and groups, and enforce price controls of basic necessities. Each official reports to the one above him unusual economic and social problems, organizational activities, and any observable changes of attitudes and loyalties among the people in his jurisdiction. The *prefecto* reports about these matters, on a provincial wide basis, to the Minister of Government and to the President. Essentially, these officials hold the same power today as was given them 130 years ago by the Constitution of 1828, and are the most powerful civil officials in the territorial subdivisions.

The governors and his lieutenants working in the smaller villages and rural areas of Peru are primarily concerned with settling family and personal disputes and maintaining local law and order in addition to the obligation of reporting changes in social, economic and organizational matters to their superiors. They also recruit labour crews when they or higher authorities need them to build or repair public facilities.

The *prefectos* and *sub-prefectos* are not necessarily native to the administrative territory they serve. They reside in the capitals of the provinces and sub-provinces, respectively, of their jurisdiction. The district governors and their lieutenants are always residents of their respective territories; in some instances, moreover, the lieutenant governors are even elected by the local population, although the *sub-prefectos* and governors need not appoint elected persons to this post if they do not so desire.

The administrative subdivisions of some of the other national ministries also coincide with the provinces, sub-provinces, and districts for purposes of extending their services and functions to the people. The officials and personnel of these other ministries do not, however, have such wide and general powers as the officials in the ministry of government appointed to the provinces, sub-provinces, and districts. Employees of these other ministries are concerned with extending such services as education, building and maintenance of highways, health, justice, post office, and social welfare.

Urban Municipalities

The municipal system in Peru provides for some of the special needs of people in cities and villages. It is responsible for such services as domestic water supply, sewage and garbage disposal, and electric lights, to build and maintain public parks and monuments, and maintain and clean city and village streets. Licenses for some types of businesses and recreation within the municipality are granted by the municipal council. Usually the public market and slaughter-house facilities are owned by the municipality and leased to private operators subject to close regulation. The munipal council employs its own police to enforce municipal ordinances.

There are two classes of municipalities in Peru corresponding to sub-provinces and districts. Each can grant services and exercise jurisdiction throughout the entire territory of its administrative unit. In practice, however, services are limited to the largest city or village of the sub-province or district which is also its capital. The municipal council in the capital of the sub-province passes on the budgets, reviews actions and has general supervisory powers over each of the district municipalities within the sub-province.

None of the officials (mayors and councilmen) of the municipalities are elected even though this is provided for by the constitution. Instead they are appointed by the central government. These officials employ their own staffs, however. The municipalities raise most of their revenues within their respective jurisdiction but all taxes, licenses, fees, and revenues from whatever source are specified by central government law or decrees. The municipal councils must obtain permission from the central government to add new sources of revenue or change existing rates. The municipal council is relatively free to allocate its income the way it wishes among various projects and services but must submit plans to the central government for approval.

Native Village Government

A third type of "local government" in Peru is that found in the native villages. This type is said to be characteristic of the native Peruvian social and economic culture that goes back long before the Spanish conquest of Peru in 1530.

There are today several thousand of these native type villages in which live about one-third of the Peruvian population. Most of them are found in the highland agricultural regions and are partially communal. This latter characteristic seems to be breaking down and changing to the extent that little of the communal aspect persists today in most villages other than use of pastures in common, family and community wide exchange of labour, and community wide participation in some improvement projects, especially those involving use of manual labour.

The village lands enjoy constitutional protection in that they cannot legally be transferred to non-members or attached for debt. Provision is also made for these native villages to become incorporated. They can then elect, subject to approval of the central government, leaders who can help mediate disputes, make representation to the central government, and assume leadership in village activities.

Summary

Officials of the Ministry of Government administer internal security in all parts of Peru through the geographical subdivisions of provinces, sub-provinces, and districts. These officials constitute the most powerful civil leadership in their respective jurisdictions. The cities and larger villages have municipal government to provide many of the needs required in urban areas. The native type village government is found in the rural highland regions to provide needs of the native Indian populations in the traditional way. None of these kinds of government in the territorial subdivisions and urban places have autonomous powers independent from the central government.

INDEX (¹)

This index needs an explanatory note. As in many other cases, it was very difficult to follow a stringent pattern in drawing it up, in particular as the same word, such as council, is often used for different levels of government. For the benefit of the reader, we give here a few indications which will be useful for a proper understanding of this index.
  (1) In general the different terms in the index refer to local government; when another level of government is meant, this is generally made clear in the index.
  (2) In many cases related concepts are mentioned under one word; e.g.: supervision, control and review, are all indexed under "control."
  (3) General concepts are sometimes indexed even if the word indicating that concept is not expressly mentioned.

Accounts, 216, 220, 221, 224, 231, 249, 250, 253, 254, 260, 262, 266, 269, 270, 273, 275, 279, 283, 284, 285, 287, 289, 300, 310, 311, 314, 316, 317, 320, 325, 326, 331, 332, 334, 337, 338, 340, 344–346, 352, 354, 358, 359, 371, 372, 376, 377, 383, 385, 397–399, 404, 410, 414, 425
Acts, 10, 34, 41, 66, 77, 208, 209, 211, 214, 215, 217, 221, 222, 226, 230, 243, 248, 252, 255, 257, 258, 260, 270, 276, 279, 288, 329, 349, 350, 354, 355, 358, 359, 380, 383, 386, 390–392, 394, 403, 412, 418
Administration, 8, 9, 12, 24, 45, 75, 76, 85, 97, 133, 136, 143, 178, 182, 208, 213, 217, 220, 239, 248, 267, 272, 368
  central, 314
  district, 263, 418
  local, 5, 7, 19, 25, 33, 37, 92, 132, 154, 155, 157–159, 166, 169, 206, 221, 223, 225, 229, 230, 236, 237, 245, 250, 253, 254, 257, 258, 265, 266, 273, 275, 278, 282, 285, 287, 296, 298, 299, 304–306, 310–312, 320, 321, 323, 325–328, 331, 332, 343, 344, 346, 347, 352, 353, 358, 364, 371, 374, 382, 384,
385, 388, 391, 392, 394, 397, 406, 413, 416, 417, 421, 422, 424, 426
  provincial, 29, 227, 249–251, 285, 315, 317, 318, 340, 355, 366, 410, 423, 424
Advisory councils, 22, 28, 74, 75, 200, 375, 401, 404, 408, 409, 421
Alderfer, Harold F., 25, 143
Alderman, 58, 210, 211, 214, 215, 218
Amalgamation of local units, 18–20, 27, 34, 163, 303
Anglo-Saxon group, 14, 21, 27, 28, 38, 41, 59, 63, 72, 76, 88, 97, 98, 182, 192–194, 196, 208–243
Annulment, including void, 39, 40, 42, 125, 140, 224, 231, 258, 259, 262, 271, 275, 277–280, 283, 289, 292, 293, 297, 300, 301, 306, 311–313, 318, 321, 338, 345, 353, 364, 373, 374, 383, 386, 423
Appeal, 40–42, 177, 178, 216, 246, 250, 251, 255, 261, 266, 269, 275, 280, 282, 283, 285, 306, 311–313, 318, 321, 326–328, 332, 338, 340, 344, 348–351, 353, 359, 372, 374, 376, 382, 383, 424
Appleby, Paul, 8
Approval, 11, 22, 40, 42, 43, 52, 66, 74, 75, 79, 96, 97, 99, 100, 101,

¹ Including an index of reference footnotes.

105, 115, 118, 123, 134, 138, 145, 152, 175, 185, 192, 215, 216, 220, 223–226, 228, 231, 236–238, 246, 250, 251, 253, 255, 258–262, 266, 270, 273, 277, 279, 282, 283, 285, 287–289, 291, 300, 301, 304, 310, 313–316, 318, 321, 325–327, 329, 330, 332, 334, 336, 338–340, 343, 347, 348, 350, 353–355, 357, 359, 364, 367–369, 372–378, 383, 385, 389, 390, 392, 398, 399, 403, 406, 409, 412, 413, 418, 420, 423, 426
Arneson, Ben, A., 37
Arnold-Baker, Charles, 75
Audit, 157, 216, 221, 224, 231, 238, 253, 262, 270, 313, 332, 344–346, 354, 358, 359, 377, 383, 389, 398, 403, 414, 427
Australia, 217–221
 committees, 102
 general, 1, 192, 193
 mayor, 101
 special purpose bodies, 25
Austria, 267–271
 board, 111, 115
 general, 2, 45, 196
 mayor, 117
 municipalities, 19
 selection, 115
Autonomous, 5, 22, 35, 37, 44, 45, 129, 133, 167, 220, 232, 247, 252, 254, 268, 269, 272, 274, 275, 281, 288, 290, 291, 309, 313, 314, 319, 335, 342, 343, 360, 365, 424–427

Barfivala, C. D., 198
Barrio, 22, 74, 332, 420–422
Basic unit, 2, 12–17, 20, 21, 25, 27–29, 72, 74, 84, 88, 127, 134, 136, 203, 204, 232, 239, 260, 268, 309, 314, 342, 343, 356, 362, 365, 370, 375, 380, 391, 393, 407
Belgium, 280–286
 board, 111
 control, 13
 councilmember, 197
 general, 45, 196, 197
 mayor, 134, 140, 197
 selection, 135, 197
Bensman, Joseph, see Vidich...
Bergh, C. van der, 59

Bicameral council, 89, 198, 303, 308
Board,
 chairman, 91, 109–112, 115–118, 121, 122, 130, 145, 175, 179, 195–197, 225, 246, 249, 265, 269, 274, 278, 282, 288, 292, 296, 300, 325, 337–339, 343, 371, 413, 416
 composition, 175, 229, 245, 248, 265, 269, 274, 277, 292, 296, 297, 300, 320, 325, 326, 331, 336, 371, 413
 definition, 109
 dismissal, 296, 336, 364, 413
 general, 25, 38, 40, 72, 76, 77, 79, 83, 88, 89, 91, 94, 96–101, 104, 106, 107–118, 119, 123, 125–127, 129, 133, 150, 155, 156, 158, 160, 161, 174–176, 179, 180, 184, 193, 195–198, 201, 226, 229, 230, 237, 238, 245, 250, 251, 253–255, 257, 258, 261, 266, 274, 276–278, 281–283, 286, 287, 291–294, 297, 299–301, 320, 331, 333, 336–338, 343, 349, 363, 364, 372, 397, 412, 413, 416, 417
 members, 104, 110–112, 114, 117, 118, 155–158, 175, 181, 184, 196, 200, 201, 225, 226, 245, 253, 258, 265, 269, 274, 277, 281, 282, 287, 288, 296, 297, 300, 320, 325, 336, 349, 363, 364, 371, 412, 413
 secretary, 114, 115, 118, 157, 159–161, 292, 296, 300
 selection, including election and appointment, 110, 111, 175, 225, 229, 245, 246, 249, 257, 261, 287, 292, 295–297, 300, 331, 336, 413
Boroughs, 14, 132, 192, 208, 210, 211, 216, 222, 234, 380
Brazil, 342–346
 chief executive, 136
 general, 2, 20, 55, 142, 201, 202
 mayor, 123, 124, 136
 municipalities, 14, 15, 38, 68
 selection, 136
 sub-municipal units, 21, 22
Bromage, Arthur, W., 155

INDEX

Budget, 2, 23, 40–42, 45, 47, 49, 75, 83, 126, 223, 229, 230, 235, 236–238, 244, 249, 252–254, 257–260, 266, 269, 270, 273, 275, 276, 279, 281, 283, 286–289, 291, 296, 300, 301, 304, 306, 310–318, 320–322, 325, 326, 328, 331–334, 336–338, 343–345, 347, 357, 363, 364, 367, 371, 372, 375, 381–383, 385, 387, 389, 397–399, 401, 403, 406, 412–414, 416, 420, 421, 425
Bulgaria, 299–302
  board, 198
  general, 45, 197
Burghs, 209, 213
Buriks, 14
Burma, 390–395
  council, 58, 76
  general, 77, 204, 205
  rural municipalities, 76
  tiers, 12
By-laws, 34, 35, 42, 43, 75, 80, 217, 224, 225, 230, 231, 244, 260, 261, 266, 279, 288, 305, 322, 332, 336, 337, 381, 388, 390, 392, 397, 399, 402, 412, 413, 416, 425

Cabinet, 33, 138, 181, 227, 251
Canada, 227–233
  board, 110, 115
  council, 87
  general, 1, 84, 192, 193
  mayor, 142
  rural municipalities, 87
  selection, 110, 115, 142
  special purpose bodies, 25
  tiers, 12
Canton, 25, 83, 271–275, 309, 314, 315, 347, 349
Central and North-West Europe, 196–197
Central government,
  administration, 310, 335
  agencies, 5, 23, 24, 28, 33, 35, 37, 40, 41, 45, 117, 127–129, 145, 179, 183, 200, 206, 220, 238, 239, 278, 280–282, 285–288, 312, 315, 323, 329, 351, 353, 355, 359, 360, 363–366, 369, 376, 377, 388, 402, 413, 422, 424, 426, 427
  control, 2, 16, 18, 31, 32, 34, 39, 41, 42, 47, 48, 50, 73, 99, 129, 138, 140, 165, 167, 176, 199, 204, 216, 217, 220, 239, 246, 251, 255, 256, 258, 264, 266–268, 270, 271, 277, 279, 285, 301, 302, 308, 312, 321, 327, 329, 330, 332, 336, 338, 340, 341, 345, 347, 354, 357, 359, 364, 366, 368, 372, 378, 380, 382–384, 386, 388, 390, 395, 398, 399, 402, 404, 413, 415, 418, 419, 422, 424, 426, 427
  definition, 2
  delegation, 26, 113, 127, 128, 196, 199, 200, 204, 257, 268, 271, 277, 278, 280, 282, 294, 296, 300, 301, 303, 324, 328, 354, 369, 402, 425–427
  departments, see Departments of central government
  general, 1–3, 6–9, 12, 13, 15, 17, 18, 20, 22, 24, 26–31, 34–42, 44–50, 53, 57, 70, 73, 75–78, 83, 85, 86, 95, 102, 109, 115, 121, 125–129, 135–138, 150–153, 163, 165–168, 182, 183, 196, 200–202, 204–206, 216–221, 234, 235, 237–241, 243, 244, 246, 247, 249, 251, 256, 258, 260, 263–269, 271, 278, 279, 288, 289, 290, 293, 294, 297, 300, 302, 303, 311, 313–322, 325, 327, 328–331, 333, 334, 337, 340, 342–345, 347, 348, 350, 351, 355, 356, 359, 360, 363–367, 369–372, 374–385, 387, 389–396, 398, 399, 401, 402, 404, 405, 409, 414, 416, 418, 419, 422–425, 427
  grants, 20, 33, 41, 44–46, 79, 165, 216, 239, 248, 251, 316, 329, 338, 389, 393, 398, 399, 427
  legislation, 43, 205, 210, 220, 243, 245, 276, 293, 294, 309, 310, 316, 329, 360, 380, 392
Ceremonial functions,
  definition, 130
  general, 91, 130, 131, 145, 179, 180, 194, 223, 225, 229, 232, 236–238, 261, 278, 282, 300, 320, 356, 358, 360, 381, 397, 413, 425

436 INDEX

Ceylon, 386–390
  chairman, 48, 120
  chief administrative officer, 120
  chief executive, 141
  council, 48
  general, 152, 204, 205
  mayor, 101, 132
Chairman of the council,
  appointment, 89, 387, 402, 404, 412, 416
  election, 90, 132, 137, 210, 212, 213, 221, 225, 244, 248, 254, 257, 259–261, 266, 291, 299, 304, 305, 325, 327, 343, 352, 369, 390, 401, 420, 425
  functions, 89, 122, 213, 219, 221, 244, 261, 276, 305, 348
  general, 23, 48, 89, 91, 92, 101, 104, 115, 120, 122, 128, 130, 131–133, 137–140, 145, 146, 179, 194–197, 202, 203, 210, 212–215, 219, 221, 225, 235, 241, 249, 253–255, 258, 265, 269, 278, 282, 286, 288, 291, 305, 311, 327, 331, 337, 348, 358, 372, 374, 381, 384, 393, 399, 412, 413, 426
Chapman, Brian, 8, 39–40, 45, 47, 160
Charter, 4, 208, 220, 228, 235–238, 241, 260, 261, 268, 269, 271, 309, 330, 343, 381, 400–403, 420, 421, 422, 424
Chief administrative officer,
  definition, 158–159
  general, 43, 47, 92, 99, 101, 105, 118, 120, 121, 126, 132, 137, 146, 151, 154–157, 158–161, 177, 179–183, 195, 202, 205, 215, 220, 223, 253, 254, 258, 259, 261, 377, 382, 388, 413, 415, 416
Chief executive,
  definition, 118–120
  general, 4, 29, 38, 41, 43, 47, 73, 74, 76–79, 91, 92, 94, 96, 106, 108–110, 113, 115–118, 119–148, 149, 150, 152, 155–160, 170, 175, 178–182, 184, 185, 193–197, 200, 201, 203, 205, 206, 219, 229, 233, 234, 236, 238, 240, 241, 250, 259, 264–266, 277, 282, 284, 311, 312, 320, 325, 327, 331, 344, 347–350, 358, 364, 367, 371, 374, 381, 382, 387, 395, 397, 406, 407, 409, 418, 421–423, 426
City, 4, 5, 7, 13, 14, 18, 19, 23, 30, 31, 46, 59, 68, 69, 77, 81, 86, 88, 102, 110–112, 114, 120, 121, 124, 132, 133, 136, 142, 146, 153–155, 157, 158, 161, 164, 174, 194, 202, 203, 211, 212, 228, 230–232, 234, 237, 247, 248, 263, 294, 299, 343, 367, 420, 421, 424, 425
Columbia, 351–356
  general, 202, 203
  mayor, 124
Commission government, see Form of local government
Commissioner, 48, 120, 205, 217, 229, 237, 240, 283, 288, 321, 322, 348, 382, 388–390
Committees,
  administering committee, 22, 97–100, 102, 104, 105, 114, 133, 160, 161, 174, 192, 195, 198, 295, 381, 392, 397
  chairman, 92, 102, 104, 105, 175, 215, 219, 223, 245, 253, 261, 287, 301, 363, 397, 402, 426
  composition, 101–103, 245, 287, 295, 305, 392, 426
  definition committee of council, 93–94
  definition administering committee 97–98
  definition preparatory committee, 97
  finance committee, 96, 100, 112, 161, 219, 245, 257–259, 387, 397, 402
  functions, 95, 96, 174, 228, 236, 237, 244, 250, 251, 295, 301, 305, 388, 392
  general, 47, 57, 76, 78, 81, 87–90, 92, 93–107, 109, 112–114, 132, 133, 154–156, 160, 174, 175, 181, 192, 193, 198, 205, 215, 220, 222, 225, 228, 229, 238, 246, 249, 253, 257, 258, 261 262, 266, 277, 287, 288, 294–297, 299, 304–306, 316, 331, 336, 337, 358, 363, 381, 388, 389, 392, 402, 404

INDEX

preparatory committee, 97–99, 102, 104, 114, 174, 196
special committee, 94, 101, 220, 223, 229, 231, 244, 245, 247, 249, 253, 295, 305, 311, 385, 387, 388, 402, 412
standing committee, 94, 95, 102, 210, 219, 228–230, 244, 247, 253, 291, 293, 295, 300, 301, 305, 311, 357, 385, 387, 388, 425
statutory committee, 95, 98, 102, 215, 245, 249, 250, 257, 259, 381, 402
Commonwealth, 53, 102, 217, 218, 386, 395, 419
Commune, 14, 24, 72, 200, 272, 273, 281, 286, 289, 303, 309, 310, 312–314, 319, 324
Community settlements, 306
Compulsory voting, 55
Constituencies, 52, 59, 60, 62–64, 67, 68, 80, 172, 173, 293, 401
Constitution, 1, 2, 26, 38, 182, 202, 208, 210, 217, 256, 264, 268, 271, 272, 281, 286, 290, 291, 293, 299, 319, 323, 330, 342, 343, 345–349, 351, 352, 355, 356, 359, 362, 368, 379, 392, 395, 398, 405, 419, 425
Control, including review and supervision
general, 1, 6, 11, 13, 16, 18, 19, 26, 28, 29, 31–34, 36, 39–43, 46–48, 50, 78, 96–100, 105, 109, 113, 114, 126–129, 132, 133, 138–141, 143, 148, 149, 152, 153, 155, 156, 158, 165, 167, 169, 170, 171, 174–176, 183, 185, 192, 195, 198, 199, 204, 217, 219, 220, 223–230, 232, 236–239, 245–247, 249–251, 253–262, 264, 268, 270, 274, 275, 280, 282, 284–286, 289, 291–294, 295–302, 305, 306, 310, 312–318, 320, 321, 323, 325–328, 330–334, 336, 337, 340, 341, 344–346, 348, 353, 354, 358–360, 364, 366, 369–372, 374–378, 380–382, 384–386, 388–390, 393–395, 398, 399, 402–410, 412–416, 418, 419, 422–424, 426, 427

legal, 39, 40, 42, 224, 249, 262, 275, 300, 301, 306, 308, 313, 318, 321, 322, 326, 332, 337, 338, 345, 349, 353, 354, 359, 364, 373, 383, 397, 398, 403, 421, 423
merit, 39, 40, 42, 246, 321, 364
post-review, 43, 113
pre-review, 43
Co-option, 215, 219, 381
Corwin, Edward S., 107, 121
Council,
chairman, see Chairman of the council
committees, see Committees
composition, 61, 63, 86, 89, 210, 213, 218, 225, 228, 230, 231, 233, 240, 257, 303, 352, 357, 387, 394, 401, 406, 416, 422
councilmembers, see Councilmembers
definition, 72
delegation, 87, 215, 223, 230, 253, 295, 305, 388, 402
dismissal, including dissolution and suspension, 48, 141, 185, 186, 221, 231, 289, 301, 314, 321, 322, 368, 373, 381–383, 389, 390, 393, 414, 426
functions, 74–76, 100, 109, 170, 174, 209–211, 219, 223, 230, 235, 238, 244, 252, 281, 283, 286, 291, 294, 300, 310, 325, 326, 335, 343, 344, 348, 352, 371, 381, 384, 391, 397, 399, 406, 412, 416, 420, 422, 425
general, 4, 5, 14, 19, 25, 28, 32, 38–43, 47–49, 57–61, 63–68, 72–92, 93–104, 108–111, 113–115, 117–119, 121–129, 132, 133, 135–141, 143–148, 150, 152, 153, 155, 156, 158, 160, 161, 164, 170–186, 192–206, 208, 210, 221, 228, 243, 246, 249, 251–253, 255, 265, 268, 273, 274, 278, 279, 281, 286–288, 290, 292–301, 303–307, 310, 311, 313, 320, 322, 325, 329–332, 335, 336, 339, 343–347, 349–355, 358, 363, 364, 367–369, 372, 373, 375, 376, 379, 381–386, 388, 389, 391,

392, 396, 398, 401–404, 412–414, 416, 420–422, 426
meeting, 76, 78–80, 89, 90, 96, 100, 113, 123, 135, 157, 211, 215, 219, 220, 222, 223, 228, 229, 238, 244, 254, 255, 259, 261, 265, 278, 286, 291, 292, 294, 296, 299, 304–306, 310, 311, 313, 320, 327, 343, 353, 357, 358, 363, 381, 384, 389, 397, 412, 413, 416, 426
secretary, 89, 92, 118, 157, 159, 160, 215, 220, 223, 291, 305, 325, 352, 423
size, 78, 85–88, 94, 109, 174, 210, 211, 214, 218, 228, 231, 233, 235, 237, 240, 244, 248, 252, 259–261, 268, 276, 277, 281, 286, 290, 294, 297, 300, 303, 310, 320, 325, 327, 330, 335, 343, 347, 352, 356, 363, 371, 381, 384, 387, 390, 397, 398, 401, 412, 420, 422, 425
term of office, 85, 88, 89, 111, 147, 210, 211, 214, 218, 221, 222, 225, 228, 231, 233, 235, 237, 240, 244, 248, 252, 257, 259–261, 265, 268, 276, 281, 286, 290, 292, 294, 297, 299, 303, 310, 320, 325, 327, 330, 331, 335, 343, 347, 352, 357, 363, 367, 381, 384, 387, 390, 396, 398, 401, 406, 412, 416, 420–422, 425
Council of elders, 23, 134, 205, 369, 372–375
Council manager, 230, 241
Councilmembers,
appointment, 47, 84–86, 157, 396, 401, 404, 406, 420
dismissal, including removal and suspension, 222, 224, 286, 314, 326, 327, 359, 369, 383, 384, 389, 390, 399, 414, 420, 422
election, 52, 58, 68, 81, 84, 85, 88, 89, 102, 127, 138, 158, 172–174, 196, 200–202, 210, 212–214, 218, 221–223, 225, 228–231, 237, 240, 244, 246, 248, 252, 257, 259–261, 264, 276, 286, 290, 294, 296, 297, 299, 303, 310, 320, 327, 330, 331,

335, 343, 347, 352, 363, 367, 369, 381, 387, 390, 392–394, 397, 398, 401, 406, 412, 416, 420, 422, 425
general, 10, 22, 43, 48, 58, 61, 74, 79–82, 86–89, 101–103, 110, 118, 124, 136, 140, 144, 146, 157, 158, 171, 174, 175, 184, 194, 197, 198, 201, 202, 229, 253, 261, 268, 281, 286, 287, 291, 293, 294, 304–306, 308, 315, 320, 347–349, 351, 357–359, 363, 388, 392, 398, 402, 412–414, 416, 421, 422
County,
administrator, 29, 241
borough, 209–212
council, 58, 86, 132, 210, 211, 213, 221, 232, 233, 240
council delegation, 210
council functions, 209, 210, 213
district, 218, 221, 232
general, 27, 29, 64, 78, 192, 193, 208, 209–211, 212, 213, 216, 221, 227, 232–234, 239–241
Court, 35, 37, 39, 40–42, 121, 152, 177, 216, 239, 244, 246, 248, 251, 255, 265, 270, 275, 282, 283, 304, 311–313, 316, 326, 332, 338, 345, 346, 349, 352, 354, 359, 365, 374, 383, 386, 408, 409

Datta, Ansu, Kumar, 134
Decentralization, 28, 29, 35–42, 77, 155, 272, 302, 309, 319, 424
Deconcentration, 22–24, 28, 33, 35–40, 73, 82, 95, 99, 102, 117
Default, 20, 217, 225, 231, 283, 367, 383, 385, 393
Delegation, 23, 24, 26, 35, 38, 87, 94, 100, 113, 117, 127, 128, 160, 179, 196, 199, 200, 204, 210, 215, 220, 221, 223, 230, 232, 238, 241, 244, 250, 253, 254, 257, 264–268, 271, 276–278, 280–284, 287, 288, 294–298, 300, 301, 302, 305, 310, 316, 324, 328, 350, 354, 355, 366, 369, 388, 395, 401, 404, 425–427
Dennison, Henry, 9
Denmark, 256–260
general, 4, 29, 37, 194
mayor, 111

INDEX

municipalities, 96
rural municipalities, 21, 195
urban municipalities, 195
Departments,
   general, 19, 84, 95, 99, 105, 110, 112, 114, 133, 154–158, 177, 193, 194, 200, 206, 207, 228–230, 236, 237, 258, 266, 269, 277, 282, 291–293, 295–297, 305, 321, 332, 344, 347, 357, 371, 398, 406, 413, 420, 421, 423
   supervision of, 126, 160, 175, 228–230, 236, 237, 282, 294, 310, 312, 320, 326, 381, 397
Departments of the central government,
   approval of, 47, 300, 301, 333, 373, 376, 388, 389, 392, 406
   control, 220, 251, 261, 271, 297, 318, 319, 327, 337, 349, 359, 367, 370, 378, 383, 384, 402, 403, 414, 419, 427
   general, 3, 7, 13, 24, 28, 32, 33, 41, 42, 76, 133, 137, 138, 181, 220, 238, 246, 247, 250, 251, 255, 256, 258–260, 262, 270, 282, 285–289, 295, 297, 302, 312–314, 316–318, 321, 322, 330–335, 340, 341, 346, 348, 350, 351, 358, 360, 364, 366–369, 373–375, 377, 385, 388, 389, 394, 402, 403, 405–410, 413–415, 418, 419, 422, 424, 425
Dismissal, including removal and discharge, 36, 47, 48, 78, 141, 145, 147, 176, 178, 186, 221, 223, 230, 231, 236–238, 250, 282, 286, 289, 296, 301, 304, 312, 314, 317, 322, 325–327, 336–338, 348, 350, 354, 357–359, 361, 364, 366, 368, 369, 382, 386, 413
Dissolution, 48, 141, 185, 226, 275, 312, 321, 322, 337, 364, 368, 373, 381, 382, 385, 386, 389, 390, 400, 414, 419, 426
District,
   board, 267, 292, 298, 375
   chief executive, 13, 40, 41, 75, 134, 135, 137, 140, 205, 206, 267, 271, 284, 360, 369, 370, 375, 376, 406, 408, 409
   civil governor, 335, 338, 340, 341
   commissioner, 269–272, 284, 289, 368, 384, 401, 402, 404
   council, see District council
   director, 324, 328
   functions, 298, 307, 308, 360, 385, 394, 404, 412
   general, 6, 13, 22, 27–29, 42, 64, 65, 68, 72, 137, 192, 212, 213, 231, 240, 256, 258–260, 262–264, 266–269, 271, 272, 281, 284, 286, 289, 290, 294, 296, 298, 303, 307, 308, 333, 335, 337, 340, 341, 352, 355, 356, 361, 362, 365–370, 374, 375, 379, 385, 386, 390, 391, 393–395, 399, 404, 405, 407–409, 411, 418, 420
   legislation, 386
   officer, 13, 251, 394, 395, 399, 412–416, 418
   rural district, 14, 132, 208–212, 267
   secretary, 386
   urban district, 14, 132, 208–212, 310
District council,
   chairman, 259, 262, 267, 375, 376, 385, 386
   committees, 298, 385
   elections, 259, 262, 267, 298, 308, 385, 394
   functions, 209, 213, 267
   general, 42, 76, 212, 214, 216, 259, 262, 306–308, 375, 386, 394, 395
   meeting, 259, 262, 267, 298, 275, 285
   size, 259, 267, 298, 385
   term of office, 259, 262, 267, 375
Diversified pattern, 16, 17
Domestic activities, 35, 38
Drucker, Peter, 180

East Asia group, 88, 206–207, 411–428
East Europe group, 14, 42, 65, 69, 72, 76, 88, 97–100, 102, 290–309
Ecuador, 346–351
   general, 202, 203
   sub-municipal units, 21

Electoral system,
  alternate vote system, 219
  consent by acclamation, 59, 64–66
  direct election, 24, 52, 57–59, 61, 78, 84, 110, 115, 142, 157, 158, 172, 182–184, 193, 202, 210–213, 238, 303, 331, 392, 401
  elections at large, 172, 173, 218, 219, 221, 225, 228–230, 235, 237, 374, 420, 422
  election by majority vote, 110, 218, 222, 235, 252, 273, 284, 286, 310, 321, 363, 371, 387
  election by ward, 218, 225, 228–230, 235, 300, 303, 381, 387, 396
  indirect election, 6, 57, 58, 84, 335, 339, 394, 401
  plurality voting, 57, 59, 62–64, 68, 89, 172, 173
  popular election, 6, 22, 52, 89, 103, 115, 133, 136, 142, 143, 147, 157, 172, 173, 182–184, 186, 192–194, 197, 201, 202, 206, 207, 229, 231, 236, 240, 241, 247, 260, 267, 268, 276, 279, 281, 284, 286, 290, 296–298, 299, 301, 310, 315, 320, 322, 325, 327, 343, 344, 347, 348, 352, 357, 367, 369, 371, 372, 374, 385, 390, 393, 396, 398, 412, 416, 417, 418, 421–423, 425, 427
  proportional representation, 57, 59, 60, 61, 64, 67–69, 110, 140, 172, 173, 219, 235, 244, 248, 252, 257, 259, 261, 268, 273, 276, 281, 284, 286, 310, 343, 347, 350
El Salvador, 356–362
  general, 158, 202
Emerson, Rupert, see Thompson
England, see United Kingdom
Ethiopia, 405–411
  chief executive, 134–136
  council, 72, 73
  general, 54, 190, 204
  rural municipalities, 73
  selection, 136
  urban municipalities, 72
  tiers, 12

Executive body, 11, 33, 35, 36, 39–42, 61, 75, 78, 87, 97, 106, 108, 109, 117, 118, 121, 126, 128, 134, 136, 156, 170, 175, 192, 196, 248, 265, 266, 269, 273, 292, 293, 300, 336, 348, 384, 416

Federal, 1, 2, 19, 40, 202, 227, 234, 263–265, 268, 270, 271, 275, 291, 302, 335, 342–346, 356, 395, 396, 398, 399
Finland, 247–251
  board, 110, 112, 115
  chief executive, 115, 145, 149
  general, 4, 157, 194, 195
  province, 28
  rural municipalities, 145
  selection, 110, 115, 145
  urban municipalities, 145
Form of local government,
  commission, 87, 114, 142, 158, 193, 194, 234–236
  council-committee, 192, 193, 205, 206, 229, 235
  council-manager, 77, 78, 87, 120, 121, 142, 145, 146, 193, 194, 230, 234, 235, 237, 238, 241
  council-mayor, 124, 142, 161, 193, 202, 235–237
  council-mayor-director, 266
  strong mayor, 77, 143, 193, 194, 202, 206, 207, 235, 236, 241, 265, 343
  weak mayor, 132, 133, 193, 235, 236
France, 309–319
  board, 110, 118
  chief administrative officer, 126, 156, 159
  chief executive, 136, 141, 156
  committees, 96, 97, 102, 160
  control, 13, 42
  council, 5, 39, 47, 72, 128, 141, 186
  districts, 28, 72, 137
  general, 4, 5, 17, 33, 42, 45, 60, 154, 197, 199, 200
  influence on other countries, 15, 191, 199–201, 203, 204, 206, 207
  intermediate unit, 27
  mayor, 49, 110, 111, 117, 127,

INDEX 441

128, 136, 139, 140, 160, 181, 186, 199
municipalities, 14, 15, 19, 72
province, 13, 28, 72, 130, 137
secretary, 181
selection, 110, 136, 140
term of office councilmembers, 88

General purpose units, 3–7, 14, 15, 23–27, 203
German Federal Republic, 263–267
chairman, 146
chief administrative officer, 146
chief executive, 110, 145–147
committees, 97
control, 40, 78
council, 77, 78
general, 2, 4, 29, 30, 194, 196
mayor, 147, 200
municipalities, 19, 83
selection, 110
special purpose bodies, 25
tiers, 13
Governor,
district, 259
province, see under P.
state, 217, 220, 221, 239, 271, 344, 381, 395
territory, 343, 344
Governor general, 217, 227
Grants, 20, 33, 41, 44–46, 79, 165, 216, 239, 244, 248, 251, 316, 329, 338, 345, 346, 385, 386, 389, 398, 399, 427
Greece, 324–329
chief executive, 130
general, 190, 199, 201
mayor, 111
province, 28

Harris, G. Montagu, 3, 4
Headman (village) 4, 22, 24, 52, 74, 134, 135, 147, 203, 204, 206, 365, 369, 393, 407, 414–418
Home rule, 167, 235, 237, 241

Iceland, 260–263
general, 194
rural municipalities, 60, 83, 195
tiers, 12
urban municipalities, 195

India, 379–386
chairman, 132
chief administrative officer, 137
chief executive, 137, 147
committees, 98
control, 41, 42
councils, 204
councilmembers, 85
district, 29
general, 2, 4, 45, 66, 86, 151, 157, 204, 205
mayor, 101, 132, 147
province, 28
selection, 85, 137
special purpose bodies, 25
tiers, 12
urban municipalities, 64, 85
Intermediate units, 2, 12, 13, 27–29, 33, 40–42, 44, 50, 58, 72, 74, 130, 136, 138, 164, 203, 204, 227, 260, 289, 335, 355, 404, 418, 427
International City Managers' Association, (ICMA), 142, 155, 158
International Union of Local Authorities, 44, 208
Iran, 366–368
chief executive, 136
control, 13
councils, 72, 73
general, 203, 204
province, 28
rural municipalities, 17, 73
selection, 136
urban municipalities, 17, 72
Italy, 319–324
board, 115
chairman, 115
chief administrative officer, 156, 159
chief executive, 156
control, 40
council, 141
general, 17, 45, 47, 60, 151, 154, 191, 199, 200
mayor, 181
province, 29
regions, 323
secretary, 181

Jackson, R. M., 38, 153
Japan, 424–428
general, 20, 34, 45, 67, 79, 80,

442 INDEX

163, 190, 194, 206, 207
mayor, 124, 142
municipalities, 67
rural municipalities, 37
selection, 142
Jennings, W. Ivor; Laski, Harold; and Robson, W. A., 15, 81, 98
Justice of the peace, 128, 208, 210, 211, 213, 214, 240, 242

Laski, Harold, see Jennings ....
Law, see also By-laws, Ordinances, Regulations
  central, 2, 18, 26, 34, 36, 38, 40, 43, 53, 55, 74, 102, 110, 124, 152, 245, 248, 250, 252, 256, 257, 264, 268, 269, 272, 274–278, 281, 282, 284–286, 292, 293, 313, 317, 319, 320, 322, 325, 329, 331, 332, 337, 348–352, 355, 356, 359, 360, 362–365, 367, 369, 370, 373, 374, 380, 381, 383, 386, 396, 401, 406, 412–415, 417, 424–427
  federal, 264, 344, 346, 396
  general, 38, 52, 72, 123, 125, 224, 228, 235, 270, 271, 279, 282, 291, 297, 299, 302, 309, 312, 344, 358, 380, 388, 403, 407, 409, 413, 416
  local, 43, 237, 271, 277, 282, 283, 285, 313, 321, 326, 343, 345, 349, 364, 371, 383, 397, 398, 402, 404, 421, 422
  provincial, 222, 227, 279, 282, 285, 293, 334, 413
Lebanon, 368–370
  board, 176
  chief executive, 134
  general, 60, 61, 203
Legislation, see Law
Legislature, 34, 39, 227, 235, 240, 345, 385
Loans, 215, 216, 220, 235, 238–240, 244, 246, 250–253, 255, 258, 259, 261, 262, 266, 269, 270, 273, 275, 276, 279, 283, 289, 313, 316–318, 321, 325, 327, 330, 332, 338, 345, 348, 363, 371, 372, 383, 387, 389, 390, 393, 398, 426
Local government,
  form of local government, see also under F, 15, 45, 162, 168, 189, 191, 193–196, 199, 200, 203, 205, 229, 230, 235, 241, 243, 265, 286, 302, 342, 405
  functions, including competence, power, services, 13, 15–25, 27–29, 32, 33, 35, 36, 44, 46, 50, 73, 76, 95, 96, 107–109, 125–127, 131, 143, 150, 153, 155, 159, 163–169, 193, 211–215, 217, 218, 220, 221, 224, 226, 228, 231, 232, 234, 235, 238, 239, 241, 244, 248, 252, 253, 257, 258, 261, 262, 264, 267, 268, 270, 274, 281, 286, 294, 298, 299, 301, 303, 319, 324, 327, 330, 335, 347, 354, 356, 360, 363, 369, 370, 373, 375, 376, 379–381, 383, 387, 388, 396, 412, 416, 420, 425
  structure, 1, 9–11, 32, 47, 86, 115, 119–121, 132, 142, 150, 151, 162, 168, 169, 171, 178, 179, 181, 186, 189, 190, 191, 193, 195, 197, 206, 207, 209, 211, 214, 217, 221, 222, 230, 233, 238, 243, 248, 252, 263, 265, 268, 290, 294, 298, 299, 301, 319, 323, 327, 330, 335, 347, 352, 356, 368, 370, 379, 387, 390, 396, 405, 419, 424
  system, see also Form of local government, 15, 20, 189–191, 193, 198–200, 202, 206, 207, 294, 307, 309, 355, 363, 381, 386, 400, 402, 424
  types, 3, 11, 193, 201, 209, 222, 386, 389
  units, 2, 7, 11, 12, 21, 23, 31, 33, 34, 38, 42, 49, 66, 70, 74, 75, 100, 196, 210, 212, 214, 218, 222, 224, 227, 228, 231, 232, 234, 239, 241, 243, 246, 247, 252, 255, 256, 260, 264, 268, 271, 272, 276, 280, 281, 284, 286, 290, 291, 297–299, 303, 309, 319, 324, 331, 347, 368, 380, 384, 385, 393, 404, 418, 424, 427
Local non-representative government, 3–7, 9, 11, 14, 18, 27–29, 31, 35, 36, 40, 51, 73, 121, 127,

INDEX 443

136, 149, 151, 156, 349, 380
Local representative government,
   3–9, 11, 14, 15, 19, 20, 22, 27–29,
   31, 32, 34–36, 38, 40, 44–46, 49–
   52, 54, 56, 57, 70, 72, 73, 75, 76,
   79, 84, 86, 94, 107, 108, 119, 121,
   122, 125–127, 129, 130, 136, 148–
   151, 153, 156, 162–186, 367, 383,
   392, 398, 400
Locke, John, 107
Lordello de Mello, Diogo, 68
Luxembourg, 286–290
   general, 190, 196, 197
   mayor, 197
   selection, 197
   tiers, 12

MacDonald, Austin, F., 57
Mackenzie, W. S. M., 51, 59, 65
Malaya, 395–400
   chairman, 137
   chief executive, 137
   councilmembers, 85
   districts, 29
   general, 2, 204, 205
   selection, 85, 137
   urban municipalities, 85
Manager, 8, 77, 110, 119–121, 136,
   139, 144–146, 149, 194, 238, 249,
   250, 254
Marx, Fritz Morstein, 178
Marxist doctrine, 65
Mayor,
   appointment, 47, 135, 137–139,
      197, 199, 235, 277, 280, 282,
      287, 331, 333, 335, 337, 343,
      353, 387, 397, 406, 421
   dismissal, 36, 141, 235, 312, 314,
      322, 327, 337, 354, 364, 373,
      382, 383, 422, 426
   election, 52, 67, 127, 128, 133,
      135, 136, 139, 141–143, 147,
      193, 199–202, 205–207, 211,
      214, 223, 229, 236–238, 265,
      304, 310, 322, 325, 344, 348,
      357, 367, 371, 381, 398, 421,
      422
   functions, 196, 211, 223, 229, 230,
      236, 238, 270, 276, 282, 311,
      313, 325, 331, 344, 353, 358,
      364, 372, 397, 406, 421, 426
   general, 22, 36, 37, 40, 49, 57, 80,
      91, 101, 105, 110–112, 115, 117,
      119, 120, 123, 124, 127, 128,
      130, 131, 133, 134, 138–141,
      147, 156, 160, 181, 185, 193,
      194, 197–199, 201, 203, 206,
      207, 211, 215, 219, 221, 223–
      225, 228, 235, 261, 266, 269,
      277, 278, 280, 281, 283, 286–
      288, 314, 315, 320, 326, 330–
      333, 335–338, 340, 343, 344–
      346, 348, 351–355, 358–360,
      363, 371–373, 382, 388, 406,
      420, 422, 423, 425
   suspension, 311, 314, 318, 322,
      326, 327, 345, 364
   term of office, 147, 148, 193, 211,
      219, 223, 236, 277, 278, 282,
      336, 337, 344, 348, 353, 371,
      381, 421, 422
Metropolitan borough, 209–211
Meyer, Ernest, 45
Mill, John Stuart, 19, 149, 165, 185
Ministries of central government,
   see Departments of central
   government,
Morgands, J. 128
Municipalities, definition, 14–15
   general, 2, 5, 6, 13–22, 25, 27, 29,
      34, 35, 38, 44, 46–49, 53, 54,
      67, 68, 70, 72, 77, 83–85, 88,
      89, 91–94, 96, 99, 100, 104,
      108–110, 112, 114, 117, 120,
      123, 124, 126, 130, 137–139,
      144, 145, 147, 151, 152, 156–
      159, 161, 163, 164, 175, 181,
      194–204, 206, 218–220, 222,
      228, 234, 235, 238–240, 242,
      247, 254, 257, 261, 263, 268,
      272, 273, 276, 281, 286, 294,
      299, 301, 302, 303, 306–309,
      314, 319, 329, 333–335, 342–
      344, 346, 347, 351, 352, 356,
      359, 360, 362, 363, 367–370,
      372, 380, 381, 386–389, 391,
      392, 396, 400, 401, 403–406,
      409, 412, 413, 418, 419, 422,
      424–427
   definition rural municipalities,
      16–17
   rural municipalities, general, 12,
      14, 16–19, 21, 22, 29, 34, 35,
      37, 43, 44, 46, 54, 60, 73, 78,

79, 83, 84, 87, 110, 115, 133, 145, 153, 161, 193, 195, 198, 201, 203–206, 209, 212, 218, 224–227, 231–234, 241, 243, 247–250, 252, 255, 256, 258–262, 264, 290, 292, 294, 297–299, 303, 324, 327, 329, 335, 370, 373, 374, 380, 383, 386, 389, 390, 395, 398, 401, 405, 409, 411, 415, 416, 418, 422–424
definition urban municipalities, 16–17
urban municipalities, general, 4, 6, 12–18, 22, 29, 43, 64, 72, 73, 85, 87, 91, 94, 109–111, 115, 120, 130, 132, 133, 137, 145, 146, 157, 193–195, 201, 203–206, 209, 212, 218, 222, 226–228, 232, 234, 239, 243, 247–250, 252, 256–258, 260, 261, 264, 290, 292, 294–299, 303, 324, 326, 327, 329, 335, 362, 370, 372, 374, 379–381, 383, 387, 388, 390, 391, 393, 395–397, 411, 412, 416–418, 420, 421

Netherlands, 275–280
board, 113–115
chairman, 115
chief executive, 110, 129, 236
committees, 102
control, 129
general, 17, 45, 55, 60, 196, 197
mayor, 117, 138, 197
municipalities, 18
province, 29
selection, 110, 115, 136. 138, 197
Nomination, 52, 67–70, 81, 101, 103, 110, 140, 282, 285, 294, 304, 381, 384, 396, 401
Non-county borough, 209–211
North Europe group, 35, 44, 76, 97, 98, 102, 136, 194–195, 196, 198, 200, 242–263
Northern Ireland, see U.K. 209, 214
Norway, 251–256
board, 112, 115
chairman, 115, 120, 146
chief administrative officer, 146
chief executive, 121, 136

committees, 104
finance committee, 96
general, 17, 84, 194, 195
mayor, 136
municipalities, 96
province, 29
selection, 104, 136

Ordinances,
general, 220, 235, 269, 285, 396, 398–401
local, 41, 49, 75, 97, 130, 198, 236, 237, 281, 282, 300, 313, 314, 318, 344, 345, 347–349, 367, 372, 389, 402, 421
provincial, 227, 280, 293, 313, 317, 350, 354, 355, 418, 419, 423

Parish,
board, 338
council, 212–214
general, 14, 15, 21, 37, 75, 83, 192, 209, 231, 232, 234, 243, 248, 256, 260–262, 337–339
meeting, 212
Parliament, 211, 213, 216, 217, 220, 222, 279, 297, 315, 388, 392, 400
Parties, 52, 56–66, 68–71, 76, 80–82, 91, 100, 106, 115, 117, 124, 139–141, 143, 166, 171, 173–175, 180, 184, 197, 199, 201, 299, 234, 282
Personnel, see Staff
Perham, Margery, 135
Philippines, 419–424
chief executive, 133, 134
council, 74
councilmembers, 85
general, 75, 142, 194, 201, 206
mayor, 133, 142
municipalities, 14
rural municipalities, 46
selection, 85, 142, 158
sub-municipal units, 21, 22, 74, 134
urban municipalities, 85
Poland, 293–299
board, 111, 115, 198
general, 30, 45, 197
rural municipalities, 83, 198

INDEX

Police, 3, 18, 24, 25, 33, 35, 47, 85, 126, 128, 133, 149, 154, 205, 210, 211, 213, 214, 218, 231, 235, 239, 244, 247, 248, 255, 261, 269, 274, 278, 281, 282, 285, 288, 295, 312–314, 316, 317, 320, 323, 330, 334, 336–340, 344, 347, 351, 353, 357, 364, 365, 367, 372, 387, 396, 398, 406–409, 414, 420, 422, 425, 427
Policy, 8, 9, 11, 12, 20, 26, 28, 35, 48, 65, 71, 73, 75, 77, 79, 82–86, 89, 90, 94, 97, 98, 103, 105, 107–109, 111, 113–115, 118–120, 122, 124–126, 130–132, 134, 139, 141, 145, 146, 149, 150, 156, 157, 159, 165–171, 175–183, 185, 195, 198, 215, 220, 228, 229, 230, 236–238, 266, 269, 276, 277, 297, 312, 315, 316, 360, 367, 368, 373, 376, 381, 387, 399–401, 413, 414, 426
Popular assembly,
    definition, 82–83
    general, 6, 51, 66, 67, 72, 74, 75, 80, 82–84, 110, 115, 125, 192, 197, 198, 212, 225, 241, 298, 330, 384, 400
Portugal, 334, 342
    board, 201
    chief executive, 201
    council, 201
    general, 53, 199, 201, 202
    influences on other countries, 201
    municipalities, 14
    province, 28
    sub-municipal units, 21
Powers, see Local government, functions
Press, 56, 57, 93
Pressure groups, 56, 57
Price, Don K., see Stone . . .
Province, 2, 13, 27–29, 53, 137, 221–223, 225–228, 232, 243, 246, 247, 252, 255, 256, 263, 267, 276, 279–281, 286, 290, 291, 293, 296, 298, 301, 302, 309, 314–319, 322–324, 328, 329, 333–335, 339, 340, 346, 348, 350, 351, 353, 355, 356, 359, 360, 362, 366–370, 374, 375, 377–380, 391, 393, 400, 404, 405, 407, 409, 411, 418, 419, 423, 424, 427
Provincial board,
    chairman, 256, 280, 285, 322, 339, 340, 377
    functions, 279, 280, 301, 339, 423
    general, 247, 255, 256, 279, 280, 282–285, 292, 339, 340, 377, 423
    selection, 255, 280, 284, 298, 322, 339, 377, 423
    size, 255, 280, 284, 298, 423
    term of office, 255, 280, 284, 377, 423
Provincial council,
    chairman, 130, 280, 284, 315, 316, 322, 333, 334, 340, 350, 376, 409, 410, 427
    committees, 247, 298, 302, 315–318, 334
    composition, 409
    control, 296, 348
    delegation, 316
    functions, 227, 279, 301, 315, 339, 366, 376
    general, 29, 42, 72, 86, 226, 227, 247, 255, 280, 282, 285, 292, 302, 315–318, 333, 334, 339, 340, 348–351, 355, 366, 370, 372, 377, 378, 409, 419
    meeting, 247, 255, 256, 298, 315–318, 340, 350, 376
    secretary, 315, 409
    selection, 137, 226, 247, 255, 279, 284, 298, 301, 315, 322, 328, 333, 339, 350, 366, 376, 418, 427
    size, 226, 247, 279, 284, 298, 315, 322, 350, 366, 376, 427
    term of office, 226, 279, 284, 315, 322, 339, 350, 366, 376, 418, 427
Provincial government,
    chief executive, 41, 134, 223, 227, 316–318, 351, 366, 375, 394, 427
    control, 13, 29, 224–226, 228, 231, 232, 246, 250, 255, 264, 279, 284, 299, 301, 302, 313, 321, 323, 326, 327, 351, 353–355, 359, 360, 364, 366, 369, 370, 372, 377, 402, 404, 405, 409, 412, 414, 415, 424, 427
    delegation, 271, 277, 282, 354, 369

general, 22, 133, 145, 204, 222, 227, 231, 247, 249, 251, 277, 284, 292, 314, 318, 366, 369, 372, 376, 404, 407, 413, 424–427
Provincial governor,
  appointment, 227, 247, 251, 255, 280, 285, 286, 317, 322, 328, 334, 351, 355, 360, 368, 370, 377, 404, 409, 418
  election, 423, 427
  functions, 227, 247, 328, 355, 360, 370, 404, 409, 427
  general, 5, 13, 24, 28, 29, 36, 40–42, 45, 102, 130, 134, 136–138, 141, 185, 223–227, 245–247, 251, 254–256, 278, 280, 282–286, 310–319, 321–324, 326–329, 331, 333, 338, 348, 350, 354, 355, 358–361, 363, 366, 368, 373–378, 392, 401–403, 405–408, 410, 412–414, 416–419, 421, 423, 426

Quasi-federal, 1, 2
Quasi-intermediate, 13, 14, 23, 29, 30
Quasi-municipal, 29
Quasi-sovereign, 1–3, 8, 12, 30, 34, 234, 395

Recall, 142, 237, 293, 294, 384
Referendum, 82–84, 237, 241, 270, 271, 273, 274, 299
Region, 319, 323
Regulations, including national and provincial, 24, 32, 34, 38, 41, 128, 220, 225, 226, 230, 238, 244, 251, 253, 258, 268, 270, 273, 275–278, 280–283, 285, 287, 288, 295, 304, 306, 319, 320, 325, 331, 332, 336, 337, 339, 355, 364, 369, 372, 383, 393, 397, 403, 406, 413, 414, 419
Removal, 47, 48, 138, 142, 147, 183, 185, 279, 310, 318, 382–384, 389, 390, 413, 415, 417, 420, 422–424, 426, 427
Representative organ, 3–6, 9, 11, 14, 15, 17, 19, 22–24, 26, 28, 29, 35, 36, 64, 72, 75, 78, 82–84, 86, 100, 103, 108, 121, 123, 125–127, 129, 133, 136, 137, 148, 149, 152, 153, 156, 160, 164, 168, 170–172, 175–177, 199, 206, 241, 248, 255–257, 259, 264, 265, 310, 311, 330, 335, 339, 349, 352, 363, 370, 376, 377, 381, 382, 384, 385, 387, 391, 394, 396, 416, 425, 426
Review, see Control
Ridley, Clarence E., 8, 123
Rigors, Paul, 108
Robson, W. A., 26, 132, 168, 169; See also Jennings . . .
Romani, John, H., 22, 75

Sanitary district, 24, 209, 411, 414, 415, 418, 419
Scandinavia, see North Europe
Scotland, see U.K. 209, 212
  indirect elections, 58
Secondary units, 27, 58, 227, 232
Secretary, 49, 76, 78, 90, 132, 133, 157, 158, 161, 181, 193, 198, 200, 205, 215, 216, 219, 220, 223–225, 229, 230, 236, 242, 250, 278, 282, 287, 288, 291, 297, 304–306, 332, 357, 358, 361, 374, 381, 382, 384, 392, 393, 397, 398, 402, 423
Secretary general, 126, 159, 160, 181, 200, 312, 321, 326
Sharma, M. P., 86, 132–133
South Africa, 221–227
  general, 192, 193
  mayor, 101
South America, 5, 17, 194
South and Central American group, 191, 202–203, 342–362
South Asia and East Africa group, 41, 192, 204–206, 379–411
South Europe group, 17, 191, 199–201, 309–342
Sovereign, 1–3, 6, 8, 28, 31, 34, 217, 229, 247, 260, 271, 272, 324, 390, 400
Spain, 329–334
  board, 115, 117, 118
  chief executive, 121
  council, 201
  general, 53, 199, 201, 202
  influence on other countries, 191, 199, 201, 202
  mayor, 121, 124, 137, 138, 199
  selection, 115, 137

INDEX 447

Special purpose bodies,
 general, 3, 4, 6, 17, 23–26, 100, 164, 193, 220, 222, 226, 234, 247, 273, 279, 280, 411, 418, 426
 inter-municipal, 6, 19, 23, 25, 164, 263, 267, 310, 323, 327, 328
 intra-municipal, 6, 21, 24, 25, 96, 164, 231
Srinivasan, N., 66, 205
Staff, including personnel,
 appointment, 47, 132, 151–153, 215, 216, 223, 230, 239, 244, 254, 269, 276, 287, 288, 296, 304, 314, 317, 321, 325, 344, 357, 358, 374, 377, 381, 384, 388, 392, 409
 control over, 109, 126, 141, 157, 195, 219, 382, 384
 dismissal, 47, 152, 153, 176, 178, 216, 223, 230, 239, 250, 282, 325, 344, 357, 358, 361
 general, 8, 11, 13, 16, 18, 19, 23, 32, 33, 42, 43, 49, 52, 75–78, 85, 91, 94, 95, 97–99, 105, 107, 108, 110, 113–115, 119, 122, 123, 125, 127, 133, 137, 140, 143–145, 149–161, 165, 166, 170, 175–177, 180–182, 186, 197, 215, 220, 239, 253, 266, 278, 281, 288, 291, 292, 305, 306, 311, 314, 320, 331, 337, 346, 354, 360, 363, 364, 373, 375, 376, 383, 384, 386, 388, 392, 407, 408, 414, 420, 421
Stannard, Harold, 182
State, see Central government
State council, 42, 297, 306, 313, 318, 322, 327, 351, 372, 376
Steiner, Kurt, 37, 45, 80
Stone, Harold; Price, Don K.; and Stone, Kathryn H., 146
Strong mayor, see under Form of local government
Sub-district, 13, 367, 368, 379, 380, 391, 405, 407–409
Sub-governor, 375–377, 409
Sub-municipal unit,
 definition, 21
 general, 21–23, 30, 72, 74, 75, 83, 95, 134, 164, 192, 202, 203, 212, 294, 296, 306, 329, 333, 335, 338, 342, 343, 346, 347, 349, 351, 354, 355, 369, 370, 372, 411, 415–417, 419, 420, 422, 425
Sub-provinces,
 control, 372, 374, 375
 council, 376, 408, 409
 general, 27, 40, 49, 309, 314, 370, 372, 374, 375, 405, 408, 409, 419, 423
Sudan, 400–405
 chief administrative officer, 137
 chief executive, 137
 committees, 98
 council, 75
 councilmembers, 85
 general, 58, 204, 206
 mayor, 101, 132
 municipalities, 15, 85
 selection, 85, 137
Suffrage, 5, 52–54, 58
Supervision, see Control
Suspension, 124, 176, 219, 278, 280, 283, 285, 293, 297, 305, 311, 314, 318, 322, 326, 327, 345, 354, 364, 366, 383, 394, 399, 402, 403, 414, 419, 423
Sweden, 242–247
 board, 110–112, 115, 116
 chairman, 91
 chief administrative officer, 160
 chief executive, 117, 130
 committees, 94, 102, 104
 control, 40, 99
 general, 4, 17, 34, 42, 154, 163, 194, 195
 mayor, 200
 municipalities, 84, 96
 province, 29
 secretary, 158
 selection, 104, 110, 115, 158
Switzerland, 271–275
 board, 110, 114–116, 158
 council, 77
 general, 16, 53, 83, 156, 196
 mayor, 117
 municipalities, 5, 19, 83, 197
 selection, 110, 115
 special purpose bodies, 25
 term of office councilmen, 88
 tiers, 12

448 INDEX

Taxes,
  including levy, rates, 2, 22, 35,
    42, 46, 54, 73, 165, 215, 216,
    219, 226, 232, 233, 235, 237–
    241, 244–246, 252, 257–262,
    269, 276, 279, 281, 283, 286,
    288, 289, 298, 300, 304, 313,
    314, 316, 318, 321, 325, 330,
    332, 334, 338, 343–345, 347,
    349, 352–357, 359, 363, 369,
    371, 373, 374, 381–383, 387–
    389, 391, 393, 397, 399, 401,
    406, 425
Term of office, 23, 78, 85, 88, 89, 91,
    111, 115, 132, 133, 139, 145–147,
    183, 185, 193, 198, 210–214, 219,
    221–223, 225–228, 231, 233, 235–
    237, 240, 241, 244–246, 248, 249,
    252–255, 257, 259–262, 264–269,
    274, 276, 277, 279, 280, 282, 287,
    290, 292–294, 296, 299, 303, 305,
    310, 315, 320, 322, 325, 327, 328,
    330, 331, 333–337, 339, 344, 346,
    348, 350, 352, 353, 355, 357, 363,
    366, 367, 369, 371–375, 377, 381,
    382, 384, 387, 390, 396, 398, 401,
    406–409, 412, 414–418, 420, 421,
    423, 425, 427
Thailand, 411–419
  board, 112, 114, 158
  general, 206
  mayor, 117
  province, 28
  special purpose bodies, 24
Thompson, Virginia, 206
Tiers, 12–14, 27, 30, 42, 67, 100,
    156, 167, 209, 217, 222, 227, 234,
    243, 247, 252, 256, 260, 263, 268,
    272, 276, 281, 286, 290, 294, 299,
    303, 307, 309, 319, 324, 329, 335,
    342, 346, 351, 356, 362, 364, 368,
    370, 379, 386, 391, 400, 401, 411,
    424, 427
Town, 14, 18, 46, 79, 228, 232, 234,
    241, 242, 247, 248, 369, 380, 381,
    396, 406, 424
Township, 15, 17, 29, 208, 224, 231–
    234, 240–242, 391, 393
Treasurer, 78, 133, 157, 193, 216,
    223, 229, 230, 236, 240, 242, 253,
    259, 279, 287, 288, 332, 352, 357,
    415, 426

Tunisia, 362–366
  council, 73
  general, 203, 204
  rural municipalities, 17, 73
  urban municipalities, 17
Turkey, 370–379
  board, 110
  chief executive, 136
  control, 13
  general, 157, 203
  mayor, 136
  rural municipalities, 34, 83, 84
  selection, 110, 136
  sub-municipal unit, 22

Ultra vires, 39, 41, 215, 383, 385,
    419
Uniform pattern, 16, 17, 195, 197,
    199, 202, 290, 319, 330
United Kingdom, 208–217
  chairman, 91, 132
  chief administrative officer, 161
  chief executive, 121, 193
  committees, 94–96, 98, 100, 102,
    104, 160
  control, 99
  council, 5
  general, 4, 6, 16, 29, 30, 33, 38,
    45, 47, 53, 62, 84, 152, 154, 156,
    181, 192, 195
  influence on other countries, 25,
    98, 132, 191, 192, 204, 205
  mayor, 101, 128, 132, 147
  municipalities, 14, 94
  selection, 104
  special purpose bodies, 25
  sub-municipal units, 21, 22, 75,
    83
  tiers, 13

United States, 233–243
  chairman, 146
  chief administrative officer, 121,
    146
  chief executive, 121, 136, 139,
    144–147, 149
  committees, 88, 93, 97, 102
  control, 78
  council, 77, 78, 86–88, 93, 114
  councilmembers, 86, 158
  counties, 29, 78, 86

general, 1, 2, 24, 29, 52–54, 56, 63, 64, 69, 84, 129, 142, 152, 157, 192–194, 202, 206
   influence on other countries, 142, 191, 194, 202, 207
   mayor, 120, 124, 133, 136, 142, 156
   municipalities, 14, 157
   rural municipalities, 78, 79, 86, 87
   secretary, 158, 161
   selection, 142, 144, 145, 157, 158
   special purpose bodies, 6, 25
   term of office councilmen, 88, 89
   urban municipalities, 94
Urwick, L. F., 108
U.S.S.R.
   board, 109, 116, 198
   chief administrative officer, 158
   chief executive, 117
   committees, 102, 104
   council, 76
   general, 2, 45, 197, 198
   influence on other countries, 191
   selection, 104, 158

Veto, 124, 227, 236, 237, 250, 261, 262, 269, 331, 333, 345, 353, 385, 421
Vidich, Arthur J. and Bensman, Joseph, 79

Village, 4, 15, 16, 24, 29, 37, 52, 66, 67, 75–77, 80, 134, 135, 147, 204, 205, 224, 228, 234, 261, 303, 306, 307, 324, 343, 368–370, 373–375, 379, 383–385, 389, 391, 393, 394, 398, 399, 407, 415–417, 424
Void, see Annulment

Wales, see U.K., 209
Ward, 21, 218, 222, 225, 228–230, 235, 299, 381, 387, 389, 391, 392, 396, 425
Weak mayor, see under Form of local government
West Asia and North Africa group, 33, 88, 137, 191, 203–204, 362–379
Wheare, K. C., 1, 10, 90, 93, 100, 171, 186
Wickwar, W. Hardy, 5, 33, 203

Yugoslavia, 302–309
   committees, 22, 94, 95
   council, 65, 89, 95
   general, 2, 45, 66, 197
   municipalities, 14, 198
   sub-municipal units, 21, 95

Date Due